PORTRAIT OF THE 50's

compiled by John Chalcraft

D427 and D429 pound through Shap Summit cutting with IM35, the 14.00 Glasgow – Euston, 16/4/71. *(John F. Medley)*

ISBN 0 906883 07 5

Published in Great Britain by

Rail Photoprints, 8 Paulmont Rise, Temple Cloud, Nr. Bristol, BS18 5DT.

Typeset by Filton Graphics, Bristol.
Origination by Radstock Reproductions Ltd., Midsomer Norton.
Printed and Bound by Oakley Press Ltd., Backfields, Bristol BS2 8QP.

Refurbished Class 50 50017 *'Royal Oak'* heads a train of Air-conditioned stock west out of Twerton tunnel, Bath, 15/4/84. *(John Chalcraft)*

Introduction

The birth of the Class 50 was largely due to the realization in 1966 that B.R. required a 'stop gap', high power, high speed class of locomotive for use on Anglo-Scottish West Coast Main Line services in pre-electrification days. It was decided that the class should be based upon the well proven English Electric DP2 prototype, but with considerably modified body shape and incorporating electric train heating, full air braking and slow speed control. All class members were also fitted for multiple working, but, initially, only D400 had jumper cables fitted.

Construction of the class commenced at English Electric's Vulcan works during early 1967 with the first loco (D400 now 50050) entering revenue earning service from Crewe in October of that year, deliveries then proceeded at a rapid rate with the final class member entering service during November 1968.

All locos were initially leased by 'English Electric Leasing Ltd', this fact being indicated by a small die cast plaque carried mid bodyside by all locos at the time. The initial agreement guaranteed on 84% availability level, Crewe depot was the prime operating base although at various times the locos were loaned to other depots for crew training or test purposes. In an effort to maintain the high availability requirement spare engines were located at Crewe, Carlisle and Polmadie depots.

During 1969 multiple working cables were fitted to the remaining class members as a prelude to the use of pairs of locos on the greatly accelerated Anglo-Scottish services which became the norm from 5th May 1970, 100 miles per hour running became commonplace with cuts of up to 45 minutes from the pre 1970 journey times.

Some indication of the planned move of the 50's to the Western Region was given on the 11th October 1972 when 400 (50050) was transferred to Bristol Bath Road to commence crew-training, 401 followed its sister loco shortly afterwards and by mid summer 1973 both locos were operating in revenue earning service on Paddington – Bristol expresses.

A further 3 class members were transferred to the W.R. during early 1974, with a mass transfer taking place to the region upon inauguration of the 'Electric Scots' WCML service in May 1974, final transfer of the 50's from the Midland taking place in May 1976.

British Rail finally purchased the locos from English Electric during the mid '70's, the small bodyside plates being removed at this time.

The class suffered from poor availability shortly after its arrival on the Western Region, partly due to lack of staff familiarity with the locos, and, partly due to the extremely sophisticated control system that had been fitted, hard work on the part of the depots led to an improvement in availability, but, during 1977 the decision was made to embark on an extensive refurbishment program based on Doncaster Works, this included removal of the inertia filtration system, the rheostatic braking and the slow speed control fittings plus complete rewiring with the fitting of the now familiar headlight. 50006 entered Doncaster in September 1977 for refurbishment, finally returning to service in September 1979, the first of the reborn locos. Refurbishment then proceeded with all other class members, the final loco to be refurbished being 50014 which was completed during late 1983.

The first six locos to be refurbished reappeared from works in their original livery, but, on 15th August 1980 50023 reappeared resplendant in the eye catching (then) 'new' livery since adopted for the Class. 50013 was the last loco to be painted in the new style appearing in September 1984, however, 50007 had in the meantime reverted back to the old style in mock 'Brunswick Green' in conjunction with its renaming.

From the enthusiasts point of view possibly the most gratifying decision was to name class members, 50035 being the first member to be adorned on 17/1/78 at Plymouth, 50006 being the last in September 1979. For reasons better known to W.R. management 50007 was renamed "Sir Edward Elgar" in a ceremony at Paddington on 25th February 1980. Other renamings seem a distinct possibility in conjunction with the Great Western 150 celebrations during 1985.

In much the same way as the 50's replaced the 52's on prime Western Region services, they themselves were replaced by HST's on the prime routes, from May 1980 they took over the haulage of the Waterloo – Exeter services over the former LSWR main line, class members can now be found in regular use on the majority of ex GW main line routes from Swansea to Birmingham, Paddington to Penzance, freight diagramming is comparatively rare, although one or two diagrams do exist and they are almost regular power for the engineers trains in the Plymouth division.

The cost of refurbishment has assured the class of a long term future, although whether the Western Region can retain its sole ownership of the class remains to be seen.

Unfortunately layout dictates that not all photographs are in strict date order but it is hoped that this does not detract from the end product.

John Chalcraft
Temple Cloud, Avon
November 1984

50034

50001 *Dreadnought*

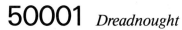

Left:
An immaculate D401 stands alongside the WCML at Crewe Diesel Depot, contrary to popular belief the photo proves that it was not fully fitted for multiple working, the small 'loan' plate is clearly visible above the bodyside shadow, 18/5/69. *(Norman Preedy)*

Left centre:
A grimy 401 stands outside Willesden depot on 7/10/73, the 50's were never common at the south end of the WCML but on this occasion as the loco was then allocated to the Western Region the occurrence was somewhat strange. *(Kevin Connolly)*

Below:
After refurbishment but still in old livery 50001 prepares to leave Bristol Temple Meads with an enthusiasts special returning to Plymouth, 3/3/84. *(John Chalcraft)*

Facing page:
In old livery, 50034 "Furious" emerges from the depths of Twerton Tunnel near Bath as it heads west with the 16.45 Paddington – Weston-super-Mare service, 20/4/80. *(John Chalcraft)*

Above:
A rare sight 50001 awaits departure from Brighton with the 09.20 Brighton – Exeter service, due to engineering work this service was 50 hauled for two Saturdays during October 1980. *(John Vaughan)*

Below:
Just ex works, repainted in the 'new' livery and accompanied by a fitter in case of problems, 50001 prepares to leave Bristol Temple Meads with the 11.25 Malago Vale – Old Oak Common empty newspaper stock. 17/8/84. *(John Chalcraft)*

50002 *Superb*

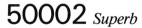

On its last months of Midland Region service 402 heads the diverted 08.55 Liverpool–Birmingham service past the ex LNWR Hednesford signal box on the Rugeley–Walsall freight line, 20/5/73. *(Geoffrey F. Bannister)*

Below:
Some ten years later the refurbished and now named 50002 climbs out of Bristol past Narroways Hill Junction with the 15.20 Weston-super-Mare – Glasgow (Su) service, 3/84.
(John Chalcraft)

50003 *Temeraire*

Right: IM27 the 08.20 Glasgow/Edinburgh – Liverpool/Manchester hurries south past Oxenholme behind D403, note the absence of multiple fittings, 27/8/69. *(A. Wyn Hobson)*

Below:
Sadly the gantry at the west end of Southampton Central has now vanished, the refurbished 50003 leaves the station with the diverted 09.10 Waterloo – Exeter, 15/2/81.
(John Chalcraft)

50004 *St. Vincent*

In the days when motorail services still carried coaching stock 50004 leans to the curve beneath Cogload flyover as it diverges from the Bristol route to take the Berks and Hants line with the up St. Austell – Kensington service, 12/8/78. *(John Chalcraft)*

Below:
The climb eases for 50004 as it breasts the summit at Buckhorn Weston with the 09.45 Exeter – Waterloo service, 19/4/81. *(John Chalcraft)*

50005 *Collingwood*

Right:
With speed approaching line maximum 50005 swings past Hungerford Common with the 12.23 Paddington – Paignton service, 29/9/79.
(John Vaughan)

Below:
On 13th April 1984 the woods of the 'Golden Valley' echo to the 16 cylinder pounding of 50005's engine as it lifts 3B42 the 09.15 Gloucester – Swindon parcels service upgrade over Frampton Mansell Viaduct.
(John Chalcraft)

50006 *Neptune*

Top: In the days after cessation of use of the 4 character headcode panels several locos displayed their own numbers, 50006 displays its number as it waits for departure from Reading with a Plymouth – Paddington service, it will be noted that the mid-bodyside 'lease' plaque has now been removed presumably indicating that the loco was in BR ownership by this time, 16/10/76. *(Norman Preedy)*

50006 was the first loco to be refurbished, returning to revenue earning service in September 1979, the loco appeared from works with a circular blanking plate covering the aperture where the headlight would later be fitted. These two views show the loco in this form *(left)* passing Clink Road Junction, Frome at the head of the (So) Barnstaple – Paddington service, 23/5/80, and *(below)* passing Dawlish with the 09.03 Penzance – Paddington, 23/8/80. *(John Chalcraft, Bert Wynn)*

Right:
Due to the supposed better reliability of the refurbished 50's the Southern Region requested that only the modified locos be used on the Waterloo – Exeter services, on 28/3/81 50006 stands at Sherborne with an up train. *(John Chalcraft)*

Below:
50006 in final livery working in multiple with 50025, the train is the (Su) 08.50 Exeter – Paddington which is seen passing the site of Box station. The train was regularly rostered for a pair of 50's at the time, 1/4/84. *(John Chalcraft)*

50007 *(Hercules)* *Sir Edward Elgar*

In original form 407 in multiple with a sister engine prepares to leave Carlisle with an Anglo-Scottish express, 17/9/73. *(H. C. Casserley)*

Below:
Three years later after transfer to the Western Region 50007 leaves Newton Abbot with the 09.20 Liverpool – Penzance, note the positioning of the BR insignia, 21/8/76. Finally *(foot)* in refurbished form *'Hercules'* passes Benhall, Cheltenham with the 07.40 Penzance – Liverpool, 7/9/83. *(Both Norman Preedy)*

During late 1983 Western Region management made the decision to name a locomotive *'Sir Edward Elgar'* in memory of the composer, and following the earlier tradition set by 'Castle' class No. 7005, rather than name a 47 it was decided to rename 50007, the loco was repainted in Brunswick Green livery with die cast BR crests, numberplate and nameplate, the official unveiling taking place at Paddington on 25th February 1984.

Top:
After the unveiling ceremony 50007 in its new guise worked the 12.15 Paddington – Oxford service, it was photographed passing West Ealing on the outward journey, 25/2/84.

Centre:
Several months later 50007 poses for the camera at Exeter St. Davids prior to working the 18.17 service to Waterloo, 15/9/84.

Foot:
7/7/84, 50007 rounds the curve to Cowley Bridge Junction, Exeter with the 17.45 Paignton – Paddington service, sadly, the semaphore signalling will soon be a thing of the past, vanishing under the Exeter MAS scheme which is due to become operational in March 1985. *(All photos John Chalcraft)*

50008 *Thunderer*

Above:
At a time when 50's were virtually unknown on the North and West route 50008 heads F & W railtours 'Crewe Invader' charter train north past Church Stretton, 22/9/79. *(Gavin Morrison)*

Below:
On Summer Sundays during 1982 the 14.40 Plymouth – Paddington service was rostered for a pair of 50's, 50008 and 50038 lean to the curve as they slow for the Totnes stop on 23/5/82. *(John Chalcraft)*

50009 *Conqueror*

Right:
The Western lines used the 50's in much the same way as the 87's are used today, freightliner working being a common overnight feature. 409 eases a freightliner bound for Gushetfaulds FLT out of the sidings alongside Polmadie depot after a stop for crew change purposes, 9/9/71.
(Norman Preedy)

Right:
The 09.20 Edinburgh – Plymouth service was the normal method of returning ex works 50's to the Western Region until it became an HST rostered working, from that time a variety of turns were used, on 26/1/84 50009 found itself rostered to work a train of MGR empties from Scunthorpe to Severn Tunnel Junction, photographed passing Walton-on-Trent. *(Bert Wynn)*

Below:
Several months later 50009 finds itself on a more normal working as it heads the 08.50 (Su) Exeter – Paddington east near Box, 15/4/84.
(John Chalcraft)

50010 *Monarch*

Left:
A grimy 50010 breasts Whiteball summit and commences the run downgrade with the 10.23 Manchester Piccadilly – Penzance, 20/5/78.
(John Chalcraft)

Left:
The intrepid photographer records 50010 as it heads past Burton Salmon towards York in bitterly cold conditions, 19/12/81.
(Gavin Morrison)

Below:
A further minor livery change for 50010 after repainting at Landore, no grey paint having been available blue was used, on 17/9/83 it was photographed at Whiteball (once again!).
(John Chalcraft)

50011 *Centurion*

Right:
Normal power for the Glasgow/Edinburgh – Bristol sleeper over recent months has been one of the ETH fitted 'Peaks' (45/1) surprisingly 50011 was supplied as power on 8/7/84, the train is seen leaving Cheltenham on the last leg of its journey. *(John Chalcraft)*

Below:
Many years earlier 411 as it was then known is seen in the company of 407 at the head of the 14.05 Euston – Glasgow service, photographed passing Bay Horse, south of Lancaster, 21/8/72. *(A. Wyn Hobson)*

50012 *Benbow*

In original condition, without multiple working jumper cables D412 heads the 11.20 Perth – Birmingham away from Oxenholme, note the position of the BR logotype. 9/9/69.
(Stanley Creer)

Below:
In the days before many of the Worcester line services were cut back to terminate at Oxford an immaculate 50012 eases the 09.55 Paddington – Worcester service out of Paddington past Ranelagh Bridge, 20/9/81.
(John Vaughan)

50013 *Agincourt*

50013 stands at Duddeston carriage sidings with the stock for the 20.40 service from Birmingham New Street to Paddington, 10/5/77. The BR logotype was carried centrally on the bodyside at the time, this position being changed to lower cabside upon naming. *(Kevin Connolly)*

Below:
A superb photograph showing D413 approaching Ais Gill summit with the diverted (Sun) 11.00 Glasgow – Birmingham (Circa 1969). The photograph clearly shows the mounting plates for the multiple fittings and the small bodyside loan plate. *(Peter J. Robinson)*

Above:
50013 was one of the first locos to be refurbished returning to service with the normal yellow front end and all blue body, the loco is seen leaving Woking with the 09.10 Waterloo – Exeter, 6/12/82. *(John Chalcraft)*

Left:
50013 was the last 50 to appear from Doncaster works in new livery. Just ex works it was photographed speeding west near Clink Road, Frome with the 10.27 Paddington – Penzance service, 18/9/84. *(Dave Brush)*

Below:
One week later the loco had been stopped at Old Oak Common with A.W.S. problems, it was photographed running light 'on test' near Ruscombe, 25/9/84. *(John Chalcraft)*

50014 *Warspite*

Right:
Norton Junction, on 13/5/83 50014 joins the Bristol – Birmingham route (via Worcester) off the Oxford line at the head of the 17.00 Paddington – Hereford service. To the local railmen the single track route is still known as 'the main', old traditions die hard! *(David Hill)*

Right:
31/7/83. Work appears to be well under way with the last 50 refurbishment as 50014 stands in grey primer in Doncaster works. *(Norman Preedy)*

Below:
In new livery 50014 passes the passing loop at Kenilworth Common with the 09.40 Poole – Leeds/Newcastle service en route Coventry, 18/2/84. *(Steve Turner)*

50015 *Valiant*

Above:
50015 heads for home as it passes Little Bedwyn with the 12.30 Paddington – Plymouth service on 8/4/80, sadly the aims of the railway photographer were not considered when the trees were planted alongside the Kennet and Avon canal, and this view is now virtually unobtainable. *(John Chalcraft)*

Below:
The beam of 50015's headlight picks up a heavy drizzle as the loco stands at Bristol Temple Meads after arrival from Cheltenham, 18/3/83. *(Steve Turner)*

50016 *Barham*

Right:
The 16.20 Swindon – Taunton transfer freight normally produced an ETH loco as power and 31/7/80 was no exception when 50016 ambled through the countryside having just left Bath. Sadly, the service was a casualty in the October freight rationalization in the area. *(Mike Miller)*

Right:
After a considerable period of crew-training at Cardiff Canton including regular turns on the Cardiff – Crewe services 50's took over certain other workings from South Wales from 14/5/84. On 25/5/84 50016 crosses the River Wye (and the anglo/welsh border) with IS61 the 08.10 Cardiff – Glasgow. *(John Chalcraft)*

Below:
Under the wires at Berkswell, 50016 heads the 08.50 Paddington – Liverpool service towards Birmingham where AC electric power will take over the service. *(Steve Turner)*

50017 *Royal Oak*

Left:
50017 poses alongside a 'duff', between duties at Ranelagh Bridge loco yard outside Paddington, 22/7/78. *(Gavin Morrison)*

Below:
In the depths of Harbury cutting 50017 hurries downgrade towards Leamington Spa with the 09.50 Paddington – Liverpool service, 14/5/82. *(John Chalcraft)*

Above:
50017 was the second 50 to be refurbished by Doncaster Works, it emerged from 'the plant' with a blanking plate covering the cab front hole where the headlight would later be fitted, the loco was photographed in this condition in Clapham Junction Yards with the stock for the 17.00 Waterloo – Exeter service, 22/12/80. *(Mike Collins)*

Below:
In final form 50017 rumbles over the Royal Albert Bridge, Saltas with an engineers train of empties bound for Tavistock Junction Yar 28/2/84. *(John Chalcraf*

50018 *Resolution*

Left:
Powering west on the L.S.W.R., 50018 heads the 13.10 Waterloo – Exeter past Byfleet and New Haw, 10/9/81. *(John Vaughan)*

Below:
The low evening sun catches the sides of 50018 and its stock as it passes through Newton Meadows (on the approach to Bath) with the (Su) 18.12 Bristol – Paddington service, 15/4/84. *(John Chalcraft)*

50019 *Ramillies*

Right:
Deep in the heart of Cornwall, 50019 leaves St. Erth with 4MO5 the 12.50 Penzance – Crewe perishables/parcels, the loco will work the train as far as Bristol Temple Meads, 30/7/75. *(Brian Morrison)*

Below:
On 10th June 1978 50019 storms past Stoneycombe signal box as it attacks the climb to Dainton summit with the down 'Cornish Riviera Express', sadly the signal box is no longer in operation and Stoneycombe Quarry no longer supplies ballast to British Rail. *(John Chalcraft)*

Left:
The refurbished and repainted 50019 breasts the climb from Par as it leaves Treverrin Tunnel with an up Penzance – Plymouth ECS working, 28/9/84. *(Steve Turner)*

Below:
In refurbished but not yet repainted condition 50019 exerts full power as it moves the 12.25 Paddington – Plymouth away from its Totnes stop on 29/5/81. *(John Chalcraft)*

50020 *Revenge*

Right:
D420 is still in ex works condition as it stands at the south end of Carlisle Citadel station with a Glasgow – Manchester/Liverpool working, 16/8/69. *(Norman Preedy)*

Right:
50020 stands at Birmingham New Street alongside 33014, 14/12/81. *(Kevin Connolly)*

Below:
'Revenge' pulls out of Temple Mills Yard with the afternoon freight to Acton Yard which apparently consists of electrification engineers stock, this being the return working of the 09.45 freight from Acton, a train which regularly produced '50' power, 6/1/84. *(Mike Collins)*

50021 *Rodney*

Left:
On a fine April morning 50021 heads the 11.20 Paignton – Paddington east, up the Berks and Hants route near West Lyng (Somerset), 3/4/80.
(John Vaughan)

Left:
50021 leaves Evesham on the Cotswold line with the 12.50 Paddington – Worcester service, sadly this train was one of the casualties of the 1982 timetable cuts which left Hereford and Worcester with only two through services to Paddington, 1/5/82. *(David Mitchell)*

Below:
On a fine September day 50021 hurries towards Paddington, through Twyford with one of the hourly loco-hauled services from Oxford, the train is running on the 'up relief' line, the 'main' lines being visible to the left of the picture.
(John Vaughan)

50022 *Anson*

Above:
The Midland retained a small stud of 50's after full electrification on the WCML although they were relegated to more mundane freight duties, on 8/4/75 50022 finds itself at Cannock Road Junction, Wolverhampton with a train of MGR empties from Ironbridge to Trentham (Stoke). *(Geoffrey F. Bannister)*

Left:
Portrait of an immaculate ex works 50, 50022 stands outside Doncaster Works on 6/3/84. *(Gavin Morrison)*

Below:
Four days later a (still) immaculate *'Anson'* slows for Paddington as it passes Westbourne Park with an up express, 10/3/84. *(Peter Marsh)*

50023 *Howe*

Left:
During the mid '70's milk traffic from the West Country to London played a large part in Western Region traffic plans, the milk trains were amongst the first freight diagrams for the newly arrived 50's 50023 heads west through West Ealing with empties bound for St. Erth, 16/5/74.
(Norman Preedy)

Below:
50023 in refurbished condition heads away from Exeter St. Davids with a down express for Paignton on a typically dull summer day. The loco was the first to be repainted in the new livery.
(John Chalcraft)

50024 *Vanguard*

Right:
Class 50's handle a large number of overnight parcels and newspaper workings on the Western Region, 50024 awaits departure from Paddington's platform 9 with a parcels working to the west. *(John Chalcraft)*

Centre:
An unusual pairing for a South Devon working 50024 being rostered to provide assistance for 33065 on the 23.37 Fawley – Plymouth Friary block oil working, the odd couple are seen passing Totnes with 33065 apparently doing all the work for the assault on Rattery, 15/4/82. *(Mike Miller)*

Foot:
When motive power shortages necessitate such action 50's have been allowed to work north of Birmingham, normally on the routes to the north-east, but, on 14/2/84 50024 found its way under the wires to Manchester, it returned south on the 13.20 Manchester – Portsmouth service which was photographed passing Cheadle Hulme. *(Steve Turner)*

50025 *Invincible*

Left:
In the days before Class 50 maintenance was transferred to Doncaster 50025 stands ex works at Crewe Works note that the logotype has now been positioned centrally on the bodyside, no longer on the cab sides, 15/12/74.
(Kevin Connolly)

Centre:
Pounding up to Buckhorn Weston tunnel 50025 heads west with the 09.10 (Su) Waterloo–Exeter service, 19/4/81. *(John Chalcraft)*

Below:
On a sunny March morning 50025 leaves Treverrin Tunnel and heads downgrade towards Lostwithiel with an up relief service from Penzance to Paddington, 2/3/84. *(John Chalcraft)*

50026 *Indomitable*

Right:
50026 accelerates away from Exeter past Cowley Bridge junction at the head of the 17.40 Paignton – Paddington service, 23/5/82.
(John Chalcraft)

Below:
During late 1983 the 08.30 Exeter – Newcastle (Su) service weaved a tortuous route via the LSWR to Yeovil, thence to Castle Cary and the Berks and Hants to Reading and Birmingham, on 27/11/83 50026 headed the train over frost coated tracks into Yeovil Pen Mill.
(John Chalcraft)

50027 *Lion*

Right:
The remains of the old Midland main line at Westerleigh now provide a home for the Civil Engineers department in the Bristol area, on 25/11/80 50027 finds itself propelling one wagon of track panels plus brake van towards Westerleigh having left the main line at Yate South Junction. *(Mike Miller)*

Below:
In refurbished condition 50027 leaves Penzance with 3S15 the 12.10 parcels to Glasgow Salkeld Street, the train will be re-engined at Bristol Temple Meads. *(John Vaughan)*

50028 *Tiger*

Right:
Hoover 50028 makes a smoky exit from Plymouth as it struggles to restart RPPR's 'Penzance Pullman' and commence the return trip to Paddington 26/4/80.
(John Chalcraft)

Below:
Late on a March afternoon 50028 scurries along the valley bottom beneath Restormel Castle as it approaches Lostwithiel with 2B34 the 16.15 Plymouth – Penzance stopping service, 1/3/84. *(John Chalcraft)*

50029 *Renown*

Left:
Early evening at Bristol Temple Meads, 50029 poses for the camera at platform 10 having arrived with the 12.10 Penzance – Glasgow Parcels, considerable remarshalling of stock will now take place before the train continues on its northward journey. *(John Chalcraft)*

Below:
In unmodified form 50029 takes the through road as it passes Tiverton Junction on an up Plymouth – Manchester service, 16/4/81. *(David Mitchell)*

Foot:
50029 hurries past Clink Road Junction, Frome at the head of a Penzance – Paddington service, the line diverging right goes to Frome Station, Whatley Quarry and Radstock, sadly the semaphore signals disappeared from the location in October 1984. *(John Chalcraft)*

50030 *Repulse*

Right:
Cowley Bridge Junction, Exeter (yet again), the recently refurbished 50030 rounds the curve and approaches the junction with the 16.15 Penzance – Paddington, 7/7/84. *(John Chalcraft)*

Below:
Two years earlier *'Repulse'* heads through lush South Devon countryside with the 10.45 (So) Newquay – Paddington service, 28/8/82. *(Gavin Morrison)*

50031 *Hood*

Above:
50031 heads the rake of 'Air-Cons' forming the 13.30 Paddington – Penzance west of Bruton, the photograph was taken from the remains of an embankment which was formerly the old Somerset and Dorset Joint Railway.
(John Vaughan)

Left:
Officially adopted by the Class 50 Locomotive Society 50031 stands at Bournemouth with the societies first railtour, appropriately named 'The Wessexman'. It is possible that this was the first visit of a class member to the south coast resort, 22/10/83. *(John Chalcraft)*

Below:
The last light of a typically foggy November Day is used to capture 50031 as it heads west through Winchfield with the 13.10 Waterloo – Exeter service, 12/11/83. *(John Chalcraft)*

50032 *Courageous*

Right:
In Western Lines condition 432 in multiple with 444 backs onto an Anglo-Scottish express at Crewe, 7/7/73. *(Kevin Connolly)*

Right:
Diverted from its normal route from Birmingham to take the freight only route over Cannock, 432 passes Brereton Sidings signal box at Rugeley shortly before rejoining the WCML, 24/2/74.
(Geoffrey F. Bannister)

Below:
50032 climbs away from Exeter Central and approaches St James' Park station with the 12.24 service to Waterloo, 30/8/82.
(Gavin Morrison)

50033 *Glorious*

Left:
A portrait of 50033 as it awaits attention at Bath Road depot. *(John Chalcraft)*

Below:
The backlighting enhances the power of 50033 as it pounds over Whiteball summit passing the signal box with 1A83, the 10.30 Penzance–Paddington service. *(John Chalcraft)*

50034 *Furious*

Right:
On 30/11/74 50034 leaves Preston with a southbound van train, as the WCML was fully electrified at this time it is likely that the trains destination was Manchester Red Bank, diesel haulage being provided from Preston.
(Kevin Connolly)

Right:
50034 heads west away from Bristol past Parson Street station with IV90 the 10.47 Glasgow Central – Plymouth service, Bristol's Malago Vale carriage sidings are just visible beyond the overbridge. *(John Chalcraft)*

Below:
Under the guard of Exeter Centrals upper quadrant semaphore signals 50034 departs from the city with the 12.20 Exeter St. Davids – Waterloo service, the semaphores were due for replacement during October '84.
(David Mitchell)

50035 *Ark Royal*

Left:
Side lighting enhances the bodylines of 50035 as power is applied to accelerate it out of the tight curve at Crofton with the 09.40 Paddington – Penzance ("Jumbo") service. Note the large bodyside crest above the nameplate, 2/6/84.
(John Chalcraft)

Below:
To the compiler 'the Ark' will always be the flagship of the class, possibly due to it being the first loco to be named in January 1978. On 12th July 1980 the loco is seen heading up the singled ex LSWR main line near West Tisbury with the 09.40 Exeter – Waterloo service. *(John Vaughan)*

50036 *Victorious*

Right:
'Victorious' leaves Gloucester and rejoins the Bristol – Birmingham main line at Barnwood Junction, should the proposed Gloucester Parkway station come to fruition then it will be situated in the vicinity of the area covered by this photograph, the train is the 07.45 Bristol – Manchester, 3/5/83. *(Norman Preedy)*

Below:
With the GPO Tower and the 'Westway' providing a backdrop 50036 leaves Paddington at the head of a West of England express, in the background a second 50 awaits to back down into the terminus, the L.T. Metropolitan Line can be seen in the bottom right foreground, 20/3/80. *(Gavin Morrison)*

50037 *Illustrious*

Left:
As the early morning mist lifts 50037 leans to the curve through Castle Cary with IB24 the 07.30 Paddington – St. Austell Motorail service, this view will shortly change drastically with the replacement of the signal box and semaphores under the Westbury MAS scheme, the station area and Weymouth line junction are also being extensively remodelled with a third platform face (for Weymouth trains) and the junction being moved to the east of the station (beyond the footbridge). 5/6/82. *(John Chalcraft)*

Below:
After a visit to Doncaster Works (presumably due to engine or generator problems – the loco has not been cleaned) 50037 heads IN21 the works test train north up the ECML near Ferryhill, 11/3/79. *(Peter J. Robinson)*

50038 *Formidable*

Above:
The tranquility of Hungerford Common is shattered as a local Berks and Hants DMU and 50038 on a Penzance – Paddington service pass to the east of Hungerford Station, 29/9/79. *(John Vaughan)*

Below:
Deep in the heart of third-rail country 50038 heads the 15.10 Waterlo – Exeter service west through Weybridge station. *(John Chalcraf*

50039 *Implacable*

Left:
On the last part of the trains journey 50039 approaches St. Austell with the 09.20 Liverpool – Penzance service, 29/2/84. *(John Chalcraft)*

Below:
439 in multiple with 437 heads the 08.00 Euston – Glasgow service north near Newton le Willows, 3/73. *(David N. Clough)*

Foot:
On 29/2/84 50039 heads the 12.10 Penzance – Glasgow parcels away from Bodmin Parkway (Road) station, the train was obviously re engined at Plymouth (see top picture). *(John Chalcraft)*

50040 *Leviathan*

Right:
A very grimy oil stained 50040 approaches Paddington past Westbourne Park on 20/3/80. *(Gavin Morrison)*

Right:
A far cry from todays 'modern railway' D440 without multiple fittings pauses at Carnforth with the 08.30 Carlisle – Euston semi-fast service, 20/8/69. Today WCML services no longer stop at Carnforth, all traffic using the Barrow line platforms (not visible) to the left of this view. *(A. Wyn Hobson)*

Below:
Storming out of Exeter past St James Park Halt, 50040 heads the 12.25 Exeter St. Davids – Waterloo service, 25/3/82. *(David Mitchell)*

50041 *Bulwark*

Right:
In old livery and not more than half a mile from the scene of its most inglorious act 50041 passes Ranelagh Bridge with the 15.00 Paddington – Hereford service, 16/5/81. *(John Vaughan)*

Centre:
Approaching Plymouth station on 17/2/83, 50041 heads for Friary Yards with a 'mixed' freight consisting of empty fuel tanks ex Penzance and empty cement wagons from Chacewater. *(David Mitchell)*

Foot:
After its derailment outside Paddington on 23/11/83 when heading the 21.35 Penzance – Paddington sleeper service *'Bulwark'* was despatched to Doncaster Works for repair assessment, it was photographed in works after stripping (March 1984). Fortunately the decision was made to repair the loco. *(Gavin Morrison)*

50042 *Triumph*

Above left:
50042 rumbles over the River Avon as it heads down the St Philips Loop with ECS from a Plymouth – Bristol working en route the carriage washing machine and the Malago Vale sidings.
(John Chalcraft)

Above right:
The final livery for the 50's(?) 50042 complete with black roof accelerates through Chepstow as it recovers from the Wye Bridge slack with the 13.20 Glasgow – Swansea service, 27/7/84.
(John Chalcraft)

Below:
On Easter Monday 1984, 50042 grinds the final yards to Dainton Summit with an unidentified eastbound ECS, 23/4/84.
(John Chalcraft)

50043 *Eagle*

Left:
'Eagle' speeds down the Berks and Hants past Lavington at the head of the 13.30 Paddington – Penzance, 3/3/80. *(John Vaughan)*

Below:
Evening at Bristol Temple Meads with 50043 waiting to leave platform 5 with the 13.20 Liverpool Lime Street – Plymouth, 20/1/84. *(John Chalcraft)*

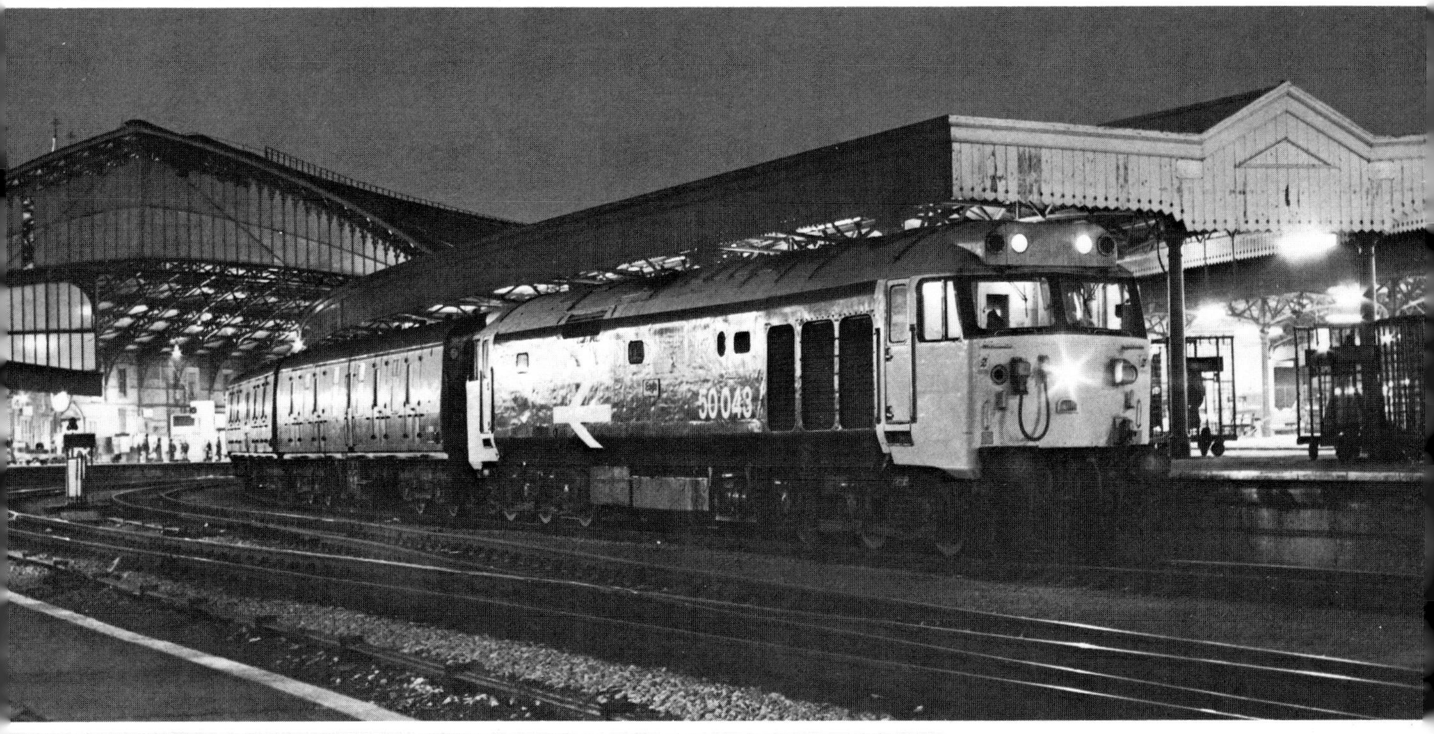

Left:
Another view at Temple Meads as *'Eagle'* leaves Platform 12 with a relief service to the 14.25 Paddington – Penzance (the HST standing at platform 10), 15/4/84. *(John Chalcraft)*

50044 *Exeter*

Right:
Having arrived from the north 444 makes for Crewe Depot and servicing on 1/6/71.
(Norman Preedy)

Right:
On 24/2/78, Bath Road depot provided 50044 (then un-named) for the Bristol East Depot – Portishead trip freight working, the train consisting of Presflos and scrap is seen passing Ashton Junction. *(Mike Miller)*

Below:
Until October '83 Hoovers were something of a rarity in South Wales although 'Ruggexes' in conjunction with Rugby Internationals at Cardiff normally produced a 50 on a train from Paddington. 50044 is seen on one of these train on 18/2/84, obviously some 'bashers' were well informed. *(John Chalcraft)*

50045 *Achilles*

Left:
Only days after naming 50045 leaves Bristol Temple Meads with the 12.30 Paddington–Plymouth service, 28/4/78. Note the patch just behind the nameplate where the BR logotype has been painted out. *(John Chalcraft)*

Left:
On the Oxford–Worcester 'Cotswold Line' 50045 pauses at Charlbury with a down train for Worcester. *(John Vaughan)*

Below:
As mentioned elsewhere at times when resources have been at full stretch 50's have been allowed to work north beyond Birmingham, 50045 slows for a stop at Derby with a summer Saturday relief train, 6/8/83. *(Gavin Morrison)*

50046 *Ajax*

Right:
Unmodified and modified 50's 50046 and 50008 exert their 5400 HP as they lift the 14.40 (Su) Plymouth – Paddington up Brewham Bank towards Westbury, at the time the working was rostered for a pair of 50's, 6/6/82. *(John Chalcraft)*

Below:
With an idiot showing all that is wrong with the enthusiast fraternity as he leans from the first coach in an effort to get himself killed, 50046 storms up to Harbury Tunnel with the 08.20 Liverpool – Paddington, 14/5/83. *(John Chalcraft)*

50047 *Swiftsure*

Above:
Before the Windermere branch was relegated to DMU only service, D447 stands at Kendal with the 16.15 Windermere – Euston service, the barrows and parcels on the platform show all the signs of thriving business, a far cry from todays money starved business, 9/9/69. *(Stanley Creer)*

Below:
Returning from refurbishment on 27/5/80, 50047 finds itself in charge of the 09.50 Edinburgh – Plymouth, due to the rebuilding of the normal route from Water Orton the train is passing Whitacre Junction, 50047 is already throwing oil and the train is some 50 minutes late. *(John Chalcraft)*

Left:
15 months later, 50047 as a refurbished lo
is obviously acceptable power for t
Southern Region authorities as it leav
Salisbury Tunnel, passing Tunnel Juncti
signal box with the 09.40 Exeter – Waterlo
17/8/81. Sadly the signal box was tak
out of service upon completion of t
Salisbury resignalling scheme.
(David Mitche

Below:
In final condition after another visit to 't
plant' on 7/7/84 50047 commences the r
down to Totnes from Dainton summit wi
the 09.45 (So) Paddington – Newquay.
(Steve Turn

50048 *Dauntless*

Left:
With its number displayed in its indicator panel and pre naming 50048 takes the Westbury avoiding line at Fairwood Junction with the up "Cornish Riviera", the 10.55 Penzance – Paddington, 23/10/76. *(Grenville Hounsell)*

Left:
50048 approaches Ealing Broadway with a westbound ballast train, 26/4/84. *(Michael J. Collins)*

Below:
'Dauntless' hurries downgrade from Harbury Tunnel towards Leamington Spa with the 14.50 Paddington – Liverpool service, 14/5/83. *(John Chalcraft)*

50049 *Defiance*

Right:
In August 1971 449 and a sister loco prepare to leave Preston with the 12.05 Euston – Glasgow service, note the patch where the locos 'D' prefix has recently been deleted. *(Eric Bullen)*

Right:
50049 leaves Penzance with the Penzance – Crewe parcels, 10/10/75. *(Kevin Connolly)*

Below:
The Tytherington branch normally sees only stone traffic, but, once a year a special train is run for quarry staff, on 3/7/83 50049 was provided to take the train to Paignton. *(Mike Miller)*

50050(D400) *Fearless*

Left:
400 stands at its new home (Laira) between crew-training duties, 2/2/74. *(Kevin Connolly)*

Left:
Two crested members of the 50 family cross the 154ft high Liskeard viaduct as they head west for Penzance, 50002 leads 50050. *(John Vaughan)*

Below:
50050 sweeps down from Whiteball summit at the head of the 10.10 Paddington – Paignton, 17/9/83. *(John Chalcraft)*

Motive Power Depots

During their seventeen years in service the 50's have only been allocated (for servicing purposes) to four depots, the Midland Region concentrated the complete class on Crewe Diesel Depot, although initially the first 26 members (400–425) were allocated to WL (Western Lines) under the regions common user policy (for book-keeping purposes), the paper transfer to DO5 being made in June '68 with final 'transfer' to Crewe Diesel Depot being made with effect from 6/5/73.

Below:
Crewe Diesel Depot: *(left to right)* 426, 404 and 439 stand outside CD on 20/2/71.
Locos allocated to depot: 50001 – 50050 (as D400 – D449)
(John Medley)

Foot:
Old Oak Common: *(left to right)* 50001 (refurbished), 50031 and 50034 (repainted but not yet numbered), 25/4/81.
Locos allocated (at various times):-
50001/2/4/5/21/2/3/4/5/6/7/8/9/30/1/2/3/4/5/6/7/8/9/40/ 8/50 *(John Chalcraft)*

Left:
Bristol Bath Road: 50022 stands outside the depots heavy lifting shed in the bitter condition of 13/1/82.
Locos allocated (at various times):-
50001/2/3/4/5/6/8/11/16/7/8/9/20/2/3/4/5/9/30/2/3/5/7/8/9/40/1/2/3/4/6/7/8/9/50. *(John Chalcraft)*

Below:
Laira (Plymouth): 50012 and 50042 stand outside the depot in company with 37142, 19/9/84.
Locos allocated (at various times): 50001–50050 *(John Chalcraft)*

Facts and Figures

New number.	Old number	Date to Traffic	Name.	Depots allocated				Date named.
50050	D400	10/67	Fearless	CD	BR	OC	LA	8/1978
50001	D401	12/67	Dreadnought	CD	BR	OC	LA	4/1978
50002	D402	12/67	Superb	CD	BR	OC	LA	3/1978
50003	D403	1/68	Temeraire	CD	BR	LA		5/1978
50004	D404	12/67	St. Vincent	CD	BR	OC	LA	5/1978
50005	D405	1/68	Collingwood	CD	BR	OC	LA	4/1978
50006	D406	3/68	Neptune	CD	BR	LA		9/1979
50007	D407	3/68	*Sir Edward Elgar	CD	LA			25/2/84
50008	D408	3/68	Thunderer	CD	BR	LA		9/1978
50009	D409	3/68	Conqueror	CD	LA			5/1978
50010	D410	2/68	Monarch	CD	LA			3/1978
50011	D411	3/68	Centurion	CD	BR	LA		8/1979
50012	D412	2/68	Benbow	CD	LA			4/1978
50013	D413	3/68	Agincourt	CD	LA			4/1978
50014	D414	4/68	Warspite	CD	LA			5/1978
50015	D415	4/68	Valiant	CD	LA			4/1978
50016	D416	4/68	Barham	CD	BR	LA		4/1978
50017	D417	4/68	Royal Oak	CD	BR	LA		4/1978
50018	D418	4/68	Resolution	CD	BR	LA		4/1978
50019	D419	4/68	Ramilles	CD	BR	LA		4/1978
50020	D420	5/68	Revenge	CD	BR	LA		7/1978
50021	D421	5/68	Rodney	CD	LA	OC		7/1978
50022	D422	5/68	Anson	CD	BR	LA	OC	4/1978
50023	D423	5/68	Howe	CD	BR	LA	OC	5/1978
50024	D424	5/68	Vanguard	CD	BR	LA	OC	5/1978
50025	D425	6/68	Invincible	CD	BR	LA	OC	6/1978
50026	D426	6/68	Indomitable	CD	LA	OC		3/1978
50027	D427	6/68	Lion	CD	BR	LA	OC	4/1978
50028	D428	6/68	Tiger	CD	LA	OC		5/1978
50029	D429	6/68	Renown	CD	BR	LA	OC	11/1978
50030	D430	6/68	Repulse	CD	BR	LA	OC	4/1978
50031	D431	7/68	Hood	CD	LA	OC		6/1978
50032	D432	7/68	Courageous	CD	BR	LA	OC	7/1978
50033	D433	7/68	Glorious	CD	BR	LA	OC	6/1978
50034	D434	7/68	Furious	CD	LA	OC		4/1978
50035	D435	7/68	Ark Royal	CD	BR	LA	OC	1/1978
50036	D436	8/68	Victorious	CD	LA	OC		5/1978
50037	D437	9/68	Illustrious	CD	BR	LA	OC	6/1978
50038	D438	9/68	Formidable	CD	BR	LA	OC	5/1978
50039	D439	9/68	Implacable	CD	BR	LA	OC	6/1978
50040	D440	9/68	Leviathan	CD	BR	LA	OC	9/1978
50041	D441	10/68	Bulwark	CD	BR	LA		5/1978
50042	D442	10/68	Triumph	CD	BR	LA		10/1978
50043	D443	10/68	Eagle	CD	BR	LA		6/1978
50044	D444	10/68	Exeter	CD	BR	LA		4/1978
50045	D445	10/68	Achilles	CD	LA			4/1978
50046	D446	10/68	Ajax	CD	BR	LA		10/1978
50047	D447	11/68	Swiftsure	CD	BR	LA		5/1978
50048	D448	11/68	Dauntless	CD	BR	LA	OC	3/1978
50049	D449	12/68	Defiance	CD	BR	LA		5/1978

*Locomotive named Hercules 4/1978 – 2/84

MICPAR0031/ENG/NC
GW00632277
Michelin and Yamaha Factory MotoGP Team celebrate Valentino Rossi's MotoGP World Championship Title. Challenge drives champions to achieve. That's why we've won 14 out of 16 races and the top five rider's places in 2004. For the track or for you, every Michelin tyre shares this glory.
MICHELIN
A better way forward

THE MOTORCYCLE

YEARBOOK

2004-2005

CHRONOSPORTS
EDITEUR

ISBN 2-84707-070-2
Also available in French under the title of "L'Année Grands Prix Moto 2004" ISBN 2-84707-084-2

Jordils Park, Chemin des Jordils 40, CH-1025 St-Sulpice, Switzerland.
Phone : (+41 21) 694 24 44.
Fax : (+41 21) 694 24 46.
E-mail: info@chronosports.com
www.chronosports.com

Printed in France by Imprimerie Clerc, 18206 St-Amand Montrond
Bound in France by SIRC, 10350 Marigny-Le-Chatel

THE MOTORCYCLE YEARBOOK 2004-2005

Photos
Stan Perec

Thanks to Nello Zoppe (Nikon France) for his valued collaboration and to Jaime Olivares and Lukasz Swiderek who have provided some of the photos in this book.

Texts
Jean-Claude Schertenleib

CONTENTS

PREFACE

"Well done Vale! But next year it's my turn!"

"Before talking about my own season, which has been a difficult one, I would first like to offer huge congratulations to Valentino Rossi. Yes Vale, you have just finished the best season of your career. I have never seen you so determined. You took risks and in fact you fell a few times, which is not really your style, but you won. You definitely deserve your place among the greats of this sport. But you also know that nothing is ever a certainty in our game, so beware, because next year, it will be my turn. In 2005, we will see red at the head of the pack.
So back to where I started – my season. Everyone knows it was a difficult season, because everyone, me most of all, expected us to show much more potential.
Should we draw a line under this year and forget everything? No, quite the contrary. We must continue to work to avoid making the same mistakes. Everyone at Ducati understands this. We stayed on at Phillip Island the day after the Australian Grand Prix, where we already tested several good ideas for 2005. Therefore the signs are promising for a championship, which for the first time, will feature seventeen races. It will be a full card.
I've already been asked if it is too much. You know, as long as you look for the fun and the pleasure of riding, there can never be too many races. So I am already looking forward to 2005. In the meantime, make the most of the break to dive once again inside the story of this fabulous 2004 season.

Enjoy reading, the *Motorcycle Grand Prix Yearbook*."

Loris Capirossi

QATAR

Riders in the land of black gold

In the Qatar capital of Doha, which is built around a quiet bay, futuristic buildings spring up like mushrooms, in a mixture of crazy Las Vegas-style follies and traditional Arab design. "Qatar is the safest country in the world. As there are no poor people, there is no lawlessness and so there is no jealousy." Hidden behind the official line however, there are two very different realities. There are the bosses, the Qataris, who drive around in luxury limos and then there are those who do the building work, looking for a little bit of shade to rest in during the hottest part of the day. They come from all over the world looking for work and a wage.

A few kilometres to the north, one gets a rude awakening: on the left, a giant university complex, on the right, the Golf Club. Then...nothing, except a ribbon of asphalt running through the desert, heading nowhere. Sand and rock, rock and sand. In the far distance, one can make out the sand dunes, where one can imagine camel caravans, oil derriks and oil springing out of the ground. The latest adventure for the GP riders is taking place in black gold country!

Then, in the middle of nowhere, is a control tower, indicating that one has arrived in Losail. In eight months a circuit was born. "It's nice, with a lot of corners, but I get the impression that it does not have much of a flow to it. Of course, with the building dust and the sand in the air, grip will be minimal, but that's not surprising at a new circuit," says the young Swiss rider, Thomas Luthi.

Head, humidity and dust, but also a superb smiling welcome, a good track layout and facilities of a very high standard. Although it was hardly a great success, with only 2000 spectators on race day, this first Qatar GP will be remembered as a sign of the times, in the eco-political sense. A high profile event like the motorcycle world championships will always have to go and seek out new markets. It needs new partners, now capable of investing huge amounts needed to stage such an event. In Qatar, the Emirs coughed up 58 million dollars to build Losail. For them it is just a drop in the ocean, a drop of oil in the desert!

Kawasaki
FUCHS
Kawasaki
Racing Team

الدوحة
Doha
Q
ق
1A

Qatar, yesterday and today

● Location: Qatar is a peninsula measuring just over 11,000 square metres, situated in the middle of the west coast of the Persian Gulf.

● Population: it currently stands at 700,000 and is growing at an annual rate of 9%. Almost half the inhabitants live in Doha, the economic and administrative capital.

● Climate: A moderate desert climate with very hot summers in July and August and quite cool winters: in January, temperatures can drop to around 7 degrees.

● History: Archaeological inscriptions prove that the region was inhabited as far back as between ten and eight thousand years BC. Drawn in the eleventh century, a map of Ptolemy, one of the first ever geographical maps, shows the name "Catara". In the sixteenth century, the Qataris formed alliance with the Turks to eject the Portuguese. The result was that, like the bulk of the Arab Peninsula, it found itself under the control of the Ottoman Empire for the best part of four centures, even though the real power remained in the hands of sheiks from different tribes. It became a British Protectorate in 1916 and gained independence on 3rd September 1971.

● The royal family: Since 27th June 1995, Sheik Hamad Bin Khalifa Al Thani has been the Emir. He rules over Qatar, along with two of his sons, Sheik Tamin Bin Hamad and Sheik Abdullah, who is also the prime-minister.

● Economy: Apart from the huge reserves of natural gas, Qatar has a stock of 15.2 billion barrels of oil.

● Colours: The national flag is burgundy, with a white band in the shape of the blade of a scythe. White is the country's official colour, with the burgundy symbolising the blood spilt by the Qataris in several wars.

First there is the picture postcard Qatar, with its capital, Doha, situated on a calm bay. Then (page 9) in the middle of the desert, the Losail circuit, immortalised on the small screen. Qatar is definitely a country with two faces. Shinya Nakano and Loris Capirossi pose for posterity, Maria, like other women in the paddock tries out the local customs, the organisers did not depart from tradition and the grid girls (opposite) came in by plane from a neighbouring country and modesty prevailed as they wore trousers.

YAMAHA

Yamaha: the real history behind the tuning fork

The story of Soichiro Honda is one pretty much known to all: a guy who was mad about things mechanical, racing and pretty women and, in general, was a turbulent representative of the Japanese cult of the Epicure. This legend went on to become the first big success story of the motorcycle industry, built on the dreams of a son of a blacksmith who hit on the idea of taking engines off the military, who were in tatters after the collapse of the empire. He fitted them to bicycle frames and in the space of a few decades, he became the biggest constructor of

Giacomo Agostini, 1975

© M. Büla

motorcycles in the world.
But what do we know of the history of Yamaha, whose path has always been linked to its great rivalry with Honda and whose whole focus of competition when it came to Europe was to beat its home-grown rival?
Yamaha versus Honda pretty much sums up a large part of the history of modern racing. The 2004 season was marked by the most important move this century, when Valentino Rossi switched allegiance and raised the stakes.

His first boss was an English clockmaker

The story of Torakusu Yamaha is even more surprising than that of Soichiro Honda, in that he did not live to see the industrial group he had created launch itself into manufacturing motorcycles.
Born in 1851, the third son of Kanosuke Yamaha, Torakusu was already twenty before he served his first technical apprenticeship in Nagasaki, working for an English master clockmaker. Ten years later and we find him in Osaka, working for a company making medical instruments, where he perfected his skills. The turning point in his life came in 1887. Now living in Hammamatsu, Yamaha was called out to an interesting repair job on the organ of a primary school. It was an American model and in dire need of restoration. He was fascinated by the technology he discovered and he went on to build a harmonium from scratch. Proud of his creation, he was canny enough to realise he had to patent his device. This involved travelling the 300 kilometres to Tokyo. He was so determined that he made the journey on foot! At first the patent office turned him down, but he made the most of the trip to the capital to take a course in tuning. It would not be long until he started a production run.

In 1892, Yamaha was already exporting to Great Britain!

The tuning forks arrive and would soon travel around the world. In 1892, his company, Yamaha Musical Instrument Manufacturing, was already exporting 80 organs to Great Britain. Buoyed by this initial success, the company diversified into making pianos. When the company founder died, in 1916 at the age of 65, he left an empire that was already well established, with Chiyomaru Amano installed as president.
The years passed. Now it was Genichi Kawakami who ran the company, now known as "Nippon Gakki." The group was expanding rapidly and logically sought to diversify. It was the start of a foray into motorcycling and the creation of "Yamaha Motor." In 1955, came the first Yamaha, the 125 YA1, which strangely enough resembled the DKW RT 125, which at the time was reckoned to be the most copied bike in the world. 1955 was also the first year of the race at the Asuma volcano, 200 kilometres to the north of Tokyo, on a twenty kilometre long track made of volcanic cinders. The YA1, soon to be called "Akatombo," (the red dragonfly) dominated the event. The 175 YC1 was yet another DKW copy, but the 250 YD1 took its inspiration from another European machine, the Adler MB 250, but it was nevertheless the first real baby produced by the in-house engineers. In 1975, twenty years after the company was founded, the motorcycle arm

Patrick Pons, 1979

© M. Büla

Top:
Phil Read, 1964

Bottom:
Jarno Saarinen, 1973

© M. Büla

Kenny Roberts, 1983

of the Yamaha empire employed over 8000 people and produced around 800,000 bikes.

The marque evolves through racing success

Just as Honda dominated through its huge investment in research, so too Yamaha soon realised the importance of racing success when it came to improving the marque's image and sales. In 1958, Yamaha made its first foreign foray on Catalina Island, in California, on a gravel circuit, which was as bumpy as a motocross track. But Yamaha wanted more and, just like Honda a few years earlier, the Japanese sent people over to Europe to study the scene. One of them was Hiroshi Naito. It was 1960 and the man who would soon head up the technical department, attended several grands prix and came home to Japan, loaded down with information.
In 1961, Yamaha entered grands prix for the first time. A fourteen strong team of ten engineers and four mechanics arrived in France with three trucks. Five riders, Fumio Itoh, Noguchi, Sunako, Masuko and Oichi rode 125s and 250s. The total budget for the operation was 60,000 dollars.
All debuts are difficult and Yamaha was no exception to the rule, especially as the Korean war had caused a serious economic crisis in Japan. Therefore the Yamaha management decided to scrub its 1962 racing programme.
However, there was no intention to give up. The engineers continued with their work and on 7th July 1963, Yamaha scored its first world championship win in the Ardennes, in Belgium at the magnificent Spa-Francorchamps circuit. They even recorded a one-two in the 250 race, with Fumio Itoh winning ahead of Yoshikazu Sunako.

Phil Read ups the stakes

Honda and Suzuki had already participated in grands prix for several years and, like its rivals, Yamaha knew that in order to win world titles, it was not enough to enter technically competent machinery. They needed to be entrusted to experienced riders who knew the European GP circuits, which are completely different to those in Japan. Thus, on 10th November 1963 at the Japanese Grand Prix, Phil Read spontaneously offered his services to the Japanese constructor and rode a Yamaha for the first time. For much of the race, he fought for the win with Jim Redman (Honda) and Funio Itoh, before having to slacken the pace because of mechanical problems. He finished third. But the deal was done and that night, Read signed a contract worth 20,000 dollars for a year, which was about ten times more than the best contract on offer from a British factory team!
At the end of 1964, Fumio Itoh had to retire from the sport after a serious accident in the Singapore GP and Phil Read was crowned 250 world champion. It was Yamaha's first title and the first for a two-stroke engine in the class. A new era had just begun. From 1965, the marque with the three tuning forks logo began selling racing bikes to privateers and the following year, the Yamaha competition department employed 35 people as things really took off from there.

In 1968, the battle between the company's two star riders, Phil Read and Bill Ivy produced an extraordinary story line. At the Tourist Trophy, Bill Ivy obeyed team orders and let Read win the 125 race. However, he chose to make his views clear on the subject with an unforgettable performance. He rode a brave, almost reckless race, pulverising the lap record, breaking the magic "ton," lapping at over 100 mph and leaving Read for dead. But then he suddenly came to a halt, turned to the mystified crowd and shrugged his shoulders, as though asking if they had seen his team-mate! He made his point: Phil Read won, but Bill Ivy was the hero of the day.
Yamaha went on to become the ultimate supplier of customer bikes par excellence. Officially, the factory had pulled out of GP racing, but the major importers and private entrants had been passed the baton. This led to some unusual combinations, like the time Rodney Gould entered a Yamataco, by putting a Yamaha TD1C engine in a Bultaco chassis, which was the best at the time.

Christian Sarron, 1984

Jarno Saarinen was on a mission to dethrone King Ago

At the start of the 70s, a blond prince from the cold north produced some of the greatest and saddest moments in Yamaha's GP history. The most striking thing about Jarno Saarinen was a new style, with a relaxed approach and excessive angles of lean, which came from his days racing on ice which is where the young

Finn had cut his teeth. His mission was to dethrone King Ago, Giacomo Agostini, the dominant force in the 500 class. At the start of 1973, no one could match Saarinen's pace, up until that terrible day, Sunday 20th May 1973 at 15h19 at the Monza circuit.

The accident was the most serious of that era and, of course it provoked a reaction from Yamaha, which withdrew its semi-works team, although continuing its development programme to come back through the front door in 1974 to take part in the blue riband category, with the best bike in the world. What was needed was the ideal rider, a star who would help heal the wound left by the untimely death of the little Finnish prince. Rodney Gould had been appointed to look after public relations for the company and suggested to the Japanese company that they take on Giacomo Agostini, who had twice made overtures to come on board and had just been beaten within the MV Agusta team by Phil Read. King Ago at Yamaha? It was a mouth watering prospect with one proviso. Such a transfer went against the company's policy at the time: "Buying the best rider in the world from the opposition is a case of buying wins and that does not suit us," declared the men at Yamaha. It certainly is not the case today, is it Mr. Rossi?

At first they did not dare contact Agostini, so a secret test at the French Le Castellet circuit was organised for another star name, Mike Hailwood, who was just starting off in Formula 1. But "Mike the Bike" was in the United States. This opened the door to an approach for Ago, especially as Phil Read had been given Number 1 status in the MV camp. Yamaha decided to move quickly to avoid the possibility of a bidding war with Honda, who planned to return to the 500 fray. The transfer of the century was about to become reality.

At the end of 1975, King Ago honoured his contract: Yamaha won its first 500 world title with Ago in the saddle of the 500 OW 20/YZR, that had been developed starting back in November 1971. The original idea behind this machine was to stick two 250 engines together! In July 1972, the engine ran for the first time. In September, the bike turned a wheel with a brave test rider, the veteran Motohashi doing the riding. Four years later, it achieved its goal.

Wayne Rainey, 1990-1993

Yamaha: the stats

- **125 cmc:** 47 GP wins, 4 world titles (Bill Ivy in 1967, Phil Read in 1968, Kent Andersson in 1973 and '74)

- **250 cc:** 165 GP wins, 14 world titles (Phil Read in 1964, '65, '68 and '71, Rodney Gould in 1970, Jarno Saarinen in 1972, Dieter Brun in 1973, Jean-Louis Tournadre in 1982, Carlos Lavado in 1983 and '86, Christian Sarron in 1984, John Kocinski in 1990, Tetsuya Harada in 1993, Olivier Jacque in 2000)

- **350 cc:** 72 GP wins, including 6 for a Yamaha engine in a Bimota chassis. 4 world titles (Giacomo Agostini in 1974, Johnny Cecotto in 1975, Takazumi Takayama in 1977 and John Ekerold in 1980, with a Yamaha-powered Bimota)

- **500 cc:** 120 GP wins, 10 world titles (Giacomo Agostini in 1975, Kenny Roberts in 1978, '79 and '80, Eddie Lawson in 1984, '86 and '88, Wayne Rainey in 1990, '91 and '92)

- **750 cc:** 55 GP wins, 6 world titles (John Dodds in 1974, Jack Findlay in 1975, Victor Palomo in 1976, Steve Baker in 1977, Johnny Cecotto in 1978 and Patrick Pons in 1979)

- **Moto GP:** 11 GP wins, 1 world title (Valentino Rossi in 2004)

A new challenge called the OW31

Yamaha did not rest on its laurels. The Japanese marque took on another challenge and created what is possibly the bike that left the biggest impression on an entire generation, the OW31 750 cc. From the very start of practice at Daytona, in 1976, Kenny Roberts was officially clocked at 291 km/h, while unofficially, the 300 barrier had been broken for the first time. Johnny Cecotto won the race, despite the fact his tyres were destroyed. He would soon become the best paid rider of his era (600,000 dollars in 1977) while the OW31 was the most coveted bike in the world. That was almost 30 years ago. At the time, no one could imagine that, come 2004, a young, headstrong and very talented rider, would bring the blue riband title back home to Yamaha after a gap of over ten years.

Olivier Jacque, 2000

TEAMS

Kawasaki
NGK
FUCHS
SHOEI
GO!!!
YAMAHA
FILA
TAMADA
BIAGGI
Spain's N°1
YAMAHA
motogp
motogp

REPSOL
REPSOL
PROTON
PROTON
namco
SHOEI
Telefónica
MoviStar
Telefónica
MoviStar
HONDA
motogp

MOTOGP

Honda

MOTOGP

Digest

On paper, the 5 cylinder RC211V was still the dominant weapon in MotoGP. But HRC was hit by an earthquake, because not only had it lost its triple world champion, but Valentino Rossi had also taken Jeremy Burgess and his team of engineers with him to Yamaha. Picking up the pieces, the Pramac and Sito Pons (Camel) teams came together. To replace Rossi, Repsol turned to the Brazilian, Alexandre Barros, the most experienced rider on the GP grid. There was another transfer, in the shape of former double world superbike champion, the American, Colin Edwards, who joined Sete Gibernau in the Fausto Gresini Telefonica camp. Finally, while Max Biaggi used Michelins, his Camel-Pons team-mate, Makoto Tamada continued his work developing the Bridgestone tyres. The team operated from two bases, in Spain with Biaggi and in Italy with Tamada. During the summer break, HRC underwent a major reorganisation. Satoru Horrike, president Kanasawa's right hand man, was brought in to turn things around and improve communications. This meant that Koij Nakajima, Rossi's sworn enemy, now had less power. Contractually, the two Repsol riders, Barrros and Hayden were guaranteed priority in terms of receiving technical evolutions. However, in the second half of the season, Gibernau and Biaggi received slightly better treatment.

Repsol Honda

HEADQUARTERS Wijngaardveld 1,
9300 Aalst (Belgium)

INTERNET SITE www.hondaracinginfo.com

TEAM MANAGER Koij Nakajima

RIDERS
Alexandre Barros (18.10.1970)
First GP: Spain, 1986 (80)
Bresilian Champion Cyclomoto (1978)
Bresilian Champion Cyclomoto (1979)
Bresilian Champion Cyclomoto (1980)
Bresilian Champion 50 cmc (1981)
Bresilian Champion 250 cmc (1985)
Number of GP wins: 6 (4/500; 2/MotoGP)

Nicky Hayden (30.7.1981)
First GP: Japan, 2003 (MotoGP)
Champion US Supersport 600 (1999)
Champion US Superbike (2002)

TEAM STRUCTURE
Sporting director Carlo Fiorani
Chief mechanics Ramon Forcada (Alexandre Barros) and Trevor Morris (Nicky Hayden)

Camel Honda

HEADQUARTERS Poligono Industrial Sta. Rita,
C/Acustica 16,
08755 Castellbisbal/Barcelona (Spain)

INTERNET SITE www.camelhonda.com

TEAM MANAGER Sito Pons

RIDERS
Massimiliano Biaggi (26.6.1971)
First GP: Europe, 1991 (250)
Italian Champion 125 Sport-Production (1990)
European Champion 250 (1991)
World Champion 250 (1994)
World Champion 250 (1995)
World Champion 250 (1996)
World Champion 250 (1997)
Number of GP wins: 42
(29/250; 8/500; 5/MotoGP)

Makoto Tamada (4.11.1976)
First GP: Japan, 1998 (250)
Japanese Champion 250 Novice (1994)
Number of GP wins: 2 (MotoGP)

TEAM STRUCTURE
The genial Antonio Cobas, who was the technical director of the Barcelona base (Biaggi) died on Wednesday 14th April, after a cruel illness.
Technical director at the Casole d'Elsa base (Tamada)
Giulio Bernadelle
Chief mechanics Santi Mulero (Massimiliano Biaggi) and Yutaka Hirano (Makoto Tamada)

Telefonica Movistar Honda

HEADQUARTERS Via Fra Domenico Paganelli 8,
48018 Faenza (Italy)

INTERNET SITE www.gresiniracing.com

TEAM MANAGER Fausto Gresini

RIDERS
Sete Gibernau (15.12.1972)
First GP: Spain, 1992 (250)
Spanish and Catalunyan Champion 125 Junior (1991)
Number of GP wins: 9 (1/500; 8/MotoGP)

Colin Edwards (27.2.1974)
First GP: Japan, 2003 (MotoGP)
US Champion 250 (1992)
World Champion Superbike (2000)
World Champion Superbike (2002)

TEAM STRUCTURE
Sporting director Fabio Barchitta
Chief mechanics Juan Martinez (Sete Gibernau) and Fabrizio Cecchini (Colin Edwards)

3 *Massimiliano Biaggi*

4 *Alexandre Barros*

6 *Makoto Tamada*

15 *Sete Gibernau*

45 *Colin Edwards*

69 *Nicky Hayden*

Repsol Honda

Camel Honda

Telefonica Movistar

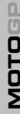

Of course, it was the big news of the year. The five times world champion, with three consecutive titles in the blue riband category, Valentino Rossi had arrived at Yamaha with some valuable baggage, in the shape of a technical team headed up by Jeremy Burgess. "It's the craziest thing I've ever taken on," reckoned the champion before the start of the season. Therefore, all Yamaha's efforts were concentrated on its star rider. All year long, he benefited from riding a YZR-M1 which was in a state of constant development. Alongside him were Carlos Checa in the factory team and Marco Melandri and Norifume Abe with Tech 3 and these guys knew they were only there to make up the numbers and they had a difficult season, as they measured up to the king of the sport. As Rossi said after taking the title, Yamaha "transformed my words into a bike." Whatever Valentino wanted, whatever he said was dealt with in double quick time. Because of this development, the Yamaha eventually matched the Honda in terms of its overall balance, even if setting it up was still rather more complex. The M1's one remaining weak point is that it is still a bit nervous over the bumps, which cost Rossi quite a few points in Brazil.

Gauloises Fortuna Yamaha

HEADQUARTERS Via Tinelli 67/69,
22050 Gerno di Lesmo, 20050 Milano (Italy)

INTERNET SITE www.yamaha-racing.com

TEAM MANAGER Davide Brivio

RIDERS
Carlos Checa (15.10.1972)
First GP: Europe, 1993 (125)
Spanish Champion 80 (1991)
Spanish Champion 250 (1995)
Number of GP wins: 2 (500)

Valentino Rossi (16.2.1979)
First GP: Malaysia, 1996 (125)
Italian Champion endurance Minibike (1992)
Italian Champion 125 Sport-Production (1994)
Italian Champion 125 (1995)
World Champion 125 (1997)
World Champion 250 (1999)
World Champion 500 (2001)
World Champion MotoGP (2002)
World Champion MotoGP (2003)
World Champion MotoGP (2004)
Number of GP wins: 68 (12/125, 14/250, 13/500, 29/MotoGP)

TEAM STRUCTURE
Technical Director Ichiro Yoda
Chief mechanics Antonio Jimenez Diaz (Carlos Checa) and Jeremy Burgess (Valentino Rossi)

7 *Carlos Checa*

17 *Norifumi Abé*

Fortuna Gauloises Tech 3

HEADQUARTERS 635 chemin du Niel,
83230 Bormes-les-Mimosas (France)

INTERNET SITE www.gauloisesracing.com

TEAM MANAGER Hervé Poncharal

RIDERS
Norifumi Abé (7.9.1975)
First GP: Japan, 1994 (500)
Japanese Champion 500 (1993)
Number of GP wins: 3 (500)

Marco Melandri (7.8.1982)
First GP: Czech Republic, 1997 (125)
Italian Champion Minibike junior A (1992)
Italian Champion Minibike junior B (1994)
Italian Champion 125 and Winner of Honda Italy Trophy (1997)
World Champion 250 (2002)
Number of GP wins: 17 (7/125, 10/250)

TEAM STRUCTURE
Chief mechanics Gilles Bigot (Norifumi Abé) and Guy Coulon (Marco Melandri)

33 *Marco Melandri*

46 *Valentino Rossi*

Gauloises Fortuna Yamaha

Fortuna Gauloises Tech 3

The Desmosedici GP4 was completely new, with around 600 of the 915 parts of the superb puzzle changed. The power of the 989 cc, 90 degree V4 engine, with desmodromic valve operation and four valves per cylinder had been increased still further and the official line is that it has 230 horsepower. A great deal of effort had been devoted to aerodynamics, with a completely enclosed saddle, from which sprouted the upper cylinders' exhaust pipe. Driveability had been seen as a weak point last year and that too had been improved. That was the pre-season theory. But almost immediately, the two riders, the same line-up as 2003, Australia's Troy Bayliss and Italy's Loris Capirossi, came up against some serious concerns. They were simply unable to transfer the power to the road. Ducati had gone too far, rather than evolving from a solid base which had proved efficient in 2003.
For its second season in MotoGP, the Borgo Panigale team, as announced at the start of the project, supported a second team run by Luis D'Antin. It ran Englishman Neil Hodgson, the reigning superbike world champion and the fiery Spaniard, Ruben Xaus on the previous year's Desmosedici.

Ducati Marlboro

HEADQUARTERS Via Cavalieri Ducati 3, 40132 Bologna (Italy)

INTERNET SITE www.ducati.com

TEAM MANAGER Livio Suppo

RIDERS
Troy Bayliss (30.3.1969)
First GP: Australia, 1997 (250)
British Superbike Champion (1999)
World Champion Superbike (2001)

Loris Capirossi (4.4.1973)
First GP: Japan, 1990 (125)
World Champion 125 (1990)
World Champion 125 (1991)
World Champion 250 (1998)
Number of GP wins: 23 (8/125,12/250, 2/500, 1/MotoGP)

TEAM STRUCTURE
Director Ducati Corse Claudio Domenicali
Technical Director Corrado Cecchinelli
Chief mechanics Bruno Leoni (Troy Bayliss) and Massimo Bracconi (Loris Capirossi)

D'Antin MotoGP

HEADQUARTERS Poligono Industrial Gitesa, C/Ramon y Cajal 25, 28814 Daganzo/Madrid (Spain)

INTERNET SITE www.dantinmotogp.com

TEAM MANAGER Luis D'Antin

RIDERS
Rubén Xaus (18.2.1978)
First GP: Great Britain, 1995 (250)
Catalunyan Supermotard 80 Champion (1993)

Neil Hodgson (20.11.1973)
First GP: Great Britain, 1992 (125)
British Champion 125 Supercup (1992)
British Champion Superbike (2000)
World Champion Superbike (2003)

TEAM STRUCTURE
Coordinator Fausto Bencivenni
Technical Director Lukas Schmidt
Chief mechanics Roberto Valetta (Rubén Xaus) and Lukas Schmidt (Neil Hodgson)

11 *Rubén Xaus*

12 *Troy Bayliss*

65 *Loris Capirossi*

50 *Neil Hodgson*

Ducati Marlboro

D'Antin MotoGP

Suzuki / Kawasaki

After two very difficult years, during which 2000 world champion Kenny Roberts lost all his motivation, the 2004 GSV-R was once again completely overhauled, this time in the right direction. The chassis now boasted a completely new rear suspension. The position of the engine had been changed, which made for a better weight distribution. There was another important technical novelty as the team switched to Bridgestone tyres. On the human front, another big change, as Freddie Spencer's former mentor, Erv Kanemoto was back. The two main riders, the Americans Kenny Roberts and John Hopkins were still on board, with frequent support from the company's test riders, Spain's Gregorio Lavilla and Japan's Yukio Kagayama.

Suzuki MotoGP

HEADQUARTERS 3 Fircroft Way, Edenbridge, Kent, TN8 6EJ (Great Britain)

INTERNET SITE www.suzuki-racing.com

TEAM MANAGER Gary Taylor

RIDERS
Kenny Roberts (25.7.1973)
First GP: United States, 1993 (250)
World Champion 500 (2000)
Number of GP wins: 8 (500)

John Hopkins (22.5.1983)
First GP: Japan, 2002 (MotoGP)
US Champion Supersport 750 (2000)
US Champion Formula Xtreme (2001)

Gregorio Lavilla (29.9.1973).
First GP: Australia, 1995 (250)
Spanish Champion Sport-Production (1993)
Spanish Champion Supersport and Sport-Production 750 (1994)

Yukio Kagayama (7.5.1974)
First GP: Japan, 1997 (250)

TEAM STRUCTURE
Director Masahito Imada
Project leader Yasuo Kamomiya
Chief mechanics Erv Kanemoto (Kenny Roberts) and Stuart Shenton (John Hopkins)

71 *Yukio Kagayama*

32 *Gregorio Lavilla*

10 *Kenny Roberts*

21 *John Hopkins*

It was year two of Kawasaki's return to the fray. The "greens" ensured they had the means to get what they wanted, by taking on a rider who was known to be quick, Japan's Shinya Nakano, while the man who was the team's test rider last year, Germany's Alexander Hofmann, was promoted to the race team. The new ZX-RR Ninja was designed and built in Switzerland by the Eskil brothers and Simon Suter. Much more compact and slimmer, it was put on a diet and gained in manoeuvrability. The engine also saw some work, including a new electronic injection and, like Suzuki, the team run by Harald Eckl had switched to Bridgestone tyres, as the Japanese company stepped up its involvement in the top category of motorcycle sport.

Kawasaki Racing

HEADQUARTERS Im Gstaudach 6, 92648 Vohenstrauss (Germany)

INTERNET SITE www.kawasaki-eckl.com

TEAM MANAGER Harald Eckl

RIDERS
Shinya Nakano (10.10.1977)
First GP: Japan, 1998 (250)
Pocket Bike regional Champion (1985)
Japanese Champion 250 (1998)
Number of GP wins: 6 (250)

Alexander Hofmann (25.5.1980)
First GP: Germany, 1997 (125)
German Champion motocross 80 (1992)
German Champion motocross 80 (1993)
German Champion motocross 125 junior (1994)
European Champion and German Champion 250 (1998)

TEAM STRUCTURE
Director Shugetsu Takata
Chief mechanics Andrea Dosoli (Shinya Nakano) and Christophe Bourguignon (Alexander Hofmann)

56 *Shinya Nakano*

66 *Alexander Hofmann*

Suzuki MotoGP

Kawasaki Racing

Aprilia / Proton

Born at Cosworth, the 3 cylinder Aprilia was further evolved at Noale, under the guidance of technical director, Dutchman Jan Witteveen. The byword was simplicity after going down some F1-type blind alleys in the recent past. "The people who came from Formula 1 thought that all a MotoGP bike's handling problems could be sorted out with electronics, but I think the complete opposite is the case," maintained Witteveen. The "ride by wire" cableless throttle remained in place, but several original features from the previous year, most notably traction control, were put to one side. The medium term goal was to come up with a brand new "made in Italy" engine. Two English riders upheld the Aprilia colours: the veteran Jeremy McWilliams and a young hopeful, Shane Byrne, who came from the British Superbike series as champion. Australia's Gary McCoy was brought in at the end of the season, as Byrne underwent surgery to his arm.

24 *Garry McCoy*

Aprilia Racing

HEADQUARTERS Via Vitalis di Giovanni 28G, 47891 Galazzano (San Marino)

INTERNET SITE www.racingaprilia.com

TEAM MANAGER Francesco Guidotti

RIDERS
Garry McCoy (18.4.1972)
First GP: Australia, 1992 (125)
Number of GP wins: 5 (2/125; 3/500)

Shane Byrne (10.12.1976)
First GP: South Africa, 2004 (MotoGP)
British Champion Superbike (2003)

Jeremy McWilliams (4.4.1964)
First GP: Australia, 1993 (500)
Irish Champion 350 Production (1988 and 1989)
Irish Champion 250 Short Circuit (1991)
Number of GP wins: 1 (250)

TEAM STRUCTURE
Technical Director Jan Witteveen
Chief mechanics Giacomo Guidotti (Shane Byrne) and Pietro Caprara (Jeremy McWilliams)

67 *Shane Byrne*

99 *Jeremy McWilliams*

For this, the second year of the four stroke project, Kenny Roberts' team started from scratch again, as had been planned. Driving the drawing board was former Formula 1 wizard, John Barnard (McLaren and Ferrari) who was the man behind several technical revolutions in motor racing. Barnard dug deep into his very full bag of ideas, coming up with a chassis that is very original and features various materials from the world of F1 and the aerospace industry. The engine was yet another evolution of last year's (a 990 cc liquid cooled V5.) Alongside faithful Japanese rider Nobuatsu Aoki was the "King's" youngest son, Kurtis Roberts. His debut in the saddle of his father's bike made people sit up, as the KR5 blew up after half a lap of the Valencia circuit in pre-season testing! The Proton uses Dunlop tyres.

9 *Nobuatsu Aoki*

Proton Digest

HEADQUARTERS 3, Lombard Way, Banbury, Oxon (Great Britain)

INTERNET SITE www.protonteamkr.com

TEAM MANAGER Kenny Roberts

RIDERS
Nobuatsu Aoki (31.8.1971)
First GP: Japan, 1990 (250)
Japanese Champion Pocket-Bike (1985)
Triple Japanese Minibike champion (1987)
Number of GP wins: 1 (250)

James Haydon (2.11.1973)
First GP: Great Britain, 1992 (250)
British Champion 125 Clubman (1990)
Champion EMRA 250 (1992, 1993 and 1994)

Kurtis Roberts (17.11.1978)
First GP: Malaysia, 1997 (250)
US Champion Formula Xtreme (1999)
US Champion Supersport 600 and Formula Xtreme (2000)

TEAM STRUCTURE
Technical Director John Barnard
Chief mechanics Nick Davis (Nobuatsu Aoki) and Tom O'Kane (Kurtis Roberts)

36 *James Haydon*

80 *Kurtis Roberts*

MS Aprilia Racing

Proton Team KR

Harris WCM

If there is one man in the paddock who deserves to have a statue erected in his honour, it is definitely New Zealander, Peter Clifford. His story began with a passion for the sport that saw him arrive in the paddock as a journalist who, once the season over, would return home to tend his flock of sheep. In 1992, when Yamaha sold the V4 engine, while ROC and Harris sold chassis, he persuaded the very rich American businessman, Bob McLean to set up a team. Thus WCM was born. The team had its moments of glory with Regis Laconi and Garry McCoy who took some GP wins. Then, last year the team developed its own bike. The chassis was made by Harris and the engine built in the team's Belgian workshop, based on a Yamaha unit. The financial situation was laughable, but the passion of a few paddock veterans such as engineers Francois Charlot, Thierry Gerin and Gerard Roussel burned brightly. In the middle of a season underscored by some fantastic performances in the rain from Michel Fabrizio, who would not see out the season, Clifford dropped another bombshell. A partnership agreement had been signed with Czech minimoto specialists, Blata who, in the not too distant future, will produce a MotoGP V6 engine!

WCM

HEADQUARTERS Parc industriel des Trois-Fontaines,
rue des Trois-Fontaines 32a,
1370 Jodoigne (Belgium)

INTERNET SITE www.harris-wcm.com

TEAM MANAGER Peter Clifford

RIDERS
Chris Burns (12.6.1980)
First GP: Great Britain, 1997 (125)
British Champion Superteen (1996)

Youichi Ui (27.11.1972)
First GP: Japan, 1995 (125)
Japanese Champion 125 (1995)
Number of GP wins: 11 (125)

James Ellison (10.9.1980)
First GP: Czech Republic, 2004 (MotoGP)
European Champion Superstock (2001)

Michel Fabrizio (17.9.1984)
First GP: Japan, 2002 (125)
Italian Champion 125 Sport-Production and
Aprilia Trophy 125 (2001)
European Champion Supersport (2003)

TEAM STRUCTURE
President Bob MacLean
Spare parts manager Mats Melander
Head of telemetry François Charlot

35 *Chris Burns*

41 *Youichi Ui*

77 *James Ellison*

84 *Michel Fabrizio*

ELLISON
Sebimoto
WISECO

TEAMS

FREE SOUL
CAMPETELLA
WURTH
Spain's Nº1
Spain's Nº1
motogp
motogp

250cc

Four riders, in three teams were accorded top status by Aprilia, in the shape of the 2004 250 RSW: they were reigning champion, Manuel Poggiali (MS Aprilia,) France's Randy De Puniet (in Lucio Cecchinello's Safilo Carrera team,) Argentina's Sebastian Porto and Spain's Alfonso "Fonsi" Gonzales-Nieto, in the Jorge "Aspar" Martinez camp. On top of that, Jan Witteveen kept a close eye on a newcomer to the category, Alex de Angelis, who was supported by the factory, just as Poggiali hit rock bottom. Apart from this group, the 250 RS remained the most popular machine in the pack.

MS Aprilia Team

HEADQUARTERS Via Vitalis di Giovanni 28G, 47891 Galazzano (San Marino)

INTERNET SITE www.racingaprilia.com

TEAM MANAGER Francesco Guidotti

RIDER
Manuel Poggiali (14.2.1983)
First GP: Imola, 1998 (125)
Italian Champion Minibike (1997)
Italian Champion 125 and Winner of Honda Italy Trophy 125 (1998)
World Champion 125 (2001)
World Champion 250 (2003)
Number of GP wins: 12 (7/125; 5/250)

TEAM STRUCTURE
Technical Director Jan Witteveen
Chief mechanic Rossano Brazzi (Manuel Poggiali)

Safilo Carrera – LCR

HEADQUARTERS Gildo Pastor Centre, 7, rue du Gabian, 98000 Monaco

INTERNET SITE www.safilocarrera.com

TEAM MANAGER Lucio Cecchinello

RIDER
Randy De Puniet (14.2.1981)
First GP: France, 1998 (125)
Winner France Cup Typhoon (1995)
French Champion 125 «national» and Winner of France Cup 125 Promosport (1997)
French Champion 125 (1998)
Number of GP wins: 4 (250)

TEAM STRUCTURE
Technical Director Massimo Biagini.

7 *Randy De Puniet*

10 *Alfonso «Fonsi» Gonzales-Nieto*

Repsol Aspar

HEADQUARTERS Poligono Industrial no 2, Avenida de los Deportes Travesia, s/n, 46600 Alzira/Valencia (Spain)

INTERNET SITE www.teamaspar.com

TEAM MANAGER Jorge Martinez

RIDERS
Alfonso «Fonsi» Gonzales-Nieto (2.12.1978)
First GP: Spain, 1997 (125)
Spanish and Catalunyan Champion 125 Junior (1995)
Spanish Champion 125 (1998)
Spanish Champion 250 (1999 and 2000)
Number of GP wins: 5 (250)

Sebastián Porto (12.9.1978)
First GP: Argentina, 1994 (125)
Argentinian Champion Minibike (1988)
Argentinian Champion Dirt-track 50 Kid (1989 and 1991)
Argentinian Champion Dirt-track 125 (1992)
Argentinian Champion 250 (1994)
European Champion 250 (1996)
Number of GP wins: 6 (250)

TEAM STRUCTURE
Technical Director Giovani Sandi
Chief mechanics Enrique Peris (Alfonso «Fonsi» Gonzales-Nieto) and Paolo Cordioli (Sebastián Porto)

19 *Sebastián Porto*

54 *Manuel Poggiali*

Repsol Aspar Team

Safilo Carrera-LCR

MS Aprilia

Aprilia Racing

HEADQUARTERS Via Vitalis di Giovanni 28G, 47891 Galazzano (San Marino)

INTERNET SITE www.racingaprilia.com

TEAM MANAGER Francesco Guidotti

RIDER
Alex De Angelis (26.2.1984)
First GP: Imola, 1999 (125)

TEAM STRUCTURE
Technical Director Jan Witteveen
Chief mechanic Giovanni Sandi (Alex De Angelis)

9 *Hugo Marchand*

11 *Joan Olivé*

Campetella Racing

HEADQUARTERS Via De Gasperi 74, 62010 Montecassiano (Italy)

INTERNET SITE www.campetella.it

TEAM MANAGER Carlo Campetella

RIDERS
Joan Olivé (22.11.1984)
First GP: Japan, 2001 (125)
Spanish Champion 50 (1998)
Winner Spanish Cup «Joven» (1999)
Spanish Champion 125 (2000)

Franco Battaini (22.7.1972)
First GP: Italy, 1996 (250)
Winner Suzuki Italy Trophy 250 (1994)

Sylvain Guintoli (24.6.1982)
First GP: France, 2000 (250)
French Champion Scooter (1995)
French Champion 250 (2000)

TEAM STRUCTURE
Technical Director Eros Braconi
Chief mechanics Fabio Braconi (Joan Olivé), Gianluca Montanari (Franco Battaini) and Christian Boudinot (Sylvain Guintoli). Christian Boudinot left the Camptella team before the end of the season

14 *Anthony West*

21 *Franco Battaini*

Freesoul Abruzzo

HEADQUARTERS Via Alfieri 102, 50013 Campi Bisenzio (Italy)

TEAM MANAGER Giordano Cerigioni

RIDERS
Hugo Marchand (22.4.1981)
First GP: France, 2000 (125)

Anthony West (17.7.1981)
First GP: Australia, 1998 (125)
Australian Champion 250 Production (1998)
Number of GP wins: 1 (250)

TEAM STRUCTURE
Technical Director Mauro Noccioli
Chief mechanics Andrea Oleari (Hugo Marchand) and Tommaso Noccioli (Anthony West)

50 *Sylvain Guintoli*

51 *Alex De Angelis*

Freesoul Abruzzo Racing

Campetella Racing

Aprilia Racing

Grefusa Aspar

HEADQUARTERS Poligono Industrial no 2, Avenida de los Deportes Travesia, s/n, 46600 Alzira/Valencia (Spain)

INTERNET SITE www.teamaspar.com

TEAM MANAGER Jorge Martinez

RIDERS
Dirk Heidolf (14.9.1976)
First GP: Germany, 1997 (125)

Hector Faubel (10.8.1983)
First GP: Spain, 2000 (125)
Winner Spanish Cup Aprilia 125 (1998)
Spanish Champion 250 (2002)

TEAM STRUCTURE
Technical Director Sergio Bonaldo
Chief mechanics Agustin Perez (Dirk Heidolf) and Sergio Bonaldo (Hector Faubel)

Matteoni Racing

HEADQUARTERS Via Larga 22, Zona artigianale, 47843 Misano Adriatico (Italy)

INTERNET SITE www.matteoniracing.net

TEAM MANAGER Massimo Matteoni

RIDER
Alex Baldolini (24.1.1985)
First GP: Italy, 2000 (125)

TEAM STRUCTURE
Chief mechanic Roberto Baglioni (Alex Baldolini)

Equipe GP de France

HEADQUARTERS Avenue des Sports, 32110 Nogaro (France)

INTERNET SITE www.scrab-competition.com

TEAM MANAGER Jean-Claude Besse

RIDERS
Arnaud Vincent (30.11.1974)
First GP: France, 1996 (125)
Provence Champion 125 (1993)
European Champion and French Champion 125 (1997)
World Champion 125 (2002)
Number of GP wins: 7 (125)

Grégory Lefort (23.6.1979)
First GP: France, 1999 (125)
French Champion 50 (1997)
French Champion 125 (2000, 2002 and 2003)

TEAM STRUCTURE
Technical Director Didier Langouët
Chief mechanics Julien Lemaire (Arnaud Vincent) and Yannis Maigret (Grégory Lefort)

Aprilia Germany

HEADQUARTERS SWS Racing AG, PO Box 23, 7205 Zizers (Switzerland)

INTERNET SITE www.250apriliagermany.com

TEAM MANAGER Dieter Stappert

RIDERS
Johan Stigefelt (17.3.1976)
First GP: Rio, 1997 (250)
Swedish Champion 125 (1994 and 1995)
Swedish Champion 250 (1996)

Chaz Davies (10.2.1987)
First GP: Japan, 2002 (125)
British Champion Minibike (1996, 1997 and 1998)

TEAM STRUCTURE
Technical Director Stefan Kurfiss
Chief mechanics Robert Reich (Johan Stigefelt) and Marco Winter (Chaz Davies)

12 *Arnaud Vincent*

16 *Johan Stigefelt*

25 *Alex Baldolini*

28 *Dirk Heidolf*

33 *Hector Faubel*

57 *Chaz Davies*

77 *Grégory Lefort*

Aprilia
Germany

Equipe GP
de France

Matteoni
Racing

Grefusa
Aspar

Honda had promised to strengthen its presence in the 250 class and it was true to its word. Four riders, in two teams, had the new RS250RW: they were Daniel Pedrosa (reigning 125 champion) and Hiroshi Aoyama with Telefonica and Toni Elias and runner up in the series, Roberto Rolfo with Fortuna. Right from the IRTA test at Catalunya, Aoyama had an evolution bike and, at first glance it was obvious that the 2004 bike had been built around Dani Pedrosa. Compact, slim and agile it was purpose built for the newcomer. The result of this was that taller and therefore heavier riders, like Roberto Rolfo were in agony for the whole season. Apart from the works bikes, three teams had private RS250R machines.

Fortuna Honda

HEADQUARTERS Potosi 38,
08030 Barcelone (Spain)

INTERNET SITE www.monlau-competicion.com

TEAM MANAGER Dani Amatriain

RIDERS
Roberto Rolfo (23.3.1980)
First GP: Italy, 1996 (250)
Number of GP wins: 3 (250)

Antonio «Toni» Elias (26.3.83)
First GP: Spain, 1999 (125)
Number of GP wins: 9 (2/125; 7/250)

TEAM STRUCTURE
Technical Director Guido Cecchini
Chief mechanics Tomasso Raponi (Roberto Rolfo) and Massimo Capanna (Toni Elias)

2 *Roberto Rolfo*

24 *Antonio "Toni" Elias*

Telefonica Movistar Honda

HEADQUARTERS c/del Puy 16 Escalera,
Andorra la Vella (Andorra)

INTERNET SITE www.telefonica.com

TEAM MANAGER Alberto Puig

RIDERS
Daniel Pedrosa (29.9.1985)
First GP: Japan, 2001 (125)
Spanish Champion Minibike (1998)
World Champion 125 (2003)
World Champion 250 (2004)
Number of GP wins: 15 (8/125; 7/250)

Hiroshi Aoyama (25.10.1981)
First GP: Pacific, 2000 (250)

TEAM STRUCTURE
Chief mechanics Mike Leitner (Daniel Pedrosa) and Ivan Bonassi (Hiroshi Aoyama)

26 *Daniel Pedrosa*

73 *Hiroshi Aoyama*

Telefonica Movistar

Fortuna Honda

Molenaar Racing

HEADQUARTERS Panoven 20,
3401 RA Ijsselstein (The Netherlands)

INTERNET SITE www.molenaarracing.com

TEAM MANAGER: Arie Molenaar

RIDER
Jakub Smrz (7.4.1983)
First GP: Czech Republic, 1998 (125)
Czech Republic Champion 125 (1998 and 1999)

TEAM STRUCTURE
Technical Director Hans Spaan
Chief mechanic Koen Van Lierop (Jakub Smrz)

6 *Alex Debon*

15 *Christian Gemmel*

Würth Honda BQR

HEADQUARTERS Mestre Nicolau, 6 Nave 4, 08440
Cardedeu (Spain)

INTERNET SITE www.hondabqr.com

TEAM MANAGER Raul Romero

RIDERS
Alex Debon (1.3.1976)
First GP: Madrid, 1998 (250)
Spanish Champion 250 (2001)

Eric Bataille (18.4.1981)
First GP: Catalunya, 2000 (125)

TEAM STRUCTURE
Chief mechanics Fausto Martinez (Alex Debon) and
Gabrielle Fontanelli (Eric Bataille)

34 *Eric Bataille*

Castrol Kiefer

HEADQUARTERS Zur Rothheck 12,
55743 Idar-Oberstein (Germany)

INTERNET SITE www.kiefer-mot.de

TEAM MANAGER Stefan Kiefer

RIDER
Christian Gemmel (9.6.1980)
First GP: Germany, 2001 (250)

TEAM STRUCTURE
Chief mechanic Jochen Kiefer (Christian Gemmel)

96 *Jakub Smrz*

Castrol Kiefer

Würth Honda BQR

Molenaar Racing

The TZM 250 was still a customer machine, with limited development. It is fair to say that, in 2004, Yamaha had other things on its mind, namely the MotoGP class and the new in-house phenomenon that was Valentino Rossi.) The three tuning forks marque therefore put its 250 programme on the back burner, but did not ignore it totally. Apart from the faithful German, Hermann Kurz, a new team entered the GP arena: NC World Team and it had a difficult start to the season. In the Kurz camp, France's Erwan Nigon did not complete the season, but he reappeared in the Equipe GP de France team, with whom he had made his debut.

Team Kurz

HEADQUARTERS Geiselroter Heidle 1, 73494 Rosenberg (Germany)

INTERNET SITE www.yamaha-kurz.de

TEAM MANAGER Hermann Kurz

RIDERS
Naoki Matsudo (25.7.1973)
First GP: Japan, 1997 (250)
Japanese Champion 1999 (250)

Erwan Nigon (27.9.83)
First GP: France, 2000 (125)
Japanese Champion 125 (2001)

TEAM STRUCTURE
Technical Director Tomohiro Saeki
Chief mechanics Uli Rölig (Naoki Matsudo) and Naoya Urakawa (Erwan Nigon)

8 *Naoki Matsudo*

36 *Erwan Nigon*

NC World Trade

HEADQUARTERS Plazza E. Enriquez 12, 47891 Dogana (San Marino)

INTERNET SITE www.ncworldtrade.com

TEAM MANAGER Loris Castellucci

RIDERS
Massimiliano Sabbatani (4.8.1975)
First GP: Imola, 1998 (125)
European Champion 125 (1998)

Taro Sekiguchi (5.12.1975)
First GP: Japan, 1999 (250)

TEAM STRUCTURE
Technical Director Franco Moro

40 *Massimiliano Sabbatani*

44 *Taro Sekiguchi*

NC World Trade

Team Kurz

TEAMS

125cc

Honda 125cc Digest

In 2003, Daniel Pedrosa was given special treatment by Honda, as sponsor, Telefonica, had done the necessary to have a "made to measure" bike built for its super-talented rider. Officially, in 2004, three riders got the best equipment, consisting of an engine kit (which other teams rented,) and a chassis kit. The recipients were Italians Andrea Dovizioso and Simone Corsi in the Scot team and Switzerland's Thomas Luthi in the Elit team. In fact, Dovizioso marked himself out as the clear number 1 for the marque, while Corsi and Luthi had all sorts of problems adapting to the new equipment. From the mid-season, Corsi reverted to the previous year's chassis and Luthi did the same for the last three races of the year.

Kopron Team Scot

HEADQUARTERS Via Brodolini 55/2,
61025 Montelabbate/Pesaro (Italy)

INTERNET SITE: www.kopron.com

TEAM MANAGER: Giancarlo Cecchini

RIDERS
Simone Corsi (24.4.1987)
First GP: Italy, 2002 (125)

Andrea Dovizioso (23.3.1986)
First GP: Italy, 2001 (125)
Italian Champion Pocket-Bike Junior B (1997 and 1998)
Winner of Challenge Aprilia 125 «under 16» (2000)
European Champion 125 (2001)
World Champion 125 (2004)
Number of GP wins: 5 (125)

TEAM STRUCTURE
Technical Director Giancarlo Cecchini

12 *Thomas Lüthi*

24 *Simone Corsi*

Elit Grand Prix

HEADQUARTERS Jeremiasova 18/1283,
15500 Prague 5-Stodulki (Czech Republic)

INTERNET SITE www.paddock.cz

TEAM MANAGER Daniel-M. Epp

RIDERS
Thomas Lüthi (6.9.1986)
First GP: Germany, 2002 (125)
Swiss Champion Pocket-Bike Junior A
(1999 and 2000)

Dario Giuseppetti (1.3.1985)
First GP: Germany, 2001 (1250)
Winner of ADAC Pro Junior Cup (2000)
German Champion 125 (2003)

TEAM STRUCTURE
Technical Director Manfred Wittenborn
Chief mechanics Stefan Fuhrer (Thomas Lüthi) and
Davide Viperino (Dario Giuseppetti)

26 *Dario Giuseppetti*

34 *Andrea Dovizioso*

Elit Grand Prix

Kopron Team Scot

Angaia Racing

HEADQUARTERS Corso Peschierai 336/1, Torini (Italy)

INTERNET SITE www.angaiaracing.com

TEAM MANAGER Giorgio Bertelli

RIDERS
Julian Simón (3.4.1987)
First GP: Spain, 2002 (125)

Mattia Angeloni (4.11.1983)
First GP: Japan, 2002 (125)
Italian Champion Minibike Senior A (1998)
Winner of Honda 125 Trophy (2000)

TEAM STRUCTURE
Technical Director Roberto Bava
Chief mechanics Simone Falconi (Julian Simón) and Romano Fusaro (Mattia Angeloni)

10 *Julian Simón*

11 *Mattia Angeloni*

Ajo Motorsports

HEADQUARTERS Erkkilankatu 11, 33100 Tampere (Finland)

INTERNET SITE www.ajo.fi

TEAM MANAGER Aki Ajo

RIDERS
Lukas Pesek (22.11.1985)
First GP: Czech Republic, 2002 (125)

Robbin Harms (9.6.1981)
First GP: Australia, 1999 (125).
Dutch Champion 125 (1996, 1997 and 1998)
Scandinavian Champion 125 (1998 and 1999)

TEAM STRUCTURE
Chief mechanics Aki Ajo (Lukas Pesek) and Jani Veijonen (Robbin Harms)

16 *Raymond Schouten*

52 *Lukas Pesek*

Molenaar Racing

HEADQUARTERS Panoven 20, 3401 RA Ijsselstein (The Netherlands)

INTERNET SITE www.molenaarracing.com

TEAM MANAGER Arie Molenaar

RIDER
Raymond Schouten (15.3.1985)

TEAM STRUCTURE
Chief mechanic Hans Spaan (Raymond Schouten)

69 *Robbin Harms*

Molenaar Racing

Ajo Motorsport

Angaia Racing

The little Austrian orange squad tackled its second season in the world championship. At the same time, riders were taken on at a lower level, most notably in the European and German championships. Technical Director, Harald Bartol created a sensation with a very unusual technical solution: "Our engine is traditional, using a carburettor, but we have added an injector which acts directly on the head depending on demand and it is all controlled electronically." After coming close on several occasions, Casey Stoner gave the Austrian bike its first GP win in Malaysia.

Red Bull KTM

HEADQUARTERS Stallhofnerstrasse 3,
5230 Mattighofen (Austria)

INTERNET SITE www.ktm.at

TEAM MANAGER Stefan Pierer

RIDERS
Casey Stoner (16.10.1985)
First GP: Great Briain, 2001 (125)
Winner of Challenge Aprilia RS125 (2000)
Number of GP wins: 2 (125)

Mika Kallio (8.11.1982)
First GP: Germany, 2001 (125)

TEAM STRUCTURE
Technical Director Harald Bartol
Chief mechanic Mario Galeotti
Research and Development Wolfgang Felber

27 *Casey Stoner*

36 *Mika Kallio*

Red Bull
36
Red Bull
KTM
KTM
Red Bull
KTM
DUNLOP
ÖHLINS

The situation was less clear at Aprilia than in the Honda camp as, officially, the Italian marque was not represented in this category. On paper therefore, the teams with the 2004 RSW all had the same equipment and it was up to them to develop it. However, the teams were not about to help one another, as could be seen by the bidding war surrounding Hector Barbera, between the team financed by footballer, Clarence Seedorf and the promising Spanish rider's former team run by Jorge "Aspar" Martinez.

3 *Hector Barbera*

Safilo Oxydo - LCR

HEADQUARTERS Gildo Pastor Centre, 7 rue du Gabian, 98000 Monaco

INTERNET SITE www.safilocarrera.com

TEAM MANAGER Lucio Cecchinello

RIDERS
Roberto Locatelli (5.7.1974)
First GP: Italy, 1994 (125)
Italian Champion d'enduro 50 Novice (1990)
Italian Champion d'enduro 80 Novice (1991)
Italian Champion 125 Sport-Production (1993)
World Champion 125 (2000)
Number of GP wins: 9 (125)

Mattia Pasini (13.8.1985)
First GP: South Africa, 2004 (125)

TEAM STRUCTURE
Technical Director Massimo Branchini
Chief mechanics Andrea Serrentino (Roberto Locatelli) and Cristian Gabarrini (Mattia Pasini)

15 *Roberto Locatelli*

19 *Alvaro Bautista*

Master Repsol

HEADQUARTERS Poligono Industrial no 2, Avenida de los Deportes Travesia, s/n, 46600 Alzira/Valencia (Spain)

INTERNET SITE www.teamaspar.com

TEAM MANAGER Jorge Martinez

RIDERS
Pablo Nieto (4.6.1980)
First GP: Catalunya, 1998 (125)
Number of GP wins: 1 (125)

Sergio Gadea (30.12.1984).
First GP: Spain, 2003 (125)

TEAM STRUCTURE
Technical Director Giovani Sandi
Chief mechanics Angel Perurena (Pablo Nieto) and Sandro Galli (Sergio Gadea)

22 *Pablo Nieto*

Seedorf Racing

HEADQUARTERS c/Fray Juan Gil no 5, 28036 Madrid (Spain)

INTERNET SITE www.seedorfracing.com

TEAM MANAGER Susana López Pichot

RIDERS
Hector Barbera (2.11.1986)
First GP: Japan, 2002 (125)
Winner of Valence Aprilia 50 Cup (2000)
Winner of Spanish Aprilia 125 Cup (2001)
Spanish Champion 125 (2002)
Number of GP wins: 6 (125)

Alvaro Bautista (21.11.1984)
First GP: Spain, 2002 (125)
Spanish Champion 125 (2003)

TEAM STRUCTURE
Technical Director Christian Lundberg
Chief mechanics Manuel Santos (Hector Barbera) and David Galacho (Alvaro Bautista)

33 *Sergio Gadea*

54 *Mattia Pasini*

Seedorf Racing

Master-Repsol

Safilo Carrera-LCR

Globet.com Racing

HEADQUARTERS Via Beltramina 3, CP 4356, 6904 Lugano Molino Nuovo (Switzerland)

INTERNET SITE www.racingworldteam.com

TEAM MANAGER Stefano Bedon

RIDERS
Gino Borsoi (11.3.1974)
First GP: Italy, 1996 (125)

Mike Di Meglio (17.2.1988)
First GP: France, 2003 (125)

TEAM STRUCTURE
Technical Director Gino Borsoi
Chief mechanics Roberto Dalla Nora (Gino Borsoi) and Maurizio Soli (Mike Di Meglio)

Rauch Bravo

HEADQUARTERS Worldwide Communications, (Italy)

INTERNET SITE www.worldwidegroup.net

TEAM MANAGER Fiorenzo Caponera

RIDERS
Steve Jenkner (31.5.1976)
First GP: Germany, 1996 (125)
German Champion Minibike (1993)
Number of GP wins: 1 (125)

Marco Simoncelli (20.1.1987)
First GP: Czech Republic, 2002 (125)
Italian Champion Minibike (1999)
European Champion Minibike (2000)
European Champion 125 (2002)
Number of GP wins: 1 (125)

TEAM STRUCTURE
Chief mechanics Aligi Deganello (Steve Jenkner) and Tommaso Rapori (Marco Simoncelli)

Matteoni Racing

HEADQUARTERS Via Larga 22, Zona artigianale, 47843 Misano Adriatico (Italy)

INTERNET SITE www.matteoniracing.net

TEAM MANAGER Massimo Matteoni

RIDERS
Mirko Giansanti (14.9.1976)
First GP: Italy, 1996 (125)

Jordi Carchano (2.7.1984)
First GP: Catalunya, 2003 (125)

TEAM STRUCTURE
Chief mechanics Claudio Macciotta (Mirko Giansanti) and Sanzio Raffaelli (Jordi Carchano)

6 *Mirko Giansanti*

21 *Steve Jenkner*

23 *Gino Borsoi*

28 *Jordi Carchano*

58 *Marco Simoncelli*

63 *Mike Di Meglio*

Matteoni Racing

Rauch Bravo

Globet.com

Abruzzo Racing

HEADQUARTERS Via del Consorzio 10,
60015 Falconara, Ancona (Italy)

TEAM MANAGER Giuliano Cerigioni

RIDERS
Youichi Ui (27.11.1972)
First GP: Japan, 1995 (125)
Japanese Champion 125 (1995)
Number of GP wins: 11 (125)

Gioele Pellino (13.8.1983)
First GP: Italy, 2002 (125)
Winner of Challenge Aprilia 125 «under 18» (1999)

Andrea Ballerini (2.7.1973)
First GP: Australia, 1995 (125)
Number of GP wins: 1 (125)

TEAM STRUCTURE
Technical Director Andrea Orlandi
Chief mechanics Alberto Bernardi (Youichi Ui,
puis Andrea Ballerini) and Stefano Cozzini (Gioele Pellino)

Sterilgarda Racing

HEADQUARTERS Via Cavou 33,
46043 Castiglione delle Stiviere/Mantova (Italy)

INTERNET SITE www.fontanaracing.com

TEAM MANAGER Italo Fontana

RIDER
Lorenzo Zanetti (10.8.1987)
First GP: Italy, 2004 (125)

TEAM STRUCTURE
Chief mechanic Roberto Materassi

Team Hungary

HEADQUARTERS 2120 Dunakeszi Foti ùt,
055 Hrsz (Hungary)

INTERNET SITE www.tothimi.com

TEAM MANAGER Imre Toth

RIDERS
Imre Toth (6.9.1985)
First GP: Japan, 2002 (125)

Vesa Kallio (6.9.1980)
First GP: Germany, 2003 (250)

TEAM STRUCTURE
Technical Director Romano Ciatti
Chief mechanics Rolando Zanni (Imre Toth) and
Ferdinando Fabiani (Vesa Kallio)

25 *Imre Toth*

41 *Youichi Ui*

42 *Gioele Pellino*

45 *Lorenzo Zanetti*

50 *Andrea Ballerini*

66 *Vesa Kallio*

Team Hungary

Sterilgarda Racing

Abruzzo Racing

As in the previous year, the Mediterranean "cousins" were entered under two different names: Derbi and Gilera, with the two marques both owned by the giant Piaggio group. There were now two teams with two riders each and, technically, huge efforts were made. Italian engineer, Luigi Dall'Igna, who had been running the Aprilia MotoGP project, rejoined the team that was still run by Giampiero Sacchi. Belgium's Olivier Liegeois was in charge of development. On the driver front, Gilera took on the experienced Stefano Perugini and a late-blooming talent, discovered the previous year riding a Malaguti, the 26 year old Fabrizio Lai.

Caja Madrid Derbi Racing

HEADQUARTERS c/La Barca 5-7, 08107 Martorelles (Spain)

INTERNET SITE www.derbiracing.com

TEAM MANAGER Giampiero Sacchi

RIDERS
Angel Rodriguez (20.5.1985)
First GP: Catalunya, 2000 (125)
Spanish Champion 125 (2001)

Jorge Lorenzo (4.5.1987)
First GP: Spain, 2002 (125)
Number of GP wins: 4 (125)

TEAM STRUCTURE
Sporting director Luca Boscoscuro
Technical Director Luigi Dall'Igna
Research and Development Olivier Liégeois
Chief mechanics Gérard Petit (Angel Rodriguez) and Juan Llansa (Jorge Lorenzo)

47 *Angel Rodriguez*

48 *Jorge Lorenzo*

Metis Gilera Racing

HEADQUARTERS Corse Sempione 43, 20145 Milan (Italy)

INTERNET SITE www.gilera.com

TEAM MANAGER Giampiero Sacchi

RIDERS
Stefano Perugini (10.9.1974)
First GP: Italy, 1993 (125)
Italian Champion 125 Sport-Production (1992)
European Champion 125 (1993)
Italian Champion 125 (1993)
Number of GP wins: 5 (125)

Fabrizio Lai (14.12.1978)
First GP: Valencia, 2001 (125)
European Champion Minibike (1996)
European Champion Minibike (1997)
Winner of Honda 125 Trophy (1999)
Italian Champion 125 (2002)

TEAM STRUCTURE
Chief mechanics Giuseppe Torcolacci (Stefano Perugini) and Luigi Naldi (Fabrizio Lai)

7 *Stefano Perugini*

32 *Fabrizio Lai*

Metis Gilera Racing

Caja Madrid Derbi Racing

Malaguti is a name that has featured on the nursery slopes of many riders' careers, as they discovered the delights of two wheels on one of the marque's mopeds. But Malaguti has also got a long competition history and this was revived on the grand prix scene last year. In 2004, the yellow machines, especially that of the Hungarian, Gabor Talmacsi, were the revelation of the category. The team's number one rider put up some strong showings on this inventive bike, which boasted possibly the best handling in the class. "We have made progress this season, but we still have much to do this winter, especially in terms of increasing the power," explained the man in charge, Nicola Casadei, in Valencia. It is a project worth watching.

Semprucci Malaguti

HEADQUARTERS Via Villagrande 228,
61024 Mombaroccio/Pesaro (Italy)

INTERNET SITE www.teamsemprucci.it

TEAM MANAGER Giorgio Semprucci

RIDERS
Manuel Manna (10.2.1984)
First GP: Portugal, 2003 (125)
Italian Champion Minibike (1993)
Italian Champion Minibike (1995)

Gabor Talmacsi (28.5.1981)
First GP: Czech Republic, 1997 (125)
Hungarian Champion 125 (1999)

TEAM STRUCTURE
Executiv Director Nicola Casadei
Technical Director Pierluigi Aldrovandi
Chief mechanics Vanni Corbara (Manuel Manna) and
Luca Battistini (Gabor Talmacsi)

8 *Manuel Manna*

14 *Gabor Talmacsi*

Semprucci Malaguti

THE CHAMPIONS

VALENTINO ROSSI
DANI PEDROSA
ANDREA DOVIZIOSO

Valentino Rossi

Sete Gibernau and Valentino Rossi bashing fairings is an image that sums up the season.

Never mind what circuit, never mind what bike, Rossi popped the champagne cork nine times this season from the top step of the podium.

The conductor and his tuning forks

Each year, for the past four years, the writer faces the same problem when it comes to discussing the champion in the blue riband category of motorcycle sport, previously known as the 500 cc class and now called MotoGP. The problem is straightforward enough to discern, but much harder to resolve. How does one talk about Valentino Rossi without sounding banal, without using terms already deployed a thousand times before: genial, extraordinary, spectacular, perfect, cunning, extra-terrestrial, cocky, communicative, perfectionist? How does one write something new about this young man who deserves his place in the pantheon of greats, even if it is impossible to compare him to those of a different generation such as Giacomo Agostini for example?

How? Well, one has to chose a theme. And the theme of this agreeable exercise for 2004 is courage. Because Valentino Rossi showed courage in taking on a new challenge, packing his bags, leaving a comfortable home which no one was forcing him to do, to take on a virtually blank sheet of paper and a bet that seemed crazy to all his peers. He decided to turn Yamaha into a winner and give the three tuning forks marque its first title since 1992. Taking on this challenge, Rossi knew that he would win new friends and supporters, who were intrigued to find out if this over-gifted lad was really capable of winning with a bike whose initials, MI, were jokingly attributed the name of "Mission Impossible," rather than its birth name of M1. Rossi knew he would also and undoubtedly make a few enemies and that the huge Honda task force would do all in its power to stop him realising his dream.

But realise it he did, despite contractual wranglings that prevented him slinging his leg over the Yamaha until early January and despite the armada of RC211V, an armada that seemed to lack an admiral, given that Barros struggled, Hayden was disappointing, although Gibernau showed plenty of courage. He triumphed and how! He sowed the seeds in the IRTA test at Catalunya and then in Jerez, at the championship dress rehearsals. Then, at the first race of the season, in South Africa, Valentino had to ride over his own limits to win his first race with Yamaha, just as he won his last with Honda. He beat Max Biaggi and showed everyone, despite speaking words of caution, that the Number 46 would already be a force to be reckoned with this season.

Sushi and pasta: the M1 project men from Yamaha, with Davide Brivio and Valentino Rossi. The mix worked.

Next came some difficulties in the rain in Jerez, he was beaten by Gibernau at Le Mans, but each time, he fired back. After being eliminated in Rio, he won at Donington. After getting a pasting in Qatar, he swept through those who thought he was their friend, by turning up the wick and winning in Malaysia. Sete Gibernau has still not recovered from that one. Then, in Phillip Island, after an enthralling duel, he took yet another title.

For the first time since the Wayne Rainey era, the orchestra had a conductor who knew how to make do with just three tuning forks. The Honda bigwigs thought they were unbeatable and they were convinced they were going to "kill" Rossi with their advanced technology. The giant discovered it had feet of clay. And all this was due to the courage of one man and one team and the work of a racing department that had rolled up its sleeves, spurred on by the arrival of Valentino Rossi.

Rossi on the deck shows just how much the greatest champion of the current era had to raise his game to achieve his objectives.

"Yamaha turned my words into a bike"

You have won eight races with this Yamaha that so many riders have criticised. What has changed?
A lot of things, but especially the work methods. Right from my first test in Malaysia, I had full confidence in the project. Maybe I didn't think it would evolve to such a high level, but it was clear that we had the means to produce a nice surprise. Right from the start, Yamaha followed my comments to the letter, with the engineers turning my words into a bike. On top of that, my team worked its magic.
But what about the rider Valentino? Because when one looks at the performance of the other Yamaha riders, the results are not so good.
(Smiles) I am a Yamaha rider, so I am happy when my team-mates do well. But if they experienced more problems, that doesn't really bother me and maybe that's the difference.
What was lacking at Yamaha when you joined?
A rider to point them in the right direction. You know, the Honda is a fantastic bike; so much so that some people thought that everything about it was easy, but that's not the case. Up to last year, there was too much disparity within the pack. With my team, we had the courage to change tack and I do not regret this choice.
And the Yamaha continued to evolve?
Yes, but the Honda is still an easier machine to fine tune. But today, I really get immense pleasure from riding the M1 and you know that for me, pleasure is the main thing. The day I don't enjoy it, I will stop.
The Formule 1?
Wait and see!

Another triumphal finish as, one week after the Qatar "affair," Rossi wins in Malaysia.

A royal setting for the biking emperor. Barcelona and the Yamaha team launch at the start of the season. The acrobat was about to perform in style.

BUSINESS CARD

Name:	Rossi
Given name:	Valentino
Born:	16 February 1979
At:	Urbino/Italy
First race:	1992
First GP:	Malaysia, 1996 (125)
Number of GP wins:	68 (12/125; 14/250; 13/500; 29/MotoGP)
First GP win:	Czech Republic, 1996 (125)
Titles:	9 (Endurance minibike 1992, Italian Champion 125 Sport-Production 1994, Italian Champion 125 1995, World champion 125 1997, World champion 250 1999, World champion 500 2001, World champion MotoGP 2002, 2003, 2004)

Career details

1990: Regional karting championship
1991: 5th Italian junior karting championship, first Minibike win
1992: Italian Champion endurance Minibike
1993: 12th Italian Championship 125 Sport-Production (Cagiva)
1994: Italian Champion 125 Sport-Production (Cagiva)
1995: 3th European Championship 125, 11th Spanish championship 125 open, Italian Champion 125 (Aprilia)
1996: 9th World championship 125, 10th European championship 125 (Aprilia)
1997: World Champion 125 (Aprilia)
1998: 2th World championship 250 (Aprilia)
1999: World Champion 250 (Aprilia)
2000: 2th World championship 500 (Honda)
2001: World Champion 500 (Honda)
2002: World Champion MotoGP (Honda)
2003: World Champion MotoGP (Honda)
2004: World Champion MotoGP (Yamaha)

A title-winning shower as Capirossi sprays Rossi at Phillip Island.

Facts and figures

- Valentino Rossi is the first rider since Eddie Lawson to win the title in the blue riband category with two different makes, in two consecutive years. He also handed Yamaha its first title, since the unfortunate Wayne Rainey did so in 1992.
- A supreme talent, early in the season, Rossi was invited to try a 2004 Ferrrari F1 car at the Fiorano circuit. He got within 3 seconds of Michael Schumacher's lap record. More and more pundits reckon that in the not too distant future, he could switch to four wheels.
- With an estimated income of 15 million Euros per year, Valentino Rossi is Italy's highest paid sportsman.

The magical number 46 and global popularity

The perfect rider is Rossi on the attack.

Daniel Pedrosa

Family photo for a second title in two years for the 250 Telefonica Movistar team.

The agility of a jockey, the courage of a rider as Dani Pedrosa plies his trade in Australia.

Dani, the titanium rider

Everyone who follows the world championship still remembers that day in early April 2001, somewhere between the amusement park and the paddock in Suzuka for the opening round of the season. Alberto Puig was limping along, thanks to a permanent souvenir of a dreadful racing accident at Le Mans. Following him like a shadow were three young men, kids really, who looked totally bemused by everything going on. The three lads were Antonio "Toni" Elias, Joan Olive and Daniel Pedrosa. As they walked past, some wag uttered a line that was to stick throughout the season as these young Spaniards began their riders' apprenticeships: "Look, there goes mother hen Alberto Puig and his three little chicks."
Alberto was there to teach them all about racing and all about life, while protecting them from a world that seems to get ever more cruel. So, when the Continental Circus returned to the Old Continent, the mother hen became even more demanding. The little chaps would not sleep at the track in a motorhome, they would return to a hotel every night. They would have dinner and breakfast together, when the mother hen would make sure they said hello to the paddock veterans and be polite.
Of the three, only one would stick with the master and that was Dani Pedrosa, now a double world champion in two different categories. "I nicknamed Dani, "Titanic," not because of the famous passenger liner, but because he is like the metal, like titanium. Pedrosa is hard, light and cold," explained Sete Gibernau, his elder.
He is definitely not one of the mad young guys of the paddock who run amok. He is calm, cold and can be calculating when he needs to. It is equally true that he is a major talent, an immeasurable talent, as the man closest to him, his mother hen, Alberto Puig relates: "The most impressive thing about this young man is that he has so much talent that I have still not worked out just how far he can go."
In 2004, he pulled off an amazing achievement in winning the 250 title at his first attempt, as did his predecessor Manuel Poggiali.

"Never settle for what you've got" is Alberto Puig's constant mantra for his gifted student, Dani Pedrosa.

It happened in Rio. For several laps, his team had told him he could settle for second, but the new world champion worried his predecessor, Manuel Poggiali, all the way to the flag.

Daniel Pedrosa

"I am very happy with the life I lead"

Dani, do you find being a professional rider a demanding job? Do you have to pass up on some of the finer things in life?
A few. There are some things I would like to do, but cannot. Take a night out in Qatar for example. I was invited to go out and eat seafood, but I turned it down. It's not that I don't like it, but I am very careful about what I eat. But don't get the wrong idea. I am very happy with the life I lead.
You still have one weak point – riding in the rain. Is it down to fear?
No, not really. But when it rains, I have always found it difficult to get the right feeling on the bike. From that point, all I'm thinking about is not falling off. But I get the impression this is gradually improving.

"Weight has always been the enemy, we know that..."

But an advantage or not?
The situation has been the same for a while now: the late Kato, Harada, Capirossi, even Sito Pons way back when; they all derived an advantage from their light weight compared to some of their rivals. This year, the discussion got heated because no one had thought we would win.
There have been some strange incidents in the races. Have you ever deliberately tried to knock off a rival's brake lever in a duel?
No, I try and win through my own ability and that's the way I like it.

First GP, first triumph: South Africa.

In the rain in Jerez, Pedrosa led for the early stages, ahead of eventual winner, Roberto Rolfo.

Rossi says the rider is more important than the bike. Your views?
I think he is absolutely right. Just like in F1, the bike is definitely very important in the top disciplines, but no way is it as important as the rider.
You seem to be a quiet sort of person and yet you have been the target of all sorts of attacks this year, some of them to do with the fact that you only weight 54 kilos, kit included.
I think that for some people, this was a way of justifying their own results. You know, before every season, the team bosses make promises, big promises to their sponsors and they don't always deliver on them.

What's the worst thing that happened to you?
Oh, there have been all sorts of incidents, but most of them were back in my motocross days.
Let's talk about crashes, including the very serious one you had in qualifying for the 2003 Australian GP.
Given what could have happened, I reckon I'm in perfect condition, although its true I still don't have total mobility in my left ankle.
Your father says you are a perfectly "normal" young man. How do you manage that in this world of glory and over-inflated egos?
There are strange people in this world who try to get under your skin. Everyone has their own qualities and faults. I think that, seen from the outside, I am pretty much alright. But believe me, I'm not perfect and I am very happy the way I am.

But doesn't this quiet image go against you in this job?
lObviously, I'm not as charismatic as some, or as popular in terms of appearing on shows or to be caught up in scandals. But there you go, I prefer to be recognised for what I do on the track and leave it at that.
What are you most proud of?
Of my consistency in performance terms, because I know that is something very difficult to achieve. Of course, it is great to win races, but consistency is more important and there are not many riders who can achieve that over the course of a season.

Champions in the plural, as Valentino Rossi joins his young fellow countryman.

BUSINESS CARD

Name:	Pedrosa
Given name:	Daniel «Dani»
Born:	29 September 1985
At:	Castellar del Vallès/Spain
First race:	1993
First GP:	Japan, 2001 (125)
Number of GP wins:	15 (8/125; 7/250)
First GP win:	Netherlands, 2002 (125)
Titles:	(Minibike 1998, 125 World championship 2003, 250 World championship 250 2004)

Career details

1996: 2nd Spanish Championship Minibike
1997: 3rd Spanish Championship Minibike
1998: Spanish Champion Minibike
1999: 8th "Joven" Cup (Honda)
2000: 4th Spanish Championship 125 (Honda)
2001: 8th Spanish Championship 125 (Honda)
2002: 3rd Spanish Championship 125 (Honda)
2003: 125 World Champion (Honda)
2004: 250 World Champion (Honda)

Facts and figures

- Crowned at the age of 19 years and 18 days, Daniel Pedrosa is the youngest ever 250 world champion (ahead of Melandri – 20 years and 74 days and a certain Valentino Rossi – 20 years and 250 days.)
- It is the first time since Carlo Ubbiali in 1960 that a 125 world champion has won the 250 category the following year.
- The product of a Spanish school created by Honda and Movistar around Alberto Puig, Dani Pedrosa did not make the cut, automatically chosen at the end of the 1999 "Joven" cup and it was Puig who insisted he was called back.

Two men for one number one: Alberto Puig and Daniel Pedrosa.

The Spanish flag flutters in the breeze as the gifted Spaniard takes another win.

125cc

Andrea Dovizioso

Crowned a week earlier in Malaysia, Andrea Dovizioso leads the way in Australia, chased by Jorge Lorenzo and Casey Stoner.

Victory and a champion is born!

He wanted a motorbike that made a noise...

A champion at 18 and a half. It is no longer a surprise, as these past few years have been marked by the arrival of what the Grand Prix world calls the "baby riders". They are young and virtually born on a mini-bike, brought up on a diet of duelling and grow by simply flying over obstacles. What is more surprising in the case of Andrea Dovizioso and it also applies to Daniel Pedrosa, who preceded him in 125 and triumphed this year in 250, is the level of self assurance these young men can demonstrate, their capacity to deal with stress and to keep a perfectly cool head and not succumb to pressure, even if they are fighting to the nearest thousandth of a second, even if much is at stake around them. "What me, do the maths and just make sure of the title? No, I am not a MotoGP class rider, I am almost nothing. At our age, just one thing matters and that is winning races, a lot of races," said the young Italian on the eve of taking the title in Malaysia. The following day, he missed out on the win by just 29 thousandths from Casey Stoner, having tried one last move at the final corner.

The story of his career is a simple but enjoyable one. As a little lad, Andrea Dovizioso had an idol, Kevin Schwantz and that's why he adopted the American's number 34. He was already an independent lad. "For his third birthday," recalls Antonio, his father, "I bought him an electric mini-moto, a copy of a Yamaha Tenere, with two stabiliser wheels at the back. Six months later, it was not enough for him: "Papa, I want a real bike, one that makes a noise..." I said okay, you will have your real bike when you can balance on your own. A few days later, he had found a way of getting the trainer wheels off..." After that, he started racing pocket bikes at the age of 8. When he was 11, he took his first Italian title. In 2001, he won the European 125 championship and took part in his first grand prix. He was spotted by Honda in 2003, who made him their number one rider that year. In South Africa, he won the first GP of his career and was leading the championship and he kept that lead until he took the title.

A 125 pulls a wheelie; something they could not do a few years back.

125cc

Andrea Dovizioso

"With my friends, I can go crazy"

Andrea, we know you as a nice but shy guy. True or false?
Maybe, but you can be sure that in normal life, with my friends, I can get out of control.
It's the same thing on track, where you very rarely make a mistake. Is it because you are a bit less aggressive than some of your rivals?
Oh, please don't talk about my weak point. It's true that I have to become a bit tougher in the middle of a tight pack.
Tell us about this decisive race in Malaysia.
It was not at all easy and it is no coincidence that there were so many fallers. The track had changed completely since the morning warm-up and it was a surprising situation. Along with Stoner, we were running between 2 or 3 seconds off our qualifying pace and we were out on our own at the front, as the others were still going quite slowly. In this situation, I settled calmly into Casey's slipstream and I tried an attack right at the very end. Unfortunately, I made a mistake.
Andrea, you are talking about the race, but what about the title?
Yes, yes I know. Now, there is so much going through my head that I'm finding it hard to say what I feel. Maybe it's because with the lead I had before coming to Malaysia, I was half expecting the title. (long pause.) Either that or, maybe that's all there is to a title and there is no more emotion to come? But there is one thing I am sure of and that is that I dedicate this to my Dad, Antonio, who has always supported me and, when I was three years old would take me out on my motocross bike. That's where it all started.

Andrea and his fan club: in Sepang, the young Italian was the first 2004 world champion to secure his crown.

"I did not think it would all be done so quickly"

Looking at the figures, you have dominated the championship right from the first race, which is very rare in this category.
Yes, and I did not think it would all be done so quickly. So far, in mini-bikes or the year of my European title, the title only came my way in the final race of the season. This year was different. At the start of the season, I was on a roll because I had a very competitive bike and immediately after my first win (South Africa,) I believed in the title. But there was always a doubt. Locatelli was also very quick, then Barbera got involved in our duel, as did several others. Then, at the Sachsenring, when I went from first to fourth place in the space of a few metres, I began to have serious doubts.
Then came Donington.
That's where I won my title. It was in England that I made a big step forward in psychological terms. Up until then, I had the better of my rivals several times, but I had never managed to lose them and go off on my own, which is the hardest thing for a rider to do. But it happened at Donington.
What is the main change between the promising Dovizioso of 2003 and the triumphant one this year?
Last year, I already felt capable of fighting for the title, but my privateer chassis was not up to it.
And next year, is it the 250 class?
A new chapter begins and I hope that Honda will give me a works bike again. I'm ready to learn something new, even though I think I could do something very good quite quickly. It's an exciting prospect. It will be very hard to win immediately, because Pedrosa is a real phenomenon and there are a lot of other quick riders. But…
With someone of his talent, anything is possible.

A gust of wind on the podium sees Dovizioso fighting with his national flag.

A duel with Stoner: they were two of the best this season.

BUSINESS CARD

Name	Dovizioso
Given name:	Andrea
Born:	23rd March 1986
At:	Forlimpopoli/Italy
First race:	1994
First GP:	Italie, 2001 (125)
Number of GP wins:	5 (125)
First GP win:	South Africa, 2004 (125).
Titles:	5 (Minibike Junior B 1997 and 1998, Challenge Aprilia "under 16" 2000, European 125 championship 2001 and 125 World Championship 2004)

Career Details

1994: 3rd Italian Championship Minibike Junior A
1995: 2nd Italian Championship Minibike Junior A
1996: 2nd Italian Championship Minibike Junior A
1997: Italian Champion Minibike Junior B
1998: Italian Champion Minibike Junior B
1999: 2nd Italian Championship Minibike Senior A
2000: Winner of the Challenge Aprilia "under 16" (Aprilia)
2001: European Champion 125 (Aprilia)
2002: 16th World championship 125 (Honda)
2003: 5th World championship 125 (Honda)
2004: World champion 125 (Honda)

Kevin Schwantz's number – 34 – and an acknowledgement of victory as Andrea Dovizioso has a bright future ahead of him.

Facts and figures

- Andrea Dovizioso is the fourth youngest world champion in history, behind Loris Capirossi, Daniel Pedrosa and Valentino Rossi
- It is the first time since 1995 (Haruchika Aoki) that a rider wins the title having led the championship from the opening round
- Andrea is engaged to Samuela De Nardi, a young rider who races in the "Trofeo Motocicliste" in Italy with an Aprilia 1000 Tuono. She attends most of the European GPs with Dovizioso, when she won't anyone else fill the role of his "brolly dolly"

Neck and neck with Jorge Lorenzo, but who has won?

Dovizioso, Lorenzo, Stoner: three different makes in the top three places of a GP sums up the 125 scene.

3
BIAGGI

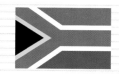

SOUTH AFRICA
Welkom

It was the win Valentino Rossi coveted the most. In his first ride on the Yamaha M1, he beat Max Biaggi at the Welkom circuit. The world champion therefore had plenty of souvenirs to bring home from his African trip, apart from the usual, yet superb post card images.

MOTOGP

South Africa Grand Prix
18th April 2004 / Welkom - 4.242 m

STARTING GRID

1.	46	V. Rossi	Yamaha	1'32.647
2.	15	S. Gibernau	Honda	1'32.682
3.	3	M. Biaggi	Honda	1'32.919
4.	69	N. Hayden	Honda	1'33.098
5.	45	C. Edwards	Honda	1'33.111
6.	56	S. Nakano	Kawasaki	1'33.276
7.	33	M. Melandri	Yamaha	1'33.296
8.	4	A. Barros	Honda	1'33.359
9.	65	L. Capirossi	Ducati	1'33.522
10.	10	K. Roberts	Suzuki	1'33.543
11.	21	J. Hopkins	Suzuki	1'33.598
12.	6	M. Tamada	Honda	1'33.679
13.	66	A. Hofmann	Kawasaki	1'33.815
14.	7	C. Checa	Yamaha	1'33.884
15.	50	N. Hodgson	Ducati	1'33.977
16.	11	R. Xaus	Ducati	1.34.103
17.	99	J. McWilliams	Aprilia	1'34.404
18.	17	N. Abé	Yamaha	1'34.484
19.	67	S. Byrne	Aprilia	1'34.703
20.	9	N. Aoki	Proton KR	1'34.845
21.	12	T. Bayliss	Ducati	1'35.804
22.	84	M. Fabrizio	Harris WCM	1'36.982

RACE: 28 LAPS = 118.776 KM

1. Valentino Rossi	43'50.218 (162.569 km/h)
2. Massimiliano Biaggi	+ 0"210
3. Sete Gibernau	+ 7"255
4. Alexandre Barros	+ 18"667
5. Nicky Hayden	+ 24"094
6. Loris Capirossi	+ 24"375
7. Colin Edwards	+ 28"855
8. Makoto Tamada	+ 36"535
9. Norifumi Abé	+ 36"643
10. Carlos Checa	+ 39"284
11. Marco Melandri	+ 43"806
12. Shinya Nakano	+ 43"920
13. John Hopkins	+ 56"028
14. Troy Bayliss	+ 56"558
15. Shane Byrne	+ 1'13.831
16. Jeremy McWilliams	+ 1'22.206
17. Nobuatsu Aoki	+ 1'26.933
18. Michel Fabrizio	+ 3 laps

Fastest lap:
Biaggi, in 1'33.208 (163.840 km/h). New record.
Previous record: Rossi, in 1'33.851 (162.717 km/h/2003)

Outright fastest lap: Rossi, in 1'32.647 (164.832 km/h/2004).

CHAMPIONSHIP

1. V. Rossi	25	(1 win)
2. M. Biaggi	20	
3. S. Gibernau	16	
4. A. Barros	13	
5. N. Hayden	11	
6. L. Capirossi	10	
7. C. Edwards	9	
8. M. Tamada	8	
9. N. Abé	7	
10. C. Checa	6	

Runners and riders:
Kurtis Roberts, King Kenny's youngest son had been the big loser of the winter, suffering a seized left shoulder. He tried it out on Friday morning but gave up after nine laps. The brave Peter Clifford's WCM team was still only entering one Harris, in the hands of Italy's Michel Fabrizio.

Qualifying:
The burning question on everyone's lips was soon answered in resounding fashion: Valentino Rossi, having switched to Yamaha, was fastest in all four sessions. Over a single lap, his main rival was still Sete Giberrnau. The expected closeness of competition had been confirmed and indeed in the ten decisive minutes of Saturday qualifying, no less than four riders occupied provisional pole: the surprising Nakano on the Bridgestone-shod Kawasaki, Biaggi, Gibernau and Hayden, before the fifth man, Rossi of course, had the final word.

Start:
Rossi, Gibernau and Biaggi take off in the lead. Hofmann starts from the pits. As they come round for the first time, the champion leads Biaggi by 0"419 followed by Gibernau, Hayden and a very good showing from Melandri.

Lap 3:
Rossi, Biaggi and Gibernau, separated by 368 thousandths have pulled out a gap over Hayden and Edwards who has got the better of Melandri.

Lap 4:
It's hotting up! Biaggi passes Rossi, who counterattacks. Gibernau infiltrates the duel and it's great scrap. Xaus (Ducati) retires.

Lap 7:
Biaggi leads.

Lap 8:
Kenny Roberts retires. Rossi is back in charge and the duel between the two racing enemies of the track is majestic.

Half distance (14 laps):
The hand to hand scrap between Rossi and Biaggi continues to enthral, as Max trails Valentino by 167 thousandths. One second further back, Gibernau has thrown in the towel. Barros is now fourth, ahead of Hayden and Edwards.

Lap 16:
Hodgson retires.

Lap 17:
Hofmann falls. The two leaders pick up the pace and the gap between the two Italians is 277 thousandths.

Rossi and Biaggi wheel to wheel. The season got off to a high octane start.

Lap 23:
Biaggi now leads by 291 thousandths.

Lap 26:
Rossi comes back forcing Max to run wide.

Finish (28 laps):
Biaggi sets the fastest time on the final lap, but it was not enough as Rossi is too strong. He stops on his victory lap, sits down in front of his bike and cries. In the Yamaha camp, it is kisses all round.

Championship:
Rossi and Yamaha lead the championship after this first round. Even the most "rossi" of fans of the number 46 rider had not dared dream of such a start to the year.

A well deserved champagne shower as Valentino Rossi gave his all to win.

Rossi – Biaggi: brilliant!

It is a question of honour for Valentino Rossi, the firecracker from Tavullia and Massimiliano Biaggi, who dreams of the jet set, Roman style. Their verbal sparring is well known and, a couple of centuries back, the two Italians would have found themselves satisfying their honour on a cold and misty dawn, pistols in hand. Two seconds dressed in black would be their only witnesses.
But these two live in the present and for their duel they have chosen the circuits of the world motorcycle championship and their honour is settled in front of tens of millions of television viewers.
This first GP of the season soon turned into the direct conflict everyone had been expecting: Rossi the champion who had left for the opposition in the shape of Yamaha, against Biaggi who dreams of getting the treatment he deserves from Honda.
The others? All beaten. Gibernau put up a good fight for a while, but he had to give best: "I have never made excuses and I'm not going to start now. Right from the start of practice, I could tell I would not be able to match that pace for the whole race. Well done Max and Valentino!"
It was a nice tribute to the two stars of the day who put on a dazzling 28 lap display, sliding and late-braking, fairing to fairing, just centimetres and thousandths of seconds separating them, never more than 300 between them as they crossed the line! It was a crazy race with honour at stake and Valentino Rossi emerged as the most valiant knight.

A historic moment as the number 46 blue Yamaha hurtles past the chequered flag.

Interview...

Valentino, after the win, you leant your bike against a tyre barrier. Were you crying?
No. But when I crossed the finish line, I felt a new emotion, different to what I had experienced in the past. I had to stop for a moment, to be alone with my bike to thank it.
So you thanked it, as though it was a living creature?
Yes, and I talk to it! Two laps from the finish, when I passed Biaggi again, I said to it, "go on, don't let me down, go on, we can do it..."
This was an incredible race. How did you see it?
I still can't find the right words. I think I have just taken the best win of my career at the end of a perfect weekend.
The win is down to Yamaha, but more than that it is down to you?
First of all, I have to say a big thank you to the technical team who supported me in this gamble. Without that, I would not have done it. Today, I have shown that in our sport, the human element is the most important factor.
Do you feel you are the greatest champion of all time?
That's a very difficult question. But I think we have just done something very important.
A final question. As you crossed the line, we saw you congratulate Max Biaggi. Is there peace between you now?
(Smiles) You know, at the end of such an intense race, run at such a pace, you can have nothing but respect for your rival, whoever he is.

The team in triumph: "Vale" never underplays the importance of his entourage, particularly his confidant and best friend, Uccio.

250cc

The 125 reigning champion, Daniel Pedrosa is about to embark on a new adventure in search of the title.

South Africa Grand Prix
18th April 2004 / Welkom - 4.242 m

STARTING GRID

1.	7	R. De Puniet	Aprilia	1'35.300
2.	19	S. Porto	Aprilia	1'35.379
3.	54	M. Poggiali	Aprilia	1'35.596
4.	26	D. Pedrosa	Honda	1'35.843
5.	51	A. De Angelis	Aprilia	1'36.251
6.	10	F. Gonzales-Nieto	Aprilia	1'36.447
7.	2	R. Rolfo	Honda	1'36.611
8.	34	E. Bataille	Honda	1'36.690
9.	73	H. Aoyama	Honda	1'36.764
10.	21	F. Battaini	Aprilia	1'36.819
11.	24	T. Elias	Honda	1'36.884
12.	33	H. Faubel	Aprilia	1'37.088
13.	57	C. Davies	Aprilia	1'37.171
14.	8	N. Matsudo	Yamaha	1'37.373
15.	6	A. Debon	Honda	1'37.382
16.	9	H. Marchand	Aprilia	1'37.386
17.	25	A. Baldolini	Aprilia	1'37.418
18.	11	J. Olive	Aprilia	1'37.605
19.	50	S. Guintoli	Aprilia	1'37.614
20.	14	A. West	Aprilia	1'37.633
21.	96	J. Smrz	Honda	1'37.688
22.	28	D. Heidolf	Aprilia	1'37.716
23.	36	E. Nigon	Yamaha	1'37.739
24.	12	A. Vincent	Aprilia	1'38.333
25.	15	C. Gemmel	Honda	1'38.406
26.	16	J. Stigefelt	Aprilia	1'38.735
27.	77	G. Lefort	Aprilia	1'38.940
28.	44	T. Sekiguchi	Yamaha	1'38.976
29.	40	M. Sabbatani	Yamaha	1'39.143

RACE: 26 LAPS = 110.292 km

1.	Daniel Pedrosa	42'04.690 (157.267 km/h)
2.	Randy De Puniet	+ 0"536
3.	Sebastian Porto	+ 5"859
4.	Manuel Poggiali	+ 24"561
5.	Alex De Angelis	+ 30"018
6.	Alex Debon	+ 30"653
7.	Alfonso Gonzales-Nieto	+ 31"458
8.	Toni Elias	+ 31"872
9.	Roberto Rolfo	+ 31"940
10.	Franco Battaini	+ 35"643
11.	Hiroshi Aoyama	+ 36"418
12.	Hector Faubel	+ 36"864
13.	Arnaud Vincent	+ 39"105
14.	Dirk Heidolf	+ 43"027
15.	Sylvain Guintoli	+ 51"493
16.	Anthony West	+ 51"699
17.	Joan Olive	+ 52"883
18.	Naoki Matsudo	+ 59"900
19.	Hugo Marchand	+ 1'02.819
20.	Erwan Nigon	+ 1'14.844
21.	Jakub Smrz	+ 1'15.026
22.	Taro Sekiguchi	+ 1'19.230
23.	Johan Stigefelt	+ 1'21.627
24.	Massimiliano Sabbatani	+ 1'28.990
25.	Gregory Lefort	+ 1'29.832

Fastest lap:
Porto, in 1'35.593 (159.752 km/h). New record.
Previous record: Poggiali, in 1'36.649 (158.006 km/h/2003).

Outright fastest lap: De Puniet, in 1'35.300 (160.243 km/h/2004).

CHAMPIONSHIP

1.	D. Pedrosa	25 (1 win)
2.	R. De Puniet	20
3.	S. Porto	16
4.	M. Poggiali	13
5.	A. De Angelis	11
6.	A. Debon	10
7.	A. Gonzales-Nieto	9
8.	T. Elias	8
9.	R. Rolfo	7
10.	F. Battaini	6

Runners and riders:
Honda was fed up with Aprilia's domination and came in to the game officially: Rolfo was joined by Elias, whose place with Aprilia had been taken by Porto. Reigning 125 world champion Pedrosa had a Japanese team-mate in the shape of Aoyama.

Qualifying:
De Puniet had been the pacesetter over the winter and he dominates the two days of qualifying, with Porto in his wake. Poggialia, the outgoing champion whom De Puniet conceded, "had to be the favourite," was not far behind. Neophyte Pedrosa sprung a surprise, taking a front position with his Honda.

Start:
Porto has the quickest reflexes and dashes into the lead ahead of De Puniet. An accident in the middle of the pack involves Davies, Batailli and Baldolini. As they cross the line for the first time, Porto leads De Puniet by 973 thousandths with Poggiali and Pedrosa giving chase.

Lap 2:
Porto goes off and finds himself on the exterior high speed oval! De Puniet leads the rookie Pedrosa. The Argentinian rejoins in 22nd place and begins to put up some impressive lap times.

Lap 4:
De Puniet has built up a 1"081 lead over Pedrosa, who is doing a great job of keeping outgoing champion Manuel Poggiali in check.

Lap 8:
Porto is already fifth and the quickest man on track. Out in front, the gap between De Puniet and Pedrosa stabilises at around one second.

Lap 11:
The De Puniet-Pedrosa gap has dropped to just 229 thousandths. As for Porto, he is absolutely flying as he chases Poggiali for third.

Lap 12:
Calm as you please, Pedrosa takes the lead.

Half distance (13 laps):
Sensational! Pedrosa leads his first ever 250 GP, heading De Puniet by 1.274. 7.5 seconds further back, after his escapade on lap 2, Porto will soon pass Poggiali.

Lap 19:
De Puniet has closed right up to Pedrosa. Porto is over 7 seconds down, having left reigning champion Poggiali trailing in his wake.

Lap 21:
De Puniet retakes the lead. Pedrosa sticks to him like glue and is about to surprise him yet again. The scrap between the two is superb.

Finish (26 laps):
Fantastic Pedrosa. His duel with De Puniet over the final two laps will go into the history books. The Spaniard becomes the youngest ever winner of a 250 GP.

Championship:
De Puniet and Poggiali had been expected to be very strong, but there was Pedrosa on the top step and Porto also made his mark. There's new blood in the class!

Randy de Puniet (7) is still in front, but Pedrosa would have the final word.

125cc

Runners and riders:
34 riders from twelve nations. Italy is in the majority with thirteen runners and six different constructors. The 125 class has lost its world champion as Pedrosa has moved up to 250 and this is to be a special year as next season the category will feature a maximum age limit of 28. This means that Giansanti, Perugini, Locatelli, Jenkner, Borsoi, Ui and Ballerini are embarking on their final season in the class.

Qualifying:
Locatelli dominated from the start of practice, but he would lose out to Dovizioso (Honda) in the final minutes of qualifying. The surprise of the weekend, although it confirmed excellent practice form in Catalunya, came from the Benjamin of the pack in the shape of France's Mike Di Meglio, who qualified fourth to record the first front row start of his career. The KTMs were quickest in a straight line and two of three works Honda riders, Italy's Corsi and Switzerland's Luthi were way back in 21st and 23rd places respectively.

Start:
Locatelli makes the best job of it, ahead of Dovizioso. Barbera has a problem on the formation lap and finally gets going from the pits. As they cross the line for the first time, Locatelli leads Dovizioso by 213 thousandths and Stoner by a second.

Lap 4:
Talmacsi retires. The order is Locatelli, Dovizioso, Stoner and Simoncelli.

Half distance (lap 12):
Locatelli, Dovizioso and Stoner all fit in a 350 thousandths handkerchief. Pablo Nieto is all on his own in fourth spot, while Simoncelli is a solitary fifth. The second group features a Borsoi and Di Meglio battle.

Lap 15:
Nieto catches up to the lead trio.

Lap 16:
Stoner goes second.

Lap 17:
Simoncelli is a faller.

Lap 18:
Luthi falls having been in the points on lap 15.

Lap 19:
Locatelli, Stoner, Dovizioso and Nieto are now covered by 387 thousandths.

A glimpse of Hungary on the start grid.

Lap 22:
There's a break: Locatelli leads Dovizioso. Nieto has just passed Stoner for third but is over a second down.

Finish (24 laps):
Dovizioso mounts a superb attack at the last braking point and surprises Locatelli. The Honda rider thus takes the first win of his career at this level. Stoner is third and France's Di Meglio deserves the applause for fifth place.

Championship:
Three different marques in the top three slots. Dovizioso is thus the first leader of what looks like being a closely fought championship.

Andrea Dovizioso takes his first GP win, but it would not be the last.

South Africa Grand Prix
18th April 2004 / Welkom - 4.242 m

STARTING GRID

1.	34	A. Dovizioso	Honda	1'40.942
2.	15	R. Locatelli	Aprilia	1'41.024
3.	6	M. Giansanti	Aprilia	1'41.193
4.	63	M. Di Meglio	Aprilia	1'41.195
5.	27	C. Stoner	KTM	1'41.204
6.	22	P. Nieto	Aprilia	1'41.373
7.	58	M. Simoncelli	Aprilia	1'41.483
8.	19	A. Bautista	Aprilia	1'41.550
9.	41	Y. Ui	Aprilia	1'41.619
10.	10	J. Simon	Honda	1'41.644
11.	3	H. Barbera	Aprilia	1'41.682
12.	23	G. Borsoi	Aprilia	1'41.754
13.	48	J. Lorenzo	Derbi	1'41.762
14.	14	G. Talmacsi	Malaguti	1'41.866
15.	36	M. Kallio	KTM	1'41.896
16.	26	D. Giuseppetti	Honda	1'41.959
17.	32	F. Lai	Gilera	1'42.038
18.	21	S. Jenkner	Aprilia	1'42.106
19.	7	S. Perugini	Gilera	1'42.143
20.	54	M. Pasini	Aprilia	1'42.194
21.	24	S. Corsi	Honda	1'42.242
22.	69	R. Harms	Honda	1'42.551
23.	12	T. Lüthi	Honda	1'42.634
24.	33	S. Gadea	Aprilia	1'42.642
25.	25	I. Toth	Aprilia	1'43.195
26.	66	V. Kallio	Aprilia	1'43.301
27.	52	L. Pesek	Honda	1'43.590
28.	47	A. Rodriguez	Derbi	1'43.864
29.	50	A. Ballerini	Aprilia	1'44.014
30.	42	G. Pellino	Aprilia	1'44.099
31.	8	M. Manna	Malaguti	1'44.115
32.	11	M. Angeloni	Honda	1'44.345
33.	28	J. Carchano	Aprilia	1'44.560
34.	16	R. Schouten	Honda	1'44.741

RACE: 24 LAPS = 101.808 km

1.	Andrea Dovizioso	40'34.318 (150.559 km/h)
2.	Roberto Locatelli	+ 0"071
3.	Casey Stoner	+ 2"203
4.	Pablo Nieto	+ 2"416
5.	Mike Di Meglio	+ 12"312
6.	Gino Borsoi	+ 13"270
7.	Mirko Giansanti	+ 14"457
8.	Steve Jenkner	+ 15"046
9.	Alvaro Bautista	+ 24"835
10.	Hector Barbera	+ 25"266
11.	Julian Simon	+ 29"356
12.	Mika Kallio	+ 33"134
13.	Mattia Pasini	+ 33"237
14.	Simone Corsi	+ 33"682
15.	Youichi Ui	+ 36"977
16.	Jorge Lorenzo	+ 43"650
17.	Stefano Perugini	+ 45"230
18.	Robbin Harms	+ 45"389
19.	Dario Giuseppetti	+ 45"590
20.	Lukas Pesek	+ 45"715
21.	Fabrizio Lai	+ 45"961
22.	Imre Toth	+ 46"129
23.	Sergio Gadea	+ 1'04.990
24.	Vesa Kallio	+ 1'05.784
25.	Mattia Angeloni	+ 1'23.541
26.	Manuel Manna	+ 1'23.753
27.	Jordi Carchano	+ 1'24.960

Fastest lap:
Locatelli, in 1'40.711 (151.633 km/h). New record.
Previous record: Pedrosa, in 1'41.006 (151.191 km/h/2003).

Outright fastest lap: Locatelli, in 1'40.711 (151.633 km/h/2004).

CHAMPIONSHIP

1.	A. Dovizioso	25 (1 win)
2.	R. Locatelli	20
3.	C. Stoner	16
4.	P. Nieto	13
5.	M. Di Meglio	11
6.	G. Borsoi	10
7.	M. Giansanti	9
8.	S. Jenkner	8
9.	A. Bautista	7
10.	H. Barbera	6

HONDA

SPAIN

Jerez de la Frontera

It's raining in Andalusia and in these terrible conditions, Sete Gibernau is untouchable. The Catalan rider is on a perfect trajectory as the Continental Circus gets back into European mode, with the stunning bowl of the Jerez de la Frontera circuit and a giant screen featuring Rossi.

Spanish Grand Prix
2nd May 2004 / Jerez - 4.423 m

STARTING GRID

1.	46	V. Rossi	Yamaha	1'40.818
2.	15	S. Gibernau	Honda	1'41.198
3.	7	C. Checa	Yamaha	1'41.427
4.	3	M. Biaggi	Honda	1'41.546
5.	6	M. Tamada	Honda	1'41.631
6.	56	S. Nakano	Kawasaki	1'41.645
7.	69	N. Hayden	Honda	1'41.911
8.	45	C. Edwards	Honda	1'42.000
9.	4	A. Barros	Honda	1'42.141
10.	10	Ke. Roberts	Suzuki	1'42.312
11.	33	M. Melandri	Yamaha	1'42.479
12.	11	R. Xaus	Ducati	1.42.945
13.	21	J. Hopkins	Suzuki	1'42.954
14.	66	A. Hofmann	Kawasaki	1'43.004
15.	65	L. Capirossi	Ducati	1'43.008
16.	67	S. Byrne	Aprilia	1'43.024
17.	12	T. Bayliss	Ducati	1'43.349
18.	50	N. Hodgson	Ducati	1'43.627
19.	99	J. McWilliams	Aprilia	1'43.730
20.	17	N. Abé	Yamaha	1'44.058
21.	9	N. Aoki	Proton KR	1'44.536
22.	80	Ku. Roberts	Proton KR	1'45.899
Did not meet qualifying minimum time (Fabrizio allowed to race):				
	84	M. Fabrizio	Harris WCM	1'48.485
	35	C. Burns	Harris WCM	1'48.602

RACE: 28 LAPS = 118.776 KM

1.	Sete Gibernau	52'01.293 (137.736 km/h)
2.	Massimiliano Biaggi	+ 5"452
3.	Alexandre Barros	+ 52"570
4.	Valentino Rossi	+ 58"556
5.	Nicky Hayden	+ 59"283
6.	Carlos Checa	+ 1'07.184
7.	Colin Edwards	+ 1'19.539
8.	Kenny Roberts	+ 1'45.057
9.	Shinya Nakano	+ 1 lap
10.	Michel Fabrizio	+ 1 lap
11.	Norifumi Abé	+ 1 lap
12.	Loris Capirossi	+ 1 lap
13.	Alex Hofmann	+ 1 lap
14.	Nobuatsu Aoki	+ 1 lap
15.	John Hopkins	+ 1 lap

Fastest lap:
Gibernau, in 1'53.508 (140.279 km/h).
Record: Rossi, in 1'42.788 (154.909 km/h/2003).

Outright fastest lap: Rossi, in 1'40.818 (157.936 km/h/2004).

CHAMPIONSHIP

1.	S. Gibernau	41 (1 win)
2.	M. Biaggi	40
3.	V. Rossi	38 (1 win)
4.	A. Barros	29
5.	N. Hayden	22
6.	C. Edwards	18
7.	C. Checa	16
8.	L. Capirossi	14
9.	N. Abé	12
10.	S. Nakano	8

Runners and riders:
As expected, the top category boasts a full pack. Having missed South Africa, Kurtis Roberts is on track, with the WCM team lining up a second Harris for Englishman, Chris Burns.

Qualifying:
"When I saw my time, 1'40"818, I said to myself that I must have got a tow from the Ducati that was just a few metres ahead of me on the track." Rossi sets a stratospheric pole on Friday, beating Capirossi's benchmark from the previous year by over a second! Gibernau is yet again his closest rival but, as in South Africa, the Spaniard knows he will not be able to match Rossi's pace...in the dry. Checa completes the front row. The works Ducatis are a long way off. The two Harris-WCM do not make the qualifying cut, but Fabrizio is reprieved.

Start:
Gibernau shows the best reflexes ahead of Rossi and Checa. Then come Biaggi, Barros, Melandri and Capirossi. England's Byrne is a faller. Gibernau leads Rossi by 0"653 and the Italian is about to be caught out by Checa.

Lap 2:
Xaus falls, followed by Bayliss. Gibernau leads Biaggi, Checa, Barros, Rossi and Melandri.

Lap 4:
365 thousandths separate Gibernau from Rossi. Melandri is now third and best Yamaha rider, ahead of Checa and Rossi. Barros has dropped back.

Lap 12:
Rossi gets a big fright, but very luckily, lands back in the saddle. McWilliams retires.

Half distance (14 laps):
Gibernau still leads from Biaggi by 338 thousandths. Melandri is 8"172 back in third, Barros is fourth, 6"643 down on the young Italian. Rossi is fifth.

Lap 16:
Biaggi takes the lead, but Gibernau gets him back one lap later.

Lap 18:
Hodgson retires.

Lap 19:
Melandri falls having been a brilliant third.

Lap 22:
Gibernau has upped the pace and Biaggi is now 1"539 back. All eyes are on Italy's Fabrizio (Harris-WCM) who, having been through a gravel trap, is now closing on Capirossi.

Finish (27 laps):
The rain is twice as heavy now, but Gibernau makes no mistake to win from Biaggi and Barros, with the works HRC rider 52 seconds behind the winner. The heart warming performance of the day comes from Michel Fabrizio with the Harris backyard special, who finishes ahead of the one remaining Ducati.

Championship:
Gibernau takes the win and the championship lead, just one little point ahead of Biaggi. Rossi is three points down in third.

Valentino Rossi's problems in the rain with the Yamaha, clearly explained in four pictures. We are on lap 12 of the Spanish GP and the decisive moment has just taken place.

(Photos: S. Kibiki).

Sete, Moses of the race track

There are those who, usually in a friendly fashion, have nicknamed him "Hollywood" for his propensity for wearing his heart on his sleeve, with grandiose gestures. This side to his character was very much on show on this wet Sunday in May at Jerez de la Frontera. Sete Gibernau stood on the pegs for his victory lap, he kissed the top step of the podium, his podium and he did not forget to kiss the trophy, dedicating it to his late lamented team-mate from the previous year, Daijiro Kato. He then captivated the audience with his well-rehearsed speech, as he thanked all the right people.

That's the way he is. For a long time, his manner and his playboy physique made him the butt of generally well intentioned jokes in the paddock. But the lad from a good family had grown up. Since last year, at the controls of his Honda RC211V, he began to command the respect of his rivals.

The main thorn in Valentino Rossi's side in 2003, Sete along with Max Biaggi was the strongest weapon in Honda's armoury this year. Now heading the championship classification for the first time in his career, the man who lives in Chatel St Denis in Switzerland, where he drives around in a red Ferrari, had for a long time been reckoned as something of a wet weather specialist.

Others ended up deciding that discretion was the better part of valour, including Massimiliano Biaggi who said, "there came a time when I reckoned it was better to settle for twenty points for second. It took a miracle to keep the king of the tracks, Valentino Rossi upright, to the extent that he used the opportunity to tell his new masters at Yamaha that they were not yet on Honda's level. But Sete Gibernau had fun, making the most of it while the others faltered. At the end of the day, the rain master had done it all, including distancing third place Alexandre Barros, on paper HRC's number one rider, by 52"570. We had not seen the like of that since the 1992 Japanese GP.

Interview...

Sete, what does this home win mean?

25 points is the most important thing. Honda helps us and gives us new parts, but I know that if the track had not been wet, I would not have won, which shows there is still some way to go. Having said that, two races, two podiums and leading the championship for the first time in my career, it's not that bad.

How far can Sete Gibernau go in 2003?

You know, when Rossi won the first GP on a Yamaha, the pressure on our shoulders got even greater. But I think I am even better than last year and I know there is still more to come.

A win at Jerez?

Total happiness. I've done it before at Valencia, now I've got to do it again in Barcelona.

A celebratory gesture while crossing the line, because Gibernau is the best rider in the world on a wet track.

Eyes on the sky, from where his mate Daijiro Kato is watching. It sums up Sete in one image!

250cc

Another wet weather specialist, the Italian Roberto Rolfo.

Spanish Grand Prix
2nd May 2004 / Jerez - 4.423 m

STARTING GRID

1.	19	S. Porto	Aprilia	1'43.673
2.	54	M. Poggiali	Aprilia	1'44.054
3.	26	D. Pedrosa	Honda	1'44.163
4.	7	R. De Puniet	Aprilia	1'44.196
5.	2	R. Rolfo	Honda	1'44.716
6.	24	T. Elias	Honda	1'44.989
7.	10	F. Gonzales-Nieto	Aprilia	1'45.222
8.	51	A. De Angelis	Aprilia	1'45.258
9.	21	F. Battaini	Aprilia	1'45.652
10.	73	H. Aoyama	Honda	1'45.822
11.	33	H. Faubel	Aprilia	1'45.976
12.	50	S. Guintoli	Aprilia	1'45.991
13.	14	A. West	Aprilia	1'46.075
14.	11	J. Olive	Aprilia	1'46.311
15.	6	A. Debon	Honda	1'46.429
16.	34	E. Bataille	Honda	1'46.514
17.	57	C. Davies	Aprilia	1'46.575
18.	96	J. Smrz	Honda	1'46.614
19.	8	N. Matsudo	Yamaha	1'46.657
20.	9	H. Marchand	Aprilia	1'46.966
21.	12	A. Vincent	Aprilia	1'47.158
22.	28	D. Heidolf	Aprilia	1'47.214
23.	41	A. Molina	Aprilia	1'47.382
24.	25	A. Baldolini	Aprilia	1'47.411
25.	15	C. Gemmel	Honda	1'47.561
26.	40	M. Sabbatani	Yamaha	1'48.204
27.	16	J. Stigefelt	Aprilia	1'48.376
28.	77	G. Lefort	Aprilia	1'48.452
29.	43	R. Rous	Aprilia	1'48.812
30.	44	T. Sekiguchi	Yamaha	1'48.995
31.	42	G. Leblanc	Aprilia	1'49.144
32.	63	J. Ronzoni	Yamaha	1'50.311

RACE: 26 LAPS = 114.998 km

1. Roberto Rolfo	52'20.145 (131.838 km/h)
2. Randy De Puniet	+ 8"740
3. Alfonso Gonzales-Nieto	+ 32"623
4. Anthony West	+ 32"844
5. Alex Debon	+ 58"884
6. Alex De Angelis	+ 1'03.950
7. Sebastian Porto	+ 1'05.322
8. Arnaud Vincent	+ 1'08.923
9. Gregory Lefort	+ 1'47.081
10. Naoki Matsudo	+ 1'49.191
11. Alex Baldolini	+ 1'55.028
12. Toni Elias	+ 2'01.756
13. Hugo Marchand	+ 1 lap
14. Johan Stigefelt	+ 1 lap
15. Taro Sekiguchi	+ 1 lap
16. Dirk Heidolf	+ 1 lap
17. Hector Faubel	+ 1 lap
18. Jarno Ronzoni	+ 1 lap
19. Radomil Rous	+ 1 lap
20. Joan Olive	+ 1 lap
21. Gregory Leblanc	+ 2 laps

Fastest lap:
Rolfo, in 1'58.815 (134.013 km/h).
Record: Kato, in 1'44.444 (152.452 km/h/2001).

Outright fastest lap: Porto, in 1'43.673 (153.586 km/h/2004).

CHAMPIONSHIP

1. R. De Puniet	40
2. R. Rolfo	32 (1 win)
3. D. Pedrosa	25 (1 win)
4. A. Gonzales-Nieto	25
5. S. Porto	25
6. A. Debon	21
7. A. De Angelis	21
8. A. West	13
9. M. Poggiali	13
10. T. Elias	12

Runners and riders:
Tough luck for France's Erwan Nigon (team UGT Kurz/Yamaha) who has broken an ankle in a scooter accident and is replaced by the virtually unknown Italian, Jarno Ronzoni (6th in the first leg of the European championship at Vallelunga.) There are three invited riders: Spain's Alvaro Molina, France's Gregory Leblanc and the Czech, Radomil Rous. On the eve of qualifying, Franco Battaini announces that this will be his final season in the 250 class, as he plans to tackle world superbikes in 2005.

Qualifying:
Argentinian Sebastian Porto is definitely on great form. After a fantastic race at Welkom, where he had gone off the track at the start of the race, he dominates the first day of qualifying before a spectacular fall, which must have been very painful. However, he hangs on to provisional pole which becomes the real thing when it rains on Saturday. Poggiali, Pedrosa and De Puniet complete the front row.

Start:
Pedrosa storms off into the lead ahead of Rolfo, Poggiali and De Puniet. Further back the world champion is a faller.

Lap 4:
Aoyama falls when second then Eric Bataille does the same. Rolfo leads De Puniet by 4"000 with Pedrosa almost 4 seconds further back.

Lap 5:
Pedrosa falls.

Lap 8:
Rolfo is solidly out in front, leading the first of his pursuers, a solitary Randy De Puniet, by 5"543. Battaini is third with French team-mate Sylvain Guintoli now fourth.

Lap 10:
Battaini falls. There is a superb dice for third place between Guintoli, West and Gonzales-Nieto.

Half distance (13 laps):
Rolfo leads De Puniet by 8"097. 20 seconds behind the Frenchman, West has got the better of Gonzales-Nieto for third place. Guintoli has just fallen and rejoined in twelfth place.

Lap 24:
Battaini falls again having climbed up to fifteenth spot after his mistake on lap 10. A bit later, Guintoli pits.

Finish (26 laps):
Two faultless performances, from the winner Rolfo and De Puniet who makes sure of the 20 points for second place.

Championship:
On the eve of first qualifying for the South African GP, De Puniet had said: "very few riders will get through the season without making mistakes." Thus Poggiali and Pedrosa end up with no points and the Frenchman with two second places, which is enough to see him lead the classification going into his home race.

Ouch, as the reigning world champion, Manuel Poggiali ends up on his knees.

FRANCE
Le Mans

Ever since Claude Michy brought the French GP back to Le Mans, the public had flocked to the historic track en masse. One of the paddock regulars, Pietro Biaggi, you know whose father, cannot resist a bit of flirting and who can blame him with young ladies like this.

MOTOGP

French Grand Prix
16th May 2004 / Le Mans - 4.180 m

STARTING GRID

1.	15	S. Gibernau	Honda	1'33.425
2.	7	C. Checa	Yamaha	1'33.575
3.	3	M. Biaggi	Honda	1'33.579
4.	46	V. Rossi	Yamaha	1'33.668
5.	45	C. Edwards	Honda	1'33.870
6.	33	M. Melandri	Yamaha	1'33.920
7.	69	N. Hayden	Honda	1'33.966
8.	6	M. Tamada	Honda	1'34.057
9.	65	L. Capirossi	Ducati	1'34.095
10.	12	T. Bayliss	Ducati	1'34.211
11.	4	A. Barros	Honda	1'34.342
12.	56	S. Nakano	Kawasaki	1'34.362
13.	10	Ke. Roberts	Suzuki	1'34.459
14.	50	N. Hodgson	Ducati	1'34.526
15.	11	R. Xaus	Ducati	1.34.578
16.	21	J. Hopkins	Suzuki	1'34.597
17.	17	N. Abé	Yamaha	1'34.665
18.	99	J. McWilliams	Aprilia	1'35.371
19.	66	A. Hofmann	Kawasaki	1'35.718
20.	9	N. Aoki	Proton KR	1'36.044
21.	80	Ku. Roberts	Proton KR	1'36.373
22.	67	S. Byrne (*)	Aprilia	1'36.543
23.	84	M. Fabrizio	Harris WCM	1'37.710
24.	35	C. Burns	Harris WCM	1'38.097

(*): Still suffering the effects of his fall in Jerez, (broken finger on the right hand,) the Englishman pulls out on Saturday after the morning's free practice.

RACE: 28 LAPS = 117.040 km

1. Sete Gibernau	44'22.750 (158.236 km/h)
2. Carlos Checa	+ 1"671
3. Massimiliano Biaggi	+ 1"908
4. Valentino Rossi	+ 4"272
5. Colin Edwards	+ 15"755
6. Marco Melandri	+ 18"225
7. Alexandre Barros	+ 27"656
8. Troy Bayliss	+ 31"530
9. Makoto Tamada	+ 33"164
10. Loris Capirossi	+ 39"512
11. Nicky Hayden	+ 47"625
12. Kenny Roberts	+ 1'12.140
13. Jeremy McWilliams	+ 1'23.391
14. Ruben Xaus	+ 1 lap
15. Kurtis Roberts	+ 1 lap
16. Michel Fabrizio	+ 1 lap
17. Nobuatsu Aoki	+ 1 lap

Fastest lap:
Biaggi, in 1'34.088 (159.935 km/h). New record.
Previous record: Haga, in 1'36.688 (155.634 km/h/2003).

Outright fastest lap: Gibernau, in 1'33.425 (161.070 km/h/2004).

CHAMPIONSHIP

1. S. Gibernau	66	(2 wins)
2. M. Biaggi	56	
3. V. Rossi	51	(1 win)
4. A. Barros	38	
5. C. Checa	36	
6. C. Edwards	29	
7. N. Hayden	27	
8. L. Capirossi	20	
9. M. Melandri	15	
10. M. Tamada	15	

The first scandal of the season, as Valentino Rossi is given a helping hand on the grid. The subject was back on the agenda several months later after the Qatar affair.

Runners and riders:
Everyone is on parade in the blue riband class; even Shane Byrne who broke a finger on the right hand in Spain, although he would pack it in after Saturday's free practice. Most of the teams stayed in Jerez after the GP – Sete Gibernau even rode all on his own on Wednesday. Developed since the start of the season by the Tech 3 team, with Marco Melandri, a new Magneti Marelli electronic injection system is fitted to Rossi's M1.

Qualifying:
The first day is characterised by a fightback for the team number twos. Edwards is quickest, Checa is already ahead of Rossi, Hayden takes the upper hand over Barros, while Bayliss precedes Capirossi. Running a temperature since arriving at Le Mans, Gibernau still manages to take pole on Saturday, ahead of fellow countryman Checa, who had been trying his hand at extreme sports at altitude between Jerez and the French GP and Max Biaggi. Rossi is thus on the second row.

Start:
Carlos Checa gets the holeshot, ahead of Gibernau, Biaggi and Rossi, who bang elbows at the chicane. The champion, who had concerns at the start of the warm-up laps as his engine stalled and he needed a push, is already third as they cross the line for the first time. Hodgson, Abe and Hopkins all crash, the latter showing his disgust by flinging dirt at the other two.

Lap 3:
Xaus falls but continues. Gibernau is just 451 thousandths off Checa.

Lap 7:
Hofmann retires (three engines in two days.)

Lap 11:
You can cover Checa and Gibernau with a 277 thousandths handkerchief. Rossi is 2.4 behind in third with Biaggi closing in on the world champion.

Lap 12:
The pace hots up. Gibernau takes the lead and at the start of lap 13, Biaggi ambushes Rossi.

Biaggi catches out Rossi round the outside. Max was on form.

Half distance (14 laps):
Three pairs head up the race. The first, Gibernau-Checa, leads the second (Biaggi-Rossi) by two seconds. Melandri and Edwards are 5 seconds back.

Lap 17:
Nakano retires.

Lap 21:
Biaggi outbrakes himself at the Dunlop chicane. As they cross the line, the four leaders, Gibernau, Checa, Biaggi and Rossi are covered by 2"498.

Lap 22:
Gibernau turns up the heat, setting the fastest lap to give himself a 1"448 breathing space.

Finish (28 laps):
Rossi has tried a final attack with three laps to go, but in vain. Gibernau has been faultless yet again, Checa takes his first podium of the season and Rossi is "only" fourth.

Championship:
Gibernau has a ten point lead, with Rossi already 15 down on the Spaniard.

37.5 degrees in the morning, champagne in the afternoon!

"Adrenalin is the best possible remedy when it comes to fixing physical problems." Sete Gibernau had been suffering with 'flu since arriving at La Sarthe, but now he had forgotten his throat problems. In the space of just over forty five minutes, the temperature and queasiness had gone. "Over the last five laps, I suffered terribly," he said before adding with a smile that, "a victory instantly makes things better." Gibernau had won, sweating on the dry track at Le Mans two weeks after swimming through the streams of Jerez de La Frontera. He was getting a taste for his role as the championship leader after a thrilling duel with his fellow countryman, Checa, having fought off his closest rival in the points, Biaggi, who was now 10 behind. "Let's keep our feet on the ground. I have said since last year that I have the best team in the world, but the championship is very long and it is far from over. As soon as a rider starts winning, he wants more. I am no exception to that rule and I am going to work flat out to get ready for the next GP in Italy. But before that, I am dreaming of two things: having a shower and going to bed." Eating a fondue in his Swiss home at Chatel Saint Denis would have to wait, as would the traditional winner's champagne. It was all part of a commotion which bubbled up on this hot Sunday in May at Le Mans, precipitating Gibernau, Checa and Biaggi into the role of pawns in a mini-scandal.

In France, the Evin legislation which controls tobacco and alcohol advertising bans the use of champagne magnums on the podium. But at Le Mans, it seemed that a nice white foam had been sprayed...Wrong! "We had replaced the champagne with fizzy water," a spokesman for the organisation was in a hurry to explain.

The French GP had also been the scene of much discussion with the star of the show at the heart of the drama. At the start of the warm-up lap, Valentino Rossi stalled his Yamaha. Four mechanics rushed onto the track and, egged on by Mike Trimby, the secretary of the teams' association, came to his assistance. The champion got going at the back of the pack, catching up with it and then taking up his place on the grid. According to article twelve of the rule book, 30 seconds before the warm-up lap, "...all assistance from mechanics is forbidden. Any rider who cannot start his machine has to push it into pit lane.... Where he can try and start it or switch to the spare....Any rider in this position will start the race from the back of the grid." In this instance, the rules were completely ignored.

As an explanation, the starter and race director, Englishman Paul Butler said:" I took the decision and I take responsibility for it, taking into account safety and sporting concerns."

In simple terms, Rossi had cheated but had been immediately absolved!

Despite a high temperature, Sete Gibernau produced a bravura performance, proving he could also win when the conditions were normal.

250cc

French Grand Prix
16th May 2004 / Le Mans - 4.180 m

STARTING GRID

1.	26	D. Pedrosa	Honda	1'37.123
2.	7	R. De Puniet	Aprilia	1'37.407
3.	19	S. Porto	Aprilia	1'37.436
4.	54	M. Poggiali	Aprilia	1'38.007
5.	24	T. Elias	Honda	1'38.536
6.	21	F. Battaini	Aprilia	1'38.674
7.	10	F. Gonzales-Nieto	Aprilia	1'38.903
8.	2	R. Rolfo	Honda	1'39.085
9.	73	H. Aoyama	Honda	1'39.088
10.	51	A. De Angelis	Aprilia	1'39.151
11.	50	S. Guintoli	Aprilia	1'39.163
12.	14	A. West	Aprilia	1'39.314
13.	6	A. Debon	Honda	1'39.360
14.	34	E. Bataille	Honda	1'39.516
15.	33	H. Faubel	Aprilia	1'39.775
16.	11	J. Olive	Aprilia	1'39.828
17.	28	D. Heidolf	Aprilia	1'39.936
18.	96	J. Smrz	Honda	1'39.976
19.	57	C. Davies	Aprilia	1'40.144
20.	8	N. Matsudo	Yamaha	1'40.201
21.	36	E. Nigon	Yamaha	1'40.249
22.	9	H. Marchand	Aprilia	1'40.302
23.	12	A. Vincent	Aprilia	1'40.616
24.	77	G. Lefort	Aprilia	1'40.778
25.	25	A. Baldolini	Aprilia	1'40.788
26.	15	C. Gemmel	Honda	1'40.942
27.	43	R. Rous	Aprilia	1'41.607
28.	42	G. Leblanc	Aprilia	1'41.855
29.	16	J. Stigefelt	Aprilia	1'42.182
30.	44	T. Sekiguchi	Yamaha	1'42.214
Not qualified:				
	45	S. Aubry	Honda	1'44.064
	46	V. Eisen	Honda	1'44.524
	47	M. Scaccia	Yamaha	1'45.659

RACE: 26 LAPS = 108.680 km

1.	Daniel Pedrosa	43'03.338 (151.450 km/h)
2.	Randy De Puniet	+ 7"711
3.	Toni Elias	+ 19"233
4.	Hiroshi Aoyama	+ 20"427
5.	Alex De Angelis	+ 21"175
6.	Anthony West	+ 24"269
7.	Alfonso Gonzales-Nieto	+ 38"537
8.	Franco Battaini	+ 39"827
9.	Alex Debon	+ 42"589
10.	Joan Olive	+ 47"541
11.	Jakub Smrz	+ 47"874
12.	Chaz Davies	+ 51"623
13.	Hector Faubel	+ 51"813
14.	Naoki Matsudo	+ 58"880
15.	Alex Baldolini	+ 1'03.261
16.	Dirk Heidolf	+ 1'05.370
17.	Hugo Marchand	+ 1'05.906
18.	Erwan Nigon	+ 1'08.323
19.	Christian Gemmel	+ 1'19.342
20.	Gregory Lefort	+ 1'21.036
21.	Taro Sekiguchi	+ 1'39.861
22.	Gregory Leblanc	+ 1 lap

Fastest lap:
Pedrosa, in 1'38.202 (153.235 km/h). New record.
Previous record: Melandri, in 1'39.648 (151.011 km/h/2002).

Outright fastest lap: Pedrosa, in 1'37.123 (154.937 km/h/2004).

CHAMPIONSHIP

1.	R. De Puniet	60
2.	D. Pedrosa	50 (2 wins)
3.	A. Gonzales-Nieto	34
4.	R. Rolfo	32 (1 win)
5.	A. De Angelis	32
6.	T. Elias	28
7.	A. Debon	28
8.	S. Porto	25
9.	A. West	23
10.	H. Aoyama	18

Pedrosa-De Puniet, the two main players in the early part of the season, have a scrap.

Runners and riders:
The works Honda riders stayed an extra two days at Jerez de la Frontera for testing duties. They were therefore able to try the new chassis, which Aoyama, the development rider, had been using since the IRTA test at Barcelona. For the French GP, Elias and Rolfo decide to use it. Daniel Pedrosa prefers to persevere with the old bike: "I still need to pick up experience in 250s," he explained. Nigon, injured in a road accident prior to Jerez, is back. There are five wild cards, including four French riders: Leblanc, Aubry, Eiesen and Scaccia.

Qualifying:
Porto, De Puniet, Poggiali and Pedrosa on the first day; Pedrosa, De Puniet, Porto and Poggiali (a fall) on the second. The class leaders kept it to themselves round the Bugatti circuit. Championship leader, De Puniet had the entire crowd on his side but he was finally beaten by little Dani Pedrosa. The first to pull out was racing's little jockey, Max Sabbatani who suffered a broken right leg after a fall on Friday morning.

Start:
Pedrosa, De Puniet and Poggiali have the quickest reflexes. Rolfo, the winner in Jerez, falls at the Dunlop chicane. Pedrosa crosses the line for the first time with a 0"145 lead over De Puniet. Poggiali is third but not for long, as he falls at Dunlop and his Aprilia almost collects Porto as it crosses the track.

Lap 3:
Pedrosa and De Puniet are locked together just 0"287 apart. Porto is third at 2.7 seconds from the Frenchman as the Argentinian sets the fastest race lap.

Lap 12:
Vincent falls at the Raccordement corner.

Half distance (13 laps):
Pedrosa rules the roost and now has a 5"962 lead over De Puniet, who heads Porto by 1"399. Fourth, but over ten seconds off the Argentinian's Aprilia we find Japan's Aoyama, the leader's team-mate.

Lap 18:
Porto falls having closed to within 1"131 of Randy De Puniet.

Finish (26 laps):
A perfect demonstration from Pedrosa who takes his second 250 bouquet. De Puniet is powerless, while Elias is third.

Championship:
Like famous French cyclist Raymond Poulidor, Randy de Puniet is playing the consistency card this year. Three second places, 60 points while Poggiali has already got it wrong twice. De Puniet leads Pedrosa, the day's winner and his main rival, by ten points. Gonzales-Nieto, consistent but not brilliant, is third.

Blast! Arnaud Vincent gets it wrong in front of the home crowd.

125cc

Andrea Dovizioso wins in majestic style from the experienced Roberto Locatelli.

Runners and riders:
Full house among the regular riders. As well as Germany's Georg Frohlich, who has a wild card for all the European races, Spain's Julian Miralles and three French riders (Alex Masbou, Yannick Deschamps and Mathieu Gines are trying their luck. A week before this GP, Switzerland's Thomas Luthi won the first leg of the German championship at the Sachsenring.

Qualifying:
World championship leader as the series reached the Sarthe, Andrea Dovizioso recalls that it was here at Le Mans the previous year that he took his first career pole position. He went on to dominate the two days of qualifying, ahead of Jorge Lorenzo, who had also been very quick twelve months earlier in France. There are no less than 17 fallers over the two practice days, including Frohlich who has to scrub with a broken right wrist.

Start:
Hector Barbera, Dovizioso and Jorge Lorenzo make the best starts. Thomas Luthi fails to complete the opening lap having been hit from behind.

Lap 2:
Jerez winner Marco Simoncelli is a faller.

Lap 4:
A superb battle for the lead between Barbera, Dovizioso, Lorenzo, Mirko Giansanti and Locatelli, all covered by just 571 little thousandths. One lap later, Dovizioso takes matters in hand, putting together the perfect lap to lead the pack across the line by 7 tenths.

Lap 9:
Locatelli has dragged the group back to Dovizioso and takes the lead.

Still Dovizio, but this time head on, tackling one of the young lions in the class, Jorge Lorenzo.

Lap 10:
An impressive crash for the young local hero, Mike Di Meglio, who had worked his way back up to ninth after an average start.

Half distance (12 laps):
Locatelli and Dovizioso are wheel to wheel (370 thousandths.) Lorenzo is all alone in third spot. Further back, Barbera is battling with the ever consistent Mirko Giansanti.

Lap 13:
Japan's Youichi Ui is a faller.

Lap 20:
The positions remain unchanged, except for the fourth place battle between Barbera and Giansanti.

Finish (24 laps):
Dovizioso times his decisive attack in the final lap, just as he had planned. There is something of a world champion about him that's for sure! Thanks to Jorge Lorenzo, Derbi takes its first podium in the discipline and also its first points of 2004.

Championship:
A fifteen point lead for Dovizioso, the strong force in the early stages of 2004 and Honda's lead rider. Chasing him is the consistent Roberto Locatelli with, like the leader, two podiums from three races and there are still nine riders who have scored points in every race.

French Grand Prix
16th May 2004 / Le Mans - 4.180 m

STARTING GRID

1.	34	A. Dovizioso	Honda	1'42.608
2.	48	J. Lorenzo	Derbi	1'42.990
3.	3	H. Barbera	Aprilia	1'43.086
4.	15	R. Locatelli	Aprilia	1'43.190
5.	6	M. Giansanti	Aprilia	1'43.282
6.	21	S. Jenkner	Aprilia	1'43.324
7.	41	Y. Ui	Aprilia	1'43.379
8.	63	M. Di Meglio	Aprilia	1'43.421
9.	58	M. Simoncelli	Aprilia	1'43.441
10.	22	P. Nieto	Aprilia	1'43.458
11.	19	A. Bautista	Aprilia	1'43.515
12.	24	S. Corsi	Honda	1'43.956
13.	27	C. Stoner	KTM	1'43.975
14.	12	T. Lüthi	Honda	1'44.194
15.	23	G. Borsoi	Aprilia	1'44.261
16.	7	S. Perugini	Gilera	1'44.324
17.	54	M. Pasini	Aprilia	1'44.342
18.	10	J. Simon	Honda	1'44.364
19.	32	F. Lai	Gilera	1'44.435
20.	36	M. Kallio	KTM	1'44.652
21.	52	L. Pesek	Honda	1'44.877
22.	14	G. Talmacsi	Malaguti	1'44.977
23.	50	A. Ballerini	Aprilia	1'45.067
24.	42	G. Pellino	Aprilia	1'45.087
25.	25	I. Toth	Aprilia	1'45.158
26.	26	D. Giuseppetti	Honda	1'45.189
27.	33	S. Gadea	Aprilia	1'45.492
28.	69	R. Harms	Honda	1'45.553
29.	8	M. Manna	Malaguti	1'45.625
30.	66	V. Kallio	Aprilia	1'45.726
31.	47	A. Rodriguez	Derbi	1'46.134
32.	20	G. Fröhlich	Honda	1'46.181
33.	16	R. Schouten	Honda	1'46.282
34.	70	J. Miralles	Aprilia	1'46.366
35.	28	J. Carchano	Aprilia	1'46.559
36.	72	A. Masbou	Honda	1'47.004
37.	11	M. Angeloni	Honda	1'47.304
38.	73	Y. Deschamps	Honda	1'48.700
39.	74	M. Gines	Honda	1'49.152

RACE: 24 LAPS = 100.320 km

1. Andrea Dovizioso	41'26.747 (145.230 km/h)
2. Roberto Locatelli	+ 0"594
3. Jorge Lorenzo	+ 6"690
4. Mirko Giansanti	+ 9"662
5. Hector Barbera	+ 10"178
6. Mika Kallio	+ 20"698
7. Pablo Nieto	+ 20"967
8. Casey Stoner	+ 21"158
9. Alvaro Bautista	+ 21"645
10. Steve Jenkner	+ 23"080
11. Gino Borsoi	+ 26"699
12. Mattia Pasini	+ 29"332
13. Julian Simon	+ 33"187
14. Lukas Pesek	+ 37"002
15. Simone Corsi	+ 40"239
16. Gabor Talmacsi	+ 40"304
17. Gioele Pellino	+ 51"919
18. Angel Rodriguez	+ 54"523
19. Dario Giuseppetti	+ 54"575
20. Fabrizio Lai	+ 54"922
21. Imre Toth	+ 1'05.458
22. Sergio Gadea	+ 1'05.610
23. Manuel Manna	+ 1'13.982
24. Jordi Carchano	+ 1'14.248
25. Julian Miralles	+ 1'14.539
26. Vesa Kallio	+ 1'24.230
27. Mattia Angeloni	+ 1'27.607
28. Raymond Schouten	+ 1'36.938
29. Mathieu Gines	+ 1 lap
30. Yannick Deschamps	+ 1 lap

Fastest lap:
Dovizioso, in 1'42.651 (146.593 km/h). New record.
Previous record: Pedrosa, in 1'43.837 (144.919 km/h/2003).

Outright fastest lap: Barbera, in 1'42.536 (146.758 km/h/2004).

CHAMPIONSHIP

1. A. Dovizioso	63 (2 wins)
2. R. Locatelli	48
3. C. Stoner	35
4. S. Jenkner	34
5. H. Barbera	33
6. P. Nieto	29
7. M. Giansanti	28
8. M. Simoncelli	25 (1 win)
9. J. Lorenzo	16
10. G. Borsoi	15

YAMAHA
THE DOCTOR

ITALY
Mugello

Valentino Rossi at work. After two rather more difficult races, the reigning champion gets it right in the hills of Mugello, a superb circuit, full of Italian charm.

MOTOGP

The race was decided over a six lap sprint, with Rossi emerging victorious.

Italian Grand Prix
6th June 2004 / Mugello - 5.245 m

STARTING GRID

1.	15	S. Gibernau	Honda	1'49.553
2.	69	N. Hayden	Honda	1'49.922
3.	46	V. Rossi	Yamaha	1'49.926
4.	4	A. Barros	Honda	1'50.058
5.	33	M. Melandri	Yamaha	1'50.315
6.	3	M. Biaggi	Honda	1'50.445
7.	6	M. Tamada	Honda	1'50.584
8.	65	L. Capirossi	Ducati	1'50.699
9.	10	Ke. Roberts	Suzuki	1'50.736
10.	56	S. Nakano	Kawasaki	1'50.807
11.	7	C. Checa	Yamaha	1'50.858
12.	45	C. Edwards	Honda	1'50.970
13.	66	A. Hofmann	Kawasaki	1'51.303
14.	11	R. Xaus	Ducati	1.51.405
15.	12	T. Bayliss	Ducati	1'51.647
16.	17	N. Abé	Yamaha	1'51.659
17.	67	S. Byrne	Aprilia	1'52.355
18.	99	J. McWilliams	Aprilia	1'52.368
19.	50	N. Hodgson	Ducati	1'52.496
20.	9	N. Aoki	Proton KR	1'52.904
21.	80	Ku. Roberts	Proton KR	1'54.066
22.	88	A. Pitt	Moriwaki	1'54.556
23.	84	M. Fabrizio	Harris WCM	1'54.695
Fastest lap:				
	35	C. Burns	Harris WCM	1'58.174

RACE: 6 LAPS = 31.470 km (*)

1.	Valentino Rossi	12'06.803 (155.877 km/h)
2.	Sete Gibernau	+ 0"361
3.	Massimiliano Biaggi	+ 1"540
4.	Troy Bayliss	+ 1"782
5.	Ruben Xaus	+ 2"389
6.	Alexandre Barros	+ 2"446
7.	Norifumi Abé	+ 5"842
8.	Loris Capirossi	+ 6"228
9.	Marco Melandri	+ 6"461
10.	Shane Byrne	+ 7"198
11.	Neil Hodgson	+ 9"048
12.	Colin Edwards	+ 9"626
13.	Nobuatsu Aoki	+ 14"201
14.	Alexander Hofmann	+ 48"091
15.	Michel Fabrizio	+ 50"498
16.	Jeremy McWilliams	+ 56"572
17.	Andrew Pitt	+ 59"267

(*): The race was stopped because of the rain. In this case, the order of the first part serves only to establish the grid order for the second decisive race.

Fastest lap:
Gibernau, in 1'51.133 (169.904 km/h). New record.
Previous record: Ukawa, in 1'52.601 (167.689 km/h/2002).

Outright fastest lap: Gibernau, in 1'49.553 (172.354 km/h/2004).

CHAMPIONSHIP

1.	S. Gibernau	86	(2 wins)
2.	V. Rossi	76	(2 wins)
3.	M. Biaggi	72	
4.	A. Barros	48	
5.	C. Checa	36	
6.	C. Edwards	33	
7.	L. Capirossi	28	
8.	N. Hayden	27	
9.	T. Bayliss	23	
10.	M. Melandri	22	

Runners and riders:
Still in pain with his right thumb, Hopkins choses to skip this GP. The Moriwaki makes its first appearance of the season; the original chassis fitted with a V5 Honda and ridden by the Australian, Andrew Pitt.

Qualifying:
On Friday, Sete Gibernau set an exceptional time, 1.7 seconds quicker than any GP bike had ever gone at the Mugello circuit, beating Rossi's 2002 time. His time would remain unbeaten on the second day of qualifying and Sete is again quickest, by 2 thousandths this time, on Saturday. Max Biaggi expressed his surprise to which the Spaniard replied: "If Max wants to swap bikes with me, no problem!" Problems were affecting Kurtis Roberts however. For the second time this year, his Proton caught fire on Saturday afternoon, this time after a fall.

Start:
Rossi, Biaggi and Capirossi make perfect starts, but not Gibernau who is only seventh at the end of the first lap.

Lap 3:
Rossi has a 194 thousandths lead over Biaggi, who is being caught by Tamada. Melandri, Hayden and Gibernau, who has just set the fastest lap are also closing in.

Lap 4:
Checa falls. Tamada is about to attack Biaggi and pass him.

Lap 6:
Tamada leads and Gibernau is already fourth.

Lap 7:
Hayden falls, but gets going again.

Lap 9:
Tamada leads Gibernau, Biaggi and Rossi, all of them wheel to wheel within 575 thousandths.

Half distance (12 laps):
Rossi has a 37 thousandths lead over the rocket of the day, Makoto Tamada with Gibernau 244 thousandths behind the Japanese rider. Biaggi is a further second down on the series leader. Having continued after his fall, Hayden comes into the pits.

Lap 13:
A frightening fall for Nakano when a tyre explodes at the end of the main straight!

Lap 14:
Tamada retires (tyre problem.)

Lap 15:
Rossi and Gibernau are just 18 thousandths apart!

Lap 19:
Rain. Red flag and it will be a six lap sprint to the flag.

Second start:
Barros leads the opening lap ahead of Biaggi and Abe as it begins to rain again.

Lap 2:
Xaus is in front with Bayliss and Barros in pursuit, chased by Gibernau and Rossi.

Lap 3:
Bayliss takes his turn at the front.

Lap 4:
Rossi takes control.

Finish (6 laps):
Even in these unusual conditions it is the usual three riders in the top three spots.

Championship:
Two wins apiece for Gibernau and Rossi means the reigning champion has closed to within ten points.

National dress for the home race: Max Biaggi on Friday morning in Mugello.

Fear on the track

Inevitably there were cries of scandal, farce and stupid rules. When a race has been so intense and of such high quality, frustration is the natural reaction to it being stopped. There was certainly plenty of discussion about a new for 2004 article in the regulations which sees a GP played out over a minimum of a five lap sprint, with the greater part of the race already run counting for virtually nothing. However, whatever the rules, be it a 13 minute GP or a "normal" forty five minute race, the strongest riders still find their way to the podium. At Mugello in 2004, as at other races, Rossi and Gibernau took the top two slots, although one wonders what Sete might have done if he had not been held up by Bayliss. Max Biaggi was also ever present, but in third place, fractionally less competitive than the two men who had shared the wins between them so far this season.
That was the sporting drama on the day, but there was another incident that deserves our attention. Shinya Nakano had a terrifying fall when the rear tyre on his Kawasaki exploded on the second half of the main straight at 315 km/h, according to the telemetry read-out. An accident for a Bridgestone runner had already happened back in winter testing when Tamada was the victim, followed by Kenny Roberts in Malaysia. It might also have had serious consequences at Mugello for that other hero of the day, Tamada, who felt abnormal vibrations coming from his rear wheel and wisely pulled in before his tyre could explode. It was a sign that it might be time to slow the continual development of the MotoGP bikes.
There was more palpable tension than usual among the riders, which was proof that everyone understood that, on these rocket ship that have over 240 horsepower and can now travel at more than 340 km/h, the fine lines between what is possible and what is a catastrophe were now converging. One only had to see a look of fright in Loris Capirossi's eyes when the race was interrupted to understand that, whatever they might say, the riders could no longer hide their concerns, indeed their fear.
At Mugello, that Sunday 6th June 2004, the gods were watching over Shinya Nakano. He got up with some heavy bruising, but he was alive. The gods were on duty that day for the Japanese rider, but that might not always be the case. What would have happened if the accident occurred ten metres earlier, where the track is lined with concrete walls? What would have happened if Tamada had suffered a similar problem when he was fighting, fairing to fairing, with Rossi, Biaggi and Gibernau? And what if the accident occurred a further ten metres earlier and the bike had been launched like a bomb at the pit wall?
These are really the only questions that needed to be asked after the 2004 Italian GP.

A scary moment in six terrifying moments: the rear tyre on Shinya Nakano's Kawasaki has just exploded. One of the nicest riders in the MotoGP class miraculously escaped serious injury.
(Photos: R. Kerian).

250cc

Italian Grand Prix
6th June 2004 / Mugello - 5.245 m

STARTING GRID

1.	19	S. Porto	Aprilia	1'53.691
2.	26	D. Pedrosa	Honda	1'53.979
3.	7	R. De Puniet	Aprilia	1'54.180
4.	24	T. Elias	Honda	1'54.635
5.	51	A. De Angelis	Aprilia	1'54.643
6.	54	M. Poggiali	Aprilia	1'54.670
7.	21	F. Battaini	Aprilia	1'54.815
8.	2	R. Rolfo	Honda	1'55.157
9.	10	F. Gonzales-Nieto	Aprilia	1'55.158
10.	11	J. Olive	Aprilia	1'55.502
11.	73	H. Aoyama	Honda	1'55.627
12.	96	J. Smrz	Honda	1'55.972
13.	33	H. Faubel	Aprilia	1'56.057
14.	8	N. Matsudo	Yamaha	1'56.247
15.	50	S. Guintoli	Aprilia	1'56.328
16.	14	A. West	Aprilia	1'56.381
17.	9	H. Marchand	Aprilia	1'56.510
18.	25	A. Baldolini	Aprilia	1'56.704
19.	34	E. Bataille	Honda	1'56.752
20.	57	C. Davies	Aprilia	1'56.926
21.	77	G. Lefort	Aprilia	1'57.146
22.	12	A. Vincent	Aprilia	1'57.330
23.	36	E. Nigon	Yamaha	1'57.363
24.	28	D. Heidolf	Aprilia	1'57.515
25.	6	A. Debon	Honda	1'57.568
26.	16	J. Stigefelt	Aprilia	1'57.796
27.	15	C. Gemmel	Honda	1'58.477
28.	63	J. Ronzoni	Yamaha	1'58.643
29.	44	T. Sekiguchi	Yamaha	1'58.690
30.	40	M. Sabbatani	Yamaha	2'01.051

RACE: 21 LAPS = 110.145 km

1.	Sebastian Porto	40'32.672 (162.998 km/h)
2.	Daniel Pedrosa	+ 6"147
3.	Manuel Poggiali	+ 8"415
4.	Randy De Puniet	+ 11"226
5.	Alfonso Gonzales-Nieto	+ 11"876
6.	Toni Elias	+ 11"888
7.	Roberto Rolfo	+ 24"398
8.	Alex De Angelis	+ 27"550
9.	Hiroshi Aoyama	+ 28"126
10.	Anthony West	+ 38"025
11.	Joan Olive	+ 38"207
12.	Franco Battaini	+ 45"788
13.	Sylvain Guintoli	+ 1'01.150
14.	Hector Faubel	+ 1'06.887
15.	Alex Debon	+ 1'07.022
16.	Naoki Matsudo	+ 1'07.037
17.	Chaz Davies	+ 1'07.196
18.	Gregory Lefort	+ 1'17.464
19.	Johan Stigefelt	+ 1'19.655
20.	Christian Gemmel	+ 1'25.112
21.	Taro Sekiguchi	+ 1'33.088

Fastest lap:
Porto, in 1'54.599 (164.765 km/h).
Record: Nakano, in 1'54.462 (164.963 km/h/2000).

Outright fastest lap: De Puniet, in 1'53.586 (166.235 km/h/2003).

CHAMPIONSHIP

1.	R. De Puniet	73
2.	D. Pedrosa	70 (2 wins)
3.	S. Porto	50 (1 win)
4.	A. Gonzales-Nieto	45
5.	R. Rolfo	41 (1 win)
6.	A. De Angelis	40
7.	T. Elias	38
8.	M. Poggiali	29
9.	A. West	29
10.	A. Debon	29

Sebastian Porto is well surrounded on the start grid...

Runners and riders:
Full house for the series regulars. Just one wildcard for Jarno Ronzoni from Bergamo, home to king Giacomo Agostini. The young rider's first name is of course his parents homage to the unforgettable Jarno Saarinen. It is Ronzini's second GP, as he had replaced the injured Frenchman, Erwan Nigon at Jerez.

Qualifying:
Argentina's Sebastian Porto is true to form, setting unbeatable times on the track, with no one on Saturday getting near his Friday time, although he makes some big mistakes including a serious fall in Saturday morning's free practice, from which he walks away uninjured. Randy De Puniet also falls, while Dani Pedrosa continues to show great form, setting second fastest time. Reigning champion, Manuel Poggiali is "only" sixth on the grid.

Start:
Pedrosa storms into the lead ahead of Porto and De Puniet. Arnaud Vincent falls at the first corner, in an incident which also involves Heidolf and Sabbatini; the former world champion gets away with bruising to his back. Pedrosa leads as they cross the line for the first time, ahead of Porto and De Puniet.

Lap 3:
A lead group forms with De Puniet, Pedrosa and Porto covered by 297 thousandths. Elias is now fourth with Poggiali glued to his back wheel, 1"765 behind the leaders.

Lap 7:
Porto steps up the pace and leads de Puniet and Pedrosa by 555 thousandths. With Poggiali dragging them along, the fourth placed group is now 1.5 seconds behind.

Lap 9:
Bataille then Baldolini fall.

Half distance (10 laps):
No change at the front, De Puniet heads Porto by 55 thousandths and Pedrosa by 86 thousandths. Elias is still fourth, 1"832 down on the leader.

Lap 13:
Smrz falls after a great climb up the order.

Lap 18:
The two Aprilia riders have made the break as Porto and De Puniet now lead Pedrosa by over a second and Poggiali is alone in fourth. Elias and "Fonsi" Nieto battle it out for fifth.

Finish (21 laps):
195 thousandths separate the top two as they attack the final lap. At the very last corner, De Puniet finds himself in neutral (the engine had seized having run out of fuel.) His team manger, Lucio Cecchinello holds his head in his hands. The Frenchman finishes fourth and heartbroken.

Championship:
De Puniet now only has a three point lead over Pedrosa. Winner on the day, Sebastian Porto closes up to 23 points behind and looks set to mount a new attack.

...and out on his own on the track on a perfect weekend.

125cc

Runners and riders:
Stefano Bianco is back as a wildcard. Two years ago, a lot of people in Italy really believed in this lad, who had been discovered by the Benetton clan. There are four other invited riders, including Alessio Aldrovani, son of a former European 125 champion, now one of the best engineers in the paddock.

Qualifying:
Barbera is flying on Friday, but the pace seriously hots up for Saturday. On a track that has always suited Aprilia, in the end it is the German, Jenkner, who has the last word, ahead of Stoner (KTM) and Pasini, who beats his team leader Locatelli by two places. Gino Borsoi suffers a bad fall on Saturday, leaving him with a dislocated right shoulder. After medical checks on Sunday morning, he lines up for the race.

Start:
Dovizioso gets the best start ahead of Stoner and Barbera. On the first lap, falls for Manna, dislocating his right collar bone, Robbin Harms (lumbar bruising) and Michele Danese (broken left wrist.) At the end of the opening lap, Dovizioso leads by 0"563 from Stoner, who is chased by Barbera, Locatelli and Pasini.

Lap 3:
A lead group shapes up consisting of Barbera, Dovizioso, Locatelli, Stoner, Jenkner, Pasini and Nieto. Di Meglio falls, hitting Simoncelli and Luthi also hits the deck, breaking his left collar bone.

Lap 7:
The falls continue with Lai and Pellino, while Perugini retires.

Half distance (10 laps):
Jerez winner Simoncelli has gone, as have Vesa Kallio and Schouten.

Lap 15:
Locatelli still has Dovizioso hanging onto his shirt tails (60 thousandths down). Nieto and Stoner are right behind the two leaders with Barbera just drifting off the back.

Lap 17:
It's a superb battle as Pablo Nieto attacks Dovizioso and Barbera and Dovizioso are also going at it.

Lap 18:
Mika Kallio retires. Giansanti joins the lead group and as they begin the final lap, six of them are covered by 282 thousandths with Locatelli leading.

Finish (20 laps):
After a first attack from Nieto and a second from Dovizioso, in the end it is the experienced Locatelli who has the last word. The others are caught out by the famous hole in the final corner and it is a miracle that there are no fallers.

Championship:
Dovizioso is still ahead, but only by three little points from Locatelli, who got the most out of the weekend. Two Italians, Honda versus Aprilia, youth versus experience: the championship is still exciting.

Roberto Locatelli in the middle of the podium at the circuit where he had made his GP debut. Stoner (on left) and Barbera don't seem too unhappy.

This is what 125 racing is all about. Note the "Italian" design of Honda no 34, belonging to future world champion, Andrea Dovizioso.

Italian Grand Prix
6th June 2004 / Mugello - 5.245 m

STARTING GRID

1.	21	S. Jenkner	Aprilia	1'58.575
2.	27	C. Stoner	KTM	1'58.877
3.	54	M. Pasini	Aprilia	1'58.941
4.	34	A. Dovizioso	Honda	1'58.964
5.	15	R. Locatelli	Aprilia	1'59.132
6.	36	M. Kallio	KTM	1'59.260
7.	3	H. Barbera	Aprilia	1'59.324
8.	48	J. Lorenzo	Derbi	1'59.341
9.	63	M. Di Meglio	Aprilia	1'59.387
10.	32	F. Lai	Gilera	1'59.451
11.	6	M. Giansanti	Aprilia	1'59.527
12.	22	P. Nieto	Aprilia	1'59.578
13.	52	L. Pesek	Honda	1'59.618
14.	41	Y. Ui	Aprilia	1'59.623
15.	10	J. Simon	Honda	1'59.899
16.	58	M. Simoncelli	Aprilia	2'00.016
17.	50	A. Ballerini	Aprilia	2'00.029
18.	19	A. Bautista	Aprilia	2'00.120
19.	23	G. Borsoi	Aprilia	2'00.155
20.	12	T. Lüthi	Honda	2'00.476
21.	24	S. Corsi	Honda	2'00.481
22.	14	G. Talmacsi	Malaguti	2'00.500
23.	47	A. Rodriguez	Derbi	2'00.565
24.	42	G. Pellino	Aprilia	2'00.582
25.	75	A. Aldrovandi	Honda	2'00.727
26.	7	S. Perugini	Gilera	2'00.780
27.	25	I. Toth	Aprilia	2'00.862
28.	76	M. Danese	Aprilia	2'01.316
29.	8	M. Manna	Malaguti	2'01.319
30.	69	R. Harms	Honda	2'01.320
31.	66	V. Kallio	Aprilia	2'01.332
32.	53	S. Bianco	Aprilia	2'01.598
33.	33	S. Gadea	Aprilia	2'01.786
34.	26	D. Giuseppetti	Honda	2'01.923
35.	16	R. Schouten	Honda	2'02.055
36.	61	M. Pirro	Aprilia	2'02.704
37.	28	J. Carchano	Aprilia	2'03.296
38.	77	L. Zanetti	Honda	2'03.357
39.	11	M. Angeloni	Honda	2'04.178

RACE: 20 LAPS = 104.900 km

1. Roberto Locatelli	40'13.158 (156.492 km/h)
2. Casey Stoner	+ 0"152
3. Hector Barbera	+ 0"197
4. Andrea Dovizioso	+ 0"573
5. Mirko Giansanti	+ 0"595
6. Pablo Nieto	+ 0"879
7. Steve Jenkner	+ 5"980
8. Mattia Pasini	+ 19"206
9. Gino Borsoi	+ 28"656
10. Jorge Lorenzo	+ 28"671
11. Simone Corsi	+ 28"717
12. Andrea Ballerini	+ 28"831
13. Gabor Talmacsi	+ 28"955
14. Dario Giuseppetti	+ 44"766
15. Lukas Pesek	+ 44"875
16. Imre Toth	+ 45"682
17. Alessio Aldrovandi	+ 56"328
18. Stefano Bianco	+ 56"658
19. Michaele Pirro	+ 56"674
20. Julian Simon	+ 1'07.291
21. Jordi Carchano	+ 1'28.660
22. Youichi Ui	+ 2'29.626
23. Sergio Gadea	+ 1 lap

Fastest lap:
Nieto, in 1'59.400 (158.140 km/h).
Record: Borsoi, in 1'58.969 (158.713 km/h/2003).

Outright fastest lap: Jenkner, in 1'58.575 (159.240 km/h/2004).

CHAMPIONSHIP

1. A. Dovizioso	76 (2 wins)
2. R. Locatelli	73 (1 win)
3. C. Stoner	55
4. H. Barbera	49
5. S. Jenkner	43
6. M. Giansanti	39
7. P. Nieto	39
8. M. Simoncelli	25 (1 win)
9. J. Lorenzo	22
10. G. Borsoi	22

GAULOISES
GAULOISES
GAULOISES
GAULOISES
GAULOISES
Circuit de Catalunya

CATALUNYA
Catalunya

The grandstands are packed for another duel between Valentino Rossi and Sete Gibernau. Spain is mad about bike racing. Over the weekend, all the 500 champions from the nineties were on parade: Wayne Rainey, Kevin Schwantz, Michael Doohan and Alex Criville enjoyed the show and were all smiles.

John Hopkins and Nicky Hayden are two of the new breed of Americans.

Catalunyan Grand Prix
13th June 2004 / Catalunya - 4.727 m

STARTING GRID

1.	15	S. Gibernau	Honda	1'42.596
2.	46	V. Rossi	Yamaha	1'42.959
3.	69	N. Hayden	Honda	1'43.124
4.	3	M. Biaggi	Honda	1'43.563
5.	33	M. Melandri	Yamaha	1'43.601
6.	4	A. Barros	Honda	1'43.647
7.	11	R. Xaus	Ducati	1.43.680
8.	21	J. Hopkins	Suzuki	1'43.693
9.	6	M. Tamada	Honda	1'43.708
10.	12	T. Bayliss	Ducati	1'43.793
11.	45	C. Edwards	Honda	1'43.832
12.	7	C. Checa	Yamaha	1'43.860
13.	56	S. Nakano	Kawasaki	1'43.948
14.	66	A. Hofmann	Kawasaki	1'44.126
15.	65	L. Capirossi	Ducati	1'44.131
16.	10	Ke. Roberts	Suzuki	1'44.175
17.	50	N. Hodgson	Ducati	1'44.761
18.	17	N. Abé	Yamaha	1'44.988
19.	99	J. McWilliams	Aprilia (*)	1'45.108
20.	67	S. Byrne	Aprilia	1'45.200
21.	32	G. Lavilla	Suzuki	1'46.142
22.	88	A. Pitt	Moriwaki	1'46.327
23.	80	Ku. Roberts	Proton KR	1'46.399
24.	9	N. Aoki	Proton KR	1'46.957
25.	84	M. Fabrizio	Harris WCM	1'47.503
26.	35	C. Burns	Harris WCM	1'48.684

(*): Having fallen in the warm-up, Jeremy McWilliams (GB, Aprilia) pulls out.

RACE: 25 LAPS = 118.175 km

1.	Valentino Rossi	44'03.255 (160.949 km/h)
2.	Sete Gibernau	+ 0"159
3.	Marco Melandri	+ 13"923
4.	Carlos Checa	+ 19"213
5.	Colin Edwards	+ 21"205
6.	Ruben Xaus	+ 22"847
7.	Shinya Nakano	+ 24"014
8.	Massimiliano Biaggi	+ 24"104
9.	Norifumi Abé	+ 35"676
10.	Loris Capirossi	+ 40"775
11.	Alexander Hofmann	+ 40"862
12.	Neil Hodgson	+ 56"157
13.	Shane Byrne	+ 1'03.679
14.	Andrew Pitt	+ 1'05.933
15.	Nobuatsu Aoki	+ 1'18.199
16.	Michel Fabrizio	+ 1'18.515
17.	Kenny Roberts	+ 1 lap
18.	Chris Burns	+ 5 laps

Fastest lap:
Gibernau, in 1'44.641 (162.624 km/h). New record.
Previous record: Ross, in 1'45.472 (161.343 km/h/2003).

Outright fastest lap: Gibernau, in 1'42.596 (165.866 km/h/2004).

CHAMPIONSHIP

1.	S. Gibernau	106 2 wins)
2.	V. Rossi	101 (3 wins)
3.	M. Biaggi	80
4.	C. Checa	49
5.	A. Barros	48
6.	C. Edwards	44
7.	M. Melandri	38
8.	L. Capirossi	34
9.	N. Abé	28
10.	N. Hayden	27

Runners and riders:
After Shinya Nakano's accident and Makoto Tamada's retirement as a result of his rear tyre losing half its tread, it had been a busy week for Bridgestone, who brought reinforced tyres to Catalunya. Suzuki test driver, Spain's Gregorio Lavilla was getting a run and John Hopkins was delighted to be back.

Qualifying:
It was a case of super Sete, as the Spaniard, despite a harmless fall on Friday morning, dominated both qualifying days. Rossi was second on Saturday, albeit 4 tenths off the pace. Hayden got himself another front row start and Xaus, who had no less than three falls on Saturday, was the best Ducati in seventh.

Start:
Rossi surprises everyone, going around the outside at the first corner. Gibernau is right behind, followed by Biaggi and Tamada. Capirossi takes a trip through the dirt. After one leap, Rossi heads the championship leader by 174 thousandths and Biaggi by 518.

Lap 2:
Rossi brakes too late and almost falls, handing the lead to Gibernau.

Lap 5:
Barros falls, having got as high as third. Gibernau and Rossi are still inseparable (69 thousandths.) Melandri is now third at 1"456. Biaggi is fighting over fourth place with team-mate Tamada. Kurtis Roberts retires.

Half distance (12 laps):
96 thousandths is the tiny gap between the two men who lead the series, still with Gibernau out in front. Melandri is a brilliant third, 5 seconds down, with Biaggi in his wake. Tamada retires.

Lap 14:
Rossi passes Gibernau, but the Spaniard gets him back one lap later.

Lap 17:
Hayden retires. Gibernau makes a mistake and drops to 832 thousandths behind Rossi.

Lap 19:
Hopkins retires. Kenny Roberts stops to change his rear tyre!

Lap 21:
Gibernau has closed to just 99 thousandths and takes the lead at the end of the straight and the fight is really underway.

Lap 22:
Bayliss has a bad fall, after he had closed on Biaggi who was struggling with a faulty tyre.

Lap 24:
Fantastic! Rossi is back in front.

Finish (25 laps):
As they start the last lap, Rossi leads by 486 thousandths. Sete tries absolutely everything but he can do nothing against the world champion, who takes his third win of the year. A superb first podium for Marco Melandri.

Championship:
106 – 101: Gibernau hangs on to a five point lead with Biaggi already dropping back so it seems that, as last year, the title will come down to a battle between Sete and Valentino.

Barros in attack mode, but his race ended on lap 5.

"This bike is in perfect health!"

Valentino Rossi and his double. His rivals can rest easy, knowing it's all nicely done with mirrors.

No matter what instrument he is given, be it a Honda or a Yamaha, Valentino Rossi can always breathe new life into a bike. In Barcelona, in front of 102,301 spectators who had come to see their hero Gibernau take the win, the Doctor stopped on his slowing down lap to cast an eye over his Yamaha M1. The verdict was that, unlike its major Japanese rival, it was full of the joys of spring.

With a white shirt over his blue leathers soaked in sweat, green rubber gloves over his race ones and a stethoscope around his neck, "Dottore" Rossi once again found the hard core of his fan club at the side of the track. "I just wanted to make sure my bike was in good health and that it did not need an urgent operation. After a quick check, I was on my way again." And, for the sixty second time in his career, he was heading for the top step of a GP podium!

The 2004 Catalunya GP was a race of rare intensity and essentially it was the story of two completely different types of Japanese temperament. In the Honda camp, there has always been a culture of arrogance, with the role of the individual sacrificed for the good of the company. Working there means living, breathing and dying for Honda. When things go badly it is bad for everyone who wears the Honda badge. But above all, hierarchy counts more than anything else and no worker will ever question a decision taken by his direct superior. Rossi's gone? "So what? We are so much stronger than the opposition that there is no risk for us," was the word from Tokyo, according to HRC boss, Koij Nakajima. More powerful, more everything... But that was no longer the case, because while the Honda RC211V engine was still the benchmark in the class, the Yamaha M1 was a better balanced machine. "In order to get as good traction as the Yamaha, we have to use softer tyres," explained Sete Gibernau, the loser on the day, even though he was the only man able to hang onto the rejuvenated M1. "Using the softer tyres, everyone knows what that means for us towards the end of the race, especially when it is so hot."

Had the lesson sunk in? Valentino Rossi had been very worried about these two races – Italy and Catalunya – and yet he put in two faultless performances. He was enjoying the moment: "you know what is fantastic at Yamaha is that we make the most of every minute of testing to progress. We are doing it step by step and we try everything we can think of. And the engineers listen and respond to all our requests. No, I have no regrets about the decision I made last year." They listen to the riders? Rossi did not need to add, "unlike those at Honda," but it was clear that he meant it totally.

The doctor has just examined his bike and is about to set off for the podium.

250cc

Catalunyan Grand Prix
13th June 2004 / Catalunya - 4.727 m

STARTING GRID

1.	7	R. De Puniet	Aprilia	1'46.292
2.	26	D. Pedrosa	Honda	1'46.434
3.	19	S. Porto	Aprilia	1'46.976
4.	51	A. De Angelis	Aprilia	1'47.184
5.	24	T. Elias	Honda	1'47.377
6.	10	F. Gonzales-Nieto	Aprilia	1'47.628
7.	50	S. Guintoli	Aprilia	1'47.725
8.	2	R. Rolfo	Honda	1'47.738
9.	54	M. Poggiali	Aprilia	1'47.823
10.	21	F. Battaini	Aprilia	1'48.115
11.	11	J. Olive	Aprilia	1'48.115
12.	77	G. Lefort	Aprilia	1'48.190
13.	73	H. Aoyama	Honda	1'48.299
14.	34	E. Bataille	Honda	1'48.488
15.	8	N. Matsudo	Yamaha	1'48.533
16.	6	A. Debon	Honda	1'48.553
17.	9	H. Marchand	Aprilia	1'48.569
18.	96	J. Smrz	Honda	1'48.659
19.	14	A. West	Aprilia	1'48.808
20.	33	H. Faubel	Aprilia	1'49.085
21.	57	C. Davies	Aprilia	1'49.122
22.	36	E. Nigon	Yamaha	1'49.319
23.	16	J. Stigefelt	Aprilia	1'49.484
24.	25	A. Baldolini	Aprilia	1'49.552
25.	28	D. Heidolf	Aprilia	1'49.659
26.	44	T. Sekiguchi	Yamaha	1'49.773
27.	63	J. Ronzoni	Honda	1'51.937
28.	40	M. Sabbatani	Yamaha	1'52.745
29.	72	D. Fouloi	Aprilia	1'52.796

RACE: 23 LAPS = 108.721 km

1.	Randy De Puniet	41'29.955 (157.189 km/h)
2.	Daniel Pedrosa	+ 0"109
3.	Toni Elias	+ 9"521
4.	Sebastian Porto	+ 20"871
5.	Alfonso Gonzales-Nieto	+ 34"337
6.	Hiroshi Aoyama	+ 37"569
7.	Sylvain Guintoli	+ 42"087
8.	Alex Debon	+ 45"850
9.	Anthony West	+ 45"938
10.	Franco Battaini	+ 46"235
11.	Eric Bataille	+ 50"694
12.	Alex Baldolini	+ 50"980
13.	Chaz Davies	+ 56"785
14.	Naoki Matsudo	+ 56"895
15.	Jakub Smrz	+ 57"366
16.	Hector Faubel	+ 58"164
17.	Erwan Nigon	+ 1'32.322
18.	Taro Sekiguchi	+ 1 lap
19.	Jarno Ronzoni	+ 1 lap
20.	David Fouloi	+ 1 lap

Fastest lap:
Pedrosa, in 1'47.302 (158.591 km/h). New record.
Previous record: Rossi, in 1'47.585 (158.174 km/h/1998).

Outright fastest lap: De Puniet, in 1'46.292 (160.098 km/h/2004).

CHAMPIONSHIP

1.	R. De Puniet	98 (1 win)
2.	D. Pedrosa	90 (2 wins)
3.	S. Porto	63 (1 win)
4.	A. Gonzales-Nieto	56
5.	T. Elias	54
6.	R. Rolfo	41 (1 win)
7.	A. De Angelis	40
8.	A. Debon	37
9.	A. West	36
10.	H. Aoyama	35

Pedrosa makes the promptest start, but right behind, De Puniet will give him a hard time.

Runners and riders:
There are two absentees; Arnaud Vincent who broke two ribs in his fall at the first corner in Mugello and Germany's Christian Gemmel, who has quit the sport citing "too much pressure". Vincent is replaced by fellow countryman David Fouloi, while Jarno Ronzoni continues his life as a replacement rider, this time on board the Castrol team's Honda. A familiar face has a wild card in the shape of Spain's Jose Luis Cardoso, on a third Yamaha with the NC World Trade team.

Qualifying:
A great duel comes to life between the two pace setters at this stage of the season, France's Randy De Puniet and Spain's Dani Pedrosa, with pole going to Randy. Reigning champion Poggiali is still in crisis and is only ninth. France's Gregory Lefort does well to come twelfth.

Start:
Pedrosa gets the holeshot, but De Puniet is soon in the lead. First time across the line and Randy leads by 228 thousandths from Pedrosa who is pursued by Elias. Then there is already a gap, with fourth placed Fonsi Gonzales-Nieto almost two seconds behind.

Lap 4:
De Puniet speeds up, but Pedrosa is still two tenths back, with Elias a whole second down on his fellow countryman. Then comes a big four second hole until Rolfo comes past in fourth place.

Lap 7:
161 thousandths separate the two leaders, who have left the others in their wake.

Lap 8:
Marchand and Stigefelt fall.

Half distance (11 laps):
Pedrosa had attacked a lap earlier, but De Puniet countered. Elias is 1"692 down in third. Porto is now alone in fourth spot, but over 8 seconds behind Elias.

Lap 12:
The crowd is on its feet as Pedrosa now leads, but only for a few hundred metres, as De Puniet gets by again.

Lap 13:
Alex de Angelis is a faller.

Lap 15:
Rolfo and Poggiali collide and fall. Out in front, De Puniet and Pedrosa are bashing fairings.

Lap 18:
Pedrosa now leads by 432 thousandths.

Lap 20:
De Puniet is back in front.

Finish (23 laps):
The Frenchman leads by 37 thousandths as they tackle the final lap and he takes his first win of the year on the circuit where he took his maiden GP victory in 2003. De Puniet had been brilliant all race long and totally masterful on the final lap, when he twice had to get heavy handed with Pedrosa- a great display.

Championship:
De Puniet consolidates his lead with an 8 point advantage over Pedrosa.

The Marseillaise is played for Randy De Puniet, who won in his rival's back yard.

Swiss duo: the injured Thomas Luthi watches the race alongside his famous elder, Jacques Cornu.

125cc

Runners and riders:
The Italian GP had left a few scarred bodies: Thomas Luthi (broken left collar bone and shoulder blade) and Raymond Schouten and Robbin Harms also forced to pull out, but only Harms is replaced, by a 21 year old Finn, Mikko Kyyhkynen. Four riders have wild cards: Manuel Hernandez Junior, Argentina's Fabrizio Perren, Jordi Planas and Enrique Jerez.

Qualifying:
Jorge Lorenzo sets the best time on Friday and no one gets near it the next day. The performance of qualifying comes from the Czech, Lukas Pesek (5th), while Fabrizio Lai is injured and has to pull out with a broken fifth metacarpal of the right hand.

Start:
Roberto Locatelli charges through to lead from the second row, ahead of Andrea Dovizioso, who has also come through from the depths of the grid, Alvaro Bautista, Casey Stoner and Steve Jenkner. As they come across the line for the first time, Locatelli has a 91 thousandths lead over Dovizioso, Stoner, Bautista and Jenkner. Pablo Nieto gets it all wrong.

Lap 2:
Simone Corsi falls after colliding with Hector Barbera and the Spaniard sets about staging a great fight back.

Lap 4:
There are now seven in the lead group, all covered by just 535 thousandths. Marco Simoncelli and Jenkner touch on the main straight and Lorenzo takes the lead.

Lap 7:
Lorenzo still in front by 237 thousandths from Dovizioso. The top seven are now covered by 1"060.

Half distance (11 laps):
Lorenzo still leads the dance. Dovizioso is 0"234 down in second, ahead of Locatelli, Bautista, Simoncelli and Stoner. Jenkner has been in trouble for the past two laps and drops to eighth. Pablo Nieto, who had been eighth is now heading the charge to the leaders.

Lap 17:
Locatelli takes matters in hand with Pablo Nieto stuck to his rear wheel. Lorenzo is 7 tenths down in third.

Lap 18:
Locatelli has a high-speed fall, leaving Pablo in the lead ahead of Barbera and Lorenzo.

Lap 20:
280 thousandths between Barbera and Nieto. Lorenzo is third, ahead of Stoner, Bautista and Dovizioso, all within a second.

Finish (22 laps):
A group of six attack the final lap within 9 tenths of one another and in the end, Barbera takes it by 16 thousandths from Dovizioso, with Nieto joining them on the podium.

Championship:
With Roberto Locatelli out, Dovizioso does well this weekend, even though he is beaten, as he extends his position as leader. The Honda rider has a 22 point advantage over his closest rival, who is now Barbera.

The crazy pack as Hector Barbera is faultless.

Catalunyan Grand Prix
13th June 2004 / Catalunya - 4,727 m

STARTING GRID

1.	48	J. Lorenzo	Derbi	1'50.497
2.	3	H. Barbera	Aprilia	1'51.219
3.	27	C. Stoner	KTM	1'51.260
4.	22	P. Nieto	Aprilia	1'51.315
5.	52	L. Pesek	Honda	1'51.357
6.	15	R. Locatelli	Aprilia	1'51.388
7.	6	M. Giansanti	Aprilia	1'51.451
8.	34	A. Dovizioso	Honda	1'51.465
9.	63	M. Di Meglio	Aprilia	1'51.579
10.	21	S. Jenkner	Aprilia	1'51.623
11.	10	J. Simon	Honda	1'51.639
12.	19	A. Bautista	Aprilia	1'51.658
13.	58	M. Simoncelli	Aprilia	1'51.666
14.	14	G. Talmacsi	Malaguti	1'51.918
15.	36	M. Kallio	KTM	1'51.928
16.	24	S. Corsi	Honda	1'51.972
17.	54	M. Pasini	Aprilia	1'51.999
18.	41	Y. Ui	Aprilia	1'52.204
19.	25	I. Toth	Aprilia	1'52.923
20.	7	S. Perugini	Gilera	1'52.982
21.	32	F. Lai (*)	Gilera	1'53.080
22.	42	G. Pellino	Aprilia	1'53.136
23.	26	D. Giuseppetti	Honda	1'53.158
24.	23	G. Borsoi	Aprilia	1'53.168
25.	50	A. Ballerini	Aprilia	1'53.357
26.	43	M. Hernandez	Aprilia	1'53.653
27.	33	S. Gadea	Aprilia	1'53.669
28.	47	A. Rodriguez	Derbi	1'54.004
29.	28	J. Carchano	Aprilia	1'54.223
30.	66	V. Kallio	Aprilia	1'54.243
31.	38	M. Kyyhkynen	Honda	1'55.045
32.	68	F. Perren	Honda	1'55.114
33.	8	M. Manna	Malaguti	1'55.182
34.	11	M. Angeloni	Honda	1'55.238
35.	71	E. Jerez	Honda	1'55.282
36.	78	J. Planas	Honda	1'56.875

(*): Having fallen on Saturday morning, the Italian pulls out.

RACE: 22 LAPS = 103.994 km

1. Hector Barbera	41'17.986 (151.081 km/h)
2. Andrea Dovizioso	+ 0"016
3. Pablo Nieto	+ 0"342
4. Casey Stoner	+ 0"400
5. Jorge Lorenzo	+ 0"548
6. Alvaro Bautista	+ 0"733
7. Marco Simoncelli	+ 7"907
8. Mike Di Meglio	+ 10"793
9. Mika Kallio	+ 13"431
10. Mirko Giansanti	+ 13"513
11. Mattia Pasini	+ 14"242
12. Steve Jenkner	+ 14"333
13. Gioele Pellino	+ 16"209
14. Julian Simon	+ 22"605
15. Angel Rodriguez	+ 22"655
16. Dario Giuseppetti	+ 22"773
17. Gabor Talmacsi	+ 22"961
18. Youichi Ui	+ 23"575
19. Imre Toth	+ 40"669
20. Andrea Ballerini	+ 42"929
21. Sergio Gadea	+ 51"446
22. Stefano Perugini	+ 58"908
23. Jordi Carchano	+ 58"995
24. Manuel Hernandez	+ 59"548
25. Mikko Kyyhkynen	+ 1'17.227
26. Enrique Jerez	+ 1'36.638
27. Vesa Kallio	+ 1'48.618
28. Jordi Planas	+ 1 lap

Fastest lap:
Barbera, in 1'50.903 (153.442 km/h). New record.
Previous record: Stoner, in 1'51.190 (153.046 km/h/2003).

Outright fastest lap: Pedrosa, in 1'50.178 (154.451 km/h/2003).

CHAMPIONSHIP

1. A. Dovizioso	96 (2 wins)
2. H. Barbera	74 (1 win)
3. R. Locatelli	73 (1 win)
4. C. Stoner	68
5. P. Nieto	55
6. S. Jenkner	47
7. M. Giansanti	45
8. M. Simoncelli	34 (1 win)
9. J. Lorenzo	33
10. A. Bautista	24

NGK

THE NETHERLANDS
Assen

A blue bike against the green backdrop of Assen: Valentino continues his tutorial in the Mecca of racing. The bikes are always feted here, the pretty girls have killer smiles and every year, the world championship reaches a critical point.

Dutch Grand Prix
26th June 2004 / Assen - 6.027 m

STARTING GRID

1.	46	V. Rossi	Yamaha	1'58.758
2.	7	C. Checa	Yamaha	1'59.440
3.	15	S. Gibernau	Honda	1'59.903
4.	33	M. Melandri	Yamaha	2'00.724
5.	56	S. Nakano	Kawasaki	2'00.755
6.	4	A. Barros	Honda	2'00.977
7.	10	Ke. Roberts	Suzuki	2'01.182
8.	6	M. Tamada	Honda	2'01.212
9.	11	R. Xaus	Ducati	2'01.312
10.	21	J. Hopkins	Suzuki	2'01.593
11.	66	A. Hofmann	Kawasaki	2'01.617
12.	3	M. Biaggi	Honda	2'01.635
13.	45	C. Edwards	Honda	2'01.642
14.	12	T. Bayliss	Ducati	2'01.707
15.	65	L. Capirossi	Ducati	2'02.029
16.	69	N. Hayden	Honda	2'02.062
17.	17	N. Abé	Yamaha	2'02.427
18.	67	S. Byrne	Aprilia	2'02.580
19.	99	J. McWilliams	Aprilia	2'02.613
20.	50	N. Hodgson	Ducati	2'02.896
21.	84	M. Fabrizio	Harris WCM	2'03.852
22.	9	N. Aoki	Proton KR	2'03.912
23.	80	Ku. Roberts	Proton KR	2'05.311
24.	35	C. Burns	Harris WCM	2'06.137

RACE: 19 LAPS = 114.513 km

1. Valentino Rossi	38'11.831 (179.876 km/h)
2. Sete Gibernau	+ 0"456
3. Marco Melandri	+ 9"909
4. Massimiliano Biaggi	+ 10"183
5. Nicky Hayden	+ 10"300
6. Colin Edwards	+ 10"801
7. Ruben Xaus	+ 13"705
8. Loris Capirossi	+ 14"091
9. Carlos Checa	+ 15"159
10. Neil Hodgson	+ 34"066
11. Norifumi Abé	+ 34"414
12. Makoto Tamada	+ 39"186
13. Alexander Hofmann	+ 41"506
14. John Hopkins	+ 54"569
15. Jeremy McWilliams	+ 1'04.761
16. Kenny Roberts	+ 1'22.266
17. Chris Burns	+ 2'00.469

Fastest lap:
Rossi, in 1'59.472 (181.609 km/h). New record.
Previous record: Rossi, in 2'00.973 (179.355 km/h/2002).

Outright fastest lap: Rossi, in 1'58.758 (182.700 km/h/2004).

CHAMPIONSHIP

1. V. Rossi	126 (4 wins)
2. S. Gibernau	126 (2 wins)
3. M. Biaggi	93
4. C. Checa	56
5. M. Melandri	54
6. C. Edwards	54
7. A. Barros	48
8. L. Capirossi	42
9. N. Hayden	38
10. N. Abé	33

Michel Fabrizio was the best Italian in the rain in qualifying!

Runners and riders:
Loris Capirossi and Troy Bayliss have finally got their hands on the Ducati "big bang" engine, which they first tried the day after the Catalunya GP. Capirossi will use it in the race, but not Bayliss. Melandri has had an operation on his right forearm, which bears the marks of 36 stitches!

Qualifying:
The rain king, Sete Gibernau, is definitely the strongest on Thursday in a session which sees an incredible performance from the young Italian, Michel Fabrizio, fourth on the WCM and best placed Italian rider. The track gradually dries out on Friday and although there are still some damp patches, the kings of the category have a field day. Valentino Rossi beats Capirossi's benchmark lap from last year by a second and once again, Gibernau is the only Honda rider to put up a fight.

Start:
Checa has the quickest reflexes, but Gibernau is soon in the lead, ahead of Rossi, Checa, Barros and Biaggi, who has powered through from the fourth row. Crossing the line for the first time, the two series leaders are separated by 131 thousandths, with Checa and Barros hanging onto their coattails.

Lap 2:
Barros passes Checa. Gibernau leads Rossi by 209 thousandths.

Lap 5:
Fabrizio has a spectacular fall after his engine seizes. Kurtis Roberts retires. Gibernau, Rossi and Barros are covered by 0"555, with the Brazilian the quickest man on track for two consecutive laps.

Lap 8:
Aoki retires. Gibernau, Rossi and Biaggi are still in line astern (423 thousandths.)

Lap 9:
Byrne and Nakano retire.

Half distance (10 laps):
Still Gibernau, by 508 thousandths from Barros, who is about to have a terrible fall.

Lap 11:
Rossi has just set the fastest race lap and is now only 160 thousandths off Gibernau. Melandri is 1"776 down.

Lap 12:
Melandri goes straight on at the chicane, but still hangs onto third place.

Lap 15:
It is clear that the win will be fought out between Gibernau and Rossi, separated by 134 thousandths.

Finish (19 laps):
Gibernau is just 309 thousandths ahead of Rossi as they embark on the final lap. The world champion pulls a stunning move and the two men brush against one another leaving the Spaniard with a damaged front mudguard.

Championship:
Gibernau and Rossi are level pegging on 126. For those who believe the saying that whoever leads after Assen goes on to win the title, one should note that the reigning champion is officially the leader, by virtue of having more race wins (4 to 2.)

Rossi has just been caught by Alexandre Barros, but the Brazilian is about to get it wrong.

Rossi – Gibernau, enemies and brothers...

It was said they were thick as thieves and the two of them would often hit the town together on a sort of royal tour for the king and the prince of bike racing.

From the moment they began to dominate the MotoGP class they even spoke the same lines, acting as the mouthpiece for their peers, overseeing safety matters, ever since the previous year's drama at Suzuka that cost the life of Daijiro Kato. However, on the podium of a fantastic GP in the Netherlands, there were no hugs or applause between them. It was just a curt handshake between a beaten and still furious Gibernau and the winner, Valentino Rossi who had nothing to complain about.

Sete Gibernau had been beaten for a third straight time on the last lap by Valentino Rossi and he was angry, angry with the man who would now be more of an enemy than a brother. "I did most of the work and so it is hard to be happy with second," sulked Gibernau. While, sitting alongside him, the winner went through his usual polished speech, the Spaniard tried to understand, with the aid of a few hand gestures, exactly what had happened in that damned Turn 13 on the greatest track in the world. He wanted to know how he was suddenly knocked off balance with his front mudguard hanging off. It fell to the winner to explain...

Valentino, what really happened over that final kilometre, just after you made your winning move?

I passed Sete at Turn 12, a high speed left hander. But it meant I came up to the next tighter right too fast. I lost the front end and I was sure I was going to fall and the bike moved to the outside and we touched.

You know Gibernau is not happy?

Yes, we spoke after the prize-giving. I can understand him. Personally, I don't like this type of situation.

Rossi had therefore won and Gibernau had this to say: "If Vale says he lost control of the front of his bike, then I have to believe him. He is not the sort of rider to try this sort of move deliberately. But..." At the Mecca of racing, Yamaha had dominated Honda once again. And Rossi was now leading the 2004 championship. Equal on points with Gibernau of course, but he was number one again, based on the number of wins. What of the fact people talk about the superstition that whoever leads after Assen will go on to be champion. "I am leading, Yamaha has also taken the lead in the constructors' which is a nice surprise for us. The bike is progressing, but be careful, it is still not on a par with the opposition in some respects which we are quickly going to improve on." Ouch! What will things be like when the Yamaha M1 will have found the few extra horsepower that it currently lacks when compared to the Honda RC211V...

The Euro football tournament is in full swing and after Italy and Spain have both been eliminated, Rossi and Gibernau are still larking around. The mood would soon change.

Final chicane: Rossi has taken the lead, colliding with Gibernau, whose front mudguard is partly broken. A strong friendship has just cooled a bit.

250cc

Dutch Grand Prix
26th June 2004 / Assen - 6.027 m

STARTING GRID

1.	19	S. Porto	Aprilia	2'03.668
2.	26	D. Pedrosa	Honda	2'04.451
3.	7	R. De Puniet	Aprilia	2'04.529
4.	24	T. Elias	Honda	2'04.838
5.	54	M. Poggiali	Aprilia	2'04.903
6.	51	A. De Angelis	Aprilia	2'04.959
7.	2	R. Rolfo	Honda	2'05.956
8.	11	J. Olive	Aprilia	2'06.107
9.	10	F. Gonzales-Nieto	Aprilia	2'06.131
10.	6	A. Debon	Honda	2'06.149
11.	14	A. West	Aprilia	2'06.311
12.	21	F. Battaini	Aprilia	2'06.386
13.	25	A. Baldolini	Aprilia	2'06.548
14.	73	H. Aoyama	Honda	2'06.595
15.	8	N. Matsudo	Yamaha	2'06.799
16.	50	S. Guintoli	Aprilia	2'06.885
17.	57	C. Davies	Aprilia	2'07.520
18.	12	A. Vincent	Aprilia	2'07.546
19.	34	E. Bataille	Honda	2'07.699
20.	33	H. Faubel	Aprilia	2'07.869
21.	96	J. Smrz	Honda	2'07.937
22.	16	J. Stigefelt	Aprilia	2'08.315
23.	9	H. Marchand	Aprilia	2'08.316
24.	36	E. Nigon	Yamaha	2'09.456
25.	44	T. Sekiguchi	Yamaha	2'10.238
26.	77	G. Lefort	Aprilia	2'10.933
27.	22	I. Silva	Aprilia	2'11.067
28.	17	K. Nöhles	Honda	2'11.793
Not qualified:				
	59	H. Smees	Honda	2'12.734
	61	R. Gevers	Aprilia	2'13.220
	58	P. Lakerveld	Yamaha	2'13.451
	60	E. Litjens	Aprilia	2'14.169
	40	M. Sabbatani	Yamaha	2'15.180
	62	J. Roelofs	Yamaha	2'16.335

RACE: 18 LAPS = 108.486 km

1.	Sebastian Porto	37'26.576 (173.842 km/h)
2.	Daniel Pedrosa	+ 2"566
3.	Toni Elias	+ 4"038
4.	Randy De Puniet	+ 8"024
5.	Alex De Angelis	+ 13"596
6.	Anthony West	+ 20"405
7.	Manuel Poggiali	+ 26"477
8.	Alfonso Gonzales-Nieto	+ 27"302
9.	Roberto Rolfo	+ 27"357
10.	Hiroshi Aoyama	+ 43"693
11.	Alex Baldolini	+ 43"945
12.	Alex Debon	+ 44"181
13.	Naoki Matsudo	+ 52"638
14.	Eric Bataille	+ 52"768
15.	Chaz Davies	+ 52"900
16.	Franco Battaini	+ 59"865
17.	Hector Faubel	+ 1'03.776
18.	Hugo Marchand	+ 1'03.994
19.	Taro Sekiguchi	+ 1'18.056
20.	Johan Stigefelt	+ 1'18.128
21.	Klaus Nöhles	+ 2'00.936
22.	Ivan Silva	+ 1 lap

Fastest lap:
Pedrosa, in 2'03.469 (175.729 km/h). New record.
Previous record: Rolfo, in 2'04.824 (173.822 km/h/2002).

Outright fastest lap: Pedrosa, in 2'03.469 (175.729 km/h/2004).

CHAMPIONSHIP

1.	R. De Puniet	111 (1 win)
2.	D. Pedrosa	110 (2 wins)
3.	S. Porto	88 (2 wins)
4.	T. Elias	70
5.	A. Gonzales-Nieto	64
6.	A. De Angelis	51
7.	R. Rolfo	48 (1 win)
8.	A. West	46
9.	H. Aoyama	41
10.	A. Debon	41

Porto and the Argentine flag: second win of the season for "Aspar" Martinez's rider.

Runners and riders:
With Christian Gemmel having decided to hang up his helmet, another German, Klaus Nohles decides to quit his job in charge of telemetry for the Aprilia Germany team, switching to the Honda Castrol squad. Yet another German, Dirk Heidolf, scratches from the event after two difficult GPs saw him fall in Italy and Catalunya. He is replaced by Spain's Ivan Silva.

Qualifying:
On the first day, Anthony West brings back memories of Assen a year ago when in difficult conditions, he took his first and so far, only GP victory. Other riders on standard Aprilia machines feature prominently. They include Guintoli, Arnaud Vincent and the surprising Silva, who is tackling Assen for the first time on his debut on a two-stroke Aprilia. The track has dried on Friday and a more usual order is established, with Porto, Pedrosa, De Puniet and Elias setting the pace.

Start:
A super move from Porto, while Pedrosa is pretty average, getting it all wrong because of a carburation problem. At the end of the first lap, the Argentinian leads De Puniet by 1"399, with Alex De Angelis next up. Dani Pedrosa has started to fight back and is already twelfth.

Lap 3:
Porto tries to go it alone, leading De Puniet by 1"358. One second behind the Frenchman, a pursuit group is gathering, with Elias, De Angelis, Pedrosa (where did he come from!) Gonzales-Nieto and Rolfo.

Lap 7:
De Puniet is on hard tyres, followed by Pedrosa on softs, with Porto on mediums. The top five are covered by 1"230: De Puniet, Porto, Elias, Pedrosa and De Angelis.

Half distance (9 laps):
Still De Puniet, but his advantage has been shredded to just 64 thousandths by Porto. Pedrosa is already third.

Happy birthday Silvain! Guintoli turns 22.

Lap 11:
Porto takes control, setting a lap record as he crosses the line with an 884 thousandths lead over the second placed man, who is now Elias. Pedrosa and De Puniet are not far behind.

Lap 13:
Nothing can stop Porto as he currently leads by 1"868.

Lap 15:
Still Porto, who has the race in the bag. Elias is second as De Puniet hangs onto his third place.

Finish: (18 laps):
No change at the front. However, Elias has the last word for the third step on the podium.

Championship:
Randy De Puniet extends his lead over Dani Pedrosa by one point. A week before the Rio GP, which marked his first GP win in 2003, Sebastian Porto, the winner on the day, is back in contention.

125cc

Mike Di Meglio goes playing in the sand and as usual at Assen there are several fallers.

Runners and riders:
The Swiss rider Thomas Luthi has finally opted to have an operation on his left collarbone and he is not replaced. As in Barcelona, Finland's Kyyhkynen rides the Honda normally allocated to Denmark's Robbin Harms. In the Angaia camp, the young Czech Marketa Janakova, who had already run at Brno, replaces Mattia Angeloni.

Qualifying:
There were only two types of weather: heavy rain or light rain! On the first day, the 125 riders fight it out in terrible conditions with no less than 18 fallers on Thursday. Barbera is quickest, but he drops back to thirteenth place on Friday, when the track is slightly less wet. Casey Stoner records his second pole position and also the second for KTM, ahead of Nieto, Dovizioso and Jenkner.

Start:
Stoner makes the perfect start, ahead of Locatelli, Dovizioso and Corsi. Locatelli completes the first lap leading Stoner by 0"469, followed by Dovizioso, Mika Kallio and Giansanti.

Lap 4:
Locatelli and Stoner have attempted to make an initial break, but a very aggressive Lorenzo will not be shaken off and is just a second off Stoner.

Lap 6:
There is now a lead group of three, tightly together in 267 thousandths: Locatelli, Lorenzo and Stoner. Further back, Dovizioso is now trying to get in on the act.

Lap 7:
Ui and Borsoi retire.

Half distance (8 laps):
Still Locatelli, 160 thousandths ahead of Lorenzo with Stoner glued to the Spaniard's back wheel. Dovizioso has closed to 1"508 off the current podium trio.

Lap 11:
Lorenzo is back in charge, leading Locatelli by 568 thousandths. Mika Kallio is now fourth, half a second behind team-mate Stoner.

Lap 14:
There is now a lead group of four: Locatelli, Lorenzo, Dovizioso and Stoner.

Lap 16:
Mika Kallio retires.

Finish (17 laps):
Lorenzo leads by 279 thousandths on the penultimate lap. The final 6 kilometres are mental: Lorenzo goes onto the grass, Dovizioso narrowly avoids hitting him as Locatelli retakes the lead. But Lorenzo fights back and with two crazy moves he takes the win. Behind them, it all goes wrong for Giuseppetti, Manna and Pesek, who fall at the chicane.

Championship:
Dovizioso strengthens his position in relation to Barbera, but journeyman Locatelli is now in second place, 16 down on his young fellow countryman. Barbera and Stoner are equal third, 25 points behind Dovizioso.

He personifies aggression on two wheels and Jorge Lorenzo takes his first win of the season.

Dutch Grand Prix
26th June 2004 / Assen - 6.027 m

STARTING GRID

1.	27	C. Stoner	KTM	2'18.592
2.	22	P. Nieto	Aprilia	2'19.046
3.	34	A. Dovizioso	Honda	2'19.972
4.	21	S. Jenkner	Aprilia	2'20.168
5.	15	R. Locatelli	Aprilia	2'20.656
6.	41	Y. Ui	Aprilia	2'20.689
7.	48	J. Lorenzo	Derbi	2'21.041
8.	24	S. Corsi	Honda	2'21.551
9.	50	A. Ballerini	Aprilia	2'21.727
10.	25	I. Toth	Aprilia	2'22.180
11.	6	M. Giansanti	Aprilia	2'22.318
12.	10	J. Simon	Honda	2'22.724
13.	3	H. Barbera	Aprilia	2'22.746
14.	58	M. Simoncelli	Aprilia	2'22.837
15.	52	L. Pesek	Honda	2'23.117
16.	63	M. Di Meglio	Aprilia	2'23.142
17.	66	V. Kallio	Aprilia	2'23.363
18.	33	S. Gadea	Aprilia	2'23.431
19.	82	J. Van Der Marel	Honda	2'23.462
20.	36	M. Kallio	KTM	2'23.823
21.	54	M. Pasini	Aprilia	2'24.329
22.	8	M. Manna	Malaguti	2'24.347
23.	26	D. Giuseppetti	Honda	2'24.455
24.	19	A. Bautista	Aprilia	2'24.865
25.	16	R. Schouten	Honda	2'24.897
26.	23	G. Borsoi	Aprilia	2'25.119
27.	32	F. Lai	Gilera	2'25.152
28.	42	G. Pellino	Aprilia	2'25.176
29.	47	A. Rodriguez	Derbi	2'25.595
30.	14	G. Talmacsi	Malaguti	2'25.604
31.	9	M. Janakova	Honda	2'25.736
32.	7	S. Perugini	Gilera	2'25.876
33.	79	A. Den Bekker	Honda	2'26.785
34.	38	M. Kyyhkynen	Honda	2'27.325
Not qualified:				
	83	G. Kok	Honda	2'28.941
	80	M. Van Kreij	Honda	2'29.005
	44	F. Van Den Dragt	Honda	2'29.010
	28	J. Carchano	Aprilia	2'29.923

RACE: 17 LAPS = 102.459 km

1.	Jorge Lorenzo	37'13.859 (165.118 km/h)
2.	Roberto Locatelli	+ 0"235
3.	Casey Stoner	+ 0"564
4.	Andrea Dovizioso	+ 0"606
5.	Steve Jenkner	+ 3"865
6.	Hector Barbera	+ 11"450
7.	Marco Simoncelli	+ 11"756
8.	Pablo Nieto	+ 11"764
9.	Mirko Giansanti	+ 11"913
10.	Imre Toth	+ 29"339
11.	Mattia Pasini	+ 29"851
12.	Mike Di Meglio	+ 30"394
13.	Gioele Pellino	+ 30"428
14.	Stefano Perugini	+ 39"233
15.	Angel Rodriguez	+ 39"346
16.	Alvaro Bautista	+ 39"583
17.	Gabor Talmacsi	+ 39"777
18.	Simone Corsi	+ 40"058
19.	Julian Simon	+ 40"711
20.	Andrea Ballerini	+ 59"377
21.	Sergio Gadea	+ 1'07.555
22.	Raymond Schouten	+ 1'07.715
23.	Vesa Kallio	+ 1'26.749
24.	Jarno Van der Marel	+ 1'51.060
25.	Mikko Kyyhkynen	+ 1 lap
26.	Adrie Den Bekker	+ 1 lap
27.	Marketa Janakova	+ 1 lap

Fastest lap:
Lorenzo, in 2'10.123 (166.743 km/h). New record.
Previous record: Olive, in 2'11.209 (165.363 km/h/2002).

Outright fastest lap: Lorenzo, in 2'10.123 (166.743 km/h/2004).

CHAMPIONSHIP

1.	A. Dovizioso	109 (2 wins)
2.	R. Locatelli	93 (1 win)
3.	H. Barbera	84 (1 win)
4.	C. Stoner	84
5.	P. Nieto	63
6.	J. Lorenzo	58 (1 win)
7.	S. Jenkner	58
8.	M. Giansanti	52
9.	M. Simoncelli	43 (1 win)
10.	M. Pasini	25

CINZANO
CINZANO CINZANO CINZANO

RIO
Jacarepagua

An incomparable setting for a GP that would go down in history. In the land of smiles, dancing, joie de vivre and plenty more besides, Makoto Tamada gives Bridgestone its first win at the highest level. The worries of Mugello are forgotten and the second half of the season will see several strong performances from Shinya Nakano in the saddle of the green Kawasaki.

(Photo: M. Paulicek)
A rarity, as Valentino Rossi is caught out by the bumps on the Rio track and falls

Rio Grand Prix
4th July 2004 / Jacarepagua – 4.933 m

STARTING GRID

1.	10	Ke. Roberts	Suzuki	1'48.418
2.	3	M. Biaggi	Honda	1'48.572
3.	69	N. Hayden	Honda	1'48.580
4.	15	S. Gibernau	Honda	1'48.618
5.	4	A. Barros	Honda	1'48.675
6.	65	L. Capirossi	Ducati	1'48.844
7.	6	M. Tamada	Honda	1'48.848
8.	46	V. Rossi	Yamaha	1'49.075
9.	56	S. Nakano	Kawasaki	1'49.153
10.	12	T. Bayliss	Ducati	1'49.546
11.	45	C. Edwards	Honda	1'49.648
12.	7	C. Checa	Yamaha	1'49.673
13.	33	M. Melandri	Yamaha	1'49.773
14.	66	A. Hofmann	Kawasaki	1'49.853
15.	17	N. Abé	Yamaha	1'50.128
16.	11	R. Xaus	Ducati	1'50.240
17.	21	J. Hopkins	Suzuki	1'50.350
18.	99	J. McWilliams	Aprilia	1'50.942
19.	50	N. Hodgson	Ducati	1'51.031
20.	67	S. Byrne	Aprilia	1'51.792
21.	9	N. Aoki	Proton KR	1'51.955
22.	80	Ku. Roberts	Proton KR	1'52.054
23.	35	C. Burns	Harris WCM	1'54.092
24.	52	D. De Gea	Harris WCM	1'54.116

RACE: 24 LAPS = 118.392 km

1. Makoto Tamada	44'21.976 (160.110 km/h)
2. Massimiliano Biaggi	+ 2"019
3. Nicky Hayden	+ 5"764
4. Loris Capirossi	+ 11"145
5. Alexandre Barros	+ 12"951
6. Colin Edwards	+ 13"904
7. Kenny Roberts	+ 23"493
8. Norifumi Abé	+ 27"498
9. Shinya Nakano	+ 27"802
10. Carlos Checa	+ 36"808
11. Alexander Hofmann	+ 37"713
12. Ruben Xaus	+ 48"924
13. Marco Melandri	+ 57"102
14. Jeremy McWilliams	+ 1'03.046
15. John Hopkins	+ 1'10.296
16. Neil Hodgson	+ 1'12.548
17. Shane Byrne	+ 1'19.734
18. Nobuatsu Aoki	+ 1'31.512
19. Kurtis Roberts	+ 1'43.627
20. Chris Burns	+ 1 lap

Fastest lap:
Tamada, in 1'49.789 (161.753 km/h). New record.
Previous record: Rossi, in 1'50.453 (160.781 km/h/2003).

Outright fastest lap: Ke. Roberts, in 1'48.418 (163.799 km/h/2004).

CHAMPIONSHIP

1. V. Rossi	126 (4 wins)
2. S. Gibernau	126 (2 wins)
3. M. Biaggi	113
4. C. Edwards	64
5. C. Checa	62
6. A. Barros	59
7. M. Melandri	57
8. L. Capirossi	55
9. N. Hayden	54
10. M. Tamada	44 (1 win)

Runners and riders:
Fabrizio is a non-starter, with a minor fracture of the left foot. At the last minute, WCM boss Peter Clifford finds a solution, replacing him with Spain's David De Gea. Barros is injured on home turf, with a minor fracture to the left shoulder. On the Wednesday before the race, Melandri has the 36 stitches removed from his right forearm.

Qualifying:
"Well, I actually prefer world championship tracks, but this seems to be a Moto X track." Valentino Rossi and his peers discover that the Jacarepagua circuit is even bumpier than before. On the plus side, the Brazilian winter has produced great weather with high temperatures. On the first day, Gibernau puts everyone in the shade. However, the Spaniard ends up starting from the second row, as the team ran into problems with a brake pad when it was time to fit qualifying tyres on Saturday afternoon. This meant Sete was late out on track. Worse still for Rossi, who was eighth as the Yamahas were struggling over the bumps. The sensation of qualifying was Kenny Roberts, who gave Bridgestone tyres their first pole position, here on the circuit where in 2003, Tamada gave the Japanese their first podium finish.

Start:
Roberts makes no mistake, leading Biaggi, Hayden, Barros and Rossi who has already moved up the order to get ahead of Gibernau.

Lap 2:
Biaggi now leads as Gibernau passes Rossi before falling a few corners later.

Lap 4:
Bayliss falls. The lead group consists of Biaggi, Hayden, Barros and Roberts. Further back, Tamada closes on Rossi.

A Honda festival: Biaggi, Tamada and Hayden, although the first two will switch places at the flag.

Lap 6:
Rossi has passed Roberts. Melandri and Checa collide, while Biaggi continues to lead.

Half distance (12 laps):
Rossi is up to a podium position with an unusual look to it as Biaggi leads his "sort of" team-mate Tamada, who is going like a train and closing.

Lap 13:
First big shock of the day as Rossi falls at the same spot where Gibernau hit the dirt eleven laps earlier.

Lap 22:
Tamada, who had closed right up on Biaggi, goes into the lead and leaves everyone for dead.

Finish (24 laps):
Makoto Tamada gives Japanese tyre company Bridgestone its maiden victory in the blue riband class.

Championship:
It is wide open again, as Biaggi is now just 13 points off the Gibernau – Rossi duo and there is still more than a half a season to go.

Makoto's strange weekend

Japan's Makoto Tamada is a surprising guy; open, always smiling and with the sort of expression that implies he is not sure what is happening. Fitting in well with his Italian team, over the past months he has made a lot of friends and he has received the occasional standing ovation from those in the press room after some of his exploits. And, on this 4th July 2004, Tamada has written another chapter in his surprising story at this ever more bumpy Jacarepagua track, where, last September, he gave Bridgestone tyres their first pole position in the blue riband class.

There is no doubt that this weekend in Rio will stick in Makoto's mind for a very long time: for better and for worse, for happiness and for a great sadness. Yes, Tamada experienced it all. On arriving in the land of the samba, Tamada and his crew realised that it was much hotter than when the race was usually held in September. Thanks to his Bridgestone tyres, he knew these conditions gave him a good chance of taking the win. Indeed, right from the start of practice and before Kenny Roberts had taken pole, Michelin's racing boss, Nicolas Goubert had stated, "we are not favourites here."

He was to be proved right. What Goubert could not predict was that the two main men in the championship, Valentino Rossi and Sete Gibernau, would bite the dust. Nor could he predict that the Rio GP would blow the championship wide open with Max Biaggi once again staking his claim as a contender.

Apart from that, it was the heart-warming and touching tale of Makoto Tamada. He caught the leaders after an average start, before swallowing them up like a cruising shark taking its prey. He was throwing his Honda around the track, while others looked like they were riding on egg shells. He passed Max Biaggi and left him standing. That was the story on the track. Then came the dedications. First off, to his mate Daijiro Kato, who would have celebrated his birthday that 4th July. Then, after the hugs and the champagne came a knowing wink: "I really must find myself an Italian girlfriend so I can learn the language." It was good to see Tamada so happy. No one could guess at the truth.

A salute to a first win: Makoto Tamada does it in Rio.

Rossi and Gibernau on the deck so the Jacarepagua podium is a distinctly yellow affair.

His crew could not understand why he had disappeared from the track so suddenly. While they had planned to party, Makoto made his excuses. He headed for the airport and a flight home to Tokyo. The reason was both simple and cruel. He wanted to hug his mother one last time, as the poor woman had been severely ill for the past few months. It was his secret and he chose not to share it with his work colleagues.

He kept that secret and kept his promise, so that he was there on that Monday 5th July, when the person he loved most in the world, passed away in her sleep.

250cc

Rio Grand Prix
4th July 2004 / Jacarepagua – 4.933 m

STARTING GRID

1.	19	S. Porto	Aprilia	1'52.503
2.	24	T. Elias	Honda	1'52.823
3.	7	R. De Puniet	Aprilia	1'52.929
4.	54	M. Poggiali	Aprilia	1'52.981
5.	51	A. De Angelis	Aprilia	1'53.157
6.	26	D. Pedrosa	Honda	1'53.227
7.	50	S. Guintoli	Aprilia	1'53.602
8.	21	F. Battaini	Aprilia	1'53.682
9.	2	R. Rolfo	Honda	1'53.776
10.	10	F. Gonzales-Nieto	Aprilia	1'53.872
11.	14	A. West	Aprilia	1'53.962
12.	6	A. Debon	Honda	1'54.392
13.	11	J. Olive	Aprilia	1'54.617
14.	8	N. Matsudo	Yamaha	1'54.666
15.	73	H. Aoyama	Honda	1'54.738
16.	25	A. Baldolini	Aprilia	1'54.791
17.	96	J. Smrz	Honda	1'54.992
18.	12	A. Vincent	Aprilia	1'54.998
19.	57	C. Davies	Aprilia	1'55.017
20.	17	K. Nöhles	Honda	1'55.059
21.	77	G. Lefort	Aprilia	1'55.105
22.	34	E. Bataille	Honda	1'55.109
23.	9	H. Marchand	Aprilia	1'55.215
24.	28	D. Heidolf	Aprilia	1'55.723
25.	36	E. Nigon	Yamaha	1'55.799
26.	16	J. Stigefelt	Aprilia	1'56.029
27.	33	H. Faubel (*)	Aprilia	1'56.375
28.	44	T. Sekiguchi	Yamaha	1'56.550
29.	40	M. Sabbatani	Yamaha	2'00.125

(*): Having fallen on the first day of practice, H, Faubel (E, Aprilia) is forced to pull out with a broken collar bone.

RACE: 22 LAPS = 108.526 km

1.	Manuel Poggiali	41'56.561 (155.249 km/h)
2.	Daniel Pedrosa	+ 0"076
3.	Toni Elias	+ 3"792
4.	Alex De Angelis	+ 4"678
5.	Alfonso Gonzales-Nieto	+ 20"393
6.	Hiroshi Aoyama	+ 20"576
7.	Roberto Rolfo	+ 30"399
8.	Randy De Puniet	+ 34"742
9.	Alex Debon	+ 36"021
10.	Franco Battaini	+ 36"476
11.	Hugo Marchand	+ 50"991
12.	Sylvain Guintoli	+ 52"196
13.	Chaz Davies	+ 53"576
14.	Naoki Matsudo	+ 1'01.641
15.	Dirk Heidolf	+ 1'02.014
16.	Klaus Nöhles	+ 1'11.756
17.	Erwan Nigon	+ 1'11.999
18.	Gregory Lefort	+ 1'20.226
19.	Arnaud Vincent	+ 1'22.037
20.	Taro Sekiguchi	+ 1 lap

Fastest lap:
Porto, in 1'53.573 (156.364 km/h). New record.
Previous record: Poggiali, in 1'54.215 (155.485 km/h/2003).

Outright fastest lap: Porto, in 1'52.503 (157.851 km/h/2004).

CHAMPIONSHIP

1.	D. Pedrosa	130 (2 wins)
2.	R. De Puniet	119 (1 win)
3.	S. Porto	88 (2 wins)
4.	T. Elias	86
5.	A. Gonzales-Nieto	75
6.	A. De Angelis	64
7.	M. Poggiali	63 (1 win)
8.	R. Rolfo	57 (1 win)
9.	H. Aoyama	51
10.	A. Debon	48

A duel between two champions: Manuel Poggiali finally got the better of Dani Pedrosa. But in three months time, the Spaniard would take the title from the San Marino rider.

Runners and riders:
Everyone is present and the rumour mill is getting up to speed. Thus, Randy de Puniet confirms that he does indeed intend switching to MotoGP for next season. The KTM 250 project is also taking shape, the Austrian marque showing great interest in the reigning world champion, Manuel Poggiali.

Qualifying:
On the subject of Poggiali, Aprilia has brought its number one rider some new parts and, right from Friday – second quickest behind De Puniet, the San Marino operator makes his presence felt. However, on Saturday, it is the Argentine, Sebastian Porto, who takes pole at the track where two years earlier, he took his first GP win. Spain's Faubel breaks a collarbone in a fall.

Start:
Pedrosa charges through from the second row to take the lead ahead of Poggiali, Elias, De Puniet and Rolfo. Eric Bataille fails to complete the opening lap.

Lap 3:
West falls. Pedrosa still leads from Poggiali, Elias, De Puniet and now Porto, as Rolfo is in trouble yet again.

Lap 4:
Poggiali has taken the lead.

Lap 6:
An excellent Alex de Angelis has caught the tightly packed lead group.

Half distance (11 laps):
A first warning for De Puniet, who suddenly drops to sixth. Out in front, Poggiali has chipped away to lead by 3 tenths from Pedrosa. Elias is third, followed by Porto, De Angelis and De Puniet.

Lap 12:
De Puniet loses 2 seconds in a single lap. It is not yet clear that his tyres will not go the distance.

Lap 14:
The Frenchman is coming under fire, having to deal with Gonzales-Nieto and then Aoyama. No change up front, as Poggiali still has the legs of Pedrosa.

Lap 18:
Another warning shot for the Aprilia camp. While Poggiali is totally in control, it is Porto who is in trouble, completing a couple of slow laps before retiring with engine problems.

Finish (22 laps):
On the penultimate lap, Alberto Puig showed Dani Pedrosa a pit board, with the message, "P2 OK," but the little Spaniard will not give up chewing at the bone. In the end he is beaten by just 76 tiny thousandths by Poggiali, who finally takes his first win in the category.

Championship:
Pedrosa is the big winner this weekend, taking the lead in the championship, heading De Puniet by 11 points, as the Frenchman eventually comes home eighth. The title will now be decided between these two men.

Arnaud Vincent in action, but the former 125 world champion is not very happy with his team.

125cc

Runners and riders:
Team Elit decides not to make the long trek: apart from the fact its number one rider, Switzerland's Luthi is injured, the team also has to do without Giuseppetti, as a result of his fall on the last lap of the Dutch GP, which had left its traces, not to mention the fact he had fallen three times during practice!

Qualifying:
Hector Barbera is on good form and watching him here is Brazilian football international, Roberto Carlos, who along with Clarence Seedorf, finances the Barbera and Bautista team. The young Spaniard dominates the two days of qualifying. Dovizioso asks Honda for more help. The championship leader is second on the grid, while the next best Honda is only thirteenth. Lorenzo also qualifies on the front row, as does Locatelli's surprising team-mate, Mattia Pasini.

Start:
Stoner (KTM) comes round at the end of the opening lap with a 4 second lead over Lorenzo. Next come Dovizioso, Locatelli, Barbera and Pasini. Lai, still suffering the effects of several falls over the past few weekend, was not even sure he would start, but he and Spaniard Gadea fail to finish the first lap.

Lap 2:
A first breakaway group has formed. In the lead, we find Stoner, Lorenzo, Barbera, Dovizioso and Locatelli.

Lap 3:
Barbera is definitely the man to beat in Rio and takes the lead.

Half distance (10 laps):
Barbera has to do it all again, having tried to shake off his pursuers, although his lead never exceeded one second. It is Stoner who leads now, from Lorenzo, Dovizioso, Locatelli, Giansanti and Barbera.

Lap 11:
Assen winner Jorge Lorenzo falls when lying second ("the front wheel was knocked out of balance by a bump.") Stoner makes the most of it to pull out a little half second lead.

Lap 16:
It is evidently not a day for making a break as Barbera is now back to 2 tenths off Stoner.

Lap 19:
The race gets even more hectic! Stoner, Barbera, Dovizioso, Locatelli and Giansanti are wheel to wheel and all of them look in with a chance.

Finish (21 laps):
Dovizioso had led on the penultimate lap as they crossed the line, Stoner retakes the lead down the straight, but it is Barbera who has the final word. Stoner is beaten by 96 thousandths, with Dovizioso 202 thousandths down in third spot.

Championship:
Dovizioso has yet to slip up, but he now sees Hector Barbera closing on him, having made up fourteen points since the Italian GP. Along with Locatelli and Stoner, the top four are within 21 points of one another.

One should always show the boss some respect. Brazilian international football player Roberto Carlos became Clarence Seedorf's partner, heading up Barbera's Aprilia team and they won in Rio.

Barbera leads Dovizioso, Stoner and Lorenzo. The Spaniard did very well out of the weekend.

Rio Grand Prix
4th July 2004 / Jacarepagua – 4.933 m

STARTING GRID

1.	3	H. Barbera	Aprilia	1'57.323
2.	34	A. Dovizioso	Honda	1'57.683
3.	48	J. Lorenzo	Derbi	1'57.793
4.	54	M. Pasini	Aprilia	1'57.923
5.	27	C. Stoner	KTM	1'58.055
6.	15	R. Locatelli	Aprilia	1'58.162
7.	6	M. Giansanti	Aprilia	1'58.254
8.	22	P. Nieto	Aprilia	1'58.639
9.	50	A. Ballerini	Aprilia	1'58.664
10.	41	Y. Ui	Aprilia	1'58.726
11.	21	S. Jenkner	Aprilia	1'58.779
12.	23	G. Borsoi	Aprilia	1'58.782
13.	10	J. Simon	Honda	1'58.806
14.	19	A. Bautista	Aprilia	1'58.828
15.	24	S. Corsi	Honda	1'58.847
16.	63	M. Di Meglio	Aprilia	1'58.979
17.	52	L. Pesek	Honda	1'59.073
18.	36	M. Kallio	KTM	1'59.094
19.	25	I. Toth	Aprilia	1'59.180
20.	58	M. Simoncelli	Aprilia	1'59.201
21.	14	G. Talmacsi	Malaguti	1'59.663
22.	42	G. Pellino	Aprilia	1'59.817
23.	33	S. Gadea	Aprilia	1'59.845
24.	7	S. Perugini	Gilera	2'00.118
25.	47	A. Rodriguez	Derbi	2'00.352
26.	32	F. Lai	Gilera	2'00.392
27.	66	V. Kallio	Aprilia	2'01.415
28.	8	M. Manna	Malaguti	2'02.226
29.	16	R. Schouten	Honda	2'02.229
30.	28	J. Carchano	Aprilia	2'02.363
31.	9	M. Janakova	Honda	2'02.885
32.	38	M. Kyyhkynen	Honda	2'03.481

RACE: 22 LAPS = 108.526 km

1.	Hector Barbera	41'41.459 (149.086 km/h)
2.	Casey Stoner	+ 0"096
3.	Andrea Dovizioso	+ 0"202
4.	Roberto Locatelli	+ 0"359
5.	Mirko Giansanti	+ 0"737
6.	Marco Simoncelli	+ 7"614
7.	Pablo Nieto	+ 7"769
8.	Mika Kallio	+ 12"725
9.	Alvaro Bautista	+ 13"950
10.	Mattia Pasini	+ 19"938
11.	Andrea Ballerini	+ 25"983
12.	Mike Di Meglio	+ 26"633
13.	Simone Corsi	+ 26"996
14.	Julian Simon	+ 27"131
15.	Lukas Pesek	+ 30"697
16.	Gioele Pellino	+ 30"806
17.	Gino Borsoi	+ 38"591
18.	Imre Toth	+ 52"505
19.	Gabor Talmacsi	+ 59"593
20.	Steve Jenkner	+ 1'07.333
21.	Vesa Kallio	+ 1'20.065
22.	Stefano Perugini	+ 1'48.237
23.	Manuel Manna	+ 1'48.311
24.	Raymond Schouten	+ 1'49.405

Fastest lap:
Barbera, in 1'57.789 (150.767 km/h). New record.
Previous record: Pedrosa, in 1'58.121 (150.344 km/h/2003).

Outright fastest lap: Barbera, in 1'57.323 (151.366 km/h/2004).

CHAMPIONSHIP

1.	A. Dovizioso	125 (2 wins)
2.	H. Barbera	109 (2 wins)
3.	R. Locatelli	106 (1 win)
4.	C. Stoner	104
5.	P. Nieto	72
6.	M. Giansanti	63
7.	J. Lorenzo	58 (1 win)
8.	S. Jenkner	58
9.	M. Simoncelli	53 (1 win)
10.	A. Bautista	31

DAINESE
SHIMANO
CORREOS
TEAM
Honda
BIAGGI

GERMANY
Sachsenring

Max the Max: at the Sachsenring, Biaggi tore the championship wide open. Just before the summer break, he came to within one little point of Rossi, which was a talking point over the holidays! Loris Capirossi continues to fight his Ducati, while Germany reminds us that it has other things to offer apart from beer. Cheers!

German Grand Prix
18th July 2004 / Sachsenring – 3.671 m

STARTING GRID

1.	3	M. Biaggi	Honda	1'22.756
2.	46	V. Rossi	Yamaha	1'22.840
3.	10	Ke. Roberts	Suzuki	1'22.961
4.	15	S. Gibernau	Honda	1'22.969
5.	56	S. Nakano	Kawasaki	1'23.009
6.	4	A. Barros	Honda	1'23.154
7.	7	C. Checa	Yamaha	1'23.336
8.	12	T. Bayliss	Ducati	1'23.372
9.	69	N. Hayden	Honda	1'23.453
10.	65	L. Capirossi	Ducati	1'23.475
11.	45	C. Edwards	Honda	1'23.583
12.	21	J. Hopkins	Suzuki	1'23.622
13.	6	M. Tamada	Honda	1'23.623
14.	33	M. Melandri	Yamaha	1'23.692
15.	17	N. Abé	Yamaha	1'24.151
16.	66	A. Hofmann	Kawasaki	1'24.172
17.	99	J. McWilliams	Aprilia	1'24.322
18.	11	R. Xaus	Ducati	1'24.377
19.	50	N. Hodgson	Ducati	1'24.599
20.	9	N. Aoki	Proton KR	1'25.038
21.	84	M. Fabrizio	Harris WCM	1'25.310
22.	80	Ku. Roberts	Proton KR	1'25.478
23.	67	S. Byrne	Aprilia	1'25.614
24.	35	C. Burns	Harris WCM	1'26.665

RACE: 30 LAPS = 110.130 km

1.	Massimiliano Biaggi	42'23.287 (155.888 km/h)
2.	Alexandre Barros	+ 0"349
3.	Nicky Hayden	+ 4"293
4.	Valentino Rossi	+ 4"500
5.	Colin Edwards	+ 16"137
6.	Makoto Tamada	+ 16"482
7.	Shinya Nakano	+ 18"477
8.	Kenny Roberts	+ 23"335
9.	John Hopkins	+ 30"705
10.	Alexander Hofmann	+ 40"540
11.	Ruben Xaus	+ 43"712
12.	Jeremy McWilliams	+ 52"791
13.	Neil Hodgson	+ 53"690
14.	Shane Byrne	+ 1'13.215
15.	Michel Fabrizio	+ 1'20.050
16.	Chris Burns	+ 1 lap

Fastest lap:
Barros, in 1'24.056 (157.223 km/h). New record.
Previous record: Biaggi, in 1'24.630 (156.157 km/h/2003).

Outright fastest lap: Biaggi, in 1'22.756 (159.693 km/h/2004).

CHAMPIONSHIP

1.	V. Rossi	139 (4 wins)
2.	M. Biaggi	138 (1 win)
3.	S. Gibernau	126 (2 wins)
4.	A. Barros	79
5.	C. Edwards	75
6.	N. Hayden	70
7.	C. Checa	62
8.	M. Melandri	57
9.	L. Capirossi	55
10.	M. Tamada	54 (1 win)

Whoops! Jeremy McWilliams is caught out in qualifying.

Runners and riders:
Michel Fabrizio is back with Harris-WCM. Alexandre Barros gets new exhausts. Edouard Michelin, the president of the French company that bears his name is in the paddock.

Qualifying:
Max Biaggi, boosted by the presence of Edouard Michelin and Kiyoshi Kawashima, Honda's "Supreme Advisor," has the last word on Saturday, ahead of Rossi. The top fourteen are all within the same second, or to be precise, 936 thousandths.

Start:
Biaggi pulls off the perfect start, swerving ahead of Rossi and Kenny Roberts. But even before the lap is over, Rossi takes the lead and Biaggi counter attacks. It sets the tone for the afternoon.

Lap 2:
Biaggi, Rossi, Gibernau, the three dominant forces are nose to tail within 402 thousandths.

Lap 4:
Aoki falls. Checa has just set the fastest lap and will soon pass Gibernau.

Lap 5:
Checa falls at the bottom of the hill. Biaggi still leads from Rossi and Gibernau.

Lap 7:
Biaggi has eked out a lead of 464 thousandths over Rossi. Gibernau has caught up with the world champion.

Lap 9:
Gibernau has a spectacular fall.

Lap 10:
Capirossi falls promoting Hayden to third, ahead of Barros, Kenny Roberts and Abe.

Lap 11:
Bayliss falls. 235 thousandths separate Biaggi and Rossi.

Lap 12:
Barros has got the better of team-mate Nicky Hayden, as they fight for third place.

Half distance (15 laps):
Biaggi still leads Rossi by 353 thousandths. Barros has just set a fastest race lap and is now less than 8 tenths off the No. 46 Yamaha. In fourth, Hayden is not far behind.

Lap 16:
The gap is closed and Barros is in touch. At the first corner on lap 17, Rossi takes the lead and tries to escape.

Lap 18:
Rossi heads the heated Biaggi-Barros tussle by 7 tenths.

Lap 22:
Fear on the track: Melandri is thrown from his bike having strayed onto the grass and team-mate, Norifumi Abe has no option but to brake hard to avoid him and the Japanese rider also flies through the air.

Lap 23:
Biaggi is back in front. Barros will soon pass Rossi who had a big moment.

Finish (30 laps):
Biaggi has the edge by 256 thousandths going into the final lap and the Roman fights off the Brazilian to the flag. Rossi is "only" fourth.

Championship:
Only 13 points for Rossi, 0 for Gibernau and 25 for Biaggi means the title fight is on once again: Rossi (139 points,) Biaggi (138) and Gibernau (126) makes it is all very close.

Barros is thirsting…to see a podium

Max, the king of the Ring!

The way Max Biaggi likes it: out in front ahead of the rest, especially that damned number 46.

For once, Max Biaggi is not fiddling with the few black hairs which serve him as a beard, but his tone of voice makes it clear that he is taking great pleasure in recounting how happy he is. He throws out a few barbed remarks aimed at those who got it wrong: "You know, the problem with these Mickey Mouse circuits which seem like fairground rides is that it is easy to make mistakes. So it is difficult to put together a perfect race. So yes, I am happy and I think we did a good job this weekend."

When he is in this sort of mood, nothing can get to Max Biaggi and he was certainly the only front runner of this fascinating season not to get caught out at the Ring of Saxe.

Gibernau was knocked out and cried at 14h13, down there at turn 9A, near the spectator-packed hill. It was the ninth lap of the German GP, the ninth round of a titanic struggle between the giants that are Rossi, Biaggi and Gibernau. The Spaniard was caught out by a well aimed direct hit and his race was over, as he wept into the inflatable crash barriers. That was that.

Rossi was on his guard and taking care at 14h32 as he reached the foot of the steep descent on lap 23 of 30. But the dreams of the champion ended abruptly as Valentino Rossi was caught out by a destroyed rear tyre and only just managed to avoid a crash. He would not finish on the podium, but unlike Gibernau he saved himself from a fall. "Here, our bike was hungrier for tyres than the Hondas and if I had pushed harder I would have fallen."

These casualties meant that Biaggi's only remaining task was to control Barros and avoid making mistakes. It all worked out well for him as he was now just one point adrift of Rossi. It had been a perfect weekend for the man who had often been the butt of criticism in the paddock over the past few seasons.

Unjustified criticism one might say. When he was a young lad, his father Pietro was an amateur football coach and he dreamed of turning his son into a "calcio" star and that's what looked like happening until Max slung a leg over a friend's motorbike. And then, according to the man himself, he discovered a magic world. Success followed and he became a star. He was never off Italian television and his name was linked to several top models. He moved to Monaco, as it was the done thing and there he met other stars and got even greater exposure.

However, there was one fly in the ointment and that was the arrival on the scene of a major pain in the backside, in the shape of Valentino Rossi. Max, who dominated totally in the 250 class, was missing out in the blue riband category. Up until this German weekend, where he scored big time in front of two major players: Edouard Michelin, the top man with the French company and Kiyoshi Kawashima. Who is Kawashima-san? Along with Soichiro Honda himself he was one of the co-founders of the giant motorcycle firm and he certainly approved of Max's faultless performance.

250cc

German Grand Prix
18th July 2004 / Sachsenring – 3.671 m

STARTING GRID

1.	19	S. Porto	Aprilia	1'25.078
2.	51	A. De Angelis	Aprilia	1'25.236
3.	2	R. Rolfo	Honda	1'25.386
4.	7	R. De Puniet	Aprilia	1'25.535
5.	26	D. Pedrosa	Honda	1'25.633
6.	54	M. Poggiali	Aprilia	1'25.652
7.	24	T. Elias	Honda	1'25.719
8.	10	F. Gonzales-Nieto	Aprilia	1'25.783
9.	8	N. Matsudo	Yamaha	1'26.195
10.	21	F. Battaini	Aprilia	1'26.256
11.	50	S. Guintoli	Aprilia	1'26.260
12.	73	H. Aoyama	Honda	1'26.300
13.	6	A. Debon	Honda	1'26.353
14.	14	A. West	Aprilia	1'26.405
15.	28	D. Heidolf	Aprilia	1'26.511
16.	11	J. Olive	Aprilia	1'26.530
17.	57	C. Davies	Aprilia	1'26.714
18.	25	A. Baldolini	Aprilia	1'26.720
19.	17	K. Nöhles	Honda	1'26.795
20.	9	H. Marchand	Aprilia	1'27.133
21.	96	J. Smrz	Honda	1'27.180
22.	44	T. Sekiguchi	Yamaha	1'27.403
23.	36	E. Nigon	Yamaha	1'27.663
24.	34	E. Bataille	Honda	1'27.731
25.	12	A. Vincent	Aprilia	1'27.752
26.	16	J. Stigefelt	Aprilia	1'27.845
27.	77	G. Lefort	Aprilia	1'29.194
28.	40	M. Sabbatani	Yamaha	1'29.384

RACE: 29 LAPS = 106.459 km

1.	Daniel Pedrosa	41'37.239 (153.470 km/h)
2.	Sebastian Porto	+ 4"279
3.	Alex De Angelis	+ 16"403
4.	Hiroshi Aoyama	+ 16"769
5.	Randy De Puniet	+ 16"966
6.	Roberto Rolfo	+ 18"135
7.	Anthony West	+ 32"141
8.	Alfonso Gonzales-Nieto	+ 32"766
9.	Franco Battaini	+ 37"726
10.	Sylvain Guintoli	+ 38"088
11.	Alex Debon	+ 50"782
12.	Chaz Davies	+ 50"934
13.	Joan Olive	+ 1'00.946
14.	Eric Bataille	+ 1'02.410
15.	Jakub Smrz	+ 1'02.527
16.	Naoki Matsudo	+ 1'02.554
17.	Taro Sekiguchi	+ 1'18.235
18.	Dirk Heidolf	+ 1'18.386
19.	Erwan Nigon	+ 1'21.155
20.	Johan Stigefelt	+ 1'21.574
21.	Klaus Nöhles	+ 1'22.048
22.	Toni Elias	+ 1 lap

Fastest lap:
Porto, in 1'25.118 (155.262 km/h). New record.
Previous record: Gonzales-Nieto, in 1'26.469 (152.836 km/h/2003).

Outright fastest lap: Porto, in 1'25.078 (155.335 km/h/2004).

CHAMPIONSHIP

1.	D. Pedrosa	155 (3 wins)
2.	R. De Puniet	130 (1 win)
3.	S. Porto	108 (2 wins)
4.	T. Elias	86
5.	A. Gonzales-Nieto	83
6.	A. De Angelis	80
7.	R. Rolfo	67 (1 win)
8.	H. Aoyama	64
9.	M. Poggiali	63 (1 win)
10.	A. West	55

It could only be in Germany!

Runners and riders:
No wild cards and one absentee in the shape of Spain's Hector Faubel, who was injured in Rio. One quirk which did not amuse the world champion, Manuel Poggiali, who was paying for his difficult start to the season, was that he found himself working out of a tent, rather than a proper pit garage.

Qualifying:
In Rio, Jorge Martinez (Porto and Gonzales-Nieto,) Dani Amatriain (Elias and Rolfo) and Lucio Cecchinello (Randy de Puniet) had gone to the race director with the suggestion that, as in the 125 class, the 250s should have a minimum weight for bike and rider, so as not to give away too much to featherweights like Pedrosa. On track, Porto sets the fastest time on Friday and no one would get near his time on Saturday. Alex de Angelis is 2nd, his best showing in the class. Pedrosa is "only" fifth.

Start:
Rolfo has the quickest reflexes, ahead of Porto and Pedrosa. At the end of the opening lap, last year's winner crosses the line with a 301 thousandths lead over Porto and 350 over Pedrosa, who will soon take the lead.

Lap 3:
Pedrosa breaks away and leads second placed De Puniet by 812 thousandths.

Lap 6:
Still Pedrosa. His closest pursuer is now Porto, 1"097 down. A great scrap for third place between De Angelis and De Puniet.

Lap 7:
Reigning champion Poggiali is a faller.

Half distance (15 laps):
Pedrosa is faultless and leads a solitary Porto by 4 seconds. De Puniet is third, still fighting Elias, De Angelis and now Rolfo.

Lap 19:
A spectacular fall for Toni Elias who rejoins.
Lap 23: All are powerless against Pedrosa. Porto is on his own. However, the fight for third is hotting up, as it is now Japan's Aoyama, the leader's team-mate, who is chasing De Puniet.

Finish (29 laps):
When the press suggests that his easy style and adaptability remind them of Valentino Rossi, Dani Pedrosa has a good answer: "You can think it, I have to make myself believe it." The young Spaniard has put on another classy demonstration. Porto was powerless. De Angelis takes his first podium in the class while De Puniet is only fifth, suffering after a qualifying fall.

Championship:
Of course, things are looking good for the winner on the day. As the season is about to slip into its second half, he leads De Puniet, the big loser on the weekend, by 25 points.

Pedrosa shows how it's done: the reigning 125 champion scores a third win and makes a first real break.

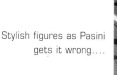

Stylish figures as Pasini gets it wrong....

Runners and riders:
Angry with his team in Rio, as his chief mechanic was none too well on the day of the race, Andrea Ballerini threw in the towel. He is replaced at Sterilgarda (a brand of mineral water) by Simone Sanna. Injured in Mugello, Thomas Luthi is back, despite a near set-back, as one week before this GP, his Brno testing was hindered by a nasty little virus which saw the Swiss rider end up in hospital to ensure he did not have appendicitis. Also back is Denmark's Robbin Harms.

Qualifying:
The Aprilia riders dominate throughout the sessions and championship leader Dovizioso grabs pole on the very last lap: "I got a tow from Ui," Behind him come Barbera, Jenkner, Giansanti and Pablo Nieto. One of the major players is injured, as Australian Casey Stoner re-fractures his left collar bone and pulls out on Saturday morning.

Start:
Dovizioso gets a superb start, ahead of Giansanti and Simoncelli. The Dutchman Schouten fails to finish the opening lap, which the championship leader completes with a 391 thousandths advantage over Giansanti. Simoncelli and Jenkner follow on.

Lap 2:
Simoncelli takes the lead.

Lap 5:
It is a great tussle with seven riders covered by just 875 thousandths with Simoncelli still in front.

Lap 8:
The whole crowd goes wild as local hero, Steve Jenkner, has grabbed the lead. The top 13 are covered by 1"726!

Lap 10:
Simoncelli is condemned to a drive-through in pit lane. Sanna falls.

Half distance (13 laps):
Pablo Nieto is the new leader by 645 thousandths. Behind come Barbera, Dovizioso and Mikka Kallio.

Lap 14:
Another punishment is dished out, this time for Steve Jenkner, who like Simoncelli overtook under the yellow flag. Lai is a faller.

Lap 17:
As things settle down, Barbera is now leading by 466 thousandths from the Dovizioso-Nieto duel. Locatelli is fourth, over 2 seconds down.

Lap 20:
Barbera, Dovizioso and Nieto are separated by 389 thousandths.

Lap 22:
Locatelli has caught the leading trio.

Lap 24:
Ui is a faller.

Finish (27 laps):
Locatelli takes the lead on the penultimate lap and does not put a foot wrong to win from Barbera and Nieto, with Dovizioso fourth.

Championship:
Dovizioso still heads the table, but his lead is now down to only seven points from Locatelli, who is still second. Barbera is 9 points down on the leader. With Stoner not racing, a gap is now growing to the rest.

...while his lead rider, Roberto Locatelli takes a second win of the season.

German Grand Prix
18th July 2004 / Sachsenring – 3.671 m

STARTING GRID

1.	34	A. Dovizioso	Honda	1'27.836
2.	3	H. Barbera	Aprilia	1'27.870
3.	21	S. Jenkner	Aprilia	1'27.881
4.	6	M. Giansanti	Aprilia	1'28.030
5.	22	P. Nieto	Aprilia	1'28.061
6.	58	M. Simoncelli	Aprilia	1'28.106
7.	10	J. Simon	Honda	1'28.202
8.	41	Y. Ui	Aprilia	1'28.333
9.	23	G. Borsoi	Aprilia	1'28.404
10.	15	R. Locatelli	Aprilia	1'28.448
11.	36	M. Kallio	KTM	1'28.542
12.	27	C. Stoner (*)	KTM	1'28.570
13.	48	J. Lorenzo	Derbi	1'28.577
14.	52	L. Pesek	Honda	1'28.882
15.	24	S. Corsi	Honda	1'28.942
16.	32	F. Lai	Gilera	1'28.986
17.	19	A. Bautista	Aprilia	1'28.994
18.	33	S. Gadea	Aprilia	1'29.055
19.	42	G. Pellino	Aprilia	1'29.217
20.	14	G. Talmacsi	Malaguti	1'29.273
21.	63	M. Di Meglio	Aprilia	1'29.366
22.	18	S. Sanna	Aprilia	1'29.416
23.	25	I. Toth	Aprilia	1'29.552
24.	54	M. Pasini	Aprilia	1'29.568
25.	69	R. Harms	Honda	1'29.693
26.	7	S. Perugini	Gilera	1'29.940
27.	12	T. Lüthi	Honda	1'30.123
28.	66	V. Kallio	Aprilia	1'30.439
29.	47	A. Rodriguez	Derbi	1'30.475
30.	39	P. Unger	Aprilia	1'30.476
31.	28	J. Carchano	Aprilia	1'30.553
32.	16	R. Schouten	Honda	1'30.909
33.	40	M. Mickan	Honda	1'31.096
34.	20	G. Fröhlich	Honda	1'31.280
35.	70	J. Miralles Jnr	Aprilia	1'31.376
36.	35	V. Bittman	Honda	1'31.388
37.	8	M. Manna	Malaguti	1'31.790
Not qualified				
	9	M. Janakova	Honda	1'36.013

RACE: 27 LAPS = 99.117 km

1. Roberto Locatelli	40'03.511 (148.458 km/h)
2. Hector Barbera	+ 0"165
3. Pablo Nieto	+ 0"706
4. Andrea Dovizioso	+ 0"715
5. Mika Kallio	+ 1"073
6. Jorge Lorenzo	+ 1"176
7. Alvaro Bautista	+ 1"283
8. Mirko Giansanti	+ 1"459
9. Julian Simon	+ 9"636
10. Marco Simoncelli	+ 11"821
11. Steve Jenkner	+ 17"967
12. Simone Corsi	+ 20"307
13. Gioele Pellino	+ 31"798
14. Sergio Gadea	+ 31"927
15. Stefano Perugini	+ 37"556
16. Gabor Talmacsi	+ 37"720
17. Lukas Pesek	+ 37"911
18. Thomas Lüthi	+ 37"920
19. Robbin Harms	+ 55"350
20. Mattia Pasini	+ 55"384
21. Patrick Unger	+ 58"942
22. Vesa Kallio	+ 59"902
23. Georg Fröhlich	+ 1'17.723
24. Jordi Carchano	+ 1'17.997
25. Vaclav Bittman	+ 1'18.297
26. Manuel Manna	+ 1'18.550
27. Manuel Mickan	+ 1 lap

Fastest lap:
Barbera, in 1'27.680 (150.725 km/h). New record.
Previous record: P. Nieto, in 1'28.490 (149.345 km/h/2003).

Outright fastest lap: Barbera, in 1'27.680 (150.725 km/h/2004).

CHAMPIONSHIP

1. A. Dovizioso	138 (2 wins)
2. R. Locatelli	131 (2 wins)
3. H. Barbera	129 (2 wins)
4. C. Stoner	104
5. P. Nieto	88
6. M. Giansanti	71
7. J. Lorenzo	68 (1 win)
8. S. Jenkner	63
9. M. Simoncelli	59 (1 win)
10. M. Kallio	40

MOTUL
Dainese

GREAT BRITAIN
Donington

Valentino Rossi turns round, but there is no one in sight. At Donington, the Italian left everyone for dead. He fulfilled his role of champion on Thursday at the traditional auction for "Riders for Health" and did it again on track and on the top step of the podium on Sunday.

MOTOGP

British Grand Prix
25th July 2004 / Donington – 4.023 m

STARTING GRID

1.	46	V. Rossi	Yamaha	1'28.720
2.	15	S. Gibernau	Honda	1'29.152
3.	65	L. Capirossi	Ducati	1'29.209
4.	12	T. Bayliss	Ducati	1'29.214
5.	45	C. Edwards	Honda	1'29.250
6.	69	N. Hayden	Honda	1'29.295
7.	7	C. Checa	Yamaha	1'29.329
8.	3	M. Biaggi	Honda	1'29.502
9.	4	A. Barros	Honda	1'29.801
10.	11	R. Xaus	Ducati	1'29.840
11.	33	M. Melandri (*)	Yamaha	1'29.900
12.	56	S. Nakano	Kawasaki	1'30.214
13.	10	Ke. Roberts	Suzuki	1'30.239
14.	50	N. Hodgson	Ducati	1'30.297
15.	6	M. Tamada	Honda	1'30.371
16.	21	J. Hopkins	Suzuki	1'30.442
17.	17	N. Abé	Yamaha	1'30.460
18.	67	S. Byrne	Aprilia	1'30.502
19.	99	J. McWilliams	Aprilia	1'30.595
20.	84	M. Fabrizio	Harris WCM	1'31.353
21.	66	A. Hofmann	Kawasaki	1'31.486
22.	9	N. Aoki	Proton KR	1'31.491
23.	80	Ku. Roberts	Proton KR	1'32.222
24.	35	C. Burns	Harris WCM	1'33.285

(*): A faller in Friday morning's free practice, M. Melandri gets up with a broken right thumb. He takes part in Saturday qualifying, but decides not to race.

RACE: 30 LAPS = 120.690 km

1.	Valentino Rossi	45'30.473 (159.124 km/h)
2.	Colin Edwards	+ 2"945
3.	Sete Gibernau	+ 4"426
4.	Nicky Hayden	+ 6"096
5.	Troy Bayliss	+ 14"711
6.	Carlos Checa	+ 17"110
7.	Loris Capirossi	+ 23"313
8.	John Hopkins	+ 28"121
9.	Alexandre Barros	+ 35"380
10.	Neil Hodgson	+ 44"468
11.	Ruben Xaus	+ 47"490
12.	Massimiliano Biaggi	+ 54"004
13.	Shane Byrne	+ 57"378
14.	Makoto Tamada	+ 1'07.158
15.	Shinya Nakano	+ 1'15.795
16.	Jeremy McWilliams	+ 1'26.485
17.	Kenny Roberts	+ 1 lap
18.	Nobuatsu Aoki	+ 1 lap
19.	Alexander Hofmann	+ 1 lap
20.	Michel Fabrizio	+ 1 lap

Fastest lap:
Edwards, in 1'29.973 (160.968 km/h). New record.
Previous record: Rossi, in 1'31.023 (159.023 km/h/2003).

Outright fastest lap: Rossi, in 1'28.720 (163.720 km/h/2004).

CHAMPIONSHIP

1.	V. Rossi	164 (5 wins)
2.	S. Gibernau	142 (2 wins)
3.	M. Biaggi	142 (1 win)
4.	C. Edwards	95
5.	A. Barros	86
6.	N. Hayden	83
7.	C. Checa	72
8.	L. Capirossi	64
9.	M. Melandri	57
10.	M. Tamada	56 (1 win)

A Ducati leads thanks to a remarkable opening lap from Loris Capirossi.

Runners and riders:
All present and correct, in part due to the courage of Norifume Abe, who takes to the track with broken ribs as a result of a fall at the Sachsenring. The news story of the week comes from the Czech minimoto marque Balta, which intends producing a 1000 cc V6 engine next year and already has an agreement in place with the WMC-Harris team.

No team orders as Colin Edwards beats his team leader, Sete Gibernau.

Qualifying:
A nice surprise on the first day, as Nicky Hayden is on provisional pole. Rossi is not far away, while Biaggi is a bit further back, complaining about the front end of his Honda. On Saturday, Rossi is unbeatable and smashes the Donington record by 2"020 and is 4 tenths quicker than the rest of the pack. Melandri is out of luck, falling on Friday morning following a misunderstanding with Hoffman. He pulls out with a broken thumb.

Start:
Rossi charges into the lead at Redgate Corner, but Capirossi shoots past, going down the hill. As they cross the line for the first time, Capirossi leads Rossi by 129 thousandths with Gibernau a further 341 thousandths behind. Biaggi is sixth.

Lap 2:
Rossi leads Gibernau by 0"356 and Capirossi by 0"910. Burns retires.

Lap 3:
Still Rossi. Edwards is now third having just set the fastest race lap. Biaggi is seventh.

Lap 5:
Rossi's advantage over Gibernau is now 899 thousandths, with the Spaniard's team-mate, Edwards, glued to his back wheel. Bayliss has passed Capirossi for fourth. Biaggi is now only eleventh.

Lap 7:
Edwards passes Gibernau for second and is 1"420 down on Rossi.

Lap 9:
A few specks of rain appear on the camera lenses. Biaggi has dropped to thirteenth. At the time, no one knows he is having gear selection problems.

Half distance (15 laps):
Rossi remains in charge and he now has a 1"457 lead over Edwards, who still has Gibernau for company. Hayden has just taken fourth place off Bayliss and is 3"923 behind Sete.

Lap 19:
Bayliss goes off the track down the hill and takes a high speed trip across the grass. Out in front, Rossi leads Edwards by 2"265, while Gibernau drops back slightly.

Lap 24:
Well done Abe, who has climbed up to ninth.

Lap 29:
Poor Abe crashes on the descent, having closed up to Capirossi.

Finish (30 laps):
Rossi crosses the line standing up on the pegs. A regal performance.

Championship:
As Rossi prepares to go on his holidays, his lead has extended to a comforting 22 points.

Day of the champions, acts I and II

A burn-out from the accomplished Valentino Rossi, for yet another triumph.

Thursday, 22nd July. As every year, the motorbike champions are on parade in the Donington Park paddock. Relaxed and smiling, they pose with their fans, signing autographs until their wrists ache. For the good cause of Riders for Health, they hand over some of their kit, which is then auctioned to their eager fans. Every grand prix Thursday at Donington is "The day of champions" and a day for generosity.
Sunday 25th July. A super-talented rider representing the new generation, Italy's Andrea Dovizioso, produces a faultless performance in the 125 class. It gives him a significant lead in the world championship, which he dominates with surprising ease. He looks the most likely winner and, like his predecessor, Daniel Pedrosa, he seems set to move up a class for the following year.
Sunday, 25th July again. A perfect start, in the lead from the first to the last lap, laps ticked off with metronomic regularity, Pedrosa, a 250 rookie, takes a fourth win. In many ways, he is the new Valentino Rossi, although he refuses to accept the fact when quizzed by the media. He is totally dominant and despite the fact he is small of stature, one cannot help but wonder if he will continue to surprise in MotoGP the following year.
Sunday 25th July once again. A "steady" first lap according to the man himself, so one has to believe him, then the pace picks up and the gaps get bigger as he pulls away from his rivals. Valentino Rossi, the doctor has just given them all another injection. It was a painful experience for some of them who tried to keep up, such as Biaggi who finished 12th with gear selector problems. Those who hung on, like third placed Sete Gibernau, were happy to settle for what they had.
Sunday, 25th July at Donington was really the "day of champions," the day of the great champions, except that this time there was no charity involved. For the top men in each category it was a case of picking up as many points as possible before the summer recess. But the holidays would have to wait for a day. "We have a day's testing planned here at Donington on Tuesday," revealed Rossi. "Because, just as we did in Rio and Germany, we came up against some serious problems with the back end and although everything went well this weekend, we have some new things we want to try."
Work and more work, despite a healthy twenty two point lead meaning pretty much a case of having one race in hand. "We are not going to settle for this as a lead, because we know there are still some circuits where we are going to really struggle against the Hondas," continued the champion, who can now claim to be the greatest in the modern era.

An all-blue podium: Edwards, Rossi and Gibernau.

British Grand Prix
25th July 2004 / Donington – 4.023 m

STARTING GRID

1.	51	A. De Angelis	Aprilia	1'32.430
2.	19	S. Porto	Aprilia	1'32.493
3.	73	H. Aoyama	Honda	1'32.557
4.	26	D. Pedrosa	Honda	1'32.643
5.	7	R. De Puniet	Aprilia	1'32.870
6.	24	T. Elias	Honda	1'33.002
7.	54	M. Poggiali	Aprilia	1'33.176
8.	14	A. West	Aprilia	1'33.213
9.	10	F. Gonzales-Nieto	Aprilia	1'33.503
10.	6	A. Debon	Honda	1'33.550
11.	8	N. Matsudo	Yamaha	1'33.724
12.	57	C. Davies	Aprilia	1'33.927
13.	21	F. Battaini	Aprilia	1'34.132
14.	11	J. Olive	Aprilia	1'34.281
15.	50	S. Guintoli	Aprilia	1'34.457
16.	16	J. Stigefelt	Aprilia	1'34.921
17.	96	J. Smrz	Honda	1'34.982
18.	2	R. Rolfo (*)	Honda	1'35.090
19.	52	D. De Gea	Honda	1'35.171
20.	12	A. Vincent	Aprilia	1'35.403
21.	25	A. Baldolini	Aprilia	1'35.543
22.	9	H. Marchand	Aprilia	1'35.697
23.	28	D. Heidolf	Aprilia	1'35.721
24.	17	K. Nöhles	Honda	1'35.823
25.	36	E. Nigon	Aprilia	1'36.184
26.	44	T. Sekiguchi	Yamaha	1'36.739
27.	64	F. Watz	Yamaha	1'37.504
28.	65	L. Dickinson	Honda	1'37.622
29.	43	R. Rous	Yamaha	1'37.795
30.	33	H. Faubel	Aprilia	1'38.294
31.	40	M. Sabbatani (*)	Yamaha	1'38.438
Not qualified:				
	66	T. Campbell	Yamaha	1'39.646
	67	B. Dunn	Honda	1'30.994

(*): R. Rolfo (dislocated left shoulder) and M. Sabbatani (broken right femur) did not start.

RACE: 27 LAPS = 108.621 km

1.	Daniel Pedrosa	42'17.705 (154.090 km/h)
2.	Sebastian Porto	+ 6"003
3.	Randy De Puniet	+ 11"463
4.	Alex De Angelis	+ 12"722
5.	Alfonso Gonzales-Nieto	+ 30"430
6.	Anthony West	+ 33"007
7.	Franco Battaini	+ 51"931
8.	Naoki Matsudo	+ 55"055
9.	Hiroshi Aoyama	+ 57"422
10.	Sylvain Guintoli	+ 59"456
11.	Joan Olive	+ 1'06.270
12.	Alex Baldolini	+ 1'06.566
13.	Hugo Marchand	+ 1'21.025
14.	Johan Stigefelt	+ 1'21.800
15.	Jakub Smrz	+ 1'29.120
16.	David De Gea	+ 1'32.733
17.	Dirk Heidolf	+ 1'33.155
18.	Klaus Nöhles	+ 1 lap
19.	Taro Sekiguchi	+ 1 lap
20.	Lee Dickinson	+ 1 lap
21.	Radomil Rous	+ 1 lap

Fastest lap:
Pedrosa, in 1'33.217 (155.366 km/h). New record.
Previous record: Kato, in 1'34.096 (153.915 km/h/2001).

Outright fastest lap: De Angelis, in 1'32.430 (156.689 km/h/2004).

CHAMPIONSHIP

1.	D. Pedrosa	180 (4 wins)
2.	R. De Puniet	146 (1 win)
3.	S. Porto	128 (2 wins)
4.	A. Gonzales-Nieto	94
5.	A. De Angelis	93
6.	T. Elias	86
7.	H. Aoyama	71
8.	R. Rolfo	67 (1 win)
9.	A. West	65
10.	M. Poggiali	63 (1 win)

Another mistake as nothing goes right for Manuel Poggiali.

Runners and riders:
GP de France team boss, Jean-Claude Besse has had enough and Gregory Lefort, who retired for no obvious reason in Germany, has been shown the door. He is replaced by fellow countryman, Erwan Nigon, whose ride with UGT Kurz falls again to the Czech, Radomil Rous. Eric Bataille, the Andorran rider is also absent, having broken a leg riding a supermoto bike. He is replaced by Spain's David de Gea.

Qualifying:
One week after taking his first 250 podium, Alex de Angelis records his first pole position, setting the best time on both Friday and Saturday. The athletic Roberto Rolfo (a dislocated left shoulder) and tiny Max Sabbatani (fracture of the head of the femur) are the main victims of qualifying.

Start:
Aoyama pulls off the perfect start, ahead of his team-leader, Pedrosa, who is about to take the lead. Nigon suffers a spectacular fall on the descent. Aoyama falls at the hairpin leading onto the straight. Pedrosa thus leads by 314 thousandths from Porto, Gonzales-Nieto, Debon, De Angelis and De Puniet.

Lap 2:
Debon is holding up De Puniet and De Angelis. Pedrosa now leads Porto by 377 thousandths.

Lap 3:
De Puniet passes Debon. Poggiali falls and so does Davies.

Lap 4:
Debon is a faller.

Lap 5:
Still Pedrosa, with Porto 804 thousandths behind. De Puniet closes on Fonsi for third place while De Angelis has passed Elias.

Lap 7:
De Puniet is third after a magnificent passing move at the chicane. Pedrosa steps up the pace, leading Porto by 1"770.

Lap 10:
De Angelis passes Gonzales-Nieto as does Elias.

Half distance (13 laps):
Elias has broken down on the previous lap and pits. Pedrosa now has a 5"175 lead over Porto, who in turn leads De Puniet by 3"165. Fonsi Nieto is still battling with De Angelis for the next place.

Finish (27 laps):
It's the same old problem when one rider is too strong for the opposition in that the spectacle is lacking. Don't blame Dani Pedrosa who is on great form and has delivered another faultless performance. Porto is over 6 seconds down and De Puniet over 11. On the way, Pedrosa has repeatedly beaten the circuit lap record, held by the late Daijiro Kato since 2001.

Championship:
Dani Pedrosa's 25 point advantage over Randy de Puniet has stretched to 34. The supremely talented Spaniard's mentor, Alberto Puig, can afford to smile on the eve of the summer break.

Another faultless performance as everything goes right for his successor, Daniel Pedrosa.

Runners and riders:
The German GP left a few marks on the pack: Casey Stoner pulls out with a broken collar bone, as does Marketa Janakova, who fell again at the Sachsenring, two weeks after a big accident at Rio, which left the Czech rider seriously concussed. She is replaced by Italy's Raffaele De Rosa, a 16 year old Neapolitan taking part in his first GP. As at the previous event, Germany's Dario Giuseppetti is still recovering from a muscle operation and is replaced by the Czech, Vaclav Bittman.

Qualifying:
World championship leader Dovizioso loves Donington and his Honda is running superbly. The Italian is way out in front on Friday and confirms that performance the next day, but only by 34 thousandths from Hector Barbera. There is another Honda on the front row, courtesy of the series leader's team-mate, Simone Corsi.

Start:
Dovizioso is best at the reflex test while Barbera and Pablo Nieto are both fallers in the first few metres. As the pack crosses the line, Dovizioso has already pulled out a 1"108 lead over Locatelli. Mika Kallio is third ahead of Corsi.

Lap 2:
Pasini is a faller. Dovizioso is out on his own ahead of a quartet made up of Locatelli, Kallio, Bautista and Corsi.

Lap 5:
Simoncelli falls. Dovizioso now has a 2"623 lead over Locatelli, who is being reeled in by Bautista, the quickest man on track at the moment.

Lap 8:
Bautista has moved up to second, 3"050 behind Dovizioso. Lorenzo is worth watching, up to sixth after messing up his start.

Half distance (12 laps):
For the first time in a long while, the 125 race is proving dull to watch as Dovizioso now leads Bautista by over 3 seconds. Locatelli is third, Lorenzo fourth. However, there is a good dice for fifth place between Mika Kallio, Corsi, Jenkner, Ui and Giansanti.

Lap 17:
Giansanti retires, while Dovizioso continues to rule the roost.

Lap 22:
Locatelli has closed on Bautista, but is still 3.5 seconds behind Dovizioso.

Lap 23:
Locatelli is a faller.

Pablo Nieto seems to be something of a plane spotter.

Finish (25 laps):
Dovizioso has ridden a perfect race. Rodriguez falls at the last corner, where moments earlier, Mika Kallio tried a daring move on Lorenzo as they fought for third place. The young Spaniard came off best.

Championship:
163 for Dovizioso, 131 for Locatelli: the Honda rider has done extremely well on the day as the five riders behind him in the classification all fail to score.

Dovizioso ahead of the rest is a common sight.

British Grand Prix
25th July 2004 / Donington – 4.023 m

STARTING GRID

1.	34	A. Dovizioso	Honda	1'37.211
2.	3	H. Barbera	Aprilia	1'37.245
3.	36	M. Kallio	KTM	1'37.687
4.	24	S. Corsi	Honda	1'37.697
5.	41	Y. Ui	Aprilia	1'37.781
6.	48	J. Lorenzo	Derbi	1'37.797
7.	15	R. Locatelli	Aprilia	1'37.831
8.	10	J. Simon	Honda	1'37.907
9.	19	A. Bautista	Aprilia	1'37.912
10.	58	M. Simoncelli	Aprilia	1'37.974
11.	21	S. Jenkner	Aprilia	1'38.064
12.	6	M. Giansanti	Aprilia	1'38.089
13.	32	F. Lai	Gilera	1'38.278
14.	22	P. Nieto	Aprilia	1'38.283
15.	23	G. Borsoi	Aprilia	1'38.425
16.	63	M. Di Meglio	Aprilia	1'38.473
17.	12	T. Lüthi	Honda	1'38.521
18.	7	S. Perugini	Gilera	1'38.834
19.	54	M. Pasini	Aprilia	1'39.071
20.	52	L. Pesek	Honda	1'39.135
21.	69	R. Harms	Honda	1'39.185
22.	14	G. Talmacsi	Malaguti	1'39.270
23.	42	G. Pellino	Aprilia	1'39.365
24.	33	S. Gadea	Aprilia	1'39.442
25.	47	A. Rodriguez	Derbi	1'39.462
26.	28	J. Carchano	Aprilia	1'39.886
27.	18	S. Sanna	Aprilia	1'40.010
28.	66	V. Kallio	Aprilia	1'40.346
29.	35	V. Bittman	Honda	1'40.379
30.	25	I. Toth	Aprilia	1'40.410
31.	49	C. Elkin	Honda	1'40.631
32.	85	E. Laverty	Honda	1'40.717
33.	30	R. De Rosa	Honda	1'40.936
34.	16	R. Schouten	Honda	1'41.417
35.	8	M. Manna	Malaguti	1'41.589
36.	20	G. Fröhlich	Honda	1'41.659
37.	51	K. Weston	Honda	1'42.689
38.	84	T. Bridewell	Honda	1'43.906

RACE: 25 LAPS = 100.575 km

1.	Andrea Dovizioso	41'14.592 (146.315 km/h)
2.	Alvaro Bautista	+ 3"807
3.	Jorge Lorenzo	+ 8"250
4.	Mika Kallio	+ 8"641
5.	Simone Corsi	+ 16"706
6.	Steve Jenkner	+ 16"993
7.	Youichi Ui	+ 22"120
8.	Julian Simon	+ 23"070
9.	Gino Borsoi	+ 23"860
10.	Gioele Pellino	+ 29"993
11.	Stefano Perugini	+ 30"475
12.	Lukas Pesek	+ 30"593
13.	Gabor Talmacsi	+ 40"502
14.	Fabrizio Lai	+ 41"140
15.	Mike Di Meglio	+ 45"295
16.	Sergio Gadea	+ 46"170
17.	Robbin Harms	+ 49"325
18.	Thomas Lüthi	+ 54"672
19.	Imre Toth	+ 1'17.223
20.	Georg Fröhlich	+ 1'20.434
21.	Christian Elkin	+ 1'23.026
22.	Simone Sanna	+ 1'24.436
23.	Vaclav Bittman	+ 1'28.933
24.	Raffaele De Rosa	+ 1'33.750
25.	Eugene Laverty	+ 1 lap
26.	Kris Weston	+ 2 laps
27.	Thomas Bridewell	+ 2 laps

Fastest lap:
Bautista, in 1'38.263 (147.388 km/h). New record.
Previous record: Cecchinello, in 1'38.312 (147.314 km/h/2002).

Outright fastest lap: Dovizioso, in 1'37.211 (148.983 km/h/2004).

CHAMPIONSHIP

1.	A. Dovizioso	163 (3 wins)
2.	R. Locatelli	131 (2 wins)
3.	H. Barbera	129 (2 wins)
4.	C. Stoner	104
5.	P. Nieto	88
6.	J. Lorenzo	84 (1 win)
7.	S. Jenkner	73
8.	M. Giansanti	71
9.	A. Bautista	60
10.	M. Simoncelli	59 (1 win)

CAMEL
CAMEL
GAULOISES

CZECH REPUBLIC
Brno

The holidays were short for the riders and teams. Everyone is back in the forest around Brno, where Biaggi, Barros, Rossi and Hayden try and keep up with Sete Gibernau. Behind the scenes some don't have such a bad job and others – don't you agree Mr. Roberts Junior – have to find the will to resist temptation.

MOTOGP

Czech Republic Grand Prix
22nd August 2004 / Brno – 5.403 m

STARTING GRID

1.	15	S. Gibernau	Honda	2'09.782
2.	4	A. Barros	Honda	2'10.090
3.	46	V. Rossi	Yamaha	2'10.470
4.	12	T. Bayliss	Ducati	2'10.923
5.	45	C. Edwards	Honda	2'11.096
6.	7	C. Checa	Yamaha	2'11.188
7.	69	N. Hayden	Honda	2'11.662
8.	3	M. Biaggi	Honda	2'11.737
9.	65	L. Capirossi	Ducati	2'11.821
10.	11	R. Xaus	Ducati	2'12.073
11.	33	M. Melandri	Yamaha	2'12.685
12.	50	N. Hodgson	Ducati	2'13.008
13.	17	N. Abé	Yamaha	2'13.327
14.	80	Ku. Roberts (*)	Proton KR	2'13.345
15.	99	J. McWilliams	Aprilia	2'13.781
16.	10	Ke. Roberts	Suzuki	2'13.817
17.	6	M. Tamada	Honda	2'14.031
18.	84	M. Fabrizio	Harris WCM	2'14.223
19.	67	S. Byrne (**)	Aprilia	2'14.304
20.	88	A. Pitt	Moriwaki	2'14.397
21.	21	J. Hopkins	Suzuki	2'14.727
22.	9	N. Aoki	Proton KR	2'15.682
23.	32	G. Lavilla	Suzuki	2'16.150
24.	77	J. Ellison	Harris WCM	2'16.715
25.	56	S. Nakano	Kawasaki	2'16.723
26.	66	A. Hofmann	Kawasaki	2'17.157

(*): A faller in Saturday afternoon's qualifying, Kurtis Roberts breaks a hand and does not race.
(**): A faller in Saturday's free practice, Shane Byrne suffers a broken wrist and bruised ribcage and does not race.

RACE: 22 LAPS = 118.866 km

1.	Sete Gibernau	44'03.480 (161.876 km/h)
2.	Valentino Rossi	+ 3"514
3.	Massimiliano Biaggi	+ 4"330
4.	Makoto Tamada	+ 16"257
5.	Loris Capirossi	+ 17"930
6.	Carlos Checa	+ 21"181
7.	Colin Edwards	+ 22"471
8.	Norifumi Abé	+ 31"079
9.	Marco Melandri	+ 31"158
10.	Kenny Roberts	+ 31"625
11.	Neil Hodgson	+ 31"625
12.	Shinya Nakano	+ 54"124
13.	Alexander Hofmann	+ 54"288
14.	Jeremy McWilliams	+ 57"471
15.	Nobuatsu Aoki	+ 1'18.515
16.	Andrew Pitt	+ 1'18.691
17.	Michel Fabrizio	+ 1'53.138

Fastest lap:
Barros, in 1'59.302 (163.038 km/h). New record.
Previous record: Rossi, in 1'59.966 (162.135 km/h/2003).

Outright fastest lap: Rossi, in 1'58.769 (163.770 km/h/2003).

CHAMPIONSHIP

1.	V. Rossi	184 (5 wins)
2.	S. Gibernau	167 (3 wins)
3.	M. Biaggi	158 (1 win)
4.	C. Edwards	104
5.	A. Barros	86
6.	N. Hayden	83
7.	C. Checa	82
8.	L. Capirossi	75
9.	M. Tamada	69 (1 win)
10.	M. Melandri	64

Runners and riders:
Honda has not been idle during the break and, two races after Barros, Biaggi and Gibernau also get the new bodywork and exhausts. However, Gibernau sticks with his original equipment for the whole weekend. "There are some test days coming up to try the new parts." In the WCM camp, 24 year old James Ellison makes an appearance, having just put on a great show in the superbike races at Brands Hatch. There are two wild card riders: Lavilla on a third Suzuka and Pitt, with the Honda-powered Moriwaki.

Qualifying:
Gibernau is untouchable in the rain. Beaten on Friday by fellow countryman, Carlos Checa, the Catalan rider puts on a demonstration on Saturday. The surprise of the day comes from Valentino Rossi, who had plenty to worry about at Jerez in the rain, but this time does what he must to grab a place on the front row. Byrne has a bad fall and has to pull out.

Start:
Gibernau gets the holeshot ahead of Barros, Biaggi, Rossi and Edwards. Sete completes the opening lap with a lead of almost four tenths (391 thousandths to be precise) over Barros, Biaggi and Rossi, the latter having just had a big moment.

Lap 3:
Gibernau still leads,
887 thousandths ahead of Biaggi.

Lap 6:
Gibernau has 514 thousandths in hand. Behind him, Biaggi, Barros and Rossi are wheel to wheel.

Lap 7:
Rossi has finally found a way past Biaggi.

Lap 8:
The gap is closed and Rossi is up Gibernau's exhausts, with the top four covered by 450 thousandths.

Lap 9:
The lead group has a fifth member as Hayden joins the party.

Half distance (11 laps):
Gibernau holds fast, leading Rossi by 277 thousandths, who in turn is 0"069 ahead of Biaggi. Barros is right there with the Roman and is about to pass him. Hayden is still in touch.

Lap 13:
Barros passes Rossi to go second. The engine in Hopkins' Suzuka blows up.

Lap 14:
Rossi counter attacks and passes Barros.

Lap 15:
Barros falls.

Lap 17:
Now the fight is between Gibernau and Rossi who swap places four times in the space of four corners. Gibernau comes off best, crossing the line 255 thousandths ahead of the Italian.

Lap 19:
Biaggi attacks Rossi and has to run wide. At the same time, Hayden falls.

Lap 21:
Xaus falls. Tamada has passed Capirossi for fourth place.

Finish (22 laps):
A perfect race and Gibernau takes the win with a 3"514 lead over Rossi. Bayliss fails to finish, falling on the last lap.

Championship:
Rossi stays at the top, but Gibernau is only 17 points adrift.

Punching the air in delight, Gibernau has his own way of acknowledging Rossi's pit board.

Ouch! Kurtis Roberts has just broken his hand.

Rossi, the man who blinded Honda!

A new boss and a new communications strategy as Satoru Horiike fills two roles.

Soichiro Honda, the mercurial and brilliant visionary who founded the company would have been spinning in his grave. On a grey Saturday in the Czech Republic, those who were now in charge of his racing division were maintaining a low profile. It was a surprising stance for a company that usually adopted an arrogant sometimes even disdainful attitude. One of their top men had been forced to admit, even if it was in a uniquely Honda way, that back in the winter they had underestimated the effect of losing Valentino Rossi. 51 year old, Satoru Horiike is the new managing director of the racing division, the HRC (Honda Racing Corporation.) Very close to president Kanazawa, he is the man who now takes the decisions, sets the policies and also the philosophy of the programme. "We are ready to answer all questions," he says, which does not sound at all like his predecessor, Koiji Nakajima, the man who had let Rossi go. A year earlier he had said: "If Mr. Rossi leaves, then we will give out riders the equipment to destroy him."

In Brno, his successor turned up to face the music. His speech was peppered with the odd joke, in itself something of a novelty, but he spent most of his time answering questions about Rossi. "He is really a super rider and even though he spent so much time winning for us, we had underestimated his importance. Now he has left, we have understood. He had blinded us! And this year, we have seen weaknesses come to light that had been hidden by Rossi's talent." Horiike-San had perfectly understood the effect of what he had said. He smiled to see the media look so surprised at his speech and his frankness. "If Mr. Rossi wants to come back to us one day, he will be welcome. I make it clear that this is if he wants to come back, because it is out of the question for us to go and get him back."

Interview...

Mr. Horiike, what exactly are your responsibilities?
They cover a vast range. We have to do what it takes to ensure Honda is world champion again, but we also want to be more open to make the public understand why we go racing.

Did you expect the Rossi-Yamaha tandem to be so tough?
Yes, absolutely.

As soon as this?
(His only response is to laugh)

Is there an anti-Rossi weapon in the pipeline?
We reckon our RC211V is currently running at 90% of its potential. With a lot of work, we should reach 95% efficiency. If we reach that target, we can use it for the next two years.

After that, 3, 4, or 6 cylinders?
(Laughs. A Japanese person who does not know how to play dumb is not Japanese...)

Has this MotoGP category already gone too far? Are the bikes too quick?
We must be aware of our responsibilities. Decisions regarding the future – reduction in fuel capacity – are a step in this direction. At Honda, we are also in favour of a reduction in capacity, let's say to between 700 and 800 cc.

Valentino Rossi at work after another front running race. "He blinded us," admit the men at Honda.

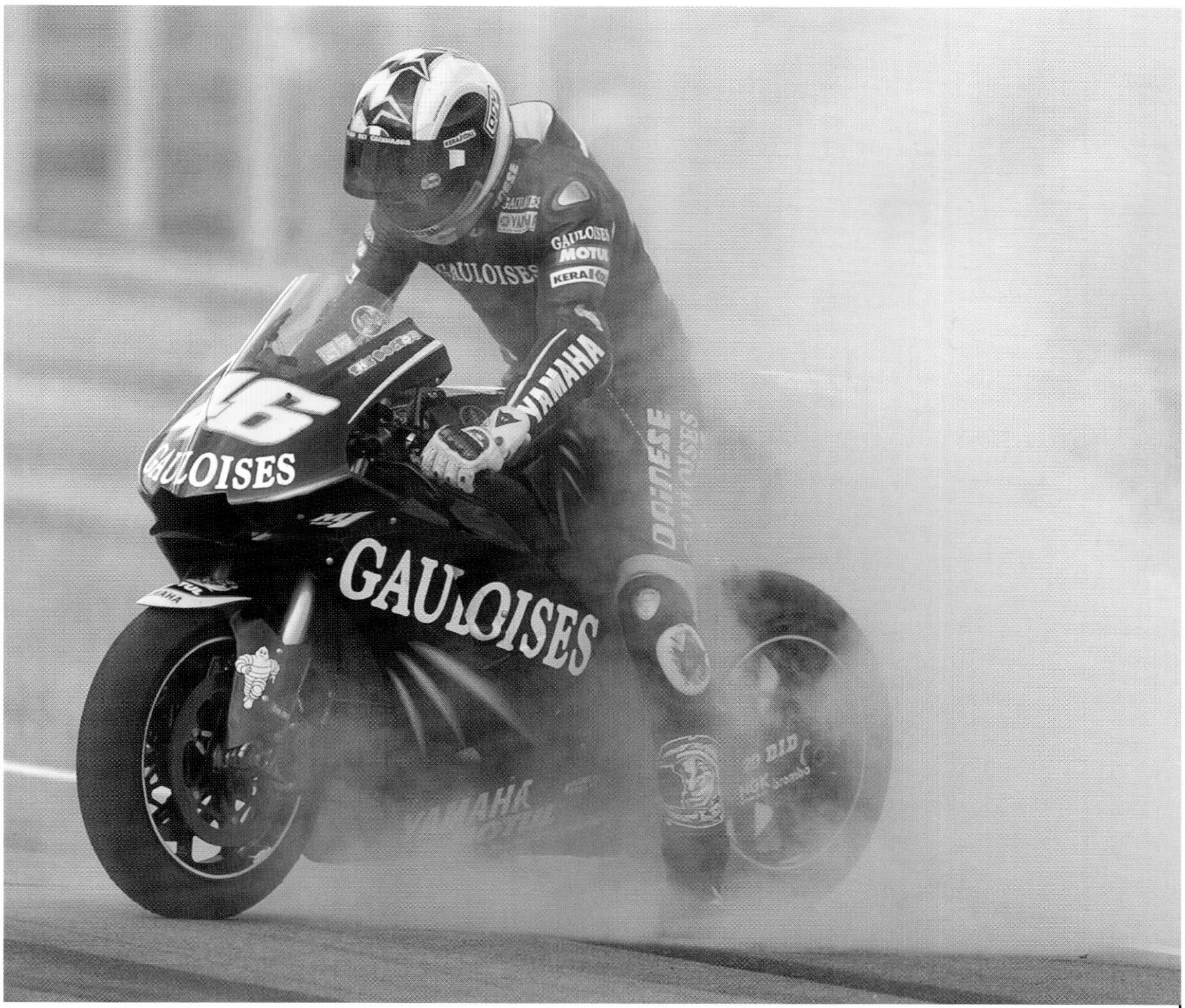

250cc

Czech Republic Grand Prix
22nd August 2004 / Brno – 5.403 m

STARTING GRID

1.	19	S. Porto	Aprilia	2'14.261
2.	10	F. Gonzales-Nieto	Aprilia	2'14.457
3.	51	A. De Angelis	Aprilia	2'14.528
4.	50	S. Guintoli	Aprilia	2'15.846
5.	2	R. Rolfo	Honda	2'15.952
6.	21	F. Battaini	Aprilia	2'16.216
7.	24	T. Elias	Honda	2'16.257
8.	73	H. Aoyama	Honda	2'16.639
9.	12	A. Vincent	Aprilia	2'16.965
10.	8	N. Matsudo	Yamaha	2'17.385
11.	7	R. De Puniet	Aprilia	2'17.542
12.	14	A. West	Aprilia	2'17.656
13.	26	D. Pedrosa	Honda	2'18.061
14.	6	A. Debon	Honda	2'18.149
15.	25	A. Baldolini	Aprilia	2'19.057
16.	96	J. Smrz	Honda	2'19.477
17.	54	M. Poggiali	Aprilia	2'19.873
18.	16	J. Stigefelt	Aprilia	2'20.175
19.	57	C. Davies	Aprilia	2'21.027
20.	34	E. Bataille	Honda	2'21.244
21.	36	E. Nigon	Aprilia	2'22.220
22.	9	H. Marchand	Aprilia	2'22.305
23.	28	D. Heidolf	Aprilia	2'22.508
24.	43	R. Rous	Yamaha	2'22.858
25.	33	H. Faubel	Aprilia	2'23.339
26.	11	J. Olive	Aprilia	2'23.502
27.	42	G. Leblanc	Aprilia	2'23.526
Did not meet qualifying minimum time, allowed to race:				
	71	H. vd Lagemaat	Aprilia	2'23.799
	17	K. Nöhles	Honda	2'24.350
	44	T. Sekiguchi	Yamaha	2'24.696
	88	Ge. Talmacsi	Yamaha	2'25.252
	27	V. Anghetti	Aprilia	2'36.226

RACE: 20 LAPS = 108.060 km

1. Sebastian Porto	42'03.061 (154.184 km/h)
2. Randy De Puniet	+ 4"309
3. Daniel Pedrosa	+ 10"919
4. Anthony West	+ 13"792
5. Toni Elias	+ 14"132
6. Roberto Rolfo	+ 21"170
7. Hiroshi Aoyama	+ 22"040
8. Chaz Davies	+ 33"426
9. Manuel Poggiali	+ 48"326
10. Hector Faubel	+ 1'03.461
11. Dirk Heidolf	+ 1'03.800
12. Hugo Marchand	+ 1'04.132
13. Gregory Leblanc	+ 1'04.630
14. Jakub Smrz	+ 1'10.960
15. Joan Olive	+ 1'11.432
16. Naoki Matsudo	+ 1'23.168
17. Johan Stigefelt	+ 1'24.665
18. Radomil Rous	+ 1'33.030
19. Henk vd Lagemaat	+ 1 lap

Fastest lap:
Pedrosa, in 2'03.332 (157.710 km/h). New record.
Previous record: Melandri, in 2'03.836 (157.069 km/h/2001).

Outright fastest lap: Harada, in 2'02.953 (158.197 km/h/2001).

CHAMPIONSHIP

1. D. Pedrosa	196 (4 wins)
2. R. De Puniet	166 (1 win)
3. S. Porto	153 (3 wins)
4. T. Elias	97
5. A. Gonzales-Nieto	94
6. A. De Angelis	93
7. H. Aoyama	80
8. A. West	78
9. R. Rolfo	77 (1 win)
10. M. Poggiali	70 (1 win)

Runners and riders:
Injured in practice at Donington, Sabbatini has had an operation on his right femur. He is replaced by Hungary's Gergo Talmacsi, the younger brother of the 125 cc Malaguti rider. Rolfo is back.

Qualifying:
It is well known that Pedrosa does not like the rain. On the first day of qualifying, he therefore languishes in twentieth spot. However, on Saturday, Dani sets the second fastest time to move himself up to thirteenth on the grid.
De Puniet is two rows ahead of him and it is the Jorge Martinez team riders who have the final word, Porto taking another pole ahead of Gonzales-Nieto. Guintoli posts a superb performance to take fourth on the semi-works Aprilia.

Start:
Porto does it best ahead of Aoyama. Battaini is a faller on the opening lap, taking Vincent with him, who is forced onto the grass. De Puniet gets a good start from the third row. At the end of the opening lap, Porto leads De Angelis by 155 thousandths, De Puniet by 320 and Pedrosa by half a second.

Lap 2:
De Angelis takes matters into his own hands to lead Porto by 0"482. De Puniet, Pedrosa and Aoyama are in touch but then comes a big gap.

Lap 6:
A few drops of rain begin to fall and while the leaders raise their arms, the race director does not react. Porto is the first to get on with it again and leads this lap by 7 tenths from De Angelis!

Half distance (10 laps):
Everything is almost back to normal, as Porto leads De Puniet by 311 thousandths. De Angelis is third, ahead of Pedrosa. Elias is 2 seconds behind in fifth spot.

Sebastian Porto showed the most cunning!

Lap 11:
Bataille and Gonzales-Nieto fall. "Fonsi" steals a flag off a marshal to show that the track is slippery. He will later be fined.

Lap 14:
De Puniet knows he has to go on the offensive, taking the lead by 208 thousandths from Porto. De Angelis and Pedrosa are third and fourth respectively.

Lap 16:
Guintoli falls as his Aprilia blows up.

Lap 17:
Another fastest lap and a break is made as Pedrosa leads De Angelis by 1"418. De Puniet and Porto are left trailing.

Lap 18:
De Angelis falls, Pedrosa raises his arm as it starts raining again. Porto and De Puniet ride past.

Finish (20 laps):
Porto had been the cleverest in this funny sort of race, as he twice made the most of the confusion. He takes the win ahead of De Puniet and Pedrosa.

Championship:
Pedrosa keeps the lead, with De Puniet now 30 points adrift, while Porto is 43 behind.

Drops of rain are falling as De Puniet, soon to be passed by Porto (19) raises an arm.

A great scrap for the win with Jorge Lorenzo having the last word.

Runners and riders:
Japan's Youichi Ui had been shown the door by Abruzzo and Andrea Ballerini picks up his ride. In the Sterilgarda camp, where Ballerini had slammed the door after Rio, we find a 17 year old Italian, Lorenzo Zanetti. For the first time this season, there's a Yamaha on track, in the hands of Japan's Tomoyoshi Koyama.

Qualifying:
While free practice on Friday and Saturday takes place in the dry, both qualifying sessions take place in the rain. It's a downpour on Friday and Simoncelli and Ballerini, the last two winners of wet races, have a great time, although less of one on Saturday. Simoncelli confirms his mastery of the difficult conditions which catch out several favourites, including Barbera (24th) and Locatelli (25th.) Series leader, Dovizioso, does the necessary, taking a front row slot with the second quickest time. Hats off to the young Zanetti, who is on his first visit to Brno and sets the eighth best time.

Start:
Dovizioso is there already. The championship leader takes no prisoners and by the end of the opening lap, he leads Stoner by 1"279. Behind them come Lorenzo, Corsi, Simoncelli and Jenkner. Barbera is already up to twelfth, while Locatelli is languishing down in thirtieth.

Lap 2:
Stoner falls and there's a crash in the pack which sees Rodriguez and Pellino fall. Dovizioso leads Lorenzo by 2"164.

Lap 3:
Simoncelli falls but rejoins.

Lap 4:
No change for Dovizioso. Barbera (2nd,) Nieto (6th) and Locatelli (15th) are all charging through the field in style. Mika Kallio retires.

Half distance (10 laps):
Having climbed to fourth, Pesek is a faller. Dovizioso is still out in front, but his lead over Barbera is down to 576 thousandths, while Jenkner is third. Nieto is 1"246 off the leader.

Lap 11:
Dovizioso has a moment and Barbera and Jenkner sneak past. Nieto is now in touch and the lead four are covered by 714 thousandths.

Lap 14:
Dovizioso is back in control, but the race is wide open as Locatelli has now joined the fray, with Lorenzo, Borsoi and Giansanti not far behind.

Lap 15:
Barbera is in the lead.

Finish (19 laps):
Lorenzo leads as they start the final lap and he has the last word after a sensational tussle. The top eight cross the line within 1"587 but there is a huge gap to the rest of the pack.

Championship:
Although he is beaten, Dovizioso increases his lead over Locatelli and Barbera who get it wrong in the final scuffle. The score looks like this: Dovizioso 183 points, Locatelli is 36 behind, while Barbera has 45 points to make up.

Barbera in qualifying as the rain fell heavily on Brno.

Czech Republic Grand Prix
22nd August 2004 / Brno – 5.403 m

STARTING GRID

1.	58	M. Simoncelli	Aprilia	2'24.458
2.	34	A. Dovizioso	Honda	2'24.638
3.	10	J. Simon	Honda	2'25.218
4.	48	J. Lorenzo	Derbi	2'25.549
5.	14	G. Talmacsi	Malaguti	2'25.831
6.	27	C. Stoner	KTM	2'25.967
7.	24	S. Corsi	Honda	2'26.232
8.	45	L. Zanetti	Aprilia	2'26.390
9.	52	L. Pesek	Honda	2'26.516
10.	23	G. Borsoi	Aprilia	2'26.605
11.	50	A. Ballerini	Aprilia	2'26.805
12.	69	R. Harms	Honda	2'26.855
13.	21	S. Jenkner	Aprilia	2'26.978
14.	6	M. Giansanti	Aprilia	2'27.128
15.	89	T. Koyama	Yamaha	2'27.131
16.	19	A. Bautista	Aprilia	2'27.402
17.	36	M. Kallio	KTM	2'27.607
18.	88	M. Ranseder	KTM	2'27.613
19.	32	F. Lai	Gilera	2'28.731
20.	33	S. Gadea	Aprilia	2'28.819
21.	12	T. Lüthi	Honda	2'28.886
22.	25	I. Toth	Aprilia	2'29.063
23.	54	M. Pasini	Aprilia	2'29.123
24.	3	H. Barbera	Aprilia	2'29.160
25.	15	R. Locatelli	Aprilia	2'29.562
26.	22	P. Nieto	Aprilia	2'29.753
27.	63	M. Di Meglio	Aprilia	2'30.189
28.	42	G. Pellino	Aprilia	2'30.390
29.	28	J. Carchano	Aprilia	2'31.002
30.	35	V. Bittman	Honda	2'31.190
31.	7	S. Perugini	Gilera	2'31.320
32.	9	M. Janakova	Honda	2'33.028
33.	26	D. Giuseppetti	Honda	2'33.158
34.	87	P. Vostarek	Honda	2'33.650
35.	16	R. Schouten	Honda	2'33.722
36.	20	G. Fröhlich	Honda	2'33.729

Did not meet qualifying minimum time, allowed to race :

8	M. Manna	Malaguti	2'34.575
66	V. Kallio	Aprilia	2'34.601
47	A. Rodriguez	Derbi	2'34.619

RACE: 19 LAPS = 102.65775 km

1.	Jorge Lorenzo	41'19.475 (149.049 km/h)
2.	Andrea Dovizioso	0"036
3.	Roberto Locatelli	0"146
4.	Pablo Nieto	0"186
5.	Gino Borsoi	+ 1"105
6.	Steve Jenkner	+ 1"197
7.	Hector Barbera	+ 1"579
8.	Mirko Giansanti	+ 1"587
9.	Simone Corsi	+ 12"488
10.	Julian Simon	+ 12"523
11.	Robbin Harms	+ 15"947
12.	Andrea Ballerini	+ 16"087
13.	Alvaro Bautista	+ 16"186
14.	Mattia Pasini	+ 25"084
15.	Fabrizio Lai	+ 28"271
16.	Michael Ranseder	+ 28"329
17.	Stefano Perugini	+ 33"895
18.	Thomas Lüthi	+ 37"754
19.	Marco Simoncelli	+ 44"541
20.	Dario Giuseppetti	+ 46"827
21.	Lorenzo Zanetti	+ 55"405
22.	Tomoyoshi Koyama	+ 55"445
23.	Vesa Kallio	+ 55"658
24.	Mike Di Meglio	+ 59"020
25.	Georg Fröhlich	+ 1'24.084
26.	Raymond Schouten	+ 1'53.072
27.	Patrik Vostarek	+ 2'14.214
28.	Marketa Janakova	+ 1 lap

Fastest lap:
Jenkner, in 2'08.891 (150.908 km/h).
Record: Cecchinello, in 2'07.836 (152.154 km/h/2003).

Outright fastest lap: Cecchinello, in 2'07.836 (152.154 km/h/2003).

CHAMPIONSHIP

1.	A. Dovizioso	183 (3 wins)
2.	R. Locatelli	147 (2 wins)
3.	H. Barbera	138 (2 wins)
4.	J. Lorenzo	109 (2 wins)
5.	C. Stoner	104
6.	P. Nieto	101
7.	S. Jenkner	83
8.	M. Giansanti	79
9.	A. Bautista	63
10.	M. Simoncelli	59 (1 win)

CAMEL
CAMEL
SHARK
Arai
45
15
4

PORTUGAL
Estoril

It's crowded at the first braking area. Admire the attacking move from Alexandre Barros on his Honda number 4, while Biaggi and Capirossi are about to be disappointed. The Portuguese GP would see Rossi take a major step forward towards another title, in a country where the fans cut their hair in quarters to show their passion.

MOTOGP

The years pass, the smile remains. Alexandre Barros is the most capped of all the GP riders and this was his fourteenth season in the blue riband category.

Portuguese Grand Prix
5th September 2004 / Estoril – 4.182 m

STARTING GRID

1.	6	M. Tamada	Honda	1'37.933
2.	46	V. Rossi	Yamaha	1'38.036
3.	15	S. Gibernau	Honda	1'38.067
4.	3	M. Biaggi	Honda	1'38.069
5.	4	A. Barros	Honda	1'38.215
6.	21	J. Hopkins	Suzuki	1'38.323
7.	33	M. Melandri	Yamaha	1'38.367
8.	45	C. Edwards	Honda	1'38.438
9.	10	Ke. Roberts	Suzuki	1'38.740
10.	7	C. Checa	Yamaha	1'38.862
11.	65	L. Capirossi	Ducati	1'39.071
12.	56	S. Nakano	Kawasaki	1'39.157
13.	12	T. Bayliss	Ducati	1'39.279
14.	17	N. Abé	Yamaha	1'39.635
15.	50	N. Hodgson	Ducati	1'39.677
16.	99	J. McWilliams	Aprilia	1'39.815
17.	66	A. Hofmann	Kawasaki	1'39.852
18.	11	R. Xaus	Ducati	1'40.259
19.	84	M. Fabrizio	Aprilia	1'40.586
20.	9	N. Aoki	Proton KR	1'41.279
21.	77	J. Ellison	Harris WCM	1'42.284
22.	35	C. Burns	Harris WCM	1'43.293

RACE: 28 LAPS = 117.096 km

1.	Valentino Rossi	46'34.911 (150.826 km/h)
2.	Makoto Tamada	+ 5"111
3.	Alexandre Barros	+ 8"157
4.	Sete Gibernau	+ 8"312
5.	Carlos Checa	+ 17"966
6.	John Hopkins	+ 18"631
7.	Loris Capirossi	+ 23"670
8.	Troy Bayliss	+ 25"126
9.	Colin Edwards	+ 25"611
10.	Norifumi Abé	+ 26"727
11.	Shinya Nakano	+ 44"704
12.	Jeremy McWilliams	+ 50"511
13.	Alexander Hofmann	+ 54"372
14.	Kenny Roberts	+ 59"518
15.	Nobuatsu Aoki	+ 1'32.853
16.	James Ellison	+ 1 lap

Fastest lap:
Rossi, in 1'38.423 (152.964 km/h). New record.
Previous record: Rossi, in 1'39.189 (151.782 km/h/2003).

Outright fastest lap: Tamada, in 1'37.933 (153.729 km/h/2004).

CHAMPIONSHIP

1.	V. Rossi	209 (6 wins)
2.	S. Gibernau	180 (3 wins)
3.	M. Biaggi	158 (1 win)
4.	C. Edwards	111
5.	A. Barros	102
6.	C. Checa	93
7.	M. Tamada	89 (1 win)
8.	L. Capirossi	84
9.	N. Hayden	83
10.	M. Melandri	64

Runners and riders:
America's Nicky Hayden broke his right collar bone the Sunday before the Portuguese Grand Prix, training on a super-motard bike in Italy. There is therefore just one Honda-Repsol on track, in the hands of Barros. Injured at Brno, Shane Byrne is replaced in the Aprilia camp by Michel Fabrizio, whose WCM ride has in turn been entrusted to James Ellison, the young British hope. Kurtis Roberts is also absent, after hurting himself in the Czech Republic.

Qualifying:
Valentino Rossi had been anxious about the Estoril event, because of the bumpy nature of the track. Nevertheless, on Friday, the world champion set the best time, which would only be beaten the following day by Makoto Tamada and his fantastic Bridgestone qualifying tyres. Better still for Rossi, in Saturday morning's wet free practice session, for the first time this season, he shines in the slippery conditions.

Start:
Capirossi comes from nowhere to take the lead ahead of Rossi and Biaggi. A bit later, Biaggi gets it all wrong and collides with Capirossi. Max crashes and Capi takes a trip off-road, while Rossi can afford to laugh as he completes the opening lap with a 492 thousandths lead over Tamada! Gibernau is already two seconds down after a fierce mano a mano with Melandri.

Lap 4:
Rossi heads Tamada by 1"307. Barros is third, 1.5 seconds off the Japanese rider, with Gibernau fourth.

Lap 8:
Marco "Spiderman" Melandri has a terrifying fall. Sete Gibernau has closed to within 426 thousandths of Barros, while Rossi strolls away in the lead.

Lap 12:
Fabrizio retires with serious pain in his arms after an opening lap tank slapper.

Half distance (14 laps):
Still Rossi, now 3"849 ahead of Tamada, who leads Barros by 2"736. Gibernau is 3 tenths off the Brazilian, while Capirossi is staging a great comeback and is up to eighth place.

Lap 17:
Hodgson retires (engine)

Lap 20:
Xaus retires (problem with the rear wheel.) Tamada has closed the gap to Rossi down to 2"6.

Finish (28 laps):
Another Rossi festival, another great showing from Tamada. It was the battle for third place that kept the crowd on its feet as Gibernau tried all he knew to get by Barros, the latest braker in the pack.

Championship:
Naturally, Rossi has done very well, making the most of the fact that, firstly, Gibernau picks up few points and is off the podium and secondly, Biaggi made a silly mistake. The outcome: a 29 point lead for the world champion, equivalent to more than one race win.

A king and his court, as Valentino Rossi wins again.

Rossi is too strong for Honda

A champagne shower for another triumph, as Rossi closes in on the title.

There can be no team orders at Honda. In Estoril, Gibernau came up against Barros.

The apparently invincible battleship has been sunk. Ever since the mid-Nineties, Honda had been the dominant force in the blue-riband category of motorcycle racing, but now it was no longer the implacable winning machine of old and it no longer had a bike to annihilate the opposition. No longer could it triumph making the most of its immense depth in terms of avant-garde technology and its heightened understanding of how to go racing.

At Estoril, on this September weekend, big boss Takeo Fukui, the Honda Motor Corporation Managing Director, had made the trip to rally his troops, breaking off his negotiations in the world of Formula 1 where, partner team BAR was fighting to hang onto its star driver, Jenson Button. Fukui soon realised that Honda was powerless against Rossi.

The story of this race? Too easy, too trouble-free for his Majesty Valentino. "I did not get a perfect start, but the first few corners went better. Then, I passed Capirossi and I could feel that something strange had happened. I did not want to turn round, as I knew that if I managed to carve out an early gap in the early stages, I would have less to worry about once the tyres began to lose grip. Everything went according to plan."

Easy was it? Max Biaggi failed to finish the opening lap, after attempting a suicidal attack on Capirossi – the incident that Rossi's sixth sense had told him about. Gibernau? A bad start and precious time lost because of Marco Melandri, before sitting on Barros' heels, with several passing attempts on the Brazilian all coming to nothing. In the space of three laps, three little laps, the Doctor had pulled out another killer cure from his little black bag. It was all too easy. Rossi was heading for the top step of the podium for the 65th time in his amazing career. From there, he could look down on his two closest pursuers, Honda men of course, but not the right ones as far as the honourable Fukui-san was concerned.

Valentino, you must at least enjoy the fact you are back on the podium alongside two Honda riders, who in terms of the championship, are already beaten?

Let's say I'm glad the opposition doesn't seem to be playing a team game.

That's understandable...

Yes, but not for the reasons you think. I mean that it would not be a good thing for the sport.

Surprised at the way things have turned out?

Oh no. Honda obviously has the advantage of strength in numbers, but as the RC211Vs are entered by three teams, each of them with different sponsors who pay the bills, you could not ask one of them to voluntarily make a sacrifice to help the other.

You now have a 29 point lead in the championship...

Yes, it's a nice margin to have in hand. Let's say that with that sort of lead, I can afford to finish a bit further back a couple of times.

Does that mean that at Motegi, in Honda's back yard in a fortnight's time, you would settle for fourth place?

Oh, no. I didn't say that. I would settle for a podium! Even if, in 2003, five Hondas filled the top five places in Japan.

250cc

Portuguese Grand Prix
5th September 2004 / Estoril – 4.182 m

STARTING GRID

1.	26	D. Pedrosa	Honda	1'41.417
2.	19	S. Porto	Aprilia	1'41.638
3.	24	T. Elias	Honda	1'41.645
4.	7	R. De Puniet	Aprilia	1'41.814
5.	51	A. De Angelis	Aprilia	1'42.226
6.	10	F. Gonzales-Nieto	Aprilia	1'42.488
7.	6	A. Debon	Honda	1'42.516
8.	54	M. Poggiali	Aprilia	1'42.520
9.	73	H. Aoyama	Honda	1'42.709
10.	21	F. Battaini	Aprilia	1'42.769
11.	14	A. West	Aprilia	1'42.781
12.	25	A. Baldolini	Aprilia	1'43.171
13.	8	N. Matsudo	Yamaha	1'43.191
14.	2	R. Rolfo	Honda	1'43.298
15.	50	S. Guintoli	Aprilia	1'43.491
16.	57	C. Davies	Aprilia	1'43.507
17.	28	D. Heidolf	Aprilia	1'43.561
18.	11	J. Olive	Aprilia	1'43.810
19.	33	H. Faubel	Aprilia	1'44.039
20.	9	H. Marchand	Aprilia	1'44.088
21.	96	J. Smrz	Honda	1'44.175
22.	36	E. Nigon	Aprilia	1'44.187
23.	16	J. Stigefelt	Aprilia	1'44.226
24.	44	T. Sekiguchi	Yamaha	1'44.312
25.	12	A. Vincent	Aprilia	1'44.318
26.	42	G. Leblanc	Aprilia	1'44.704
27.	34	E. Bataille	Honda	1'44.733
28.	17	K. Nöhles	Honda	1'45.269
29.	43	R. Rous	Yamaha	1'46.649
Did not meet qualifying minimum time:				
	88	Ge. Talmacsi	Yamaha	1'48.666

RACE: 26 LAPS = 108.732 km

1. Toni Elias	44'23.399 (146.968 km/h)
2. Sebastian Porto	+ 0"323
3. Randy De Puniet	+ 9"918
4. Daniel Pedrosa	+ 9"935
5. Alex De Angelis	+ 21"441
6. Anthony West	+ 27"638
7. Manuel Poggiali	+ 27"866
8. Alex Debon	+ 34"673
9. Hiroshi Aoyama	+ 45"923
10. Roberto Rolfo	+ 54"238
11. Hector Faubel	+ 58"751
12. Franco Battaini	+ 59"123
13. Eric Bataille	+ 1'11.620
14. Jakub Smrz	+ 1'11.785
15. Dirk Heidolf	+ 1'12.305
16. Chaz Davies	+ 1'14.925
17. Taro Sekiguchi	+ 1'14.982
18. Joan Olive	+ 1'22.255
19. Hugo Marchand	+ 1'25.071
20. Johan Stigefelt	+ 1'26.573
21. Erwan Nigon	+ 1'28.740
22. Gregory Leblanc	+ 1 lap
23. Klaus Nöhles	+ 1 lap

Fastest lap:
Elias, in 1'41.595 (148.188 km/h). New record.
Previous record: Poggiali, in 1'42.215 (147.289 km/h/2003).

Outright fastest lap: Pedrosa, in 1'41.417 (148.448 km/h/2004).

CHAMPIONSHIP

1. D. Pedrosa	209 (4 wins)
2. R. De Puniet	182 (1 win)
3. S. Porto	173 (3 wins)
4. T. Elias	122 (1 win)
5. A. De Angelis	104
6. A. Gonzales-Nieto	94
7. A. West	88
8. H. Aoyama	87
9. R. Rolfo	83 (1 win)
10. M. Poggiali	79 (1 win)

A breathtaking duel between Toni Elias and Sebastian Porto.

Runners and riders:
Gergo Talmacsi has secured a seat in the NC World Trade team, replacing Max Sabbatani. Just one wild card for Frenchman, Gregory Leblanc.

Qualifying:
Dani Pedrosa definitely has the knack of making life difficult for his rivals. While some of the managers in this category are pushing for a combined minimum weight (rider and machine, as is the case in the 125 class,) the championship leader does the necessary on the last lap of qualifying on Saturday to take another pole position, ahead of Porto, Elias, whose season as usual is following a crescendo-like rise, and Randy De Puniet.

Start:
With Sebastian Porto, Pedrosa, Toni Elias and "Fonsi" Gonzales-Nieto, it's a case of speaking Spanish through the early corners, especially as Debon is glued to the rear wheel of Frenchman Randy De Puniet's Aprilia. Porto dashes off the opening lap with a 931 thousandths lead over Pedrosa.

Lap 2:
Arnaud Vincent falls.

Lap 6:
Porto still enjoys a comfortable lead. He is now pursued by Elias (at 714 thousandths.) De Puniet and Pedrosa follow, then comes a fantastic Anthony West, who has taught a lesson to Gonzales-Nieto who is struggling once again.
De Puniet is over 2 seconds behind.

Half distance (13 laps):
Elias has just picked up the pace and Porto is struggling to keep up, with the result that the gap between them has grown to 566 thousandths. De Puniet is third, 2"275 behind, heading Pedrosa who is a full second further back.

Lap 18:
Porto has got back down to business, taking matters in hand by almost half a second with De Puniet way back, 4 seconds behind.

Lap 22:
As they cross the line, Porto swarms over Elias in a superb dice. Behind them, Pedrosa has closed up to De Puniet in the fight for third place.

Finish (26 laps):
Elias takes his first win of the season, while De Puniet just grabs third spot by 17 thousandths, thus nibbling away at Pedrosa's points advantage.

A kiss for a winner as Mother Elias is proud of her little lad.

Championship:
A super rider from Pedrosa means he keeps the championship lead, 27 points clear of De Puniet. Porto is third, 9 points off the Frenchman. With five grands prix to go, the title should be fought out between these three.

Runners and riders:
Italy's Lorenzo Zanetti is now a permanent replacement for Youichi Ui in the Sterilgarda camp. Three riders have wild cards: Spain's Manuel Hernandez Junior and Switzerland's Vincent Braillard who this year is competing in the European and Spanish championships, as well as Portugal's Carlos Ferreira.

Qualifying:
A veritable deluge hit the paddock on Thursday evening and, on Friday morning, seven 125 riders were caught out at the same spot at the bottom of the hill. Unfortunately, one of the revelations of the season, Julian Simon dislocated and broke his shoulder and had to scratch. The track was at its quickest on Friday afternoon and the Kopron Scot team riders, Dovizioso and Corsi put up a nice one-two.

Start:
Corsi, Locatelli and Stoner are quickest away. Jenkner and Pasini are fallers. As they cross the line for the first time, Stoner has a 50 thousandths lead over Corsi, who heads Mika Kallio on the second KTM.

Lap 3:
Giansanti and Ballerini fall.

Lap 4:
Dovizioso has made the break and leads Kallio and Stoner by 838 thousandths. They are followed by a flying Corsi.

Lap 5:
Corsi had been pushing too hard and falls. A bit later, Stoner has to retire with a broken exhaust, after a collision with the young Italian.

Lap 10:
A warning shot as Dovizioso's Honda has problems, handing the lead to Barbera.

Lap 11:
Locatelli is in the gravel trap.

Half distance (12 laps):
Things settle down for a moment as Dovizioso heads for the pits with a puncture caused when he unfortunately rode over a screw from an advertising hoarding! Barbera has almost a second (963 thousandths) over Kallio. Simoncelli is third, but over 4 seconds off the leader. He heads Pablo Nieto and Lorenzo.

Lap 15:
Kallio has closed right up to Barbera and takes the lead at the end of the straight.

Lap 19:
Barbera counter attacks and now leads the Finn by 472 thousandths. A thrilling fight for third place between Nieto, Simoncelli and Lorenzo.

Finish (23 laps):
Barbera has been faultless in front of his employer, the soccer player Clarence Seedorf. Lorenzo has the last word in the battle for third.

Championship:
No points for Dovizioso, but he still keeps the lead, 20 points clear of the winner on the day, Hector Barbera. Next up is Locatelli.

Giansanti-Ballerini: call it a misunderstanding.

A furious tussle at the first corner is a regular feature of the 125 races.

Portuguese Grand Prix
5th September 2004 / Estoril – 4.182 m

STARTING GRID

1.	34	A. Dovizioso	Honda	1'46.280
2.	24	S. Corsi	Honda	1'46.338
3.	27	C. Stoner	KTM	1'46.380
4.	15	R. Locatelli	Aprilia	1'46.496
5.	58	M. Simoncelli	Aprilia	1'46.572
6.	6	M. Giansanti	Aprilia	1'46.691
7.	48	J. Lorenzo	Derbi	1'46.735
8.	21	S. Jenkner	Aprilia	1'46.851
9.	36	M. Kallio	KTM	1'46.877
10.	3	H. Barbera	Aprilia	1'46.965
11.	22	P. Nieto	Aprilia	1'47.111
12.	32	F. Lai	Gilera	1'47.132
13.	52	L. Pesek	Honda	1'47.251
14.	7	S. Perugini	Gilera	1'47.270
15.	14	G. Talmacsi	Malaguti	1'47.320
16.	19	A. Bautista	Aprilia	1'47.452
17.	47	A. Rodriguez	Derbi	1'47.508
18.	54	M. Pasini	Aprilia	1'47.533
19.	23	G. Borsoi	Aprilia	1'47.544
20.	33	S. Gadea	Aprilia	1'47.861
21.	12	T. Lüthi	Honda	1'47.875
22.	50	A. Ballerini	Aprilia	1'48.135
23.	63	M. Di Meglio	Aprilia	1'48.693
24.	25	I. Toth	Aprilia	1'48.751
25.	69	R. Harms	Honda	1'48.782
26.	26	D. Giuseppetti	Honda	1'48.818
27.	66	V. Kallio	Aprilia	1'48.876
28.	42	G. Pellino	Aprilia	1'48.998
29.	45	L. Zanetti	Aprilia	1'50.346
30.	8	M. Manna	Malaguti	1'50.716
31.	28	J. Carchano	Aprilia	1'51.210
32.	16	R. Schouten	Honda	1'51.489
33.	43	M. Hernandez Jnr	Aprilia	1'51.834
34.	9	M. Janakova	Honda	1'52.777
Not qualified:				
	91	V. Braillard	Honda	1'54.414
	90	C. Ferreira	Honda	1'57.086
	10	J. Simon (*)	Honda	

(*): J. Simon breaks a collar bone in Friday's free practice.

RACE: 23 LAPS = 96.186 km

1. Hector Barbera	41'01.272 (140.687 km/h)
2. Mika Kallio	+ 0"151
3. Jorge Lorenzo	+ 8"824
4. Pablo Nieto	+ 8"888
5. Alvaro Bautista	+ 9"666
6. Marco Simoncelli	+ 10"347
7. Gabor Talmacsi	+ 11"919
8. Lukas Pesek	+ 11"962
9. Roberto Locatelli	+ 19"186
10. Stefano Perugini	+ 19"548
11. Mike Di Meglio	+ 26"981
12. Fabrizio Lai	+ 31"708
13. Sergio Gadea	+ 32"492
14. Dario Giuseppetti	+ 32"896
15. Gino Borsoi	+ 34"820
16. Thomas Lüthi	+ 34"845
17. Mattia Pasini	+ 58"409
18. Vesa Kallio	+ 1'00.159
19. Lorenzo Zanetti	+ 1'26.362
20. Jordi Carchano	+ 1'26.498
21. Raymond Schouten	+ 1'36.654
22. Manuel Manna	+ 1'36.716
23. Manuel Hernandez	+ 1 lap
24. Marketa Janakova	+ 1 lap

Fastest lap:
Barbera, in 1'45.573 (142.604 km/h). New record.
Previous record: Barbera, in 1'46.225 (141.729 km/h/2003).

Outright fastest lap: Barbera, in 1'45.573 (142.604 km/h/2004).

CHAMPIONSHIP

1. A. Dovizioso	183 (3 wins)
2. H. Barbera	163 (3 wins)
3. R. Locatelli	154 (2 wins)
4. J. Lorenzo	125 (2 wins)
5. P. Nieto	114
6. C. Stoner	104
7. S. Jenkner	83
8. M. Giansanti	79
9. A. Bautista	74
10. M. Kallio	73

CAMEL

JAPAN
Motegi

Makoto Tamada leads the way, ahead of Valentino Rossi. At Motegi, Bridgestone recorded its second win of the season, in front of a knowledgeable, enthusiastic yet polite crowd. With his plastic Asimo robot covered in autographs this young Rossi fans can now take a breather. The Italian's fans grow in number every year in Japan, even if the most moving section of the crowd was that bearing the colours of the late Daijiro Kato.

MOTOGP

Just for a weekend, Olivier Jacque was back on the GP trail, riding the Moriwaki-Honda.

Japanese Grand Prix 19th September 2004 / Motegi – 4.801 m

STARTING GRID

1.	6	M. Tamada	Honda	1'46.673
2.	21	J. Hopkins	Suzuki	1'47.230
3.	46	V. Rossi	Yamaha	1'47.275
4.	3	M. Biaggi	Honda	1'47.401
5.	45	C. Edwards	Honda	1'47.821
6.	33	M. Melandri	Yamaha	1'47.845
7.	65	L. Capirossi	Ducati	1'47.886
8.	10	Ke. Roberts	Suzuki	1'47.929
9.	69	N. Hayden	Honda	1'47.940
10.	4	A. Barros	Honda	1'47.963
11.	7	C. Checa	Yamaha	1'47.982
12.	56	S. Nakano	Kawasaki	1'48.042
13.	15	S. Gibernau	Honda	1'48.107
14.	72	T. Ukawa	Honda	1'48.154
15.	17	N. Abé	Yamaha	1'48.154
16.	12	T. Bayliss	Ducati	1'48.174
17.	50	N. Hodgson	Ducati	1'48.656
18.	11	R. Xaus	Ducati	1'48.859
19.	66	A. Hofmann	Kawasaki	1'48.885
20.	99	J. McWilliams	Aprilia	1'49.139
21.	19	O. Jacque	Moriwaki	1'49.545
22.	9	N. Aoki	Proton KR	1'51.388
23.	67	S. Byrne	Aprilia	1'51.466
Not finished:				
	41	Y. Ui	Harris WCM	1'54.743

RACE: 24 LAPS = 115.224 km

1.	Makoto Tamada	43'43.220 (158.128 km/h)
2.	Valentino Rossi	+ 6"168
3.	Shinya Nakano	+ 13"396
4.	Alexandre Barros	+ 15"435
5.	Marco Melandri	+ 23"577
6.	Sete Gibernau	+ 27"378
7.	Carlos Checa	+ 35"834
8.	Neil Hodgson	+ 47"976
9.	Ruben Xaus	+ 49"881
10.	Alexander Hofmann	+ 56"107
11.	Olivier Jacque	+ 1'21.237
12.	Jeremy McWilliams	+ 1'27.683
13.	Shane Byrne	+ 1 lap
14.	Nobuatsu Aoki	+ 1 lap
15.	Youichi Ui	+ 1 lap

Fastest lap:
Tamada, in 1'48.524 (159.260 km/h). New record.
Previous record: Rossi, in 1'48.885 (158.732 km/h/2003).

Outright fastest lap: Tamada, in 1'46.673 (162.024 km/h/2004).

CHAMPIONSHIP

1.	V. Rossi	229 (6 wins)
2.	S. Gibernau	190 (3 wins)
3.	M. Biaggi	158 (1 win)
4.	A. Barros	115
5.	M. Tamada	114 (2 wins)
6.	C. Edwards	111
7.	C. Checa	102
8.	L. Capirossi	84
9.	N. Hayden	83
10.	M. Melandri	75

Runners and riders:
Current HRC test rider, Tohru Ukawa has been given a super RC211V. Olivier Jacque is back on the GP scene, in the saddle of a Moriwaki-Honda. Injured in Brno, Kurtis Roberts has returned to the United States. The big surprise comes courtesy of WCM, as riding the Harris is none other than Youichi Ui, who had lost his 125 ride a month earlier.

Qualifying:
Bridgestone has got the better of Michelin when it comes to qualifying tyres. Riders using the Japanese product put on some impressive angles of lean and some equally impressive lap times. On the first day of qualifying, its Hopkins who hoists himself to the top of the time sheet, but his time is smashed by Tamada at the very end of Saturday's session. It is the second consecutive pole for the Japanese Honda rider. Rossi does very well to qualify third, while Gibernau, struggling with his new Michelins, does much worse and finds himself on the fifth row down in 13th place.

Start:
Rossi is the quickest off the line. Behind him comes a huge pack with Capirossi pursued by Hopkins, Biaggi, Roberts, Edwards and Hayden, while Barros loses a lot of time. At the end of the opening lap, Rossi leads Tamada by two tenths, with Melandri third, two seconds down, ahead of Nakano, Abe and Gibernau.

Lap 5:
It's still Rossi versus Tamada (92 thousandths between them.) Melandri is trailing the Japanese rider by 3"720.

Lap 6:
Tamada goes into the lead.

Lap 9:
Tohru Ukawa is a faller.

Lap 10:
Abe is slowing and comes into the pits. Out in front, Tamada now leads Rossi by 594 thousandths.

Half distance (12 laps):
Still Tamada, by 1"283 from Rossi, while third placed Melandri is 9"166 off the leader, fighting an on-form Nakano. Gibernau has moved ahead of Bayliss to go fifth.

Lap 15:
Bayliss re-passes Gibernau.

Lap 16:
Barros finds a way past Gibernau.

Lap 19:
The fans in the green Kawasaki grandstand go wild as Nakano dispenses with Melandri to take third place.

Lap 20:
Bayliss is a faller.

Lap 21:
Barros passes Melandri and the Brazilian closes to within 2"307 of Nakano.

Finish (24 laps):
Super Tamada and super Bridgestone, as Nakano completes the podium, Kawasaki's first since returning to racing.

Championship:
Things are still going Rossi's way, as he now leads Gibernau by 39 points. Biaggi is 71 points in arrears and the title now seems very close to a conclusion.

It's skittles at the first corner: Loris Capirossi has just hit John Hopkins and six riders are eliminated.

There really is a tyre war!

Impressive lean angles with perfect grip as the Tamada-Bridgestone combo prepares to strike.

When he had visited his troops at the German GP, Edouard Michelin had stressed how much he liked the idea of competition and how important it was in racing to be able to pit your wits and your product against an opponent. The president even went so far as to say that he had appreciated Tamada's win three weeks earlier in Rio de Janeiro. He said all this and there was not even a murmur from his men at the track, who were aware that they had been dominant for over ten years.

However, with each passing race, the Bridgestone menace was growing. First off with some great qualifying lap times, as the super soft Japanese tyres allowed its riders to push the risk envelope when it came to looking for the limit. Then, in Rio and also in Portugal, where Tamada finished second, the Bridgestones had gone the distance.

The crisis in the Italian GP at Mugello, when the rear tyre on Nakano's Kawasaki had exploded on the straight and Tamada was forced to stop to avoid a disaster, had been forgotten. The second half of the season was full of good surprises.

In the light of this, the Motegi event was looking interesting. The results speak for themselves: Tamada and Hopkins first and second in qualifying, two riders on the podium with Tamada the winner and Nakano third. It was party time for Bridgestone, just as there was talk of a crisis in the Michelin camp. "I think that everyone who came to Motegi and all the fans of the Bridgestone riders were happy with the result. We are extremely proud of our riders who, using our tyres, have got such good results in this the most demanding of motor cycle racing disciplines," declared Bridgestone Corporation president, Shigeo Watanabe.

The president's comments were backed up by the two stars of the day. "You can imagine how happy we are," commented Bridgestone motor sport manager, Hiroshi Yamada. "Today, we had 380 guests in a special grandstand, plus seventy of our staff. Being able to celebrate our first double podium with all these fans is quite simply fantastic."

As for the future, Michelin wanted competition and it looked as though Bibendum was going to get it. "In less than three years involvement in the MotoGP class, we have become competitive. Now, our aim, given that the contract tying Bridgestone to HRC was due to expire at the end of this season, is to increase our presence. We are now going to study all our options to support teams in the blue riband category next season," added Yamada.

Michelin's motorcycle racing boss, Nicolas Goubert, was paying attention. "It wasn't a great day for us, but no one should forget that we are dominating the championship."

That might be true, but the writing was on the wall.

Charming smiles from the girls at the start and a joyful smile from Nakano at the finish. Kawasaki took its first podium since returning to the sport.

250cc

Elias late brakes as Pedrosa prepares to go round the outside as the Japanese 250 GP gets underway.

Japanese Grand Prix 19th September 2004 / Motegi – 4.801 m

STARTING GRID

1.	26	D. Pedrosa	Honda	1'52.137
2.	73	H. Aoyama	Honda	1'52.366
3.	7	R. De Puniet	Aprilia	1'52.453
4.	24	T. Elias	Honda	1'52.534
5.	19	S. Porto	Aprilia	1'52.550
6.	55	Y. Takahashi	Honda	1'52.638
7.	51	A. De Angelis	Aprilia	1'52.809
8.	14	A. West	Aprilia	1'53.642
9.	21	F. Battaini	Aprilia	1'53.694
10.	54	M. Poggiali	Aprilia	1'53.786
11.	10	F. Gonzales-Nieto	Aprilia	1'53.798
12.	2	R. Rolfo	Honda	1'53.835
13.	76	S. Aoyama	Honda	1'53.893
14.	6	A. Debon	Honda	1'54.027
15.	78	Y. Fujioka	Honda	1'54.242
16.	8	N. Matsudo	Yamaha	1'54.423
17.	70	C. Kameya	Honda	1'54.571
18.	33	H. Faubel	Aprilia	1'54.655
19.	57	C. Davies	Aprilia	1'54.670
20.	36	E. Nigon	Aprilia	1'54.784
21.	96	J. Smrz	Honda	1'54.811
22.	34	E. Bataille (*)	Honda	1'54.867
23.	28	D. Heidolf	Aprilia	1'55.135
24.	50	S. Guintoli	Aprilia	1'55.143
25.	9	H. Marchand	Aprilia	1'55.286
26.	11	J. Olive	Aprilia	1'55.606
27.	12	A. Vincent	Aprilia	1'55.678
28.	79	K. Nakasuga	Yamaha	1'55.721
29.	16	J. Stigefelt	Aprilia	1'55.795
30.	44	T. Sekiguchi	Yamaha	1'55.813
31.	25	A. Baldolini	Aprilia	1'56.020
32.	43	R. Rous	Yamaha	1'56.949
33.	17	K. Nöhles	Honda	1'57.256
Not finished:				
	88	Ge. Talmacsi	Yamaha	2'02.836

(*): Laid low by a serious intestinal problem, Bataille (F. Honda) does not start.

RACE: 23 LAPS = 110.423 km

1.	Daniel Pedrosa	43'36.798 (151.911 km/h)
2.	Toni Elias	+ 3"174
3.	Hiroshi Aoyama	+ 15"991
4.	Sebastian Porto	+ 20"075
5.	Yuki Takahashi	+ 25"450
6.	Alex De Angelis	+ 33"451
7.	Roberto Rolfo	+ 43"084
8.	Shuhei Aoyama	+ 43"270
9.	Franco Battaini	+ 48"773
10.	Alex Debon	+ 52"000
11.	Randy De Puniet	+ 1'00.707
12.	Yuzo Fujioka	+ 1'01.472
13.	Naoki Matsudo	+ 1'02.120
14.	Hugo Marchand	+ 1'06.488
15.	Hector Faubel	+ 1'09.070
16.	Choujoun Kameya	+ 1'12.091
17.	Manuel Poggiali	+ 1'15.444
18.	Taro Sekiguchi	+ 1'17.484
19.	Sylvain Guintoli	+ 1'17.753
20.	Katsuyuki Nakasuga	+ 1'27.294
21.	Dirk Heidolf	+ 1'44.246
22.	Erwan Nigon	+ 1'45.825

Fastest lap:
Pedrosa, in 1'52.788 (153.239 km/h).
Record: Nakano, in 1'52.253 (153.970 km/h/2000).

Outright fastest lap: Pedrosa, in 1'52.137 (154.129 km/h/2004).

CHAMPIONSHIP

1.	D. Pedrosa	234 (5 wins)
2.	R. De Puniet	187 (1 win)
3.	S. Porto	186 (3 wins)
4.	T. Elias	142 (1 win)
5.	A. De Angelis	114
6.	H. Aoyama	103
7.	A. Gonzales-Nieto	94
8.	R. Rolfo	92 (1 win)
9.	A. West	88
10.	M. Poggiali	79 (1 win)

Runners and riders:
There are five Japanese wild cards, including Hiroshi Aoyama's young brother, Shuhei.

Qualifying:
Pedrosa gave himself a fright on Friday, when he fell heavily and broke a little toe. It was not enough to stop the Spaniard putting together the perfect lap on Saturday so that he and Aoyama produce a solid one-two for the Telefonica Movistar team. De Puniet is third and the only Aprilia rider on the front row.

Start:
Pedrosa and Elias show the quickest reflexes, with Toni taking the lead, while De Puniet then goes second with Fonsi Gonzales-Nieto ending up in the gravel trap.

Lap 2:
Pedrosa catches out De Puniet to go second, while Elias leads across the line by 328 thousandths.

Lap 5:
Elias signals to Pedrosa to go past as it seems the two Spaniards have worked out that the best way to shake off Randy De Puniet is to join forces. It appears to work, because while Pedrosa and Elias are still wheel to wheel (106 thousandths,) the Frenchman is already lagging behind by 1.6 seconds.

Lap 6:
De Puniet has lost another whole second and Aoyama and Takahashi are now on a charge.

Lap 7:
Aoyama passes De Puniet so that three Hondas lead the way.

Lap 9:
De Puniet falls and rejoins 19th. Out in front, Pedrosa and Elias now lead the third placed man by over 6 seconds.

Lap 11:
Elias retakes the lead. Poggiali rides through a gravel trap and as he comes back onto the track, he narrowly avoids hitting De Puniet as they fight for 18th place!

Half distance (12 laps):
Pedrosa has just made a small mistake and Elias extends his lead to 449 thousandths. Aoyama is third, 7"499 behind the leader. Takahashi is fourth and is being caught by Sebastian Porto. Fonsi has just pulled up.

Lap 14:
Porto has passed Takahashi and De Puniet is up to 15th and back in the points.

Lap 15:
West falls, having been sixth.

Lap 17:
Pedrosa has no intention of letting Elias get the upper hand and goes back in the lead.

A young master (Pedrosa) and a good pupil (Aoyama) mean it's party time for Telefonica.

Lap 18:
Fastest lap for Pedrosa, with Elias 652 thousandths adrift.

Lap 21:
Davies falls.

Finish (23 laps):
The Pedrosa festival continues. He does as he pleases to take another victory, while Aoyama is delighted to join his team-mate on the podium.

Championship:
Porto is only fourth and in the end, De Puniet picks up some points in 11th place. Let's do the maths. Dani Pedrosa leads the Frenchman by 47 points and the Argentinian by 48. The gap is a huge chasm; almost two races worth.

Sergio Gadea and Thomas Luthi raise a hand and the race is about to be stopped.

Japanese Grand Prix 19th September 2004 / Motegi – 4.801 m

Runners and riders:
Having injured a shoulder in Portugal, the Spanish hope, Julian Simon, is replaced by Manuel Hernandez Junior, whom we have already seen running as a wild card on several occasions. On the subject of invited riders, we have five here, including Thailand's Suhathai Chaemsap, who had made an appearance in Malaysia back in 2000. Since then, he has been competing in the Japanese 125 championship.

Qualifying:
There was no way the riders could know it, but the track would turn out to be at its quickest on Friday, as the higher humidity on Saturday, in the early afternoon, had an effect on grip levels. As a result, apart from a strong performance from Roberto Locatelli, who took second place by 42 thousandths from Dovizioso, the final qualifying session was mainly marked by falls, most notably for Stoner, Luthi and Simoncelli.

Start:
Barbera, Stoner and Dovizioso take off in the lead and at the end of the opening lap, Stoner leads Dovizioso by 99 thousandths. In third place, Barbera is already half a second adrift.

Lap 2:
Stoner retires, handing the lead to Dovizioso, who has a comfortable 904 thousandths advantage over Barbera, chased by Locatelli.

Lap 6:
Pablo Nieto retires. Dovizioso puts in some fastest laps to extend his lead to 2"037.

Lap 7:
Di Meglio is a faller.

Lap 9:
Hatano is a faller and Toth runs into the Japanese rider's bike which is in the middle of the track. The race is red flagged. The order at the end of lap 8 is used to decide the new grid and the race will be decided over 13 laps.

Second start:
Barbera and Lorenzo have trouble firing up the bikes and start at the back of the grid, with Barbera using his spare bike. Yet again, Dovizioso makes the best start, from Locatelli and Corsi. Locatelli takes the lead as they cross the line, ahead of Dovizioso. Bautista is a faller.

Lap 4:
Pesek falls.

Half distance (lap 7):
Locatelli and Dovizioso are still wheel to wheel (78 thousandths.) Six riders fight for third place, as Kallio falls.

Lap 8:
Dovizioso takes the lead, but Locatelli gets him back a bit later.

Lap 9:
Barbera retires.

Finish (13 laps):
Locatelli falls on the last lap, gets back on and picks up points for fourteenth place. Dovizioso has ridden a perfect race, while Lai takes his first ever podium ahead of Corsi.

Championship:
Dovizioso has made up for failing to score in Estoril and his lead over Barbera is back up to 45 points.

Fabrizio Lai flat out on his Gilera as the Italian takes his first world championship podium.

STARTING GRID

1.	34	A. Dovizioso	Honda	1'58.385
2.	15	R. Locatelli	Aprilia	1'58.427
3.	27	C. Stoner	KTM	1'58.576
4.	3	H. Barbera	Aprilia	1'58.678
5.	36	M. Kallio	KTM	1'58.750
6.	48	J. Lorenzo	Derbi	1'58.964
7.	14	G. Talmacsi	Malaguti	1'58.997
8.	52	L. Pesek	Honda	1'59.174
9.	22	P. Nieto	Aprilia	1'59.243
10.	24	S. Corsi	Honda	1'59.622
11.	58	M. Simoncelli	Aprilia	1'59.627
12.	32	F. Lai	Gilera	1'59.694
13.	23	G. Borsoi	Aprilia	1'59.735
14.	21	S. Jenkner	Aprilia	1'59.827
15.	6	M. Giansanti	Aprilia	1'59.905
16.	50	A. Ballerini	Aprilia	1'59.919
17.	89	T. Koyama	Yamaha	1'59.944
18.	19	A. Bautista	Aprilia	2'00.271
19.	12	T. Lüthi	Honda	2'00.296
20.	54	M. Pasini	Aprilia	2'00.324
21.	63	M. Di Meglio	Aprilia	2'00.477
22.	47	A. Rodriguez	Derbi	2'00.589
23.	7	S. Perugini	Gilera	2'00.687
24.	62	T. Kuzuhara	Honda	2'00.773
25.	33	S. Gadea	Aprilia	2'01.281
26.	69	R. Harms (*)	Honda	2'01.322
27.	26	D. Giuseppetti	Honda	2'01.330
28.	25	I. Toth	Aprilia	2'01.607
29.	64	S. Norikane	Yamaha	2'01.941
30.	66	V. Kallio	Aprilia	2'01.942
31.	28	J. Carchano	Aprilia	2'02.092
32.	67	S. Chaemsap	Honda	2'02.128
33.	43	M. Hernandez Jnr	Aprilia	2'02.129
34.	45	L. Zanetti	Aprilia	2'02.151
35.	95	Y. Hatano	Honda	2'02.286
36.	16	R. Schouten	Honda	2'02.857
37.	8	M. Manna	Malaguti	2'02.972
38.	42	G. Pellino	Aprilia	2'02.990
39.	9	M. Janakova	Honda	2'04.002

(*):R. Harms breaks his right femur and scaphoid in Friday afternoon's qualifying.

RACE: 13 LAPS = 62.413 km (*)

1.	Andrea Dovizioso	25'52.175 (144.756 km/h)
2.	Fabrizio Lai	+ 11"082
3.	Simone Corsi	+ 11"101
4.	Mirko Giansanti	+ 11"341
5.	Steve Jenkner	+ 11"519
6.	Marco Simoncelli	+ 14"491
7.	Jorge Lorenzo	+ 25"279
8.	Gabor Talmacsi	+ 25"320
9.	Tomoyoshi Koyama	+ 25"863
10.	Toshihisa Kuzuhara	+ 30"172
11.	Gino Borsoi	+ 30"432
12.	Thomas Lüthi	+ 30"562
13.	Sergio Gadea	+ 32"170
14.	Roberto Locatelli	+ 32"971
15.	Vesa Kallio	+ 41"950
16.	Gioele Pellino	+ 42"058
17.	Suhathai Chaemsap	+ 44"536
18.	Manuel Hernandez	+ 51"234
19.	Jordi Carchano	+ 51"283
20.	Raymond Schouten	+ 1'04.719
21.	Lorenzo Zanetti	+ 1'11.829
22.	Manuel Manna	+ 1'13.894
23.	Marketa Janakova	+ 1'36.250

(*) : The race was red flagged after two crashes on lap 8. The order of this "first leg" serves to establish the grid for the decisive race now run over 13 laps.

Fastest lap:
Dovizioso, in 1'58.766 (145.526 km/h).
Record: Pedrosa, in 1'58.354 (146.033 km/h/2002).

Outright fastest lap: Pedrosa, in 1'57.736 (146.799 km/h/2003).

CHAMPIONSHIP

1.	A. Dovizioso	208 (4 wins)
2.	H. Barbera	163 (3 wins)
3.	R. Locatelli	156 (2 wins)
4.	J. Lorenzo	134 (2 wins)
5.	P. Nieto	114
6.	C. Stoner	104
7.	S. Jenkner	94
8.	M. Giansanti	92
9.	M. Simoncelli	79 (1 win)
10.	A. Bautista	74

Losail International
Circuit 2
MICHELIN
74

QATAR
Losail

A victory salute from Sete Gibernau on the top step of the podium and hugging his team-manager, Fausto Gresini. The Spanish rider has just rekindled his championship hopes under strange circumstances. The first ever Qatar GP was played against a background of strange goings-on. It was also an opportunity to discover a sports-mad country. For example, Frank Leboeuf, who won the football World Cup with France, earns a handy living in Doha and he is about to be scared witless on the back of the two-seater Ducati, ridden by Randy Mamola.

MOTOGP

Qatar Grand Prix
2nd October 2004 / Losail – 5.380 m

STARTING GRID

1.	7	C. Checa	Yamaha	1'58.988
2.	4	A. Barros	Honda	1'59.119
3.	15	S. Gibernau	Honda	1'59.126
4.	69	N. Hayden	Honda	1'59.187
5.	56	S. Nakano	Kawasaki	1'59.232
6.	65	L. Capirossi	Ducati	1'59.281
7.	11	R. Xaus	Ducati	1'59.352
8.	12	T. Bayliss	Ducati	1'59.551
9.	45	C. Edwards	Honda	1'59.582
10.	21	J. Hopkins	Suzuki	1'59.944
11.	6	M. Tamada	Honda	2'00.638
12.	99	J. McWilliams	Aprilia	2'00.660
13.	50	N. Hodgson	Ducati	2'00.826
14.	33	M. Melandri	Yamaha	2'00.924
15.	17	N. Abé	Yamaha	2'01.303
16.	66	A. Hofmann	Kawasaki	2'01.531
17.	71	Y. Kagayama	Suzuki	2'02.151
18.	9	N. Aoki	Proton KR	2'03.281
19.	36	J. Haydon	Proton KR	2'03.845
20.	77	J. Ellison	Harris WCM	2'04.627
21.	46	V. Rossi (*)	Yamaha	2'05.494
12.	3	M. Biaggi (**)	Honda	2'06.063
Not qualified:				
	41	Y. Ui	Harris WCM	2'07.466

(*): Having set the eighth fastest time (1'59 "494) V. Rossi is given a 6 second penalty after one of his team attempted to lay rubber down on his starting position.
(**): Having set the twelfth fastest time (2'00 "063) M. Biaggi is given a 6 second penalty, after one his team washed and brushed his starting place on the grid.

RACE: 22 LAPS = 118.360 km

1. Sete Gibernau	44'01.741 (161.293 km/h)
2. Colin Edwards	+ 1"315
3. Ruben Xaus	+ 23"844
4. Alexandre Barros	+ 25"458
5. Nicky Hayden	+ 31"417
6. Massimiliano Biaggi	+ 39"209
7. Norifumi Abé	+ 53"373
8. John Hopkins	+ 58"006
9. Alexander Hofmann	+ 1'04.320
10. Makoto Tamada	+ 1'18.518
11. Yukio Kagayama	+ 1'49.438
12. James Haydon	+ 1'52.158
13. James Ellison	+ 1'53.900

Fastest lap:
Edwards, in 1'59.293 (162.356 km/h).
New record (nouveau circuit).

Outright fastest lap: Checa, in 1'58.988 (162.772 km/h/2004).

CHAMPIONSHIP

1. V. Rossi	229 (6 wins)
2. S. Gibernau	215 (4 wins)
3. M. Biaggi	168 (1 win)
4. C. Edwards	131
5. A. Barros	128
6. M. Tamada	120 (2 wins)
7. C. Checa	102
8. N. Hayden	94
9. L. Capirossi	84
10. M. Melandri	75

All smiles between Edwards, Gibernau and Xaus during the post-race press conference.

Runners and riders:
Kenny Roberts (dislocated elbow) is replaced by Yukio Kagayama. In the WCM camp, Ui is yet again riding the second Harris. At Proton, Kurtis Roberts' machine is now entrusted to England's James Haydon. Shane Byrne (Aprilia) has brought his season to a premature end to undergo a wrist operation. As from the Malaysian Grand Prix, he will be replaced by Gary McCoy.

Qualifying:
"it will be very interesting to see which rider will be the quickest at learning a brand new circuit," said Valentino Rossi at Motegi. At the end of the first day of practice, it was Ruben Xaus who had something to smile about. On Friday, (the weekend programme was shifted forward a day) when the track is quicker by almost 4 seconds, it is Checa and Barros who are quickest, with Gibernau completing the front row. Rossi is "only" eighth and Biaggi further back still in 12th spot, but there is worse to come. The two Italians are each given a six second penalty: Rossi because his crew went and put some rubber down on his grid position and Biaggi, because his boys cleaned up his grid slot. The mortal enemies thus find themselves together on the back row.

Start:
Checa is first away from the front row, but of course, all the excitement centres on Rossi, who is already ninth at the first split. Gibernau crosses the line to lead the first lap, with Checa glued to his back wheel. These two have already built up a slight gap with Xaus in third. Rossi is eighth at 3"153.

Lap 2:
Fastest lap for Rossi, now seventh.

Lap 4:
Rossi leans on Barros to get past and, still cranked over, turns to wave an apology. At that moment, for the fourth time this weekend, Nakano's Kawasaki engine blows up. Gibernau leads Checa by 878 thousandths, with Rossi fourth.

Lap 5:
Capirossi goes to play in the sand.

Lap 6:
Rossi falls, having clipped a kerb. Gibernau has a 1"954 lead over Checa, who is being caught by Edwards, the quickest man on track.

Lap 7:
Aoki falls.

Lap 9:
Edwards passes Checa and the American is now 4"016 down on team-mate Gibernau.

Half distance (11 laps):
Edwards has closed to 2"246. Checa is still third and Xaus has just relieved Melandri of fourth spot.

Out on his own against a backdrop of sand, Gibernau does not yet realise he will be portrayed as the "bad man" of a scandal for which he was not responsible.

Lap 14:
Melandri retires followed by Capirossi.

Lap 17:
Gibernau is still in charge. Barros passes Biaggi.

Lap 20:
Checa retires. Xaus is now in a podium position.

Finish (22 laps):
Gibernau kept it all together. Only 13 riders see the flag.

Championship:
Rossi's lead over Gibernau has come down to a mere 14 points.

Scores settled at the Qatar Corral!

"If Sete enjoys winning races in the Stewards room, then that's his lookout. This weekend he seemed like a goody goody who goes and tells on his neighbour to the boss because he saw him do something abnormal. I know we made a mistake on Friday evening. It was after we saw Nakano's mechanics cleaning up his grid slot two weeks ago in Japan that we got the idea of doing the same." Valentino Rossi does not like losing, not one bit of it...

And the world champion lost big time, as his only rival for the title, Sete Gibernau, rode a faultless race. The result was that on the night of the first ever Qatar GP in history, just 14 little points separated the two top men in the category!

The scenario at this grand premier was worthy of Machiavelli and would make a great holiday read, the sort of book one ploughs through at a single sitting on the sun lounger. It all began on the night before the race. And cue,,, action!

It is dusk and the day is woken up to the noise of engines. One of Rossi's crew turns up on a scooter and travels to his start place on the grid. He spins the rear wheel to put rubber on the track, to improve grip come start time. But the culprit is spotted and he is told to go and clean away the rubber. Which he does with enthusiasm using an acetone detergent that improves the grip still further! The Repsol Honda team, Rossi's former employers, reckon this act should be punished and they lodge a protest. The stewards penalise the champion by adding 6 seconds to his qualifying time, as per article 3.3.1.2 of the rules, which mentions "actions prejudicial to the sport." Rossi thus ends up on the back row, soon to be joined by Biaggi. The race can begin and the world champion faces a challenge worthy of his talents, as he is about to try and overtake the entire field.

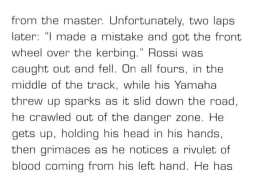

By the first corner, he is already ninth and as they cross the line he has made up another place. On lap 4, here he is leaning on Barros to overtake him, before turning round to wave an apology to the Brazilian, while still taking the corner at 100 km/h. It is insane and without precedent and another demonstration from the master. Unfortunately, two laps later: "I made a mistake and got the front wheel over the kerbing." Rossi was caught out and fell. On all fours, in the middle of the track, while his Yamaha threw up sparks as it slid down the road, he crawled out of the danger zone. He gets up, holding his head in his hands, then grimaces as he notices a rivulet of blood coming from his left hand. He has lost the race that Gibernau has yet to win. But most of all, he has lost a golden opportunity to set himself up for a first match point in Malaysia.

Sete Gibernau is not bothered. Officially, the Spaniard had nothing to do with it. What do you think?

It was a Saturday like any other. Valentino Rossi was penalised when one of his team tried to improve the grip on the starting grid. He found himself on the back row, alongside Max Biaggi. Also there, James Ellison (Harris WCM no. 77) had never started in such good company. Rossi risked all to fight his way back to the front and ended up on the deck.

250cc

Qatar Grand Prix
2nd October 2004 / Losail – 5.380 m

STARTING GRID

1.	19	S. Porto	Aprilia	2'02.710
2.	26	D. Pedrosa	Honda	2'03.181
3.	51	A. De Angelis	Aprilia	2'03.894
4.	7	R. De Puniet	Aprilia	2'04.385
5.	24	T. Elias	Honda	2'04.391
6.	73	H. Aoyama	Honda	2'04.568
7.	21	F. Battaini	Aprilia	2'04.837
8.	10	F. Gonzales-Nieto	Aprilia	2'05.364
9.	50	S. Guintoli	Aprilia	2'05.998
10.	14	A. West	Aprilia	2'06.244
11.	6	A. Debon	Honda	2'06.425
12.	33	H. Faubel	Aprilia	2'06.513
13.	57	C. Davies	Aprilia	2'06.531
14.	11	J. Olive	Aprilia	2'06.817
15.	25	A. Baldolini	Aprilia	2'06.842
16.	2	R. Rolfo	Honda	2'06.862
17.	96	J. Smrz	Honda	2'06.971
18.	36	E. Nigon	Aprilia	2'07.067
19.	28	D. Heidolf	Aprilia	2'07.180
20.	8	N. Matsudo	Yamaha	2'07.290
21.	44	T. Sekiguchi	Yamaha	2'07.322
22.	16	J. Stigefelt	Aprilia	2'07.359
23.	9	H. Marchand	Aprilia	2'08.185
24.	52	D. De Gea	Honda	2'08.345
25.	42	G. Leblanc	Aprilia	2'08.815
26.	17	K. Nöhles	Honda	2'09.014
27.	43	R. Rous	Yamaha	2'11.115
Not qualified:				
	88	Ge. Talmacsi	Yamaha	2'12.963

RACE: 20 LAPS = 107.600 km

1.	Sebastian Porto	41'17.343 (156.361 km/h)
2.	Daniel Pedrosa	+ 1"614
3.	Hiroshi Aoyama	+ 43"312
4.	Franco Battaini	+ 45"127
5.	Alfonso Gonzales-Nieto	+ 47"182
6.	Toni Elias	+ 59"471
7.	Roberto Rolfo	+ 1'11.413
8.	Alex Debon	+ 1'22.120
9.	Hugo Marchand	+ 1'22.162
10.	Joan Olive	+ 1'29.038
11.	Sylvain Guintoli	+ 1'40.121
12.	Erwan Nigon	+ 1'43.016
13.	Taro Sekiguchi	+ 1'43.056
14.	Johan Stigefelt	+ 1'50.884
15.	David De Gea	+ 1'53.027
16.	Chaz Davies	+ 1'53.335
17.	Jakub Smrz	+ 1'54.871
18.	Alex Baldolini	+ 2'25.588
19.	Klaus Nöhles	+ 1 lap

Fastest lap:
De Angelis, in 2'03.015 (157.444 km/h).
New record (new circuit).

Outright fastest lap: Porto, in 2'02.710 (157.835 km/h/2004).

CHAMPIONSHIP

1.	D. Pedrosa	254 (5 wins)
2.	S. Porto	211 (4 wins)
3.	R. De Puniet	187 (1 win)
4.	T. Elias	152 (1 win)
5.	H. Aoyama	119
6.	A. De Angelis	114
7.	A. Gonzales-Nieto	105
8.	R. Rolfo	101 (1 win)
9.	A. West	88
10.	M. Poggiali	79 (1 win)

Porto, Pedrosa, De Angelis were the dominant forces in the Qatar GP, although De Angelis sadly had to retire with a holed radiator.

Runners and riders:
Former 125 world champion, Arnaud Vincent, who is know to have been in conflict with his team for several weeks, announces that he will not be taking part in the final run of flyaway races that make up the end of the season. Officially, Vincent injured himself in the gym and he is replaced by fellow countryman Gregory Leblanc, who has already appeared at several grands prix, as a wild card. Other absentees: the Andorran rider, Eric Bataille, has suddenly decided to bring his career to an end and is replaced by David De Gea. Tough luck for outgoing champion, Manuel Poggiali, who sustains an injury playing squash in his Doha hotel, after the glass partition he lent on shattered. Poggiali sustained a serious cut to an ankle, requiring 50 stitches!

Qualifying:
Sebastian Porto is the dominant force on both Thursday and Friday. The gaps are significant, with fourth placed De Puniet 1"675 behind and there are plenty of off-track excursions. As is the case with Dovizioso in the 125s, Dani Pedrosa, the championship leader does enough to get on the front row.

Start:
Germany's Dirk Heidolf and Spain's Toni Elias start from the pits, after the field has got away. Pedrosa is the quickest, ahead of Porto and Aoyama. At the end of the first lap, 16 thousandths separate Pedrosa and Porto, with the latter about to take the lead. Gregory Leblanc is a faller.

Lap 2:
Porto leads Pedrosa by 235 thousandths. De Angelis has just taken second place. Elias is already nineteenth.

Lap 5:
Randy De Puniet falls, having been sixth. Elias is up to tenth.

Half distance (10 laps):
Porto has built his lead up to 1"816. De Angelis is on Pedrosa's back wheel. Toni Elias is superb and already seventh!

Lap 14:
Porto is in charge, while Elias has a scary moment.

Lap 19:
Alex De Angelis retires after a front wheel balance weight goes through his radiator.

Finish (20 laps):
Porto has a trouble free afternoon. In the end, he wins by 1"614 from Pedrosa, but as he fails to see the chequered flag, he completes another lap at racing pace! A great fight for third place between Aoyama and Battaini sees the Japanese rider have the last word.

Championship:
Pedrosa leads Porto by 43 points, with Randy de Puniet now relegated to third. The Spaniard needs to score seven points more than the Argentinian in Malaysia to be crowned champion in Sepang.

Lap five and Randy De Puniet gets up to see second place in the championship slipping away.

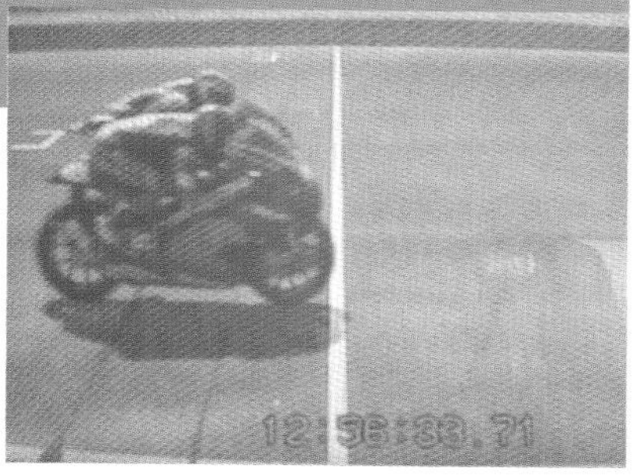

So who won? Lorenzo and Dovizioso indulge in sign language after crossing the finish line and it took a photo finish to split them.

125cc

Runners and riders:
Injured in Japan, Robbin Harms is replaced by Max Sabbatani, who had started the season in the 250 category, before sustaining a serious fall during qualifying at Donington and breaking his pelvis. Frenchman Mike Di Meglio arrives in Qatar with a plaster cast, having broken a fibula at Motegi. He gives it a go on Friday afternoon, but wisely decides to call it a day.

Qualifying:
The 125 riders have the honour of being first to discover this new circuit at Losail. It also falls to them to start the job of cleaning the track. Obviously, none of Friday's times meant much come the following day. On Saturday, the track had improved by roughly 4 seconds for all riders. Lorenzo (Derbi) did the best job, leading Dovizioso, the ever-present front runner whatever the conditions, followed by Jenkner and Stoner. There are therefore four different marques on the front row.

Start:
Stoner and Dovizioso rush into the lead. Vesa Kallio and Rodriguez are fallers. Locatelli makes a complete hash of it, while Simoncelli is a non-starter, having fallen in the warm-up. At the end of the first lap, the two leaders have already pulled out a gap of almost a second on the chasing pack.

Lap 3:
Lorenzo and Bautista have caught the Stoner-Dovizioso duo.

Lap 5:
Lorenzo goes into the lead, taking Bautista with him.

Lap 6:
Bautista has taken charge, leading Lorenzo by 404 thousandths. The top four are covered by less than a second.

Half distance (9 laps):
Stoner had been slowing for the past couple of laps and now he stops with engine problems. Out in front, Bautista leads Lorenzo by 212 thousandths. Dovizioso is third, 8 tenths off the young Spaniard. Mika Kallio is up to fourth, trailing by 6 seconds.

Lap 15:
Barbera goes off the track after a collision.

Lap 16:
Corsi retires. Bautista runs wide, leaving just Lorenzo and Dovizioso to fight for the win.

Finish (18 laps):
89 thousandths is the gap as they cross the line to start the final lap. Dovizioso pulls out of the slipstream on the straight. The two men are classified equal on time to the nearest thousandth. It is a first in the history of the sport. It is down to a photo finish and the rule that the win goes to whoever had done the fastest race lap, the result going in favour of Lorenzo.

Championship:
Another good day for Dovizioso, who now leads Barbera by 61 points. The Italian seems to have an appointment with the title crown in Malaysia.

Lorenzo gets on the podium and indicates that the crowd ought to make more noise.

Qatar Grand Prix
2nd October 2004 / Losail – 5.380 m

STARTING GRID

1.	48	J. Lorenzo	Derbi	2'09.644
2.	34	A. Dovizioso	Honda	2'09.928
3.	21	S. Jenkner	Aprilia	2'10.496
4.	27	C. Stoner	KTM	2'10.519
5.	15	R. Locatelli	Aprilia	2'10.807
6.	22	P. Nieto	Aprilia	2'10.875
7.	58	M. Simoncelli	Aprilia	2'10.956
8.	10	J. Simon	Honda	2'11.466
9.	6	M. Giansanti	Aprilia	2'11.615
10.	36	M. Kallio	KTM	2'11.784
11.	24	S. Corsi	Honda	2'11.878
12.	19	A. Bautista	Aprilia	2'11.977
13.	12	T. Lüthi	Honda	2'12.067
14.	3	H. Barbera	Aprilia	2'12.139
15.	54	M. Pasini	Aprilia	2'12.408
16.	32	F. Lai	Gilera	2'12.414
17.	14	G. Talmacsi	Malaguti	2'12.606
18.	7	S. Perugini	Gilera	2'12.759
19.	33	S. Gadea	Aprilia	2'12.760
20.	66	V. Kallio	Aprilia	2'12.820
21.	50	A. Ballerini	Aprilia	2'13.249
22.	23	G. Borsoi	Aprilia	2'13.403
23.	47	A. Rodriguez	Derbi	2'13.432
24.	26	D. Giuseppetti	Honda	2'14.088
25.	45	L. Zanetti	Aprilia	2'14.628
26.	28	J. Carchano	Aprilia	2'15.659
27.	42	G. Pellino	Aprilia	2'15.659
28.	25	I. Toth	Aprilia	2'16.050
29.	16	R. Schouten	Honda	2'16.056
30.	52	L. Pesek	Honda	2'16.406
31.	8	M. Manna	Malaguti	2'17.474
32.	31	M. Sabbatani	Honda	2'17.569
Not qualified:				
	9	M. Janakova	Honda	2'19.184
	63	M. Di Meglio	Aprilia	2'30.098

RACE: 18 LAPS = 96.840 km

1. Jorge Lorenzo (*)	39'11.620 (148.248 km/h)
2. Andrea Dovizioso (*)	0"000
3. Alvaro Bautista	+ 4"018
4. Mika Kallio	+ 18"753
5. Fabrizio Lai	+ 35"458
6. Pablo Nieto	+ 37"890
7. Julian Simon	+ 39"023
8. Gino Borsoi	+ 39"409
9. Mattia Pasini	+ 42"901
10. Mirko Giansanti	+ 42"918
11. Steve Jenkner	+ 47"425
12. Hector Barbera	+ 48"015
13. Thomas Lüthi	+ 52"652
14. Andrea Ballerini	+ 1'03.092
15. Gioele Pellino	+ 1'06.804
16. Stefano Perugini	+ 1'07.043
17. Lukas Pesek	+ 1'20.718
18. Sergio Gadea	+ 1'23.808
19. Dario Giuseppetti	+ 1'26.869
20. Roberto Locatelli	+ 1'28.482
21. Lorenzo Zanetti	+ 1'29.779
22. Jordi Carchano	+ 1'37.395
23. Manuel Manna	+ 1'37.540
24. Raymond Schouten	+ 1'38.401
25. Imre Toth	+ 1'54.617

(*) : It is the first time ever that two riders are credited with identical times to the nearest thousandth. Lorenzo was declared the winner in a photo finish.

Fastest lap:
Lorenzo, in 2'09.569 (149.480 km/h).
New record (new circuit).

Outright fastest lap: Lorenzo, in 2'09.569 (149.480 km/h/2004).

CHAMPIONSHIP

1. A. Dovizioso	228 (4 wins)
2. H. Barbera	167 (3 wins)
3. J. Lorenzo	159 (3 wins)
4. R. Locatelli	156 (2 wins)
5. P. Nieto	124
6. C. Stoner	104
7. S. Jenkner	99
8. M. Giansanti	98
9. A. Bautista	90
10. M. Kallio	86

GAULOISES
YAMAHA
THE DOCTOR

MALAYSIA
Sepang

Italy wins, Italy triumphs and it's Valentino Rossi. Against the futuristic backdrop of the Sepang circuit, the world champion puts on another demonstration of his immense talent. All over the world, the grandstands are always full of "Vale" fans.

MOTOGP

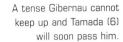

A tense Gibernau cannot keep up and Tamada (6) will soon pass him.

Malaysian Grand Prix
10th October 2004 / Sepang – 5.548 m

STARTING GRID

1.	46	V. Rossi	Yamaha	2'01.833
2.	4	A. Barros	Honda	2'02.228
3.	56	S. Nakano	Kawasaki	2'02.278
4.	15	S. Gibernau	Honda	2'02.283
5.	6	M. Tamada	Honda	2'02.394
6.	69	N. Hayden	Honda	2'02.399
7.	3	M. Biaggi	Honda	2'02.446
8.	21	J. Hopkins	Suzuki	2'02.588
9.	7	C. Checa	Yamaha	2'02.602
10.	33	M. Melandri	Yamaha	2'02.852
11.	65	L. Capirossi	Ducati	2'02.860
12.	45	C. Edwards	Honda	2'03.014
13.	66	A. Hofmann	Kawasaki	2'03.321
14.	12	T. Bayliss	Ducati	2'03.384
15.	11	R. Xaus	Ducati	2'03.956
16.	17	N. Abé	Yamaha	2'04.284
17.	50	N. Hodgson	Ducati	2'04.738
18.	99	J. McWilliams	Aprilia	2'04.830
19.	24	G. McCoy	Aprilia	2'04.875
20.	71	Y. Kagayama	Suzuki	2'05.285
21.	9	N. Aoki	Proton KR	2'06.126
22.	36	J. Haydon	Proton KR	2'06.443
23.	77	J. Ellison	Harris WCM	2'08.554
24.	41	Y. Ui	Harris WCM	2'08.995

RACE: 21 LAPS = 116.508 km

1.	Valentino Rossi	43'29.146 (160.753 km/h)
2.	Massimiliano Biaggi	+ 3"666
3.	Alexandre Barros	+ 9"299
4.	Nicky Hayden	+ 19"069
5.	Makoto Tamada	+ 21"155
6.	Loris Capirossi	+ 21"268
7.	Sete Gibernau	+ 21"881
8.	Shinya Nakano	+ 22"167
9.	Carlos Checa	+ 23"150
10.	Troy Bayliss	+ 32"615
11.	Colin Edwards	+ 33"958
12.	Norifumi Abé	+ 44"302
13.	Ruben Xaus	+ 55"235
14.	Yukio Kagayama	+ 1'09.580
15.	Jeremy McWilliams	+ 1'10.376
16.	Garry McCoy	+ 1'16.134
17.	Nobuatsu Aoki	+ 1'55.097
18.	James Ellison	+ 1 lap
19.	Youichi Ui	+ 1 lap

Fastest lap:
Rossi, in 2'03.253 (162.947 km/h). New record.
Previous record: Rossi, in 2'03.822 (161.302 km/h/2003).

Outright fastest lap: Rossi, in 2'01.833 (163.935 km/h/2004).

CHAMPIONSHIP

1.	V. Rossi	254 (7 wins)
2.	S. Gibernau	224 (4 wins)
3.	M. Biaggi	188 (1 win)
4.	A. Barros	144
5.	C. Edwards	136
6.	M. Tamada	131 (2 wins)
7.	C. Checa	109
8.	N. Hayden	107
9.	L. Capirossi	94
10.	M. Melandri	75

Runners and riders:
In the Suzuka camp, Kagayama is still standing in for Kenny Roberts, while brother Kurtis has gone home to the States, handing his Proton to Haydon. Ui rides the second Harris-WCM, but the big news of the weekend comes from Aprilia, where we find Garry McCoy back in the saddle, having just completed his first season in world superbikes: here he replaces Shane Byrne.

Qualifying:
After a war of words, or rather a war of silence between Rossi and Gibernau, the battle over hundredths of a second is dominated by Valentino Rossi. He is the most consistent rider and also the one who gets the most out of his qualifying tyres. The result is that Barros is almost 4 tenths slower and Gibernau is on the second row. Nakano produces another great performance and after giving Kawasaki its first podium in Motegi, he put the green mean machine on the front row for the first time.

Start:
Barros makes the best of it ahead of Rossi, Hayden, Checa, Biaggi, Capirossi and Gibernau. Barros ends the opening lap with a 287 thousandths lead over Rossi and is almost 8 tenths ahead of Checa. Gibernau is sixth at 1"350.

Lap 2:
The top six are covered by a handkerchief measuring precisely one second. Rossi has just mounted an initial attack, but does not succeed. James Haydon is deemed to have jumped the start and has to pit for a stop and go penalty.

Lap 3:
Hopkins retires.

Lap 4:
It's a case of third time lucky for Rossi, who takes the lead. Further back, Gibernau passes Checa for fifth place.

Lap 7:
After an exciting duel with Barros, Biaggi moves up to second. He crosses the line 796 thousandths behind Rossi. First Hodgson and then Hofmann retire.

Checa leads the charge through the first difficult double corner at the Sepang circuit. Barros and Rossi have already gone through.

Lap 10:
Melandri is a faller.

Half distance (11 laps):
The signs were there in qualifying and, sure enough, Rossi is too strong. He leads Biaggi by 1"372. Gibernau is 10 seconds back in fifth.

Lap 15:
The ever spectacular Capirossi passes Checa, who is about to be caught out by Tamada.

Lap 16:
Capirossi gets the better of Gibernau, while Rossi still controls the gap to Biaggi.

Lap 19:
Gibernau has lost another place, as Tamada sails by.

Finish (21 laps):
Rossi has put on another faultless performance on track and then produces another comedy routine with his fans.

Championship:
Valentino has a 30 point lead, with two races remaining and the title looks like being in his pocket.

When Rossi cleans up

The night after the Qatar GP controversy, ten days earlier, Valentino Rossi had changed his schedule. He cancelled the short holiday he had planned on an island in the China Sea. "Vale" and Uccio, his shadow, his general factotum, had headed home for Italy. "To treat my little finger," explained Valentino when he arrived in Malaysia. But hidden behind this urgent "medical" repatriation was another more surprising reason, namely a rapidly orchestrated call to arms for his ever so colourful fan club: "Gentlemen, I need you in Sepang." So Flavio, the president Rino and a few others did not hesitate. They jumped on the first plane, their luggage packed with a few surprises...But in order for the stunt to take place, Valentino Rossi had to fulfil his part of the deal by winning in Sepang. A not too difficult task for him under normal circumstances, but it proved a bit harder that sunny Sunday, as the temperature suddenly shot up, causing the usual problems in terms of tyre performance. Mission impossible? It was for Sete Gibernau – "I don't want to make excuses. Both me and the team had a difficult weekend," – but not for Rossi, who was so keen to regain the upper hand as quickly as possible. It was yet another impressive demonstration and the post-race stunt went ahead as planned. On his victory lap, "Vale" stopped at the point where is accomplices were waiting. One of them pulled out a broom, which Rossi used to clean the track in front of his Yamaha's front wheel, to ensure that the route that would lead to the podium was not too scruffy. Then, he was handed a specially designed T-shirt sporting a picture of Rossi and his chief engineer, Jeremy Burgess, each of them holding a broom. It bore the slogan: "The Rapida cleans up in the world championship!" With, of course, those specialist cleaning processes, "disinfection, stain removal, especially of black marks on start grids. All done in 6 seconds. Night service." Ouch, it was enough to rub salt in the wounds of Gibernau and the men at Honda.
The doctor was once again the crazy "Vale." Here's the interview...

After demonstrating his riding skills, it is time for Rossi and his fans to put on another show.

Valentino, what about this win in Malaysia?
....It's a response to a lot of things and the Sepang circuit was the ideal place to deliver it.
A 30 point lead (there were 50 still to play for) is a nice insurance policy, isnt' it?
Let's say we have regained the advantage we deserve. But careful, don't make the mistake of assuming it's a done deal. Already, after Motegi, when I led by 39 points, one could have thought that I had done the hard part. And look at what happened in Qatar ten days later.
So Sete Gibernau is still in the running?
As soon as you lower your guard, he comes back at you. We thought he was definitely beaten after Japan, but he won and I fell in Qatar. So, it's a case of being patient.

Malaysian Grand Prix
10th October 2004 / Sepang – 5.548 m

STARTING GRID

1.	19	S. Porto	Aprilia	2'06.940
2.	26	D. Pedrosa	Honda	2'07.644
3.	7	R. De Puniet	Aprilia	2'08.287
4.	51	A. De Angelis	Aprilia	2'08.345
5.	24	T. Elias	Honda	2'08.501
6.	73	H. Aoyama	Honda	2'08.510
7.	10	F. Gonzales-Nieto	Aprilia	2'08.905
8.	14	A. West	Aprilia	2'08.948
9.	21	F. Battaini	Aprilia	2'09.051
10.	2	R. Rolfo	Honda	2'09.364
11.	6	A. Debon	Honda	2'09.760
12.	9	H. Marchand	Aprilia	2'09.892
13.	37	M. Lucchi	Aprilia	2'10.010
14.	36	E. Nigon	Aprilia	2'10.494
15.	96	J. Smrz	Honda	2'10.533
16.	25	A. Baldolini	Aprilia	2'10.847
17.	8	N. Matsudo	Yamaha	2'10.902
18.	57	C. Davies	Aprilia	2'11.043
19.	16	J. Stigefelt	Aprilia	2'11.084
20.	33	H. Faubel	Aprilia	2'11.114
21.	28	D. Heidolf	Aprilia	2'11.160
22.	52	D. De Gea	Honda	2'11.231
23.	50	S. Guintoli	Aprilia	2'11.518
24.	11	J. Olive	Aprilia	2'11.707
25.	42	G. Leblanc	Aprilia	2'12.364
26.	44	T. Sekiguchi	Yamaha	2'12.623
27.	43	R. Rous	Yamaha	2'14.901
Not qualified:				
	88	Ge. Talmacsi	Yamaha	2'15.922
	17	K. Nöhles (*)	Honda	

(*): K. Nöhles (D, Honda), is injured in Friday's free practice.

RACE: 20 LAPS = 110.960 km

1.	Daniel Pedrosa	43'03.507 (154.617 km/h)
2.	Sebastián Porto	+ 13"513
3.	Toni Elias	+ 13"585
4.	Alex De Angelis	+ 25"027
5.	Randy De Puniet	+ 49"978
6.	Franco Battaini	+ 1'02.582
7.	Alfonso Gonzales-Nieto	+ 1'02.670
8.	Hugo Marchand	+ 1'09.360
9.	Chaz Davies	+ 1'09.492
10.	Naoki Matsudo	+ 1'20.994
11.	Alex Baldolini	+ 1'25.105
12.	Dirk Heidolf	+ 1'28.030
13.	Hector Faubel	+ 1'30.746
14.	Jakub Smrz	+ 1'31.221
15.	Johan Stigefelt	+ 1'31.561
16.	Marcellino Lucchi	+ 1'32.219
17.	David De Gea	+ 1'43.502
18.	Joan Olive	+ 1'48.609
19.	Gregory Leblanc	+ 1'48.812
20.	Radomil Rous	+ 2'07.022

Fastest lap:
Pedrosa, in 2'08.015 (156.019 km/h). New record.
Previous record: Elias, in 2'08.566 (155.350 km/h/2003).

Outright fastest lap: Porto, in 2'06.940 (157.340 km/h/2004).

CHAMPIONSHIP

1.	D. Pedrosa	279 (6 wins)
2.	S. Porto	231 (4 wins)
3.	R. De Puniet	198 (1 win)
4.	T. Elias	168 (1 win)
5.	A. De Angelis	127
6.	H. Aoyama	119
7.	A. Gonzales-Nieto	114
8.	R. Rolfo	101 (1 win)
9.	A. West	88
10.	F. Battaini	80

A perfect start and an exemplary race: Daniel Pedrosa got the job done. But he is not yet champion.

Runners and riders:
De Gea continues to replace Bataille and once again, Le Blanc takes the place of Vincent, but the big news is the return of the veteran Aprilia test rider, Marcellino Lucchi. At 47 years of age – his birthday was back on 13th March – he takes over the bike of the outgoing champion, Manuel Poggiali, who was injured playing squash in Qatar.

Qualifying:
The new king of pole position, Argentina's Sebastian Porto, once again puts on a demonstration right from the first day of practice. As a few drops of rain fall on Sepang on Saturday in the second half of the afternoon session, his time is never beaten. The star of the second session is Randy De Puniet. He had encountered carburetion problems the previous day, but the Frenchman does the necessary to get onto the front row. Apart from him, only one other rider improves his time on Saturday – Australia's Anthony West, who ends up eighth.

Start:
Pedrosa pulls off the perfect start, ahead of Elias and Porto.
De Puniet has lost ground in an accident that eliminates Rolfo, in his one hundredth grand prix and West. At the end of the first lap, Pedrosa has a 699 thousandths lead over Elias, who heads Porto and De Angelis. If the race were to end at this point, the little Spaniard would already be champion!

Lap 5:
While Pedrosa enjoys a solid lead of 4"850, he is no longer virtual champion, as Porto has just made the most of a mistake from Elias, to take second place.

Lap 8:
This time, it's Porto who gets it wrong and Elias is back up to second. Porto is champion again.

Lap 9:
De Bon retires.

Half distance (10 laps):
Still Pedrosa, who is riding faultlessly. He has a substantial 10"853 over Porto, who has just moved back up to second. Pedrosa is now 2 points short of his title.

Lap 12:
Elias moves up to second again, Pedrosa has the title in his pocket again.

Lap 13:
Let's start all over again as Porto goes second.

Lap 16:
Aoyama is a faller.

Finish (20 laps):
Pedrosa leads the final lap by over 14 seconds, with all eyes glued on the battle for second between Porto and Elias, as this is where the title will be decided. Pedrosa has done his job and Toni Elias has had to give best to Porto. The title will have to wait another week.

Championship:
Pedrosa has a 48 point lead, with 50 still to play for. Dani is not yet world champion.

Pedrosa and Tonia Elias: champagne!

And here is the first champion to be crowned in 2004: Andrea Dovizioso dominated the 125 season.

Runners and riders:
As in Qatar, Italy's Max Sabbatani stands in for Denmark's Robbin Harms in the Ajo Motorsport team, Switzerland's Thomas Luthi (Elit) follows the example set by Simone Corsi (Kopron-Scot) a few weeks back and chops in his 2004 Honda frame for a 2003 model, which he feels more comfortable with. One wild card, Japan's Toshihisa Kuzuhara has a third Honda in the Angaia team. Mike Di Meglio is back, having packed it in after the first day of practice in Losail.

Qualifying:
Andrea Dovizioso could have settled for a safe place, but he flew his way through qualifying; a true champion in the making. On Saturday night, when asked if he will be racing for points here, he burst out laughing: "I'm not fighting for the MotoGP title! I just want to win races. Oh, if I could be champion by winning this race, after an ace move at the final corner..." The result of this mastery was that second placed Barbera was almost 9 tenths off Dovizioso in qualifying.

Start:
It's a tussle right from the off between Barbera and Dovizioso. Corsi fails to finish the first lap, which Barbera completes leading Dovizioso by 223 thousandths.

Lap 2:
At 12h35 and 11 seconds, Dovizioso can smell the title as Barbera has just fallen. The Spaniard had to risk all up against the hero of the year, but he went too far. Casey Stoner has closed right up to the series leader. Further back, Lorenzo is already drifting 2 seconds off the leaders. Mika Kallio is a faller.

Barbera had to risk everything, but he got it wrong.

Lap 3:
Perugini, Pablo Nieto and Simoncelli all fall.

Lap 6:
Giansanti falls.

Lap 8:
Lorenzo retires.

Half distance (10 laps):
Stoner and Dovizioso are on another planet. They are separated by 284 thousandths, with the Australian leading. There is a good battle for third place, with Bautista joining the fray, albeit 9 seconds behind Dovizioso.

Lap 16:
Pellino falls from 16th spot.

Finish (19 laps):
110 thousandths separate the two men who dominated the race as they crossed the line at the end of the penultimate lap. As he had predicted, Dovizioso went for it all the way to the line, but in the end he was beaten by just 29 thousandths, with KTM taking its first win.

Championship:
A 79 point lead with only 50 left on the table, so Andrea Dovizioso is the first champion to be crowned in 2004. He led the series from start to finish, from the end of the season opener in South Africa.

Malaysian Grand Prix
10th October 2004 / Sepang – 5.548 m

STARTING GRID

1.	34	A. Dovizioso	Honda	2'12.684
2.	3	H. Barbera	Aprilia	2'13.576
3.	27	C. Stoner	KTM	2'13.718
4.	58	M. Simoncelli	Aprilia	2'13.843
5.	48	J. Lorenzo	Derbi	2'13.969
6.	36	M. Kallio	KTM	2'14.346
7.	15	R. Locatelli	Aprilia	2'14.479
8.	22	P. Nieto	Aprilia	2'14.487
9.	6	M. Giansanti	Aprilia	2'14.534
10.	32	F. Lai	Gilera	2'14.568
11.	14	G. Talmacsi	Malaguti	2'14.664
12.	7	S. Perugini	Gilera	2'14.680
13.	19	A. Bautista	Aprilia	2'14.915
14.	24	S. Corsi	Honda	2'15.015
15.	10	J. Simon	Honda	2'15.281
16.	21	S. Jenkner	Aprilia	2'15.316
17.	54	M. Pasini	Aprilia	2'15.379
18.	23	G. Borsoi	Aprilia	2'15.379
19.	12	T. Lüthi	Honda	2'15.519
20.	52	L. Pesek	Honda	2'15.876
21.	47	A. Rodriguez	Derbi	2'16.123
22.	50	A. Ballerini	Aprilia	2'16.150
23.	33	S. Gadea	Aprilia	2'16.358
24.	63	M. Di Meglio	Aprilia	2'16.428
25.	42	G. Pellino	Aprilia	2'16.444
26.	26	D. Giuseppetti	Honda	2'16.552
27.	45	L. Zanetti	Aprilia	2'16.649
28.	62	T. Kuzuhara	Honda	2'17.058
29.	25	I. Toth	Aprilia	2'17.741
30.	66	V. Kallio	Aprilia	2'17.751
31.	8	M. Manna	Malaguti	2'18.154
32.	28	J. Carchano	Aprilia	2'18.516
33.	16	R. Schouten	Honda	2'18.554
34.	31	M. Sabbatani	Honda	2'18.902
35.	9	M. Janakova	Honda	2'19.389

RACE: 19 LAPS = 105.412 km

1. Casey Stoner	43'10.360 (146.498 km/h)
2. Andrea Dovizioso	+ 0"029
3. Alvaro Bautista	+ 6"547
4. Roberto Locatelli	+ 11"579
5. Fabrizio Lai	+ 17"136
6. Julian Simon	+ 17"146
7. Mattia Pasini	+ 24"985
8. Gabor Talmacsi	+ 25"057
9. Gino Borsoi	+ 25"262
10. Steve Jenkner	+ 26"905
11. Thomas Lüthi	+ 36"819
12. Sergio Gadea	+ 45"558
13. Dario Giuseppetti	+ 47"997
14. Andrea Ballerini	+ 48"441
15. Toshihisa Kuzuhara	+ 1'06.926
16. Jordi Carchano	+ 1'18.854
17. Mike Di Meglio	+ 1'18.898
18. Imre Toth	+ 1'24.061
19. Raymond Schouten	+ 1'27.129
20. Lorenzo Zanetti	+ 3 laps

Fastest lap:
Stoner, in 2'14.928 (148.025 km/h).
Record: Cecchinello, in 2'13.919 (149.140 km/h/2002)

Outright fastest lap: Lorenzo, in 2'09.569 (149.480 km/h/2004).

CHAMPIONSHIP

1. A. Dovizioso	248 (4 wins)
2. R. Locatelli	169 (2 wins)
3. H. Barbera	167 (3 wins)
4. J. Lorenzo	159 (3 wins)
5. C. Stoner	129 (1 win)
6. P. Nieto	124
7. A. Bautista	106
8. S. Jenkner	105
9. M. Giansanti	98
10. M. Kallio	86

GAULOISES
46
THE DOCTOR
YAMAHA
MOTUL
agv
KERAKOLL
DAINESE

AUSTRALIA
Phillip Island

A dream décor for a king. At the Phillip Island circuit that he loves because it favours the human element in the sport, Valentino Rossi makes sure of his sixth world title by winning the race after a magical duel with Sete Gibernau. Even though their rider is beaten, our Spanish colleagues maintain their sense of humour as they take to the waves in the Bass straights. It made Miss Suzuka smile...

MOTOGP

Australian Grand Prix 17th October 2004 / Phillip Island – 4.448 m

STARTING GRID

1.	15	S. Gibernau	Honda	1'30.122
2.	46	V. Rossi	Yamaha	1'30.222
3.	65	L. Capirossi	Ducati	1'30.613
4.	45	C. Edwards	Honda	1'30.625
5.	6	M. Tamada	Honda	1'30.716
6.	4	A. Barros	Honda	1'30.757
7.	3	M. Biaggi	Honda	1'30.767
8.	66	A. Hofmann	Kawasaki	1'30.819
9.	12	T. Bayliss	Ducati	1'30.873
10.	33	M. Melandri	Yamaha	1'30.927
11.	56	S. Nakano	Kawasaki	1'31.093
12.	11	R. Xaus	Ducati	1'31.191
13.	7	C. Checa	Yamaha	1'31.359
14.	69	N. Hayden	Honda	1'31.377
15.	99	J. McWilliams	Aprilia	1'31.491
16.	32	G. Lavilla	Suzuki	1'31.846
17.	21	J. Hopkins	Suzuki	1'31.911
18.	17	N. Abé	Yamaha	1'32.452
19.	50	N. Hodgson	Ducati	1'32.531
20.	24	G. McCoy	Aprilia	1'32.712
21.	9	N. Aoki	Proton KR	1'32.857
22.	36	J. Haydon	Proton KR	1'33.317
23.	77	J. Ellison	Harris WCM	1'33.608
24.	41	Y. Ui	Harris WCM	1'35.280

RACE: 27 LAPS = 120.096 km

1.	Valentino Rossi	41'25.819 (173.924 km/h)
2.	Sete Gibernau	+ 0"097
3.	Loris Capirossi	+ 10"486
4.	Colin Edwards	+ 10"817
5.	Alexandre Barros	+ 10"851
6.	Nicky Hayden	+ 12"210
7.	Massimiliano Biaggi	+ 12"847
8.	Makoto Tamada	+ 12"965
9.	Troy Bayliss	+ 18"607
10.	Carlos Checa	+ 21"245
11.	Ruben Xaus	+ 23"173
12.	Shinya Nakano	+ 25"718
13.	Alex Hofmann	+ 35"137
14.	Jeremy McWilliams	+ 45"155
15.	John Hopkins	+ 45"197
16.	Gregorio Lavilla	+ 52"205
17.	Norifumi Abé	+ 52"665
18.	Neil Hodgson	+ 1'11.394
19.	Nobuatsu Aoki	+ 1 lap
20.	James Haydon	+ 1 lap
21.	Youichi Ui	+ 1 lap
22.	James Ellison	+ 3 laps

Fastest lap:
Capirossi, in 1'31.102 (175.767 km/h). New record.
Previous record: Rossi, in 1'31.421 (175.154 km/h/2003).

Outright fastest lap: : Rossi, in 1'30.068 (177.785 km/h/2003).

CHAMPIONSHIP

1.	V. Rossi	279 (8 wins)
2.	S. Gibernau	244 (4 wins)
3.	M. Biaggi	197 (1 win)
4.	A. Barros	155
5.	C. Edwards	149
6.	M. Tamada	139 (2 wins)
7.	N. Hayden	117
8.	C. Checa	115
9.	L. Capirossi	110
10.	R. Xaus	77

It takes two champions to put on a great show, but having led for most of the race, Sete Gibernau had to give best as the honourable loser.

Runners and riders:
The Roberts brothers are still absent. After Kagayama had stepped in twice in the Suzuka camp, this time, the team's test rider, Spaniard Gregorio Lavilla is in the saddle. The day before qualifying, the first transfer for next year is confirmed: Colin Edwards is to join his mate Valentino Rossi in the works Yamaha team.

Qualifying:
Rossi and Gibernau continue to ignore one another for yet another week and the only thing they swap is fastest times. Rossi is quickest on Friday, but Gibernau robs him of pole by exactly one tenth on Saturday. The scene is therefore set. In the Kawasaki camp, Alex Hoffman, whose future is in doubt, is quicker than Shinya Nakano for the first time. Capirossi hoists the works Ducati onto the front row.

Start:
Capirossi is off like a jack-in-the-box, but Gibernau is pumped up and takes the lead, while Rossi gets his wheels on the dirt as he pushes to keep up with his new "enemy." By the end of an action packed opening lap, Gibernau leads Rossi by 1"195, with Capirossi already dropping back and heading Bayliss, Barros and Biaggi.

Lap 3:
Rossi has closed to within 703 thousandths.

Lap 5:
Garry McCoy has retired. Capirossi sets the fastest lap and is back in touch with the lead pair, bringing Barros with him, but not for long.

Lap 10:
Gibernau and Rossi are out on their own again, with 232 thousandths between them. Barros has got the better of Capirossi and is trying to close the gap.

Half distance (13 laps):
Gibernau still leads Rossi. At this point, 25 points separate the two men, so that Rossi is virtually world champion. He won't be if Barros, or anyone else for that matter, manages to get between the two leaders.

A Ducati on the podium after Capirossi got the better of Barros.

Lap 16:
Marco Melandri is an ignominious retirement with dirt in his eye.

Lap 18:
Rossi attempts a first attack when there is just 60 thousandths between the two men and the champion blasts past at the end of the straight.

Lap 20:
Rossi leads by a quarter of a second.

Lap 21:
The number 46 bike runs slightly wide and the two men touch. The fight would be fantastic all the way to the flag.

Finish (27 laps):
On the last lap, Rossi finds a gap that is too small to see, Sete fights back, but Valentino has one last passing move up his sleeve and takes his eighth win of 2004.

Championship:
With 35 points in hand, Rossi is champion with one race still to go.

Rossi: the icing on the cake

He could so easily have been spooked, thrown into the turquoise skies above Phillip Island, landing with a bump and hurting himself in those first few decisive moments of the Australian GP, as he put both wheels of his blue Yamaha on the dirt, by a few centimetres.
He could also have taken his time and settled for second place, where he had been for much of the race, locked into the slipstream of Sete Gibernau's Honda. Valentino Rossi could have done all those things and he would still have become world champion for a sixth time. But he did not, precisely because he is Valentino Rossi, "Valentinik," "The Doctor," "The Master," "Rossifumi," or whatever you want to call him by flicking through his already extensive list of nicknames.
But for this crucial grand prix, "I wanted to do all I could to avoid having to fight for the title in Valencia on my main rival's home turf." He had vowed to take his sixth and supreme title with a win, to serve notice that he was not the sort to compromise by doing the maths. He wanted to celebrate by putting the icing on his new and tasty cake.
At Phillip Island, a track he loves, he made two clear attacking moves and they proved decisive. He turned up the pressure at just the right time and just the right place. With a job well done, those watching from behind the small television screens on the pit wall were taking bets on what Rossi would come up with for his lap of honour. What would the king of comedy have in store for the fans who love him, after this emotional end to his perfect season on board the Yamaha M1, that had been written off as uncompetitive just twelve short months ago?
Typically of Valentino Rossi, a complex sort of guy who can be as hard to read as he can sometimes be unpredictable, he chose dignity. He donned a white helmet that he would later toss into the crowd from the top step of the podium. Then came a simple white T-shirt, with a simple message that spoke more than any hymn, motto or poem: "Che spettacolo!" Yes, what a spectacle! It is never ending with this young man who is now being courted by Formula 1, who is the highest paid sportsman in Italy, but still has a sense of values. He shared his victory with his clan of six or seven friends who have been together since primary school in Tavullia. Valentino likes to know they are there when the going gets tough and likes to chat about other things than racing. It helps him forget he is the centre of attention for millions and that the man with the number 46 is quite simply a unique phenomenon. And yet still a simple man.

"Que spettacolo!" Yes, Valentino Rossi is always spectacular.

Gibernau attacks immediately, but Rossi does not let him get away with it. At one braking point, he deals with both works Ducati riders; Capirossi and Bayliss.

250cc

Australian Grand Prix
17th October 2004 / Phillip Island – 4.448 m

STARTING GRID

1.	19	S. Porto	Aprilia	1'32.099
2.	51	A. De Angelis	Aprilia	1'32.986
3.	54	M. Poggiali	Aprilia	1'33.210
4.	26	D. Pedrosa	Honda	1'33.225
5.	7	R. De Puniet	Aprilia	1'33.764
6.	10	F. Gonzales-Nieto	Aprilia	1'34.240
7.	73	H. Aoyama	Honda	1'34.358
8.	21	F. Battaini	Aprilia	1'34.576
9.	24	T. Elias	Honda	1'34.583
10.	57	C. Davies	Aprilia	1'35.027
11.	6	A. Debon	Honda	1'35.084
12.	16	J. Stigefelt	Aprilia	1'35.217
13.	50	S. Guintoli	Aprilia	1'35.339
14.	96	J. Smrz	Honda	1'35.568
15.	8	N. Matsudo	Yamaha	1'35.574
16.	36	E. Nigon	Aprilia	1'35.658
17.	2	R. Rolfo	Honda	1'35.824
18.	52	D. De Gea	Honda	1'35.863
19.	9	H. Marchand	Aprilia	1'35.890
20.	25	A. Baldolini	Aprilia	1'36.227
21.	11	J. Olive	Aprilia	1'36.675
22.	42	G. Leblanc	Aprilia	1'36.814
23.	14	A. West (*)	Aprilia	1'36.949
24.	43	R. Rous	Yamaha	1'37.090
25.	28	D. Heidolf	Aprilia	1'37.144
26.	44	T. Sekiguchi	Yamaha	1'37.249
27.	33	H. Faubel	Aprilia	1'37.376
28.	82	J. Waters	Honda	1'38.149
Not qualified:				
	88	Ge. Talmacsi	Yamaha	1'38.728
	81	M. Rowling	Yamaha	1'41.268
	80	P. Taplin	Honda	1'44.428
	84	B. Ried	Yamaha	1'48.308

(*) A. West (AUS, Aprilia) suffered a frightening fall in qualifying and pulled out.

RACE: 25 LAPS = 111.200 km

1.	Sebastian Porto	39'24.604 (169.296 km/h)
2.	Alex De Angelis	+ 5"941
3.	Manuel Poggiali	+ 13"289
4.	Daniel Pedrosa	+ 14"966
5.	Toni Elias	+ 46"083
6.	Chaz Davies	+ 55"140
7.	Hiroshi Aoyama	+ 1'01.014
8.	Sylvain Guintoli	+ 1'04.684
9.	Johan Stigefelt	+ 1'07.656
10.	Roberto Rolfo	+ 1'09.889
11.	Alex Debon	+ 1'13.572
12.	Hugo Marchand	+ 1'13.608
13.	Jakub Smrz	+ 1'14.681
14.	David De Gea	+ 1'21.473
15.	Naoki Matsudo	+ 1'21.515
16.	Hector Faubel	+ 1'26.860
17.	Gregory Leblanc	+ 1'30.317
18.	Joshua Waters	+ 1 lap
19.	Radomil Rous	+ 1 lap

Fastest lap:
Porto, in 1'33.381 (171.478 km/h). New record.
Previous record: Rossi, in 1'33.556 (171.157 km/h/1999).

Outright fastest lap: Porto, in 1'32.099 (173.099 km/h/2004).

CHAMPIONSHIP

1.	D. Pedrosa	292 (6 wins)
2.	S. Porto	256 (5 wins)
3.	R. De Puniet	198 (1 win)
4.	T. Elias	179 (1 win)
5.	A. De Angelis	147
6.	H. Aoyama	128
7.	A. Gonzales-Nieto	114
8.	R. Rolfo	107 (1 win)
9.	M. Poggiali	95 (1 win)
10.	A. West	88

Intelligence in the shape of a rider, as Daniel Pedrosa takes the 250 world championship title.

Runners and riders:
Poggiali is back. Germany's Klaus Nohles is absent, injured at Sepang and he is replaced by Australia's Joshua Waters.

Qualifying:
Even though he is known for his calm approach, championship leader Dani Pedrosa, who needs two points to be crowned, is bristling with tension on arrival at Phillip Island, which has bad memories for him. Twelve months ago, having just been crowned 125 cc world champion, he fractured both ankles in Friday morning's free practice. Pedrosa was in cautious mood, but it did not prevent him giving himself a fright on Saturday, when he fell at the end of the session, with the marshals having to carry him away from danger. But there were no serious injuries and the Spaniard kept his place on the grid. Porto was yet again on top form. De Puniet had to fight a recalcitrant engine that seized three times during practice.

Start:
De Angelis is promptest off the blocks, followed by Pedrosa and Porto, who soon takes the lead. "Fonsi" Gonzales-Nieto gets it all wrong, falling and taking Debon with him, although the latter keeps going, as well as Battaini, who also manages to continue, but not for long. At the end of the first lap, Pedrosa leads De Angelis and Porto.

Lap 4:
Porto is the strongest man in the closing stages of the championship. In the space of two laps, he pulls out a lead of 2"068 over his closest pursuers, Pedrosa and De Angelis.

Lap 5:
Randy De Puniet's miserable end of season continues with a fall.

Lap 8:
Battaini retires as a result of his fall on the opening lap. Erwan Nigon is shown the black flag for jumping the start and not pitting for his drive through penalty.

Half distance (13 laps):
Porto's lead is now over 4 seconds. De Angelis is having a lonely race in second place, while Pedrosa is controlling his fight with Poggiali.

Lap 20:
Porto now leads De Angelis by 5"863. Pedrosa is 8 seconds off the San Marino rider.

Lap 22:
Poggiali passes Pedrosa, who does not put up much of a fight.

Finish (25 laps):
It's been Porto's show and a great delight for Pedrosa, who finishes fourth. The Spaniard thus becomes the youngest ever 250 world champion at the age of 19 years and 18 days.

Championship:
Pedrosa is duly crowned and Porto is sure of second place. De Puniet is still under threat from a final assault from Elias.

A mistake in the shape of a rider: Alfonso Gonzales-Nieto has just knocked over his team-mate, Alex Debon.

I've made my mind up. When I grow up I will be a racer like Hector Barbera.

Runners and riders:
The Malaysian GP has left its mark: Marco Simoncelli scratches from the meeting, undergoing treatment in Italy. Marketa Janakova is also a non-starter and the Angaia team replace her with an Australian rider, Matthew Kuhne.

Qualifying:
It rained overnight on Thursday to Friday and the track is still damp for the morning's free practice. On Saturday, conditions are perfect and there's an entertaining scrap between Locatelli, Lorenzo and Stoner. Dovizioso is "only" fifth.

Start:
Stoner had a terrible start to the day, with a fall in the warm-up. However, the Australian has no intention of missing his home race and he is so pumped up that he leads through the first corner, ahead of Dovizioso, who will soon take command.

Lap 3:
Lorenzo takes the lead, with Dovizioso and Stoner glued to his back wheel. Slightly off the group is fourth placed Locatelli who tries to close the gap. The pack fighting for fifth is already over 4 seconds down.

Lap 5:
The gap is closed and four of them run wheel to wheel: Lorenzo, Stoner, Dovizioso and Locatelli.

Lap 7:
Dovizioso sets the fastest time and pulls out a slight lead. Angel Rodriguez retires with a clutch problem.

Lap 10:
Dovizioso now leads the chasing pack of Lorenzo, Stoner and Locatelli by 232 thousandths. Jenkner heads the second group, 5"398 behind.

Half distance (12 laps):
Stefano Perugini commits the cardinal sin of motorised sport by falling and collecting his team-mate Fabrizio Lai on the way down. Locatelli is dropped and that leaves three in the fight for the win: Dovizioso, Lorenzo and Stoner.

Lap 17:
Incredibly, Lorenzo is moving around his bike, indicating that Stoner and Dovizioso should pass, which sees Locatelli close to within 1"145.

Lap 18:
Mika Kallio retires (rear tyre.)

Finish (23 laps):
The final lap is crazy, as Lorenzo passes with a slipstreaming move at the end of the straight, but Dovizioso counterattacks immediately, taking Stoner with him. The world champion crosses the line 123 thousandths ahead of his two rivals, who are given the same time to the nearest thousandth. (as happened in Qatar, it is Lorenzo who is given second place thanks to a photo finish.)

Championship:
With the title already decided, attention focuses on second place, where three riders – Locatelli, Lorenzo and Barbera are separated by five points.

There was only one way that a guy like Andrea Dovizioso, seen here ahead of Lorenzo and Locatelli, was going to celebrate the fact he was world champion and that was by winning a race.

Australian Grand Prix 17th October 2004 / Phillip Island – 4.448 m

STARTING GRID

1.	15	R. Locatelli	Aprilia	1'37.417
2.	48	J. Lorenzo	Derbi	1'37.543
3.	27	C. Stoner	KTM	1'37.590
4.	21	S. Jenkner	Aprilia	1'38.147
5.	34	A. Dovizioso	Honda	1'38.238
6.	23	G. Borsoi	Aprilia	1'38.375
7.	36	M. Kallio	KTM	1'38.386
8.	3	H. Barbera	Aprilia	1'38.389
9.	6	M. Giansanti	Aprilia	1'38.643
10.	10	J. Simon	Honda	1'38.674
11.	52	L. Pesek	Honda	1'38.725
12.	14	G. Talmacsi	Malaguti	1'38.790
13.	22	P. Nieto	Aprilia	1'38.854
14.	33	S. Gadea	Aprilia	1'38.865
15.	7	S. Perugini	Gilera	1'38.870
16.	63	M. Di Meglio	Aprilia	1'38.907
17.	47	A. Rodriguez	Derbi	1'39.072
18.	32	F. Lai	Gilera	1'39.263
19.	50	A. Ballerini	Aprilia	1'39.298
20.	25	I. Toth	Aprilia	1'39.357
21.	24	S. Corsi	Honda	1'39.366
22.	12	T. Lüthi	Honda	1'39.637
23.	54	M. Pasini	Aprilia	1'39.708
24.	19	A. Bautista	Aprilia	1'39.865
25.	45	L. Zanetti	Aprilia	1'39.938
26.	26	D. Giuseppetti	Honda	1'40.135
27.	66	V. Kallio	Aprilia	1'40.264
28.	8	M. Manna	Malaguti	1'40.801
29.	42	G. Pellino	Aprilia	1'41.265
30.	46	M. Kuhne	Honda	1'41.792
31.	92	B. Staring	Honda	1'41.896
32.	16	R. Schouten	Honda	1'42.237
33.	31	M. Sabbatani	Honda	1'42.563
34.	28	J. Carchano	Aprilia	1'42.592
Not qualified:				
	94	B. Rigoli	Honda	1'44.503
	93	M. Esler	Honda	1'45.397
	56	M. Simmonds	Honda	1'45.803

RACE: 23 LAPS = 102.304 km

1. Andrea Dovizioso	38'01.877 (161.399 km/h)
2. Jorge Lorenzo	+ 0"123
3. Casey Stoner	+ 0"123
4. Roberto Locatelli	+ 2"480
5. Steve Jenkner	+ 5"336
6. Hector Barbera	+ 5"415
7. Gino Borsoi	+ 5"448
8. Mike Di Meglio	+ 17"976
9. Alvaro Bautista	+ 18"404
10. Sergio Gadea	+ 18"427
11. Gabor Talmacsi	+ 18"501
12. Lukas Pesek	+ 18"530
13. Mirko Giansanti	+ 18"739
14. Andrea Ballerini	+ 19"331
15. Pablo Nieto	+ 19"826
16. Simone Corsi	+ 27"971
17. Gioele Pellino	+ 27"983
18. Mattia Pasini	+ 27"996
19. Thomas Lüthi	+ 28"006
20. Julian Simon	+ 28"892
21. Imre Toth	+ 40"943
22. Dario Giuseppetti	+ 41"080
23. Vesa Kallio	+ 48"127
24. Lorenzo Zanetti	+ 55"439
25. Max Sabbatani	+ 1'28.474
26. Raymond Schouten	+ 1'28.656
27. Matthew Kuhne	+ 1'28.730
28. Jordi Carchano	+ 1'36.917
29. Bryan Staring	+ 3 laps

Fastest lap:
Dovizioso, in 1'38.024 (163.355 km/h).
Record: Pedrosa, in 1'37.983 (163.424 km/h/2002)

Outright fastest lap: Perugini, in 1'37.342 (164.500 km/h/2003).

CHAMPIONSHIP

1. A. Dovizioso	273 (5 wins)
2. R. Locatelli	182 (2 wins)
3. J. Lorenzo	179 (3 wins)
4. H. Barbera	177 (3 wins)
5. C. Stoner	145 (1 win)
6. P. Nieto	125
7. S. Jenkner	116
8. A. Bautista	113
9. M. Giansanti	101
10. M. Kallio	86

MoviStar
GAULOISES
46
GAULOISES
GAULOISES

VALENCIA
Cheste

It was one big party and the atmosphere was contagious. As Valentino Rossi embarked on a victory lap, a track marshal grabbed a chequered flag and played at race director, in a personal tribute to the champion. The season ended on a high, not just for Rossi, but for the championship as a whole, which welcomed another world star, the giant American basketball player, Michael Jordan, here surrounded by Sete Gibernau and Kenny and Kurtis Roberts. The other hero of the day? Daniel Pedrosa and this colourful fan.

Valencia Grand Prix
31st October 2004 / Cheste – 4.005 m

STARTING GRID

1.	6	M. Tamada	Honda	1'32.815
2.	3	M. Biaggi	Honda	1'32.831
3.	46	V. Rossi	Yamaha	1'32.913
4.	15	S. Gibernau	Honda	1'32.936
5.	69	N. Hayden	Honda	1'32.999
6.	12	T. Bayliss	Ducati	1'33.083
7.	21	J. Hopkins	Suzuki	1'33.422
8.	45	C. Edwards	Honda	1'33.438
9.	7	C. Checa	Yamaha	1'33.504
10.	56	S. Nakano	Kawasaki	1'33.557
11.	66	A. Hofmann	Kawasaki	1'33.723
12.	4	A. Barros	Honda	1'33.773
13.	65	L. Capirossi	Ducati	1'33.781
14.	99	J. McWilliams	Aprilia	1'34.104
15.	17	N. Abé	Yamaha	1'34.175
16.	33	M. Melandri	Yamaha	1'34.209
17.	11	R. Xaus	Ducati	1'34.280
18.	50	N. Hodgson	Ducati	1'34.602
19.	32	G. Lavilla	Suzuki	1'34.974
20.	24	G. McCoy	Aprilia	1'35.064
21.	9	N. Aoki	Proton KR	1'35.082
22.	19	O. Jacque	Moriwaki	1'36.394
23.	77	J. Ellison	Harris WCM	1'37.143
24.	80	Ku. Roberts (*)	Proton KR	1'37.922
25.	35	C. Burns	Harris WCM	1'38.661

(*):Ku. Roberts (USA, Proton KR) withdrew after Friday practice.

RACE: 30 LAPS = 120.150 km

1.	Valentino Rossi	47'16.145 (152.509 km/h)
2.	Massimiliano Biaggi	+ 0"425
3.	Troy Bayliss	+ 3"133
4.	Sete Gibernau	+ 6"128
5.	Makoto Tamada	+ 7"768
6.	Alexandre Barros	+ 14"675
7.	Shinya Nakano	+ 23"315
8.	Colin Edwards	+ 27"441
9.	Loris Capirossi	+ 29"403
10.	Norifumi Abé	+ 31"537
11.	Alex Hofmann	+ 40"951
12.	John Hopkins	+ 1'02.014
13.	Jeremy McWilliams	+ 1'04.637
14.	Carlos Checa	+ 1'08.042
15.	Neil Hodgson	+ 1'09.364
16.	Garry McCoy	+ 1'15.022
17.	Gregorio Lavilla	+ 1'15.274
18.	Nobuatsu Aoki	+ 1 lap
19.	James Ellison	+ 1 lap

Fastest lap:
Biaggi, in 1'33.582 (154.068 km/h).
Record: Rossi, in 1'33.317 (154.505 km/h/2003).

Outright fastest lap: Rossi, in 1'32.478 (155.907 km/h/2003).

CHAMPIONSHIP

1.	V. Rossi	304 (9 wins)
2.	S. Gibernau	257 (4 wins)
3.	M. Biaggi	217 (1 win)
4.	A. Barros	165
5.	C. Edwards	157
6.	M. Tamada	150 (2 wins)
7.	C. Checa	117
8.	N. Hayden	117
9.	L. Capirossi	117
10.	S. Nakano	83

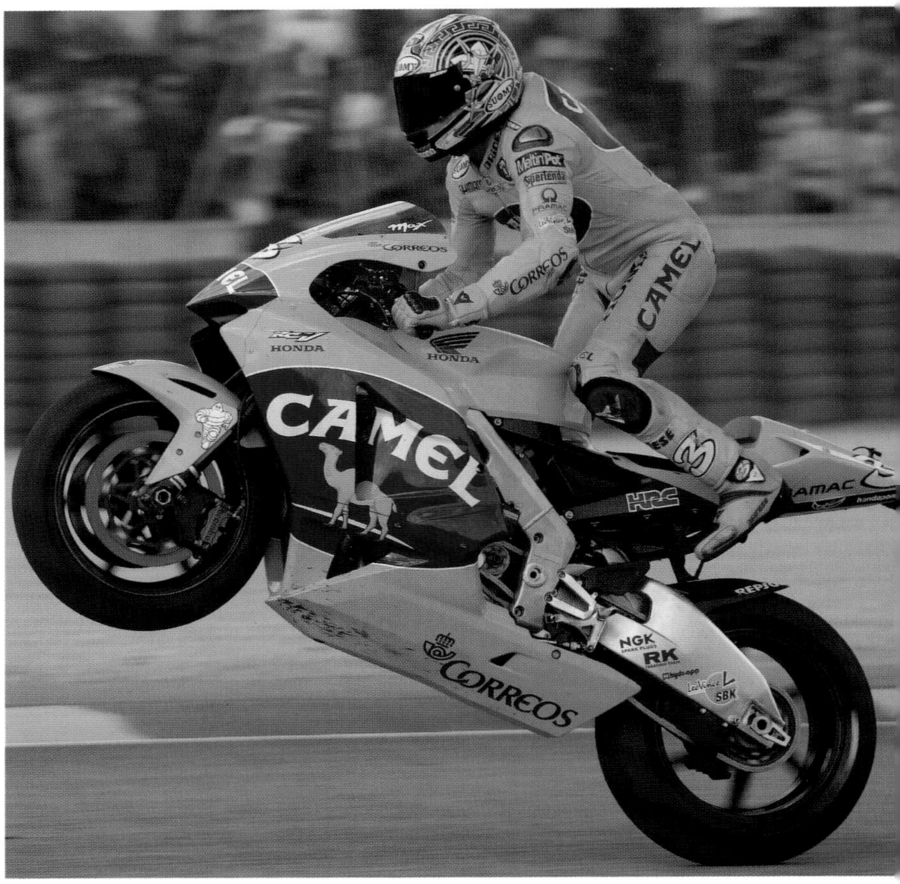

Max Biaggi after the finish. The man from Rome is already ready for 2005!

Runners and riders:
The Roberts brothers are finally back in action. Having set the fastest time in Friday's free practice, Kenny decides his elbow is hurting too much and he is replaced by Lavilla. Brother Kurtis takes part in qualifying on the first day, but he too throws in the towel. As expected, Olivier Jacque is here with Moriwaki on a wild card.

Qualifying:
Gibernau is fastest on Friday by just 3 thousandths. On Saturday, it's Tamada who puts everyone in the shade. On the first day, Rossi tries a new exhaust configuration on his Yamaha. Troy Bayliss, who has lost his Ducati ride, is much in evidence.

Start:
An on-form Tamada makes the perfect start, ahead of Biaggi, Bayliss and Gibernau. Rossi is "only" sixth at the first split. Tamada's opening lap is exceptional and he leads Biaggi by 627 thousandths.

Lap 3:
Biaggi and Gibernau lean on one another, allowing Rossi to whiz past both of them. So Tamada still leads, 869 thousandths ahead of Rossi.

A nice story from this weekend was the third place for Troy Bayliss, who has been shown the door by Ducati.

Lap 5:
Rossi has closed the gap to Tamada down to 208 thousandths. Further back, Gibernau and Biaggi fight tooth and nail over fourth place.

Lap 6:
Rossi has found a chink in Tamada's armour and does not need to be asked twice.

Lap 8:
Tamada slipstreams back into the lead. Hayden has caught up and Biaggi is not far back either, having dropped Gibernau, who is now fending off Bayliss. Checa is a faller.

Lap 9:
The lead four; Tamada, Rossi, Hayden and Biaggi are now covered by just over a second (1"164.)

Lap 11:
First Xaus and then Melandri fall.

Half distance (15 laps):
Rossi has just gone back in front. He leads Tamada by 96 thousandths as they cross the line. Biaggi is third, right behind his sort of team-mate. Hayden still hangs on.

Lap 17:
Rossi has built up a lead over Tamada of 738 thousandths. An impressive Bayliss has closed to within half a second of the lead pair. At this point, he is the quickest man on track.

Lap 18:
Max goes second and Hayden is also about to pass Tamada.

Lap 22:
Hayden gets it all wrong and only just avoids colliding with Biaggi. Bayliss finds himself back in third.

Lap 23:
Hayden is a faller and fellow countryman and spectator, Michael Jordan, shakes his head. Lap 28: Gibernau passes Tamada to go fourth as the Bridgestones have failed to go the distance this time.

Finish (30 laps):
And it's win number 9 for his majesty "Vale" Rossi!

Rossi's ninth symphony

It was a memorable event and a great day, with no less than 122,034 spectators hollering from the stands in their inimitable way. One of the marshals at the Ricardo Tormo track took it upon himself to play race director. As the winner on the day and the hero of 2004, Valentino Rossi went past on his victory lap, the marshal got hold of a chequered flag and waved it. It was a symbolic gesture which was a perfect way to end a season that belonged to just one man, the diabolically quick Rossi. He switched from the challenge of winning with the giant that is Honda to doing the same on a Yamaha, that was reckoned to be far from competitive. He won by his own efforts. He was the master of the game, a genial composer who, like Beethoven, composed yet another masterpiece on this unique Cheste track. It was his ninth win from sixteen grands prix, a ninth superb composition. Rossi had won his bet two weeks earlier in Australia and he rounded it off this October weekend with a ninth victory: "as many as with Honda, not bad is it?" He won here in Valencia, where twelve months earlier he had announced he was quitting the dominant force in the sport. At the time, because of the usual contractual wrangling, he had not been able to say where he was going. "My day?.... I just fell asleep a bit at the start and I lost quite a lot of time in the opening minutes. Also, it has to be said that in the early stages, Tamada and his Bridgestones were very incisive." Typical Rossi.

Valentino Rossi, the man in charge, is about to tackle Tamada. Once again, no one could match him.

After that, it was pure Rossi at his best. He attacked when he wanted to, stepped up the pace and then fought off the advances of Biaggi, before opening yet another magnum of champagne. "A year ago here in Valencia I was full of doubt," recalled Valentino. "I was sitting in this same seat and I had just taken an important decision about my future and I could never have imagined it would all turn out so well." On that final Sunday night, he picked up his diploma for a sixth world title, but two days later he was back in the saddle to prepare for 2005. "I am convinced that Honda will make huge efforts to try and get the title back next year. But, rest assured that, at Yamaha, we are not about to go to sleep. We have a very clear idea of where we have to improve."
That's Rossi for you, a tireless worker. A few hours after the Phillip Island race, he went through the race with his engineers, sitting in front of the computer screens and a few days after the final day of the 2004 season, he was back at work. "In our job, the winner is always right," commented a certain Max B on Sunday night of the 31st October 2004, a former enemy of the six times world champion. "Rossi and Yamaha have won this year and I hope others will understand why." We eagerly await next year to see if the message has got through to Honda.

Front view of a champion...

... and from behind, with Tamada, Biaggi and Hayden left in his wake.

250cc

Valencia Grand Prix
31st October 2004 / Cheste – 4.005 m

STARTING GRID

1.	26	D. Pedrosa	Honda	1'36.367
2.	19	S. Porto	Aprilia	1'36.535
3.	51	A. De Angelis	Aprilia	1'36.800
4.	7	R. De Puniet	Aprilia	1'36.813
5.	24	T. Elias	Honda	1'36.900
6.	21	F. Battaini	Aprilia	1'37.071
7.	73	H. Aoyama	Honda	1'37.123
8.	54	M. Poggiali	Aprilia	1'37.307
9.	8	N. Matsudo	Yamaha	1'37.446
10.	57	C. Davies	Aprilia	1'37.461
11.	6	A. Debon	Honda	1'37.482
12.	52	D. De Gea	Honda	1'37.944
13.	33	H. Faubel	Aprilia	1'38.184
14.	96	J. Smrz	Honda	1'38.354
15.	11	J. Olive	Aprilia	1'38.383
16.	10	F. Gonzales-Nieto	Aprilia	1'38.541
17.	50	S. Guintoli	Aprilia	1'38.684
18.	2	R. Rolfo	Honda	1'38.688
19.	28	D. Heidolf	Aprilia	1'38.916
20.	12	A. Vincent	Aprilia	1'38.952
21.	25	A. Baldolini	Aprilia	1'39.021
22.	9	H. Marchand (*)	Aprilia	1'39.590
23.	16	J. Stigefelt	Aprilia	1'39.680
24.	44	T. Sekiguchi	Yamaha	1'39.748
25.	36	E. Nigon (**)	Aprilia	1'39.905
26.	42	G. Leblanc	Aprilia	1'40.043
27.	41	A. Molina	Aprilia	1'40.329
28.	64	F. Watz	Honda	1'40.384
29.	43	R. Rous	Yamaha	1'40.712
30.	75	H. Smees	Aprilia	1'40.916
31.	63	J. Ronzoni	Aprilia	1'41.369
Not qualified:				
	88	Ge. Talmacsi	Yamaha	1'43.375

(*): H. Marchand (F, Aprilia) withdrew from the race suffering from concussion.
(**): E. Nigon (F, Aprilia) was withdrawn from the race by his team, after his Saturday afternoon accident.

RACE: 27 LAPS = 108.135 km (*)

1. Daniel Pedrosa	44'10.176 (146.890 km/h)
2. Toni Elias	+ 8"086
3. Randy De Puniet	+ 27"412
4. Franco Battaini	+ 31"620
5. Chaz Davies	+ 34"059
6. A. Gonzales-Nieto	+ 34"784
7. Roberto Rolfo	+ 40"352
8. Naoki Matsudo	+ 46"761
9. Hector Faubel	+ 46"770
10. Alex Baldolini	+ 58"235
11. David De Gea	+ 1'03.287
12. Arnaud Vincent	+ 1'05.615
13. Jakub Smrz	+ 1'06.024
14. Alex Debon	+ 1'06.858
15. Joan Olive	+ 1'10.842
16. Alvaro Molina	+ 1'13.946
17. Johan Stigefelt	+ 1'14.621
18. Dirk Heidolf	+ 1'15.103
19. Radomil Rous	+ 1'40.045
20. Gregory Leblanc	+ 1 lap
21. Hans Smees	+ 1 lap
22. Jarno Ronzoni	+ 1 lap

(*): Hiroshi Aoyama (J, Honda,) had finished third in the race, but was disqualified by the Stewards for an infringement of article 2.5.1. His bike was 500 grammes under the minimum weight limit.

Fastest lap:
Pedrosa, in 1'36.957 (148.705 km/h).
Record: Nakano, in 1'36.398 (149.567 km/h/2000).

Outright fastest lap: Melandri, in 1'35.885 (150.367 km/h/2002).

CHAMPIONSHIP

1. D. Pedrosa	317 (7 wins)
2. S. Porto	256 (5 wins)
3. R. De Puniet	214 (1 win)
4. T. Elias	199 (1 win)
5. A. De Angelis	147
6. H. Aoyama	128
7. A. Gonzales-Nieto	124
8. R. Rolfo	116 (1 win)
9. M. Poggiali	95 (1 win)
10. F. Battaini	93

The last start of the season with Porto and Pedrosa out in front.

Runners and riders:
Arnaud Vincent is back in the Equipe GP de France team, while his stand-in for the past weeks, Leblanc, is also riding thanks to a wild card. Injured at Phillip Island, Australia's Anthony West is replaced by Italy's Jarno Ronzoni, last seen at Mugello. In the German Castrol-Honda team, this time it's the Swede Frederik Watz who replaces Klaus Nohles.

Qualifying:
After a serious fall which leaves him concussed, France's Hugo Marchand scratches from the race after visiting the medical centre. Erwan Nigon also calls it a day. Dani Pedrosa beats Mr. Pole Position, Sebastian Porto, by 168 thousandths.

Aoyama is all smiles on the podium, but he would later be disqualified.

Start:
Porto shoots into the lead ahead of Pedrosa, De Angelis, De Puniet and Elias. As they cross the line for the first time, the Argentinian counts a 342 thousandths lead over the world champion, who has already made a break of half a second over the pack.

Lap 2:
Manuel Poggiali falls, while lying twelfth.

Lap 3:
Pedrosa has just set the fastest time and closed to within 213 thousandths of Porto.

Lap 4:
Alex de Angelis is a faller and Elias and De Puniet only just avoid running into him, with the Frenchman having to take to the gravel trap. The result is that Porto and Pedrosa are now out of reach, 4"774 ahead of the new third placed man, Aoyama.

Lap 5:
Elias passes Aoyama, but the Japanese rider hangs on.

Lap 8:
Alex Debon is a faller.

Lap 11:
Pedrosa has taken the lead, but he loses it again.

Half distance (13 laps):
The world champion had been playing with the opposition, but now it had gone on long enough and so he steps up the pace to cross the line with a lead of 1"130. In third spot, Aoyama is 7"445 behind, still fighting with Elias. De Puniet is a lonely fifth.

Lap 19:
He had got to within just over 2 seconds of Pedrosa, but Porto found himself on the tarmac. There are three Hondas in the lead, as Sylvain Guintoli joins the list of fallers.

Lap 25:
After two failed attempts, Elias takes second place and is the quickest rider on track at this time. Aoyama lets him go.

Finish (27 laps):
We find three HRC riders on the podium, but Aoyama would later be disqualified as his bike was 500 grammes underweight. However, Honda has done enough to take the constructors' world title. A special mention for Englishman, Chaz Davies, who is a brilliant fifth ahead of "Fonsi" Gonzales-Nieto, who has disappointed once again.

Pedrosa defines man and machine in perfect harmony.

125cc

Sergio Gadea, seen here in front of eventual winner, Hector Barbera and Pablo Nieto, was the revelation of the weekend on a circuit that he knows like the back of his hand.

Runners and riders:
Marco Simoncelli is in the paddock, but as predicted, he is not riding and his bike is handed to 18 year old Michele Pirro, the newly crowned European champion in the category. A surprise absentee however is the youngest of all the GP riders, Frenchman Mike Di Meglio, who broke a fibula in Motegi. He made a comeback in Malaysia and had shone in Australia, but now he had undergone another operation two days before practice.

Qualifying:
It is the last grand prix in the category for several riders as, apart from the compulsory retirements, several young lions intend making the move up to the 250 class: Dovizioso, Barbera, Lorenzo, Stoner, the most notable names on the move. The world champion has the final word ahead of a motivated Spanish mob, including Sergio Gadea, a brilliant fifth.

Start:
For his last grand prix, Borsoi charges off into the lead. Further back, Rodriguez and Ballerini hit the tarmac. As they cross the line for the first time, Borsoi leads Dovizioso by 161 thousandths. Then come Stoner, Barbera and Lorenzo.

Lap 2:
Pesek and Perugini retire.

Lap 3:
Dovizio takes command. He is followed by Barbera, Lorenzo and Borsoi.

Lap 4:
The fans are cheering as Barbera is now in the lead. The first four are covered by less than 7 tenths.

Lap 6:
Mika Kallio is a faller.

Lap 7:
Dovizioso just about controls a rodeo moment and so the world champion drops to twelfth. Barbera has pulled out a lead of 852 thousandths over Lorenzo.

Lap 9:
Lorenzo and Borsoi brush fairings and Barbera makes the most of it to pull further ahead. He leads his pursuers by 2"051 and they are fellow countrymen Lorenzo and Bautista. Giuseppetti falls and Dovizioso is back up to eighth.

Half distance (12 laps):
Still Barbera with a lead of just over 2 seconds (2"096.) The top five are all Spaniards: Barbera, Lorenzo, Gadea, Bautista and Pablo Nieto.

Lap 15:
Lorenzo and Stoner fall and so Gadea is now second.

Lap 17:
Barbera has a solid lead, but the battle for second is intense, between Nieto, Gadea, Bautista, Locatelli and Dovizioso who has tagged onto the group.

Lap 21:
Barbera's lead over Nieto is down to 1"817. Dovizioso is third.

Finish (24 laps):
1"209 the gap between Barbera and Dovizioso as they attack the final lap. The Spaniard holds it together to record his fourth win of the season. Bautista is third.

Team-mates Bautista and Barbera share the champagne.

Valencia Grand Prix
31st October 2004 / Cheste – 4.005 m

STARTING GRID

1.	34	A. Dovizioso	Honda	1'39.927
2.	3	H. Barbera	Aprilia	1'40.146
3.	48	J. Lorenzo	Derbi	1'40.413
4.	23	G. Borsoi	Aprilia	1'40.461
5.	33	S. Gadea	Aprilia	1'40.523
6.	27	C. Stoner	KTM	1'40.562
7.	15	R. Locatelli	Aprilia	1'40.571
8.	10	J. Simon	Honda	1'40.662
9.	21	S. Jenkner	Aprilia	1'40.726
10.	14	G. Talmacsi	Malaguti	1'40.909
11.	19	A. Bautista	Aprilia	1'40.971
12.	32	F. Lai	Gilera	1'41.023
13.	24	S. Corsi	Honda	1'41.116
14.	22	P. Nieto	Aprilia	1'41.333
15.	54	M. Pasini	Aprilia	1'41.473
16.	52	L. Pesek	Honda	1'41.487
17.	12	T. Lüthi	Honda	1'41.705
18.	50	A. Ballerini	Aprilia	1'41.736
19.	26	D. Giuseppetti	Honda	1'41.766
20.	36	M. Kallio	KTM	1'41.881
21.	45	L. Zanetti	Aprilia	1'42.229
22.	43	M. Hernandez	Aprilia	1'42.236
23.	47	A. Rodriguez	Derbi	1'42.278
24.	59	N. Terol	Aprilia	1'42.363
25.	6	M. Giansanti	Aprilia	1'42.468
26.	25	I. Toth	Aprilia	1'42.471
27.	7	S. Perugini	Gilera	1'42.508
28.	37	M. Pirro	Aprilia	1'42.647
29.	57	A. Espargaro	Honda	1'42.759
30.	8	M. Manna	Malaguti	1'42.949
31.	66	V. Kallio	Aprilia	1'43.019
32.	42	G. Pellino	Aprilia	1'43.110
33.	70	J. Miralles Jnr	Aprilia	1'43.444
34.	71	E. Jerez	Honda	1'43.578
35.	28	J. Carchano	Aprilia	1'43.594
36.	88	M. Ranseder	KTM	1'43.620
37.	16	R. Schouten	Honda	1'45.069
38.	31	M. Sabbatani	Honda	1'45.161
Not qualified:				
	9	M. Janakova	Honda	1'48.282

RACE: 24 LAPS = 96.120 km

1.	Hector Barbera	40'45.283 (141.510 km/h)
2.	Andrea Dovizioso	+ 0"761
3.	Alvaro Bautista	+ 0"979
4.	Pablo Nieto	+ 1"285
5.	Sergio Gadea	+ 1"338
6.	Roberto Locatelli	+ 3"708
7.	Gino Borsoi	+ 8"782
8.	Simone Corsi	+ 12"425
9.	Gabor Talmacsi	+ 12"515
10.	Steve Jenkner	+ 16"655
11.	Mattia Pasini	+ 19"936
12.	Mirko Giansanti	+ 20"076
13.	Julian Simon	+ 20"127
14.	Thomas Lüthi	+ 31"001
15.	Fabrizio Lai	+ 38"040
16.	Michele Pirro	+ 39"610
17.	Lorenzo Zanetti	+ 39"951
18.	Michael Ranseder	+ 45"884
19.	Julian Miralles Jnr	+ 46"171
20.	Gioele Pellino	+ 46"357
21.	Imre Toth	+ 46"403
22.	Nicola Terol	+ 46"803
23.	Vesa Kallio	+ 56"536
24.	Aleix Espargaro	+ 56"557
25.	Manuel Hernandez Jnr	+ 59"931
26.	Enrique Jerez	+ 1'02.191
27.	Jordi Carchano	+ 1'02.284

Fastest lap:
Nieto, in 1'40.581 (143.347 km/h).
Record: Jenkner, in 1'40.252 (143.817 km/h/2002)

Outright fastest lap: Pedrosa, in 1'39.426 (145.012 km/h/2002).

CHAMPIONSHIP

1.	A. Dovizioso	293 (5 wins)
2.	H. Barbera	202 (4 wins)
3.	R. Locatelli	192 (2 wins)
4.	J. Lorenzo	179 (3 wins)
5.	C. Stoner	145 (1 win)
6.	P. Nieto	138
7.	A. Bautista	129
8.	S. Jenkner	122
9.	M. Giansanti	105
10.	M. Kallio	86

RESULTS AND RANKINGS

MotoGP

(1) RIDER	NATION	(2)	(3)	(4)	(5)	(6)	(7)	(8)	(9)	(10)
1. ROSSI Valentino	ITA	304	16	5	13	9	11	14	1	2
2. GIBERNAU Sete	ESP	257	16	5	11	4	10	14	1	2
3. BIAGGI Max	ITA	217	16	1	5	1	9	14	1	2
4. BARROS Alex	BRÉ	165	16	-	3	-	4	13	2	3
5. EDWARDS Colin	USA	157	16	-	-	-	2	15	2	1
6. TAMADA Makoto	JAP	150	16	3	3	2	3	13	1	3
7. CHECA Carlos	ESP	117	16	1	4	-	1	13	2	3
8. HAYDEN Nicky	USA	117	15	-	3	-	2	10	3	5
9. CAPIROSSI Loris	ITA	117	16	-	2	-	1	13	3	3
10. NAKANO Shinya	JAP	83	16	-	1	-	1	12	3	4
11. XAUS Ruben	ESP	77	16	-	-	-	1	11	3	5
12. MELANDRI Marco	ITA	75	15	-	-	-	2	8	3	7
13. ABÉ Norifumi	JAP	74	16	-	-	-	-	11	7	4
14. BAYLISS Troy	AUS	71	16	-	-	-	1	8	3	8
15. HOFMANN Alex	ALL	51	16	-	-	-	-	12	9	3
16. HOPKINS John	GB	45	15	-	1	-	-	10	6	5
17. HODGSON Neil	GB	38	16	-	-	-	-	8	8	6
18. ROBERTS Kenny	USA	37	12	1	2	-	-	6	7	3
19. MCWILLIAMS Jeremy	GB	26	16	-	-	-	-	10	12	3
20. BYRNE Shane	GB	18	9	-	-	-	-	6	10	2
21. AOKI Nobuatsu	JAP	10	16	-	-	-	-	6	13	3
22. FABRIZIO Michel	ITA	8	10	-	-	-	-	3	10	2
23. KAGAYAMA Yukio	JAP	7	2	-	-	-	-	2	11	-
24. JACQUE Olivier	FRA	5	2	-	-	-	-	1	11	1
25. HAYDON James	GB	4	3	-	-	-	-	1	12	1
26. ELLISON James	GB	3	6	-	-	-	-	1	13	1
27. PITT Andrew	AUS	2	3	-	-	-	-	1	14	-
28. UI Youichi	JAP	1	3	-	-	-	-	1	15	-
29. ROBERTS Kurtis	USA	1	9	-	-	-	-	1	15	7

(1) Final Championship Classification
(2) Number of points
(3) Number of qualifications (out of 16 GP)
(4) Number of pole positions
(5) Number of front row starts
(6) Number of victories
(7) Number of podiums
(8) Scored points (top 15)
(9) Best race finish
(10) Number of retirements

FINAL CONSTRUCTOR'S WORLS CHAMPIONSHIP CLASSIFICATION

1. Honda	355
2. Yamaha	328
3. Ducati	169
4. Kawasaki	95
5. Suzuki	73
6. Aprilia	39
7. Proton KR	15
8. Harris WCM	12
9. Moriwaki	7

ROOKIE OF THE YEAR

1. XAUS Ruben	77
2. HOFMANN Alex	51
3. BYRNE Shane	18
4. ROBERTS Kurtis	1

FINAL TEAMS WORLS CHAMPIONSHIP CLASSIFICATION

1. Gauloises Fortuna Yamaha	421
2. Telefonica Movistar Honda	414
3. Camel Honda	367
4. Repsol Honda Team	282
5. Ducati Marlboro Team	188
6. Fortuna Gauloises Tech 3	149
7. Kawasaki Racing Team	134
8. D'Antin MotoGP	115
9. Team Suzuki MotoGP	89
10. MS Aprilia Racing	44
11. Proton Team KR	15
12. WCM	12

RESULTS AND RANKINGS

250cc

(1) RIDER	NATION	(2)	(3)	(4)	(5)	(6)	(7)	(8)	(9)	(10)
1. PEDROSA Daniel	ESP	317	16	4	13	7	13	15	1	1
2. PORTO Sebastián	ARG	256	16	9	15	5	10	13	1	3
3. DE PUNIET Randy	FRA	214	16	2	13	1	8	14	1	2
4. ELIAS Antonio	ESP	199	16	-	5	1	8	14	1	1
5. DE ANGELIS Alex	SMA	147	16	1	8	-	2	12	2	4
6. AOYAMA Hiroshi	JAP	128	16	-	2	-	2	13	3	3
7. GONZALES-NIETO Fonsi	ESP	124	16	-	1	-	1	12	3	4
8. ROLFO Roberto	ITA	116	15	-	1	1	1	12	1	3
9. POGGIALI Manuel	SMA	95	14	-	5	1	3	7	1	6
10. BATTAINI Franco	ITA	93	16	-	-	-	-	12	4	3
11. WEST Anthony	AUS	88	14	-	-	-	-	9	4	4
12. DEBON ALEX	ESP	82	15	-	-	-	-	13	5	2
13. DAVIES Chaz	GB	51	16	-	-	-	-	9	5	4
14. GUINTOLI Sylvain	FRA	42	16	-	1	-	-	8	7	7
15. MATSUDO Naoki	JAP	41	16	-	-	-	-	9	8	2
16. MARCHAND Hugo	FRA	36	15	-	-	-	-	8	8	3
17. FAUBEL Hector	ESP	31	13	-	-	-	-	8	9	1
18. BALDOLINI Alex	ITA	30	16	-	-	-	-	7	10	8
19. OLIVÉ Joan	ESP	27	16	-	-	-	-	7	10	5
20. SMRZ Jakub	TCH	20	16	-	-	-	-	9	11	5
21. VINCENT Arnaud	FRA	15	13	-	-	-	-	3	8	8
22. STIGEFELT Johan	SUÈ	14	15	-	-	-	-	5	9	4
23. HEIDOLF Dirk	ALL	13	15	-	-	-	-	5	11	4
24. BATAILLE Eric	FRA	12	10	-	-	-	-	4	11	6
25. TAKAHASHI Yuki	JAP	11	1	-	-	-	-	1	5	-
26. AOYAMA Shuhei	JAP	8	1	-	-	-	-	1	8	-
27. DE GEA David	ESP	8	5	-	-	-	-	3	11	-
28. LEFORT Gregory	FRA	7	8	-	-	-	-	1	9	3
29. NIGON Erwan	FRA	4	14	-	-	-	-	1	12	6
30. FUJIOKA Yuzo	JAP	4	1	-	-	-	-	1	12	-
31. SEKIGUCHI Taro	JAP	4	16	-	-	-	-	2	13	4
32. LEBLANC Gregory	FRA	3	8	-	-	-	-	1	13	1

(1) Final Championship Classification
(6) Number of victories
(2) Number of points
(7) Number of podiums
(3) Number of qualifications (out of 16 GP)
(8) Scored points (top 15)
(4) Number of pole positions
(9) Best race finish
(5) Number of front row starts
(10) Number of retirements

ROOKIE OF THE YEAR

1. PEDROSA Daniel	317
2. DE ANGELIS Alex	147
3. AOYAMA Hiroshi	128
4. VINCENT Arnaud	15

FINAL CONSTRUCTOR'S WORLS CHAMPIONSHIP CLASSIFICATION

1. Honda	354
2. Aprilia	344
3. Yamaha	44

RESULTS AND RANKINGS

125cc

(1) RIDER	NATION	(2)	(3)	(4)	(5)	(6)	(7)	(8)	(9)	(10)
1. DOVIZIOSO Andrea	ITA	293	16	8	13	5	11	15	1	1
2. BARBERA Hector	ESP	202	16	1	8	4	7	13	1	3
3. LOCATELLI Roberto	ITA	192	16	1	5	2	6	13	1	2
4. LORENZO Jorge	ESP	179	16	2	7	3	7	11	1	4
5. STONER Casey	AUS	145	14	1	9	1	6	9	1	5
6. NIETO Pablo	ESP	138	16	-	3	-	2	13	3	3
7. BAUTISTA Alvaro	ESP	129	16	-	1	-	4	12	2	3
8. JENKNER Steve	ALL	122	16	1	5	-	1	14	2	1
9. GIANSANTI Mirko	ITA	105	16	-	2	-	-	13	4	3
10. KALLIO Mika	FIN	86	16	-	1	-	1	8	2	8
11. SIMONCELLI Marco	ITA	79	13	2	3	1	1	7	1	5
12. BORSOI Gino	ITA	79	16	-	1	-	-	11	5	3
13. CORSI Simone	ITA	61	16	-	2	-	1	10	3	4
14. SIMON Julian	ESP	60	14	-	1	-	-	10	6	-
15. PASINI Mattia	ITA	54	16	-	2	-	-	10	7	3
16. LAI Fabrizio	ITA	53	14	-	-	-	1	8	2	4
17. TALMACSI Gabor	HON	43	16	-	-	-	-	7	7	4
18. DI MEGLIO Mike	FRA	41	14	-	1	-	-	7	5	5
19. GADEA Sergio	ESP	29	16	-	-	-	-	6	5	2
20. BALLERINI Andrea	ITA	29	14	-	-	-	-	7	6	5
21. PESEK Lukas	TCH	20	16	-	-	-	-	6	8	7
22. UI Youichi	JAP	19	9	-	-	-	-	3	7	4
23. PELLINO Gioele	ITA	16	16	-	-	-	-	5	10	5
24. PERUGINI Stefano	ITA	14	16	-	-	-	-	4	10	7
25. LÜTHI Thomas	SUI	14	13	-	-	-	-	4	11	4
26. GIUSEPPETTI Dario	ALL	8	13	-	-	-	-	4	13	3
27. KOYAMA Tomoyoshi	JAP	7	2	-	-	-	-	1	9	-
28. KUZUHARA Toshihisa	JAP	7	2	-	-	-	-	2	10	-
29. TOTH Imre	HON	6	16	-	-	-	-	1	10	4
30. HARMS Robbin	DAN	5	8	-	-	-	-	1	11	4
31. CARCHANO Jordi	ESP	2	14	-	-	-	-	1	14	2
32. RODRIGUEZ Angel	ESP	2	16	-	-	-	-	2	15	13
33. KALLIO Vesa	FIN	1	16	-	-	-	-	1	15	4

(1) Final Championship Classification (2) Number of points (3) Number of qualifications (out of 16 GP) (4) Number of pole positions (5) Number of front row starts
(6) Number of victories (7) Number of podiums (8) Scored points (top 15) (9) Best race finish (10) Number of retirements

ROOKIE OF THE YEAR

1. Aprilia	329
2. Honda	301
3. KTM	204
4. Derbi	179
5. Gilera	61
6. Malaguti	43
7. Yamaha	7

FINAL CONSTRUCTOR'S WORLS CHAMPIONSHIP CLASSIFICATION

1. PASINI Mattia	54
2. GADEA Sergio	29
3. PESEK Lukas	20
4. GIUSEPPETTI Dario	8
5. HARMS Robbin	5
6. CARCHANO Jordi	2
7. KALLIO Vesa	1

RESULTS OF OTHER CHAMPIONSHIPS

9. Okada/Kameya (J, Honda), 7 laps; 10. Arakaki/Ohishi (J, Honda).

14th-15th August – 24 Hours of Oschersleben – Germany
1. D. Checa/Gimbert/Costes (E/F/F, Yamaha), 883 laps, 24 h 00'55.745 (134.828 km/h); 2. Saiger/Hinterreiter/Jerman (A/A/SLO, Yamaha), 18 laps; 3. Giabbani/Duterne/Scarnato (F, Yamaha), 24 laps; 4. Monot/Jaggi/Waldmeier (CH, Suzuki), 32 laps; 5. Tode/Röthig/Czyborra (D, Suzuki), 42 laps; 6. Hepelmann/Krächter/Wrede (D, Yamaha), 50 laps; 7. Kraft/König/Steinebach (D, Suzuki), 54 laps; 8. Brüning/Dähler/Wehran (D, Kawasaki), 56 laps; 9. Gabillon/Thurel/Chéron (F, Suzuki), 59 laps; 10. Seefeldt/Platacis/Reinmann (D, Suzuki), 64 laps.

3rd October – 200 Miles of Vallelunga – Italy
1. Philippe/Cogan/Four (F, Suzuki), 100 laps, 2 h 16'00.655 (143.062 km/h); 2. Costes/Guyot/D. Checa (F/F/E, Yamaha), 48"732; 3. Giabbani/Mulot/Protat (F, Yamaha), 1'12.054; 4. Scarnato/Mertens (F/B, Yamaha), 1 tour; 5. Moreira/D. Ellison (F/GB, Honda); 6. Liverani/M. Garcia/Marchetti (I/F/I, Ducati); 7. Thomas/Edwards (AUS/GB, Yamaha); 8. Kellenberger/Morillon (CH/F, Kawasaki), 2 laps; 9. Hutchins/Falcke (GB, Kawasaki), 3 laps; 10. Tode/Röthig (D, Suzuki), 4 laps.

FINAL CLASSIFICATION

1. Yamaha GMT 94	169
2. Suzuki Castrol Team	110
3. Moto 38	104

4. Yamaha Austria, 100; 5. Suzuki Jet Team, 56; 6. Bridgestone Bikers Profi, 39; 7. WRT-Honda Austria, 39; 8. Seven Stars Honda, 38; 9. Kawasaki Bolliger, 38; 10. Yamaha Phase One, 35.

MASTERS

3rd-4th April – Le Mans 24 Hours – France
1. S. Chambon/Kitagawa/Nowland (F/J/AUS, Suzuki), 793 laps, 24 h 00'53.645 (138.028 km/h); 2. Gimbert/Costes/D. Checa (F/F/E, Yamaha), 11 laps; 3. Giabbani/Duterne/Louis (F, Yamaha), 24 laps; 4. Dietrich/Fouloi/Fremy (F, Suzuki), 27 laps; 5. M. Kellenberger/Stamm/Morillon (CH/CH/F, Kawasaki), 29 laps; 6. Donischal/Fourcadet/Bonhuil (F, Honda), 32 laps; 7. Jolivet/Amalric/Neff (F, Suzuki), 38 laps; 8. Metro/Hars/Legname (F, Suzuki), 41 laps; 9. Bocquet/Baker/Giles (F/GB/GB, Yamaha), 43 laps; 10. Philippe/Four/Lagrive (F, Suzuki), 43 laps.

11th-12th September – Bol d'Or – France
1. Philippe/Lagrive/Kitagawa (F/F/J, Suzuki), 715 laps; 2. Four/Cogan/Watanabe (F/F/J, Suzuki), 6 laps; 3. Moreira/Duterne/Da Costa (F, Kawasaki), 14 laps; 4. Dietrich/Frémy/Fouloi (F, Suzuki), 20 laps; 5. Fissette/Weynand/Fastre (B/B/F, Yamaha), 32 laps; 6. Thuret/Cheron/Baratin (F, Suzuki), 35 laps; 7. Nyström/Sotter/Tangre (S/B/F, Suzuki), 37 laps; 8. Nickmans/Van Lindschloot/D'Hondt/Raas (B, Yamaha), 42 laps; 9. Herveux/Naire/Radeff (F, Suzuki), 43 laps; 10. Guersillon/Hars/Legname/Binois (F, Suzuki), 44 laps.

Side-Cars World Cup (*)

4th September – Schleiz – Germany
Race I: 1. Webster/Woodhead (LCR-Suzuki), 17'23.195 (144.425 km/h); 2. M. Van Gils/T. Van Gils (NL, LCR-Suzuki), 6"397; 3. Roscher/Hänni (D/CH, LCR-Suzuki), 11"001; 4. Gatt/Randall (GB, LCR-Suzuki), 12"257; 5. Pedder/Steadman (GB, LCR-Suzuki), 23"863; 6. Päivärinta/Wall (SF/S, LCR-Suzuki), 24"780; 7. Manninen(Kuismanen (SF, LCR-Suzuki), 28"186; 8. Moser/Wäfler (A/CH, LCR-Suzuki), 28"359; 9. Gällros/Berglund (S, LCR-Suzuki), 28"393; 10. Doppler/Wagner (A, LCR-Yamaha), 31"135; 11. J. Cluze/G. Cluze (F, LCR-Suzuki), 46"829; 12. Ti. Reeves/Tr. Reeves (GB, LCR-Suzuki), 59"298; 13. Foukal/Pertlicek (CZ, LCR-Suzuki), 1'00.242; 14. Hauzenberger/Hilderbrand (A/D, RSR-Yamaha), 1'17.045; 15. M. Grabmüller/B. Grabmüller (A, LCR-Yamaha), 1'36.679. 15 finishers.
Race II: 1. Webster/Woodhead (LCR-Suzuki), 26'53.962 (144.282 km/h); 2. M. Van Gils/T.Van Gils (NL, LCR-Suzuki), 6"3976"840; 3. Hanks/P. Biggs (GB, Windle-Yamaha), 13"261; 4. Roscher/Hänni (D/CH, LCR-Suzuki), 13"720; 5. Päivärinta/Wall (SF/S, LCR-Suzuki), 16"455; 6. Pedder/Steadman (GB, LCR-Suzuki), 16"573; 7. Moser/Wäfler (A/CH, LCR-Suzuki), 38"359; 8. Doppler/Wagner (A, LCR-Yamaha), 56"419; 9. J. Cluze/G. Cluze (F, LCR-Suzuki), 1'08.131; 10. Gatt/Randall (GB, LCR-Suzuki), 1 tour; 11. M. Grabmüller/B. Grabmüller (A, LCR-Yamaha); 12. Hauzenberger/Hilderbrand (A/D, RSR-Yamaha); 13. B. Fleury/J. Fleury (NZ, LCR-Suzuki), 2 laps. 13 finishers.
Race III: 1. Webster/Woodhead (LCR-Suzuki), 34'50.562 (144.150 km/h); 2. Ti. Reeves/Tr. Reeves (GB, LCR-Suzuki), 12"605; 3. Roscher/Hänni (D/CH, LCR-Suzuki), 19"326; 4. M. Van Gils/T. Van Gils (NL, LCR-Suzuki), 24"486; 5. Schlosser/Helbig (CH, LCR-Suzuki), 24"521; 6. Pedder/Steadman (GB, LCR-Suzuki), 35"097; 7. Päivärinta/Wall (SF/S, LCR-Suzuki), 55"034; 8. Moser/Wäfler (A/CH, LCR-Suzuki), 1'16.354; 9. J. Cluze/G. Cluze (F, LCR-Suzuki), 1 tour; 10. Hauzenberger/Hilderbrand (A/D, RSR-Yamaha); 11. Doppler/Wagner (A, LCR-Yamaha); 12. M. Grabmüller/B. Grabmüller (A, LCR-Yamaha), 2 laps; 13. 13. B. Fleury/J. Fleury (NZ, LCR-Suzuki), 2 laps. 13 finishers.
(*): For the first time in history, a side car world cup was run in three legs, at the same circuit.

European Championship

125 cc

4th April – Vallelunga – Italy
1. Pirro (I, Aprilia), 19 laps, 26'11.078 (141.191 km/h); 2. Danese (I, Aprilia), 3"956; 3. Miralles Junior (E, Aprilia), 13"391; 4. Braillard (CH, Honda), 14"368; 5. Magda (H, Honda), 14"453; 6. De Rosa (I, Aprilia), 14"602; 7. Bittman (CZ, Honda), 14"677; 8. Bianchi (I, Honda), 17"075; 9. Romboli (I, Aprilia), 17"363; 10. Giugliano (I, Aprilia), 26"615; 11. Zanetti (I, Honda), 30"072; 12. Perotti (I, Aprilia), 32"656; 13. D'Amelio (I, Honda), 35"979; 14. S. Bradl (D, KTM), 36"771; 15. Conti (I, Aprilia), 41"084.

11th April – Assen – The Netherlands
1. Miralles Junior (E, Aprilia), 18 laps, 26'33.615 (157.810 km/h); 2. Pirro (I, Aprilia), 0"438; 3. Kalab (CZ, Honda), 0"514; 4. Romboli (I, Aprilia), 7"443; 5. Jerez (E, Honda), 7"513; 6. Conti (I, Aprilia), 7"767; 7. Braillard (CH, Honda), 7"923; 8. Litjens (NL, Honda), 10"624; 9. Planas (E, Honda), 19"389; 10. Magda (H, Honda), 27"181; 11. Mickan (D, Honda), 30"929; 12. Masbou (F, Honda), 31"301; 13. Cortese (I, Honda), 31"392; 14. Van Den Dragt (NL, Honda), 32"399; 15. Baroni (I, Aprilia), 36"682.

30th May – Hungaroring – Hungary
1. Ranseder (A, KTM), 15 laps, 29'32.400 (133.477 km/h); 2. Magda (H, Honda), 8"473; 3. Bittman (CZ, Honda), 11"607; 4. Kalab (CZ, Honda), 13"244; 5. Jerez (E, Honda), 25"546; 6. Masbou (F, Honda), 25"761; 7. D'Amelio (I, Honda), 40"816; 8. Romboli (I, Aprilia), 41"011; 9. Lacalendola (I, Aprilia), 43"184; 10. Planas (E, Honda), 44"567; 11. Mickan (D, Honda), 45"249; 12. Gnani (I, Gnani), 48"614; 13. Conti (I, Aprilia), 50"219; 14. Litjens (NL, Honda), 50"380; 15. Kaulamo (SF, Honda), 1'10.572.

13th June – Rijeka – Croatia
Race cancelled because of a tornado.

11th July – Most – Czech Republic
1. Fröhlich (D, Honda), 18 laps, 29'14.278 (153.220 km/h); 2. Mickan (D, Honda), 0"047; 3. Kalab (CZ, Honda), 0"155; 4. Miralles Junior (E, Aprilia), 0"387; 5. Litjens (NL, Honda), 0"610; 6. Bittman (CZ, Honda), 0"749; 7. Cortese (I, Honda), 11"044; 8. Wirsing (D, Honda), 19"150; 9. Magda (H, Honda), 19"473; 10. Krummenacher (D, Honda), 32"456; 11. Lacalendola (I, Aprilia), 32"496; 12. Magnoni (I, Honda), 33"005; 13. Masbou (F, Honda), 37"820; 14. Vostarek (CZ, Honda), 41"168; 15. Abraham (CZ, Honda), 41"480.

8th August – Anderstorp – Sweden
1. Pirro (I, Aprilia), 16 laps, 26'47.888 (144.189 km/h); 2. Miralles Junior (E, Aprilia), 0"340; 3. Kalab (CZ, Honda), 1"584; 4. Magda (H, Honda), 21"447; 5. Masbou (F, Honda), 23"222; 6. Jerez (E, Honda), 23"330; 7. Braillard (CH, Honda), 24"037; 8. Bianchi (I, Honda), 25"310; 9. Litjens (NL, Honda), 27"828; 10. D'Amelio (I, Honda), 31"756; 11. Van der Marel (NL, Honda), 35"315; 12. Van Den Berg (NL, Aprilia), 39"969; 13. Bittman (CZ, Honda), 44"581; 14. Olagnon (F, Honda), 55"002; 15. Kaulamo (SF, Honda), 55"194.

19th September – Schleiz – Germany
1. Pirro (I, Aprilia), 19 laps, 30'08.736 (143.891 km/h); 2. Miralles Junior (E, Aprilia), 0"586; 3. Hommel (D, Honda), 9"766; 4. Baroni (I, Aprilia), 19"874; 5. Kalab (CZ, Honda), 19"897; 6. Mickan (D, Honda), 21"202; 7. Conti (I, Aprilia), 28"865; 8. D'Amelio (I, Honda), 30"900; 9. Lacalendola (I, Aprilia), 39"630; 10. Masbou (F, Honda), 46"686; 11. Abraham (CZ, Honda), 46"796; 12. Magda (H, Honda), 47"292; 13. Jerez (E, Honda), 47"358; 14. Bittman (CZ, Honda), 47"801; 15. Litjens (NL, Honda), 49"710.

10th October – Cartagena – Spain
1. Hernandez Junior (E, Aprilia), 20 laps, 33'14.100 (126.589 km/h); 2. Pirro (I, Aprilia), 1"800; 3. Miralles Junior (E, Aprilia), 5"100; 4. Magda (H, Honda), 25"300; 5. Fröhlich (D, Honda), 25"310; 6. Minnerop (D, Honda) 26"000; 7. Kalab (CZ, Honda), 27"900; 8. Masbou (F, Honda), 38"800; 9. Wirsing (D, Honda), 49"300; 10. Braillard (CH, Honda), 50"800; 11. Bittman (CZ, Honda), 51"500; 12. Localendola (I, Aprilia), 53"800; 13. Abraham (CZ, Honda), 1'02.100; 14. Conti (I, Aprilia), 1'14.800; 15. Kyyhkynen (SF, Honda), 1'16.200.

FINAL CLASSIFICATION

1. Michele Pirro	(I, Aprilia)	115
2. Julian Miralles Junior	(E, Aprilia)	110
3. Igor Kalab	(CZ, Honda)	81

4. Magda (H, Honda), 74; 5. Bittman (CZ, Honda), 45; 6. Masbou (F, Honda), 42; Mickan (D, Honda), 40; 8. Braillard (CH, Honda), 37 ; 9. Fröhlich (D, Honda), 36; 10. Jerez (E, Honda), 35.

250 cc

4th April – Vallelunga – Italy
1. Rous (CZ, Aprilia), 22 laps, 29'39.381 (144.345 km/h); 2. Molina (E, Aprilia), 0"168; 3. Leblanc (F, Aprilia), 9"333; 4. Watz (S, Yamaha), 19"616; 5. Aggerholm (DK, Yamaha), 34"727; 6. Ronzoni (I, Yamaha), 44"370; 7. Lakerveld (NL, Yamaha), 44"479; 8. Matikainen (SF, Yamaha), 57"184; 9. Binucci (I, Yamaha), 58"650; 10. Lindfors (S, Aprilia), 1'11.525; 11. Eisen (F, Honda), 1'11.587; 12. Polzer (A, Honda), 1'11.640; 13. Nordgren (S, Honda), 1 tour; 14. Martensson (S, Yamaha); 15. Scaccia (F, Yamaha).

30th May – Hungaroring – Hungary
1. Molina (E, Aprilia), 16 laps, 31'06.674 (135.185 km/h); 2. Rous (CZ, Aprilia), 11"140; 3. Leblanc (F, Aprilia), 25"991; 4. Martensson (S, Yamaha), 27"926; 5. Zanette (I, Yamaha), 39"524; 6. Polzer (A, Honda), 40"528; 7. Aubry (F, Honda), 42"127; 8. Castka (SLO, Yamaha), 42"267; 9. Lindfors (S, Aprilia), 58"206; 10. Heierli (CH, Honda), 1'00.959; 11. Eisen (F, Honda), 1'09.763; 12. Menghi (I, Honda), 1'16.557; 13. Tibori (H, Yamaha), 1'21.521; 14. Hudovernik (SLO, Honda), 1'54.121; 15. Stella (I, Honda), 1'54.242.

13th June – Rijeka – Croatia
Race cancelled because of a tornado.

26th June – Assen – The Netherlands
1. Watz (S, Yamaha), 30'50.577; 2. Molina (E, Aprilia), 15"664; 3. Leblanc (F, Aprilia), 17"976; 4. Aggerholm (DK, Yamaha), 19"194; 5. Polzer (A, Honda), 22"116; 6. Van De Lagemaat (NL, Aprilia), 22"206; 7. Filla (CZ, Yamaha), 33"791; 8. Lindfors (S, Aprilia), 36"671; 9. Rank (D, Honda), 49"709; 10. Zanette (I, Yamaha), 1'01.291; 11. Scaccia (F, Yamaha), 1'15.199; 12. Heierli (CH, Honda), 1'15.423; 13. Campbell (GB, Yamaha), 1'16.756; 14. Oldenziel (NL, Yamaha), 1'16.895; 15. Cajback (S, Yamaha), 1'28.489.

11th July – Most – Czech Republic
1. Watz (S, Yamaha), 20 laps, 35'49.782 (138.924 km/h); 2. Walther (D, Honda), 9"744; 3 Martensson (S, Yamaha), 11"821; 4. Molina (E, Aprilia), 12"789; 5. Polzer (A, Honda), 27"877; 6. Aggerholm (DK, Yamaha), 48"953; 7. Eisen (F, Honda), 1'26.420; 8. Srdanov (NL, Aprilia), 1'47.316; 9. Scaccia (F, Yamaha), 1 tour; 10. Stella (I, Honda); 11. Sjoestroen (S, Yamaha); 12. Zanette (I, Yamaha). 12 finishers.

8th August – Anderstorp – Sweden
1. Molina (E, Aprilia), 19 laps, 30'54.239 (148.476 km/h); 2. Polzer (A, Honda), 7"820; 3. Watz (S, Yamaha), 8"543; 4. Aggerholm (SK, Yamaha), 29"767; 5. Zanette (I, Yamaha), 30"041; 6. Castka (SLO, Yamaha), 30"960; 7. Lakerveld (NL, Yamaha), 45"245; 8. Lindfors (S, Aprilia), 45"582; 9. Gevers (NL, Aprilia), 45"759; 10. Roelofs (NL, Yamaha), 46"549; 11. Cajback (S, Yamaha), 1'14.120; 12. Nordgren (S, Honda), 1'14.957; 13. Autio (SF, Honda), 1'15.431; 14. Corneliusson (S, Honda), 1'15.630; 15. Scaccia (F, Yamaha), 1'21.940.

19th September – Schleiz – Germany
1. Leblanc (F, Aprilia), 21 laps, 32'21.279 (148.179 km/h); 2. Polzer (A, Honda), 11"029; 3. Watz (S, Yamaha), 22"470; 4. Filla (CZ, Yamaha), 25"729; 5. Lakerveld (NL, Yamaha), 26"462; 6. Lougher (GB, Honda), 28"432; 7. Aggerholm (DK, Yamaha), 32"972; 8. Walther (F, Honda), 50"231; 9. Rank (D, Honda), 1'04.247; 10. Zanette (I, Yamaha), 1'10.480; 11. Molina (E, Aprilia), 1'12.148; 12. Appelo (NL, Honda), 1'14.546; 13. Voit (D, Aprilia), 1'15.325; 14. Martensson (S, Yamaha), 1'15.799; 15. Velthuijzen (NL, Honda), 1'21.206.

10th October – Cartagena – Spain
1. Molina (E, Aprilia), 24 laps, 39'06.581 (129.089 km/h); 2. Martensson (S, Yamaha), 52"900; 3. Zanette (I, Yamaha), 53"000; 4. Rank (D, Honda), 1'34.200; 5. Bellucci (I, Honda), 1 tour; 6. Cajback (S, Yamaha), 1 tour; 7. Aubry (F, Honda), 1 tour; 8. Heierli (CH, Honda), 1 tour; 9. Voit (D, Aprilia), 2 laps; 10. Stella (I, Honda), 2 laps. 10 finishers.

FINAL CLASSIFICATION

1. Alvaro Molina	(E, Aprilia)	133
2. Fredrik Watz	(S, Yamaha)	95
3. Yves Polzer	(A, Honda)	76

4. Leblanc (F, Aprilia), 73; 5. Aggerholm (DK, Yamaha), 56; 6. Zanette (I, Yamaha), 54; 7. Martensson (S, Yamaha), 53; 8. Rous (CZ, Aprilia), 45; 9. Lakerveld (NL, Yamaha), 29; 10. Lindfors (S, Aprilia), 29.

Supersport

4th April – Vallelunga – Italy
1. Giugovaz (I, Honda), 25 laps, 33'50.936 (143.712 km/h); 2. Carlacci (I, Yamaha), 4"393; 3. Prattichizzo (I, Honda), 14"863; 4. Proietto (I, Honda), 17"914; 5. Mariottini (I, Yamaha), 19"376; 6. Folkesson (S, Honda), 20"063; 7. Berta (I, Honda), 42"941; 8. Haarala (SF, Kawasaki), 43"814; 9. Magnani (I, Yamaha), 52"986; 10. Penna (SF, Honda), 55"048; 11. T. Lauslehto (SF, Honda), 1'11.369; 12. Nocetti (I, Yamaha), 1'12.720; 13. Bresciani (I, Honda), 1'16.465; 14. Bisconti (I, Yamaha), 1'21.531; 15. M. Müller (D, Yamaha), 1'21.677.

30th May – Hungaroring – Hungary
1. Giugovaz (I, Honda), 20 laps, 39'07.044 (134.395 km/h); 2. Penna (SF, Honda), 14"187; 3. T. Lauslehto (SF, Honda), 14"512; 4. Haarala (SF, Kawasaki), 14"660; 5. Pellizzon (I, Yamaha), 16"861; 6. Manici (I, Yamaha), 21"933; 7. Grammer (A, Kawasaki), 24"157; 8. Ger. Talmacsi (H, Suzuki), 24"928; 9. M. Jerman (SLO, Kawasaki), 29"135; 10. Szekely (H, Honda), 33"048; 11. M. Müller (D, Yamaha), 52"374; 12. Heyndrickx (B, Honda), 1'10.857; 13. Anello (I, Yamaha), 1'22.456; 14. Juhasz (H, Honda), 1'22.784; 15. Broz (CZ, Kawasaki), 1'23.839.

13th June – Rijeka – Croatia
Race cancelled because of a tornado.

11th July – Most – Czech Republic
1. Folkesson (S, Honda), 22 laps, 36'58.712 (148.069 km/h); 2. Vos (NL, Kawasaki), 2"587; 3. Kaldowski (POL, Yamaha), 5"026; 4. M. Jerman (SLO, Kawasaki), 11"334; 5. Haarala (SF, Kawasaki), 19"516; 6. T. Lauslehto (SF, Honda), 26"881; 7. M. Müller (D, Yamaha), 27"084; 8. Prinz (D, Yamaha), 27"179; 9. Kerbl (A, Honda), 27"596; 10. Ouda (CZ, Honda), 46"101; 11. Bergau (D, Yamaha), 1 tour; 12. Lukaseder (A, Honda); 13. Domke (D, Yamaha); 14. Broz (CZ, Kawasaki); 15. Roncoroni (I, Yamaha), 2 laps.

8th August – Anderstorp – Sweden
1. Solberg (N, Yamaha), 22 laps, 35'51.277 (148.182 km/h); 2. Folkesson (S, Honda), 0"152; 3. Vos (NL, Kawasaki), 5"903; 4. Penna (SF, Honda), 7"503; 5. T. Lauslehto (SF, Honda), 7"552; 6. Haarala (SF, Kawasaki), 31"544; 7. Aarnes (N, Yamaha), 1'13.284; 8. Bengtsson (S, Ducati), 1 tour; 9. Aromaa (SF, Honda); 10. Roncoroni (I, Yamaha); 11. Torittu (SF, Yamaha); 12. Vesterberg (S, Ducati). 12 finishers.

5th September – Assen – The Netherlands
1. T. Lauslehto (SF, Honda), 14 laps, 30'32.475 (165.765 km/h); 2. Folkesson (S, Honda), 0"841; 3. Giugovaz (I, Honda), 4"042; 4. Solberg (N, Yamaha), 25"203; 5. Penna (SF, Honda), 25"316; 6. Van Beek (NL, Yamaha), 25"812; 7. Haarala (SF, Kawasaki), 25"855; 8. Vanlandschoot (B, Yamaha), 26"072; 9. Ophey (NL, Yamaha), 30"651; 10. Kerkhoven (NL, Yamaha), 30"791; 11. M. Jerman (SLO, Kawasaki), 32"594; 12. Bakker (NL, Yamaha), 36"530; 13. Ahnendorp (NL, Kawasaki), 36"753; 14. Veijer (NL, Honda), 46"867; 15. Lenters (NL, Yamaha), 56"394.

19th September – Schleiz – Germany
1. T. Lauslehto (SF, Honda), 23 laps, 35'15.050 (148.958 km/h); 2. Giugovaz (I, Honda), 0"314; 3. Penzkofer (D, Yamaha), 8"036; 4. M. Müller (D, Yamaha), 22"143; 5. Penna (SF, Honda), 24"393; 6. Haarala (SF, Kawasaki), 34"052; 7. Korpiaho (SF, Suzuki), 35"198; 8. Valjan (CRO, Honda), 49"075; 9. M. Jerman (SLO, Kawasaki), 58"992; 10. Prinz (D, Yamaha), 1'10.503; 11. Heyndrickx (B, Honda), 1'27.075; 12. Beinlich (D, Yamaha), 1 tour; 13. Roncoroni (I, Yamaha); 14. Düssel (D, Suzuki). 14 finishers.

10th October – Cartagena – Spain
1. T. Lauslehto (SF, Honda), 24 laps, 40'09.187 (125.735 km/h); 2. Castellejo (E, Honda), 2"500; 3. Haarala (SF, Kawasaki), 8"600; 4. Giugovaz (I, Honda), 18"000; 5. Penna (SF, Honda), 23"900; 6. Abellan (D, Yamaha), 39"600; 7. M. Jerman (SLO, Kawasaki), 44"300; 8. Valjan (CRO, Honda), 58"300; 9. Hidalgo (E, Suzuki), 1 tour; 10. Aromaa (SF, Honda), 1 tour; 11. Castro (E, Yamaha), 1 tour; 12. Roncoroni (I, Yamaha), 1 tour; 13. Pascual (E, Suzuki), 2 laps.

FINAL CLASSIFICATION

1. Tatu Lauslehto	(SF, Honda)	117
2. Diego Giugovaz	(I, Honda)	99
3. Topi Haarala	(SF, Kawasaki)	77

4. Folkesson (S, Honda), 75; 5. Penna (SF, Honda), 72; 6. M. Jerman (SLO, Kawasaki), 41; 7. Solberg (N, Yamaha), 38; 8. Vos (NL, Kawasaki), 36; 9. M. Müller (D, Yamaha), 28; 10. Castillejo (E, Honda), 20.

Superstock

29th February – Valencia – Spain
1. Vizziello (I, Yamaha), 13 laps, 21'46.950 (143.413 km/h); 2. Alfonsi (I, Yamaha), 0"357; 3. Chiarello (I, Suzuki), 2"621; 4. Silva (E, Yamaha), 9"404; 5. Rocamora (E, Kawasaki), 11"725; 6. Sofuoglu (TUR, Yamaha), 18"857; 7. Scassa (I, Kawasaki), 20"712; 8. Bianco (I, Suzuki), 26"564; 9. Hurtado (E, Suzuki), 27"101; 10. Lombardo (E, Suzuki), 27"677; 11. De Noni (I, Suzuki), 28"819; 12. W. De Angelis (RSM, Ducati), 29"479; 13. J. Laverty (IRL, Suzuki), 33"779; 14. A. Martinez (E, Honda), 42"427; 15. Miksovsky (CZ, Honda), 42"590.

18th April – Misano – San Marino
1. Alfonsi (I, Yamaha), 15 laps, 28'14.947 (129.349 km/h); 2. Vizziello (I, Yamaha), 0"468; 3. Polita (I, Ducati), 2"456; 4. Vankeymeulen (B, Yamaha), 3"587; 5. Lunadei (I, Suzuki), 9"786; 6. Scassa (I, Kawasaki), 25"433; 7. Brannetti (I, Aprilia), 27"073; 8. A. Martinez (E, Honda), 29"249; 9. Lerat-Vanstaen (F, Suzuki), 36"697; 10. Rocamora (E, Kawasaki), 40"963; 11. B. Martinez (E, Yamaha), 41"205; 12. Saelens (B, Ducati), 41"588; 13. Vermonden (B, Suzuki), 41"684; 14. W. De Angelis (RSM, Ducati), 44"088; 15. Sofuoglu (TUR, Yamaha), 44"121.

16th May – Monza – Italy
1. Vizziello (I, Yamaha), 11 laps, 20'30.818 (186.382 km/h); 2. Alfonsi (I, Yamaha), 5"435; 3. Vankeymeulen (B, Yamaha), 9"635; 4. Dionisi (I, Suzuki), 14"255; 5. B. Martinez (E, Yamaha), 17"519; 6. J. Laverty (IRL, Suzuki), 27"483; 7. Sofuoglu (TUR, Yamaha), 28"122; 8. Rocamora (E, Kawasaki), 31"895; 9. W. De Angelis (RSM, Ducati), 35"570; 10. Lerat-Vanstaen (F, Suzuki), 41"817; 11. De Noni (I, Suzuki), 46"410; 12. Vermonden (B, Suzuki), 53"245; 13. Hurtado (E, Suzuki), 53"873; 14. Badovini (I, Ducati), 1'01.337; 15. R. De Vries (NL, Yamaha), 1'03.877.

30th May – Oschersleben – Germany
1. Vizziello (I, Yamaha), 15 laps, 23'00.720 (143.416 km/h); 2. Vankeymeulen (B, Yamaha), 0"346; 3. Sofuoglu (TUR, Yamaha), 3"372; 4. B. Martinez (E, Yamaha), 3"817; 5. Chiarello (I, Suzuki), 4"069; 6. Rocamora (E, Kawasaki), 5"141; 7. Alfonsi (I, Yamaha), 5"629; 8. Dionisi (I, Suzuki), 9"872; 9. Polita (I, Ducati), 15"179; 10. J. Laverty (IRL, Suzuki), 15"327; 11. W. De Angelis (RSM, Ducati), 15"593; 12. Badovini (I, Ducati), 15"929; 13. Miksovsky (CZ, Honda), 16"944; 14. De Noni (I, Suzuki), 20"996; 15. Saelens (B, Ducati), 21"360.

13th June – Silverstone – Great Britain
1. Alfonsi (I, Yamaha), 12 laps, 23'39.709 (153.239 km/h); 2. Vizziello (I, Yamaha), 0"077; 3. Dionisi (I, Suzuki), 3"649; 4. Chiarello (I, Suzuki), 5"781; 5. B. Martinez (E, Suzuki), 12"459; 6. Scassa (I, Kawasaki), 15"196; 7. Hurtado (E, Suzuki), 15"560; 8. Wilson (GB, Suzuki), 16"265; 9. A. Martinez (E, Kawasaki), 16"562; 10. W. De Angelis (RSM, Ducati), 17"249; 11. Miksovsky (CZ, Honda), 30"072; 12. Badovini (I, Ducati), 30"427; 13. Saelens (B, Ducati), 32"263; 14. Perilli (*) (I, Yamaha), 33"401; 15. De Noni (I, Suzuki), 33"605.

1st August – Brands Hatch – Great Britain
1. Vizziello (I, Yamaha), 15 laps, 22'36.698 (167.051 km/h); 2. Alfonsi (I, Yamaha), 2"297; 3. Sofuoglu (TUR, Yamaha), 2"317; 4. Dionisi (I, Suzuki), 13"039; 5. Chiarelli (I, Suzuki), 13"441; 6. A. Martinez (E, Kawasaki), 14"409; 7. Scassa (I, Kawasaki), 17"457; 8. J. Laverty (IRL, Yamaha), 17"751; 9. B. Martinez (E, Suzuki), 20"942; 10. Polita (I, Ducati), 30"825; 11. Rocamora (E, Kawasaki), 30"844; 12. Badovini (I, Ducati), 30"939; 13. Lerat-Vanstaen (F, Suzuki), 34"117; 14. W. De Angelis (RSM, Ducati), 42"192; 15. Lombardo (E, Suzuki), 44"181.

5th September – Assen – The Netherlands (*)
1. Alfonsi (I, Yamaha), 8 laps, 17'08.919 (168.699 km/h); 2. Vizziello (I, Yamaha), 0"333; 3. Sofuoglu (TUR, Yamaha), 1"852; 4. Chiarello (I, Suzuki), 2"645; 5. Vankeymeulen (B, Yamaha), 5"243; 6. Rocamora (E, Suzuki), 8"490; 7. Polita (I, Ducati), 13"069; 8. A. Martinez (E, Kawasaki), 13"479; 9. J. Laverty (IRL, Yamaha), 14"496; 10. Scassa (I, Kawasaki), 16"546; 11. Lerat-Vanstaen (F, Suzuki), 16"760; 12. Badovini (I, Ducati), 21"116; 13. Withag (NL, Yamaha), 22"361; 14. Perilli (*) (I, Yamaha), 22"597; 15. Hurtado (E, Suzuki), 23"827.
(*): Race stopped on lap 9, after an accident which cost the life of Alessio Perilli (I, Yamaha.)

26th September – Imola – Italy
1. Chiarello (I, Suzuki), 13 laps, 24'43.684 (155.602 km/h); 2. Sofuoglu (TUR, Yamaha), 0"742; 3. Scassa (I, Kawasaki), 10"598; 4. J. Laverty (IRL, Yamaha), 15"134; 5. Roccoli (I, Yamaha), 15"874; 6. Vankeymeulen (B, Yamaha), 19"874; 7. Dionisi (I, Suzuki), 24"819; 8. Polita (I, Ducati), 25"286; 9. A. Martinez (E, Kawasaki), 25"374; 10. Brannetti (I, Aprilia), 29"744; 11. Cooper (GB, Honda), 30"406; 12. Miksovsky (CZ, Honda), 36"631; 13. Badovini (I, Ducati), 36"729; 14. W. De Angelis (RSM, Ducati), 37"654; 15. Hurtado (E, Suzuki), 49"691.

3rd October – Magny-Cours – France
1. Alfonsi (I, Yamaha), 12 laps, 21'04.287 (150.721 km/h); 2. Vankeymeulen (B, Yamaha), 0"400; 3. Sofuoglu (TUR, Yamaha), 1"319; 4. J. Laverty (IRL, Yamaha), 2"307; 5. Iannuzzo (I, Suzuki), 14"372; 6. Dionisi (I, Suzuki), 14"463; 7. Scassa (I, Kawasaki), 17"562; 8. Miksovsky (CZ, Honda), 18"650; 9. Hurtado (E, Suzuki), 20"562; 10. Brannetti (I, Aprilia), 21"309; 11. De Noni (I, Suzuki), 21"789; 12. Polita (I, Ducati), 23"090; 13. Fouloi (F, Suzuki), 23"567; 14. Cooper (GB, Honda), 26"675; 15. W. De Angelis (RSM, Ducati), 28"669.

FINAL CLASSIFICATION

1. Lorenzo Alfonsi	(I, Yamaha)	169
2. Gianluca Vizziello	(I, Yamaha)	160
3. Kenan Sofuoglu	(TUR, Yamaha)	104

4. Vankeymeulen (B, Yamaha), 90; 5. Chiarello (I, Suzuki), 89; 6. Dionisi (I, Suzuki), 69; 7. Scassa (I, Kawasaki), 69; 8. J. Laverty (IRL, Yamaha), 60; 9. Polita (I, Ducati), 50; 10. Rocamora (E, Suzuki), 50.

SIDE-CARS

15th May – Vallelunga – Italy
1. S. Webster/Woodhead (GB, LCR-Suzuki), 20 laps, 27'34.373; 2. Hanks/P. Biggs (GB, Windle-Yamaha), 2"886; 3. Ti. Reeves/Tr. Reeves (GB, LCR-Suzuki), 3"862; 4. M. Van Gils/T. Van Gils (NL, LCR-Suzuki), 6"482; 5. Gällros/Berglund (S, LCR-Suzuki), 50"178; 6. Morrisey/R. Biggs (GB, LCR-Yamaha), 1'00.928; 7. Williams/Hill (GB, LCR-Suzuki), 1'05.409; 8. Foukal/Pertlicek (CZ, LCR-Yamaha), 1 tour; 9. B. Fleury/J. Fleury (NZ, LCR-Suzuki), 2 laps; 10. G. Lazzarini/Polidori (I, WLZ-Suzuki), 2 laps. 10 finishers.

29th May – Hungaroring – Hungary
1. S. Webster/Woodhead (GB, LCR-Suzuki), 15 laps, 29'19.281; 2. Ti. Reeves/Tr. Reeves (GB, LCR-Suzuki), 6"975; 3. Hanks/P. Biggs (GB, Windle-Yamaha), 22"577; 4. Gällros/Berglund (S, LCR-Suzuki), 46"640; 5. M. Van Gils/T. Van Gils (NL, LCR-Suzuki), 47"669; 6. Päivärinta/Wall (SF/S, LCR-Suzuki), 1'00.507; 7. Roscher/Hänni (D/CH, LCR-Suzuki), 1'01.158; 8. Doppler/Wagner (A, LCR-Yamaha), 1'46.636; 9. Foukal/Pertlicek (CZ, LCR-Suzuki), 1 tour; 10. B. Fleury/J. Fleury (NZ, LCR-Suzuki), 1 tour; 11. Hauzenberger/Dagnino (A/I, RSR-Yamaha), 1 tour. 11 finishers.

12th June – Rijeka – Croatia
Race cancelled because of a tornado.

10th July – Most – Czech Republic
1. S. Wesbter/Woodhead (GB, LCR-Suzuki), 25'25.836 (156.587 km/h); 2. Hanks/P. Biggs (GB, Windle-Yamaha), 4"590; 3. Ti. Reeves/Tr. Reeves (GB, LCR-Suzuki), 5"117; 4. Päivärinta/Wall (SF/S, LCR-Suzuki), 22"544; 5. Pedder/Steadman (LCR-Suzuki), 23"345; 6. Manninen/Kuismanen (SF, LCR-Suzuki), 27"829; 7. M. Van Gils/T. Van Gils (NL, LCR-Suzuki), 40"193; 8. Norbury/Parnell (GB, Windle-Yamaha), 57"228; 9. Morrissey/R. Biggs (GB, LCR-Suzuki), 57"527; 10. G. Knight/D. Knight (GB, LCR-Suzuki), 1'17.061; 11. Hauzenberger/Hilderbrand (A/D, RSR-Yamaha), 1'17.404; 12. Foukal/Pertlicek (CZ, LCR-Suzuki), 1'43.388; 13. B. Fleury/J. Fleury (NZ, LCR-Suzuki), 1 tour. 13 finishers.

7th August – Anderstorp – Sweden
1. Ti. Reeves/Tr. Reeves (GB, LCR-Suzuki), 29'06.934 (141.007 km/h); 2. Hanks/P. Biggs (GB, Windle-Yamaha), 4"294; 3. Gällros/Berglund (S, LCR-Suzuki), 25"608; 4. Manninen/Kuismanen (SF, LCR-Suzuki), 25"867; 5. M. Van Gils/T. Van Gils (NL, LCR-Suzuki), 26"484; 6. Morrisey/R. Biggs (GB, LCR-Suzuki), 35"710; 7. Päivärinta/Wall (SF, LCR-Yamaha), 40"081; 8. G. Knight/D. Knight (GB, LCR-Suzuki), 42"640; 9. Roscher/Hänni (D/CH, LCR-Suzuki), 54"130; 10. B. Fleury/J. Fleury (NZ, LCR-Suzuki), 1 tour; 11. Foukal/Pertlicek (CZ, LCR-Yamaha); 12. Pedder/Steadman (LCR-Suzuki); 13. Nurmi/Söldeberg (S, Suzuki), 4 laps. 13 finishers.

18th September – Schleiz – Germany (*)
1. Ti. Reeves/Tr. Reeves (GB, LCR-Suzuki), 4'46.680 (143.344 km/h); 2. S. Webster/Woodhead (GB, LCR-Suzuki), 0"182; 3. M. Van Gils/T. Van Gils (NL, LCR-Suzuki), 0"604; 4. Hanks/P. Biggs (GB, Windle-Yamaha), 1"644; 5. Päivärinta/Wall (SF/S,LCR-Yamaha), 5"969; 6. Pedder/Steadman (LCR-Suzuki), 6"808; 7. G. Knight/D. Knight (GB, LCR-Suzuki), 10"651; 8. Gällros/Hill (S/GB, LCR-Suzuki), 12"602; 9. Laidlow/Farrance (GB, Suzuki), 15"014; 10. Foukal/Pertlicek (CZ, LCR-Yamaha), 17"073; 11. Hauzenberger/Dagnino (A/I, RSR-Yamaha), 17"654; 12. Roscher/Hänni (D/CH, LCR-Suzuki), 22"145; 13. B. Fleury/Graham (NZ/GB, LCR-Suzuki), 25"691. 13 finishers.
(*): Race stopped after three laps.

9th October – Cartagena – Spain
Race I (replacement Rijeka): 1. Gällros/Briggs (S/GB, LCR-Suzuki), 34'13.309; 2. M. Van Gils/T. Van Gils (NL, LCR-Suzuki), 4"216; 3. Päivärinta/Wall (SF/S, LCR-Yamaha), 10"711; 4. Hanks/P. Biggs (GB, Windle-Yamaha), 18"456; 5. Roscher/Hänni (D/CH, LCR-Suzuki), 56"808; 6. Manninen/Kuismanen (SF LCR-Suzuki), 1'15.711; 7. B. Fleury/J. Fleury (NZ, LCR-Suzuki), 1 tour; 8. Foukal/Pertlicek (CZ, LCR-Yamaha), 1 tour. 8 finishers.
Race II: 1. Ti. Reeves/Tr. Reeves (GB, LCR-Suzuki), 33'39.048; 2. S. Webster/Woodhead (B, LCR-Suzuki), 0"980; 3. Päivärinta/Wall (SF/S, LCR-Yamaha), 27"641; 4. Manninen/Kuismanen (SF, LCR-Suzuki), 28"200; 5. Gällros/Briggs (S/GB, LCR-Suzuki), 36"664; 6. Roscher/Hänni (D/CH, LCR-Suzuki), 1'09.220,; 7. M. Van Gils/T. Van Gils (NL, LCR-Suzuki), 1'24.511; 8. B. Fleury/Hilderbrand (NZ/D, LCR-Suzuki), 1'33.33; 9. J. Cluze/G. Cluze (F, Windle-Yamaha), 1 tour; 10. Foukal/Pertlicek (CZ, LCR-Yamaha), 1 tour. 10 finishers.

FINAL CLASSIFICATION
1. S. Webster/P. Woodhead	(GB, LCR-Suzuki)	130
2. Tim Reeves/Tristan Reeves	(GB, LCR-Suzuki)	114,5
3. T. Hanks/P. Biggs	(GB, Windle-Yamaha)	111,5

4. M. Van Gils/T. Van Gils (NL, LCR-Suzuki), 101; 5. Päivärinta/Wall (SF/S, LCR-Yamaha), 80,5; 6. Gällros/Berglund (S, LCR-Suzuki), 80; 7. Roscher/Hänni (D/CH, LCR-Suzuki), 52; 8. Maninnen/Kuismanen (SF, LCR-Suzuki), 46; 9. B. Fleury/J. Fleury (NZ, LCR-Suzuki), 44,5; 10. Foukal/Pertlicek (CZ, LCR-Yamaha), 41.

France

125 cc

21st March – Le Mans
1. Perdriat (Aprilia); 2. Deschamps (Honda); 3. Gautier (Honda); 4. Masbou (Honda); 5. Lougassi (Aprilia); 6. Lemarie (Honda); 7. Lussiana (Honda); 8. Berger (Moto Axxe); 9. Roma (Honda); 10. Servaes (Honda).

28th March – Magny-Cours
1. Lougassi (Aprilia); 2. Masbou (Honda); 3. Gautier (Honda); 4. Gines (Honda); 5. Burdin (Honda); 6. Leleu (Honda); 7. Berger (Moto Axxe); 8. Frink (Honda); 9. Basseville (Honda); 10. Bellaire (Honda).

2nd May – Nogaro
1. Masbou (Honda); 2. Gautier (Honda); 3. Olagnon (Honda); 4. Black (Honda); 5. Berger (Moto Axxe); 6. F. Millet (Honda); 7. Gines (Honda); 8. Deschamps (Honda); 9. Larrive (Honda); 10. Michel (Honda).

9th May – Carole
1. Olagnon (Honda); 2. K. Foray (Yamaha); 3. Masbou (Honda); 4. Gautier (Honda); 5. Perdriat (Aprilia); 6. Black (Honda); 7. Burdin (Honda); 8. Deschamps (Honda); 9. Lougassi (Aprilia); 10. Basseville (Honda).

23rd May – Le Vigeant
1. Masbou (Honda); 2. Gautier (Honda); 3. Gines (Honda); 4. Deschamps (Honda); 5. Burdin (Honda); 6. F. Millet (Honda); 7. Leleu (Honda); 8. Berger (Moto Axxe); 9. Lougassi (Aprilia); 10. Black (Honda).

20th June – Lédenon
1. Deschamps (Honda); 2. Perdriat (Aprilia); 3. Masbou (Honda); 4. Gines (Honda); 5. Leleu (Honda); 6. Berger (Moto Axxe); 7. Black (Honda); 8. Burdin (Honda); 9. F. Millet (Honda); 10. Michel (Honda).

25th July – Dijon
1. Masbou (Honda); 2. Gines (Honda); 3. Gautier (Honda); 4. Leleu (Honda); 5. Perdriat (Aprilia); 6. Lougassi (Aprilia); 7. Burdin (Honda); 8. Berger (Moto Axxe); 9. K. Foray (Yamaha); 10. Olagnon (Honda).

FINAL CLASSIFICATION
1. Alexis Masbou	Honda	140
2. William Gautier	Honda	101
3. Yannick Deschamps	Honda	74

4. Gines (Honda), 71; 5. Perdriat (Aprilia), 67; 6. Lougassi (Aprilia), 60; 7. Berger (Moto Axxe), 54; 8. Burdin (Honda), 48; 9. Olagnon (Honda), 47; 10. Leleu (Honda), 43.

Supersport

21st March – Le Mans
1. Lussiana (Yamaha); 2. J. Enjolras (Yamaha); 3. Diss (Honda); 4. Tiberio (Yamaha); 5. De Rosa (Kawasaki); 6. Muscat (Ducati); 7. Stey (Honda); 8. Mizera (Honda); 9. Bouan (Yamaha); 10. Donischal (Honda).

28th March – Magny-Cours
1. Tiberio (Yamaha); 2. Muscat (Ducati); 3. Bouan (Yamaha); 4. Lussiana (Yamaha); 5. Diss (Honda); 6. De Rosa (Kawasaki); 7. Metro (Suzuki); 8. Mizera (Honda); 9. Donischal (Honda); 10. Gomez (Suzuki).

2nd May – Nogaro
1. Muscat (Ducati); 2. Tiberio (Yamaha); 3. De Rosa (Kawasaki); 4. Lussiana (Yamaha); 5. Metro (Suzuki); 6. Stey (Honda); 7. Holon (Kawasaki); 8. Diss (Honda); 9. Bouan (Yamaha); 10. Gomez (Suzuki).

9th May – Carole
1. Muscat (Ducati); 2. Tiberio (Yamaha); 3. Stey (Honda); 4. De Rosa (Kawasaki); 5. Diss (Honda); 6. Donischal (Honda); 7. Holon (Kawasaki); 8. Mizera (Honda); 9. J. Petit (Honda); 10. Metro (Suzuki).

23rd May – Le Vigeant
1. Tiberio (Yamaha); 2. Muscat (Ducati); 3. Bouan (Yamaha); 4. Lussiana (Yamaha); 5. Stey (Honda); 6. Donischal (Honda); 7. Metro (Suzuki); 8. Diss (Honda); 9. De Rosa (Kawasaki); 10. Gomez (Suzuki).

20th June – Lédenon
1. Tiberio (Yamaha); 2. Muscat (Ducati); 3. Lussiana (Yamaha); 4. Bouan (Yamaha); 5. Metro (Suzuki); 6. Donischal (Honda); 7. Mizera (Honda); 8. De Rosa (Kawasaki); 9. J. Petit (Honda); 10. Mécène (Yamaha).

25th July – Dijon
1. Muscat (Ducati); 2. Protat (Ducati); 3. Lagrive (Suzuki); 4. Metro (Suzuki); 5. Bouan (Yamaha); 6. Stey (Honda); 7. Lussiana (Yamaha); 8. J. Enjolras (Yamaha); 9. Donischal (Honda); 10. Pavoine (Honda).

FINAL CLASSIFICATION
1. David Muscat	Ducati	145
2. Yoann Tiberio	Yamaha	128
3. Yann Lussiana	Yamaha	89

4. Bouan (Yamaha), 75; 5. De Rosa (Kawasaki), 65; 6. Metro (Suzuki), 64; 7. Stey (Honda), 56; 8. Diss (Honda), 54; 9. Donischal (Honda), 52; 10. Mizera (Honda), 39.

Superproduction/Stocksport

21st March – Le Mans
1. Gimbert (Yamaha SPP); 2. Da Costa (Kawasaki SPP); 3. Tangre (Suzuki STK); 4. Protat (Ducati SPP); 5. Lerat-Vanstaen (Suzuki STK); 6. Descoings (Kawasaki STK); 7. Fremy (Suzuki STK); 8. Lalevée (Suzuki STK); 9. Moreira (Kawasaki SPP); 10. Jolivet (Suzuki STK).

28th March – Magny-Cours
1. Gimbert (Yamaha SPP); 2. Da Costa (Kawasaki SPP); 3. Fremy (Suzuki STK); 4. Dietrich (Suzuki STK); 5. Duterne (Yamaha STK); 6. Gibet (Yamaha STK); 7. F. Jond (Suzuki SPP); 8. Hernandez (Suzuki STK); 9. Fouloi (Suzuki STK); 10. Gomez (Suzuki STK).

2nd May – Nogaro
1. Da Costa (Kawasaki SPP); 2. Gimbert (Yamaha SPP); 3. Moreira (Kawasaki SPP); 4. Duterne (Yamaha STK); 5. Protat (Ducati SPP); 6. Dietrich (Suzuki STK); 7. Gomez (Suzuki STK); 8. Fouloi (Suzuki STK); 9. Cazade (Yamaha SPP); 10. Descoings (Kawasaki STK).

9th May – Carole
1. Da Costa (Kawasaki SPP); 2. Gimbert (Yamaha SPP); 3. Moreira (Kawasaki SPP); 4. Protat (Ducati SPP); 5. Duterne (Yamaha STK); 6. Dietrich (Suzuki STK); 7. Fouloi (Suzuki STK); 8. Tangre (Suzuki STK); 9. Moisan (Kawasaki STK); 10. Lerat-Vanstaen (Suzuki STK).

23rd May – Le Vigeant
1. Da Costa (Kawasaki SPP); 2. Gimbert (Yamaha SPP); 3. Moreira (Kawasaki SPP); 4. Duterne (Yamaha STK); 5. Dietrich (Suzuki STK); 6. Protat (Ducati SPP); 7. Moisan (Kawasaki STK); 8. Gibet (Yamaha STK); 9. Tangre (Suzuki STK); 10. Gomez (Suzuki STK).

20th June – Lédenon
1. Gimbert (Yamaha SPP); 2. Da Costa (Kawasaki SPP); 3. Duterne (Yamaha STK); 4. Moreira (Kawasaki SPP); 5. Dietrich (Suzuki STK); 6. Tangre (Suzuki STK); 7. Di Foggia (Suzuki STK); 8. Rulfo (Suzuki STK); 9. Gibet (Yamaha STK); 10. Lalevée (Suzuki STK).

25th July – Dijon
1. Da Costa (Kawasaki SPP); 2. Duterne (Yamaha STK); 3. Dietrich (Suzuki STK); 4. Moisan (Kawasaki STK); 5. Delhalle (Kawasaki STK); 6. Mulot (Yamaha SPP); 7. Fouloi (Suzuki STK); 8. Di Foggia (Suzuki STK); 9. Guerouah (Kawasaki SPP); 10. Tangre (Suzuki STK).

FINAL CLASSIFICATION SUPER PRODUCTION
1. Julien Da Costa	Kawasaki	160
2. Sébastien Gimbert	Yamaha	135
3. Stéphane Duterne	Yamaha	84

4. Dietrich (Suzuki), 73; 5. Moreira (Kawasaki), 68; 6. Tangre (Suzuki), 52; 7. Protat (Ducati), 47; 8. Fouloi (Suzuki), 38; 9. J.-E. Gomez (Suzuki), 32; 10. Moisan (Kawasaki), 29.

FINAL CLASSIFICATION STOCKSPORT

1. Stéphane Duterne	Yamaha	126
2. Guillaume Dietrich	Suzuki	110
3. Frédéric Moreira	Kawasaki	105

4. Tangre (Suzuki), 76; 5. J.-E. Gomez (Suzuki), 56; 6. Fouloi (Suzuki), 54; 7. Moisan (Kawasaki), 39; 8. Gibet (Yamaha), 39; 9. Fremy (Suzuki), 38; 10. Di Foggia (Suzuki), 37.

Side-Cars

21st March – Le Mans
1. Delannoy/Capon (Windle-Suzuki); 2. Minguet/Bidault (LCR-Suzuki); 3. Le Bail/Chaigneau (LCR-Yamaha); 4. Dernoncourt/Lailheugue (LCR-Suzuki); 5. Cluze/Cluze (LCR-Motul); 6. Bessy/Bessy (LCR-Suzuki); 7. Baer/Rault (LCR-Suzuki); 8. Huet/Nicolas (Shelbourne-Honda); 9. Piroutet/Goubet (Windle); 10. Bourchis/Scellier (Windle-Yamaha).

28th March – Magny-Cours
1. Le Bail/Chaigneau (LCR-Yamaha); 2. Cluze/Cluze (LCR-Motul); 3. Baer/Rault (LCR-Suzuki); 4. Bessy/Bessy (LCR-Suzuki); 5. Lacour/Lebeau (Seymaz-JPX); 6. Piroutet/Goubet (Windle); 7. Ducouret/Prijent (Suzuki); 8. Hachet/Darras (Windle); 9. Wilmes/Vannier (LCR); 10. Leblond/Leblond (Baker-Honda).

2nd May – Nogaro
1. Delannoy/Capon (Windle-Suzuki); 2. Cluze/Cluze (LCR-Motul); 3. Le Bail/Chaigneau (LCR-Yamaha); 4. Bessy/Bessy (LCR-Suzuki); 5. Dernoncourt/Lailheugue (LCR-Suzuki); 6. Baer/Rault (LCR-Suzuki); 7. Gallerne (LCR-Suzuki); 8. Beneteau (LCR-Yamaha); 9. Leblond/Leblond (Baker-Honda); 10. Bourchis/Scellier (Windle-Yamaha).

9th May – Carole
1. Delannoy/Capon (Windle-Suzuki); 2. Minguet/Bidault (LCR-Suzuki); 3. Cluze/Cluze (LCR-Motul); 4. Le Bail/Chaigneau (LCR-Yamaha); 5. Dernoncourt/Lailheugue (LCR-Suzuki); 6. Baer/Rault (LCR-Suzuki); 7. Hachet/Darras (Windle); 8. Bourchis/Scellier (Windle-Yamaha); 9. Gallerne (LCR-Suzuki); 10. Piroutet/Goubet (Windle).

23rd May – Le Vigeant
1. Minguet/Bidault (LCR-Suzuki); 2. Dernoncourt/Lailheugue (LCR-Suzuki); 3. Delannoy/Capon (Windle-Suzuki); 4. Le Bail/Chaigneau (LCR-Yamaha); 5. Cluze/Cluze (LCR-Motul); 6. Bessy/Bessy (LCR-Suzuki); 7. Gallerne (LCR-Suzuki); 8. Lacour/Lebeau (Seymaz-JPX); 9. Wilmes/Vannier (LCR); 10. Beneteau (LCR-Yamaha).

20th June – Lédenon
1. Dernoncourt/Lailheugue (Windle-Suzuki); 2. Minguet/Bidault (LCR-Suzuki); 3. Delannoy/Capon (LCR-Suzuki); 4. Cluze/Cluze (LCR-Motul); 5. Le Bail/Chaigneau (LCR-Yamaha); 6. Lacour/Lebeau (Seymaz-JPX); 7. Gallerne (LCR-Suzuki); 8. Wilmes/Vannier (LCR); 9. Leblond/Leblond (Baker-Honda); 10. Bourchis/Scellier (Windle-Yamaha).

25th July – Dijon
1. Minguet/Bidault (LCR-Suzuki); 2. Dernoncourt/Lailheugue (LCR-Suzuki); 3. Cluze/Cluze (LCR-Motul); 4. Delannoy/Capon (Windle-Suzuki); 5. Le Bail/Chaigneau (LCR-Yamaha); 6. Lacour/Lebeau (Seymaz-JPX); 7. Pilault (Suzuki); 8. Beneteau (LCR-Yamaha); 9. Marzelle (Belazi-Suzuki); 10. Wilmes/Vannier (LCR).

FINAL CLASSIFICATION

1. Delannoy/Capon	Windle-Suzuki	120
2. Minguet/Bidault	LCR-Suzuki	110
3. Cluze/Cluze	LCR-Motul	107

4. Le Bail/Chaigneau (LCR-Yamaha), 105; 5. Dernoncourt/Lailheugue (LCR-Suzuki), 100; 6. Bessy/Bessy (LCR-Suzuki), 46; 7. Baer/Rault (LCR-Suzuki), 45; 8. Lacour/Lebeau (Seymaz-JPX), 41; 9. Gallerne (LCR-Suzuki), 34; 10. Leblond/Leblond (Baker-Honda), 34.

Italy

125 cc

25th April – Mugello
1. A. Aldrovandi (Honda); 2. Zanetti (Honda); 3. Pirro (Aprilia); 4. Danese (Aprilia); 5. Conti (Aprilia); 6. Fröhlich (D, Honda); 7. Giugliano (Aprilia); 8. Bianchi (Honda); 9. Antonelli (Aprilia); 10. Bertelli (Honda).

9th May – Imola
1. Talmacsi (H, Malaguti); 2. Pirro (Aprilia); 3. A. Aldrovandi (Honda); 4. Danese (Aprilia); 5. Giugliano (Aprilia); 6. Petrini (Aprilia); 7. Antonelli (Aprilia); 8. Venturi (Honda); 9. Moretti (Honda); 10. Perotti (Aprilia).

4th July – Vallelunga
1. A. Aldrovandi (Honda); 2. Petrini (Aprilia); 3. D'Amelio (Honda); 4. Conti (Aprilia); 5. Bianchi (Honda); 6. Lacalendola (Aprilia); 7. Baroni (Aprilia); 8. Danese (Aprilia); 9. Magnoni (Honda); 10. Verdini (Aprilia).

29th August – Misano
1. Pirro (Aprilia); 2. Di Meglio (F, Aprilia); 3. Danese (Aprilia); 4. Ferro (F, Honda); 5. A. Aldrovandi (Honda); 6. Iannone (Aprilia); 7. Morelli (Aprilia); 8. Baroni (Aprilia); 9. Petrini (Aprilia); 10. Giorgi (Honda).

12th September – Vallelunga
1. Pirro (Aprilia); 2. G. Ferro (Honda); 3. Danese (Aprilia); 4. Petrini (Aprilia); 5. A. Aldrovandi (Honda); 6. De Rosa (Honda); 7. D'Amelio (Honda); 8. Morelli (Aprilia); 9. Antonelli (Aprilia); 10. Conti (Aprilia).

FINAL CLASSIFICATION

1. Alessio Aldrovandi	(Honda)	94
2. Michele Pirro	(Aprilia)	91
3. Michele Danese	(Aprilia)	73

4. Petrini (Aprilia), 52; 5. G. Ferro (Honda), 36; 6. Baroni (Aprilia), 32; 7. D'Amelio (Honda), 31; 8. Conti (Aprilia), 30; 9. Antonelli (Aprilia), 30; 10. Giugliano (Aprilia), 23.

Supersport

25th April – Mugello
1. Giugovaz (Honda); 2. Goi (Yamaha); 3. Antonello (Kawasaki); 4. Carlacci (Yamaha); 5. C. Migliorati (Kawasaki); 6. Scalvini (Yamaha); 7. Cruciani (Kawasaki); 8. Tortoroglio (Suzuki); 9. Baiocco (Yamaha); 10. Mariottini (Yamaha).

9th May – Imola
1. Giugovaz (Honda); 2. C. Migliorati (Kawasaki); 3. Lanzi (Ducati); 4. Goi (Yamaha); 5. Scalvini (Yamaha); 6. Carlacci (Yamaha); 7. Mariottini (Yamaha); 8. Tortoroglio (Suzuki); 9. Malatesta (Kawasaki); 10. Roccoli (Yamaha).

4th July – Vallelunga
1. Antonello (Kawasaki); 2. C. Migliorati (Kawasaki); 3. Roccoli (Yamaha); 4. Carlacci (Yamaha); 5. Mariottini (Yamaha); 6. Goi (Yamaha); 7. Cruciani (Kawasaki); 8. Morreale (Yamaha); 9. Boccolini (Honda); 10. Pratichizzo (Honda).

29th August – Misano
1. Roccoli (Yamaha); 2. C. Migliorati (Kawasaki); 3. Cruciani (Kawasaki); 4. Pratichizzo (Honda); 5. Giugovaz (Honda); 6. Mariottini (Yamaha); 7. Scalvini (Yamaha); 8. Tortoroglio (Suzuki); 9. Valia (Ducati); 10. Baiocco (Yamaha).

12th September – Vallelunga
1. Roccoli (Yamaha); 2. Antonello (Kawasaki); 3. C. Migliorati (Kawasaki); 4. Giugovaz (Honda); 5. Goi (Yamaha); 6. Baiocco (Yamaha); 7. Cruciani (Kawasaki); 8. Tumminello (Yamaha); 9. Pratichizzo (Honda); 10. Scalvini (Yamaha).

FINAL CLASSIFICATION

1. Cristiano Migliorati	(Kawasaki)	87
2. Diego Giugovaz	(Honda)	74
3. Massimo Roccoli	(Yamaha)	72

4. Antonello (Kawasaki), 61; 5. Goi (Yamaha), 54; 6. Cruciani (Kawasaki), 43; 7. Carlacci (Yamaha), 41; 8. Mariottini (Yamaha), 40; 9. Scalvini (Yamaha), 36; 10. Pratichizzo (Honda), 26.

Superstock

25th April – Mugello
1. Scassa (Kawasaki); 2. Conforti (Yamaha); 3. Pellizzon (Aprilia); 4. Dionisi (Suzuki); 5. De Noni (Suzuki); 6. Polita (Ducati); 7. Rocamora (E, Kawasaki); 8. Masoni (Suzuki); 9. Antonello (Kawasaki); 10. Addamo (Yamaha).

9th May – Imola
1. Polita (Ducati); 2. Rocamora (E, Kawasaki); 3. Conforti (Yamaha); 4. Dionisi (Suzuki); 5. Antonello (Kawasaki); 6. Pellizzon (Aprilia); 7. Buzzi (Suzuki); 8. W. De Angelis (Ducati); 9. Mauri (Ducati); 10. Sanna (Yamaha).

4th July – Vallelunga
1. Conforti (Yamaha); 2. Dionisi (Suzuki); 3. Ricci (Kawasaki); 4. A. Martinez (E, Kawasaki); 5. Addamo (Yamaha); 6. Lunadei (Suzuki); 7. Buzzi (Suzuki); 8. De Noni (Suzuki); 9. Rufolini (Kawasaki); 10. Tocca (Kawasaki).

29th August – Misano
1. Pellizzon (Aprilia); 2. Scassa (Kawasaki); 3. Guareschi (Kawasaki); 4. Polita (Ducati); 5. A. Martinez (E, Kawasaki); 6. Conforti (Yamaha); 7. De Noni (Suzuki); 8. Segoni (Yamaha); 9. Dionisi (Suzuki); 10. Sassaro (Suzuki).

12th September – Vallelunga
1. Pellizzon (Aprilia); 2. Guareschi (Kawasaki); 3. Lunadei (Yamaha); 4. Scassa (Kawasaki); 5. Rocamora (E, Suzuki); 6. Dionisi (Suzuki); 7. A. Martinez (E, Kawasaki); 8. Polita (Ducati); 9. Sanna (Yamaha); 10. Antonello (Kawasaki).

FINAL CLASSIFICATION

1. Luca Conforti	(Yamaha)	82
2. Fabrizio Pellizzon	(Aprilia)	77
3. Ilario Dionisi	(Suzuki)	67

4. Scassa (Kawasaki), 58; 5. Polita (Ducati), 57; 6. Lunadei (Yamaha), 42; 7. Guareschi (Kawasaki), 36; 8. De Noni (Suzuki), 30; 9. Antonello (Kawasaki), 28; 10. Sanna (Yamaha), 24.

Superbike

25th April – Mugello
1. Borciani (Ducati); 2. Gramigni (Yamaha); 3. Clementi (Kawasaki); 4. M. Sanchini (Kawasaki); 5. Sala (Suzuki); 6. Blora (Ducati); 7. Alfonsi (Yamaha); 8. Pedersoli (Ducati); 9. Di Maso (Suzuki); 10. Liverani (Ducati).

9th May – Imola
1. Martin (AUS, Ducati); 2. Nannelli (Ducati); 3. Gramigni (Yamaha); 4. Pedercini (Ducati); 5. Vizziello (Yamaha); 6. Borciani (Ducati); 7. Sanchini (Kawasaki); 8. Romboni (Yamaha); 9. Alfonsi (Yamaha); 10. Blora (Ducati).

4th July – Vallelunga
1. Borciani (Ducati); 2. Gramigni (Yamaha); 3. Pedercini (Ducati); 4. Vizziello (Yamaha); 5. Clementi (Kawasaki); 6. Di Maso (Suzuki); 7. Pini (Suzuki); 8. Alfonsi (Yamaha); 9. Pedersoli (Ducati); 10. Liverani (Ducati).

29th August – Misano
1. Pedercini (Ducati); 2. Gramigni (Yamaha); 3. Borciani (Ducati); 4. Vizziello (Yamaha); 5. Romboni (Yamaha); 6. Clementi (Kawasaki); 7. Pedersoli (Ducati); 8. Liverani (Ducati); 9. Alfonsi (Yamaha); 10. Pini (Suzuki).

12th September – Vallelunga
1. Gramigni (Yamaha); 2. Vizziello (Yamaha); 3. Borciani (Ducati); 4. Alfonsi (Yamaha); 5. Clementi (Kawasaki); 6. Brignola (Suzuki); 7. Liverani (Ducati); 8. Pini (Suzuki); 9. Pedercini (Ducati); 10. Blora (Yamaha).

FINAL CLASSIFICATION

1. Alessandro Gramigni	(Yamaha)	105
2. Marco Borciani	(Ducati)	93
3. Lucio Pedercini	(Ducati)	64

4. Vizziello (Yamaha), 59 ; 5. Clementi (Kawasaki), 48 ; 6. Alfonsi (Yamaha), 45 ; 7. Pedersoli (Ducati), 29 ; 8. Liverani (Ducati), 29 ; 9. Pini (Suzuki), 28 ; 10. Blora (Yamaha), 26.

Great Britain

125 cc

28th March – Silverstone
1. Elkin (Honda); 2. Weston (Honda); 3. E. Laverty (Honda); 4. Neate (Honda); 5. Pearson (Honda); 6. Wilcox (Honda); 7. Grant (Honda); 8. Kinton (Honda); 9. Cooper (Honda); 10. Saxelby (Honda).

12 April – Brands Hatch
1. Wilcox (Honda); 2. E. Laverty (Honda); 3. Beech (Honda); 4. Pearson (Honda); 5. Saxelby (Honda); 6. Weston (Honda); 7. Neate (Honda); 8. Bridewell (Honda); 9. Walker (Aprilia); 10. Dickinson (Honda).

25th April – Snetterton
1. E. Laverty (Honda); 2. Pearson (Honda); 3. Elkin (Honda); 4. Weston (Honda); 5. Neate (Honda); 6. Wilcox (Honda); 7. Saxelby (Honda); 8. Clark (Honda); 9. P. Robinson (Honda); 10. Guiver (Honda).

3rd May – Oulton Park
1. Wilcox (Honda); 2. Elkin (Honda); 3. Neate (Honda); 4. Dickinson (Honda); 5. Bridewell (Honda); 6. Murphy (Honda); 7. P. Robinson (Honda); 8. J. Vincent (Honda); 9. Kinton (Honda); 10. Ford (Honda).

23rd May – Mondello – Ireland
1. E. Laverty (Honda); 2. P. Robinson (Honda); 3. Elkin (Honda); 4. Bridewell (Honda); 5. Guiver (Honda); 6. Clark (Honda); 7. Dickinson (Honda); 8. Grant (Honda); 9. Stott (Honda); 10. Beech (Honda).

6th June – Thruxton
1. E. Laverty (Honda); 2. Wilcox (Honda); 3. Elkin (Honda); 4. Clark (Honda); 5. Pearson (Honda); 6. Dickinson (Honda); 7. Weston (Honda); 8. Bridwell (Honda); 9. Beech (Honda); 10. Webb (Honda).

20th June – Brands Hatch
1. Elkin (Honda); 2. Wilcox (Honda); 3. Pearson (Honda); 4. Guiver (Honda); 5. Weston (Honda); 6. Webb (Honda); 7. Clark (Honda); 8. Bridewell (Honda); 9. E. Laverty (Honda); 10. Grant (Honda).

4th July – Knockhill
1. P. Robinson (Honda); 2. Elkin (Honda); 3. Guiver (Honda); 4. Wilcox (Honda); 5. Clark (Honda); 6. Bridewell (Honda); 7. E. Laverty (Honda); 8. Pearson (Honda); 9. Beech (Honda); 10. Ford (Honda).

18th July – Mallory Park
1. Elkin (Honda); 2. Beech (Honda); 3. E. Laverty (Honda); 4. Clark (Honda); 5. Weston (Honda); 6. Dickinson (Honda); 7. Bridewell (Honda); 8. Morris (Honda); 9. Grant (Honda); 10. Tinmouth (Honda).

15th August – Croft
1. E. Laverty (Honda); 2. Weston (Honda); 3. Elkin (Honda); 4. Dickinson (Honda); 5. Wilcox (Honda); 6. Webb (Honda); 7. Cooper (Honda); 8. Bridewell (Honda); 9. Linfoot (Honda); 10. P. Robinson (Honda).

30th August – Cadwell Park
1. Beech (Honda); 2. Elkin (Honda); 3. E. Laverty (Honda); 4. Weston (Honda); 5. Morris (Honda); 6. Clark (Honda); 7. Wilcox (Honda); 8. Dickinson (Honda); 9. Guiver (Honda); 10. Neate (Honda).

12th September – Oulton Park
1. Beech (Honda); 2. E. Laverty (Honda); 3. Weston (Honda); 4. Neate (Honda); 5. Clark (Honda); 6. Wilcox (Honda); 7. Cooper (Honda); 8. A. Walker (Aprilia); 9. Webb (Honda); 10. Linfoot (Honda).

19th September – Donington
1. Elkin (Honda); 2. Gines (F, Honda); 3. Morris (Honda); 4. Dickinson (Honda); 5. Pearson (Honda); 6. A. Walker (Aprilia); 7. Webb (Honda); 8. Clark (Honda); 9. Cooper (Honda); 10. Hayward (Honda).

FINAL CLASSIFICATION

1. Christian Elkin	(Honda)	224
2. Eugene Laverty	(Honda)	203
3. Mark Wilcox	(Honda)	153

4. Weston (Honda), 127; 5. Beech (Honda), 106; 6. Pearson (Honda), 98; 7. Clark (Honda), 92; 8. Bridewell (Honda), 88; 9. Dickinson (Honda), 84; 10. Neate (Honda), 73.

Supersport

28th March – Silverstone
1. K. Harris (Honda); 2. Jones (Triumph); 3. M. Laverty (Ducati); 4. Riba (E, Kawasaki); 5. Camier (Honda); 6. Murphy (Honda); 7. Crutchlow (Honda); 8. J. Vincent (Honda); 9. Coates (Suzuki); 10. Sykes (Suzuki).

12th April – Brands Hatch
1. J. Vincent (Honda); 2. Quigley (Suzuki); 3. Andrews (Yamaha); 4. Riba (E, Kawasaki); 5. Tunstall (Honda); 6. M. Laverty (Ducati); 7. Murphy (Honda); 8. Jackson (Honda); 9. Robinson (Yamaha); 10. Norval (SA, Honda).

25th April – Snetterton
1. M. Laverty (Ducati); 2. K. Harris (Honda); 3. Riba (E, Kawasaki); 4. Quigley (Suzuki); 5. Andrews (Yamaha); 6. J. Vincent (Honda); 7. Sykes (Suzuki); 8. Coates (Suzuki); 9. Jones (Triumph); 10. Llewellyn (Ducati).

3rd May – Oulton Park
1. K. Harris (Honda); 2. M. Laverty (Ducati); 3. J. Vincent (Honda); 4. Andrews (Yamaha); 5. Crutchlow (Honda); 6. Camier (Honda); 7. Riba (E, Kawasaki); 8. Jones (Triumph); 9. Quigley (Suzuki); 10. Coates (Suzuki).

23rd May – Mondello – Irlande
1. Andrews (Yamaha); 2. M. Laverty (Ducati); 3. K. Harris (Honda); 4. Sykes (Suzuki); 5. Crutchlow (Honda); 6. Riba (E, Kawasaki); 7. J. Vincent (Honda); 8. Camier (Honda); 9. Quigley (Suzuki); 10. Jones (Triumph).

6th June – Thruxton
1. K. Harris (Honda); 2. Camier (Honda); 3. M. Laverty (Ducati); 4. Quigley (Suzuki); 5. Riba (E, Kawasaki); 6. Rea (Honda); 7. J. Vincent (Honda); 8. Young (Honda); 9. Norval (SA, Honda); 10. Sykes (Suzuki).

20th June – Brands Hatch
1. K. Harris (Honda); 2. J. Vincent (Honda); 3. Riba (E, Kawasaki); 4. Llewellyn (Ducati); 5. Andrews (Yamaha); 6. Beaumont (Honda); 7. M. Laverty (Ducati); 8. Rea (Honda); 9. Buckles (Yamaha); 10. Jackson (Honda).

4th July – Knockhill
1. Young (Honda); 2. K. Harris (Honda); 3. M. Laverty (Ducati); 4. Riba (E, Kawasaki); 5. Sykes (Suzuki); 6. Murphy (Honda); 7. Crutchlow (Honda); 8. Jones (Triumph); 9. Jackson (Honda); 10. Grant (Honda).

18th July – Mallory Park
1. K. Harris (Honda); 2. J. Vincent (Honda); 3. Camier (Honda); 4. M. Laverty (Ducati); 5. Young (Honda); 6. Llewellyn (Ducati); 7. Crutchlow (Honda); 8. Coates (Suzuki); 9. Sykes (Suzuki); 10. Murphy (Honda).

15th August – Croft
1. J. Vincent (Honda); 2. Camier (Honda); 3. K. Harris (Honda); 4. Sykes (Suzuki); 5. Quigley (Suzuki); 6. Coates (Suzuki); 7. Llewellyn (Ducati); 8. Easton (Ducati); 9. Crutchlow (Honda); 10. J. Robinson (Yamaha).

30th August – Cadwell Park
1. J. Vincent (Honda); 2. Sykes (Suzuki); 3. Easton (Ducati); 4. M. Laverty (Ducati); 5. Llewellyn (Ducati); 6. Quigley (Suzuki); 7. Riba (E, Kawasaki); 8. Jones (Triumph); 9. Andrews (Yamaha); 10. Young (Honda).

12th September – Oulton Park
1. K. Harris (Honda); 2. Sykes (Suzuki); 3. J. Vincent (Honda); 4. Camier (Honda); 5. Jones (Triumph); 6. Easton (Ducati); 7. Crutchlow (Honda); 8. Coates (Suzuki); 9. Riba (E, Kawasaki); 10. Murphy (Honda).

19th September – Donington
1. Jones (Triumph); 2. M. Laverty (Ducati); 3. Sykes (Suzuki); 4. J. Vincent (Honda); 5. Riba (E, Kawasaki); 6. K. Harris (Honda); 7. Crutchlow (Honda); 8. Young (Honda); 9. Quigley (Suzuki); 10. Andrews (Yamaha).

FINAL CLASSIFICATION

1. Karl Harris	(Honda)	232
2. Jason Vincent	(Honda)	196
3. Michael Laverty	(Ducati)	178

4. Riba (E, Kawasaki), 128; 5. Sykes (Suzuki), 123; 6. Quigley (Suzuki), 102; 7. Camier (Honda), 99; 8. Jones (Triumph), 93; 9. Andrews (Yamaha), 89; 10. Crutchlow (Honda), 75.

Superstock

28th March – Silverstone
1. Wilson (Suzuki); 2. Tinsley (Suzuki); 3. Allan (Kawasaki); 4. Palmer (Suzuki); 5. Shand (Yamaha); 6. Morley (Suzuki); 7. Beaumont (Yamaha); 8. Fitzpatrick (Suzuki); 9. Reilly (Ducati); 10. Heckles (Yamaha).

12th April – Brands Hatch
1. Tinsley (Suzuki); 2. Beaumont (Yamaha); 3. Palmer (Suzuki); 4. Wilson (Suzuki); 5. Mitchell (*) (Suzuki); 6. Heckles (Yamaha); 7. Shand (Yamaha); 8. Reilly (Ducati); 9. Crockford (Suzuki); 10. Fitzpatrick (Suzuki).

25th April – Snetterton
1. Beaumont (Yamaha); 2. Wilson (Suzuki); 3. Palmer (Suzuki); 4. Tinsley (Suzuki); 5. Shand (Yamaha); 6. J. Laverty (Yamaha); 7. Mitchell(*) (Suzuki); 8. Allan (Suzuki); 9. Thompson (Suzuki); 10. R. Rainey (Yamaha).

3rd May – Oulton Park
1. Tinsley (Suzuki); 2. Heckles (Yamaha); 3. Palmer (Suzuki); 4. Shand (Yamaha); 5. Beaumont (Yamaha); 6. Allan (Kawasaki); 7. Mainwaring (Yamaha); 8. Wilson (Suzuki); 9. Reilly (Ducati); 10. J. Laverty (Yamaha).

6th June – Thruxton
1. Palmer (Suzuki); 2. Tinsley (Suzuki); 3. Beaumont (Yamaha); 4. Mainwaring (Yamaha); 5. J. Laverty (Yamaha); 6. Wilson (Suzuki); 7. Crockford (Suzuki); 8. Shand (Yamaha); 9. Cowie (Kawasaki); 10. Mitchell(*) (Suzuki).

20th June – Brands Hatch
Race cancelled after an accident at Hawthorn Hill, which cost the life of Darren Mitchell.

4th July – Knockhill
Race cancelled because of problems with track safety.

10th August – Oulton Park
1. Allan (Kawasaki); 2. Tinsley (Suzuki); 3. Shand (Yamaha); 4. MacDonald (Suzuki); 5. Palmer (Suzuki); 6. Wilson (Suzuki); 7. N. MacLeod (Suzuki); 8. MacFadyen (Suzuki); 9. Reilly (Ducati); 10. Houston (Suzuki).

15th August – Croft
1. Da Costa (F, Kawasaki); 2. Tinsley (Suzuki); 3. Shand (Yamaha); 4. Jackson (Yamaha); 5. Beaumont (Yamaha); 6. Palmer (Suzuki); 7. Wilson (Suzuki); 8. Johnson (Yamaha); 9. Ingram (Suzuki); 10. Hutchinson (Suzuki).

30th August – Cadwell Park
1. Da Costa (F, Kawasaki); 2. Beaumont (Yamaha); 3. Neill (Suzuki); 4. Allan (Kawasaki); 5. Wilson (Honda); 6. Mainwaring (Yamaha); 7. Fitzpatrick (Suzuki); 8. Zanotti (I, Suzuki); 9. Jackson (Yamaha); 10. Tinsley (Suzuki).

12th September – Oulton Park
1. Beaumont (Yamaha); 2. Wilson (Suzuki); 3. Jackson (Yamaha); 4. Tinsley (Suzuki); 5. J. Laverty (Yamaha); 6. Neill (Suzuki); 7. Hutchinson (Suzuki); 8. Zanotti (I, Suzuki); 9. M. Davies (Yamaha); 10. R. Rainey (Yamaha).

19th September – Donington
Race I: 1. Tinsley (Suzuki); 2. Da Costa (F, Kawasaki); 3. Beaumont (Yamaha); 4. Wilson (Suzuki); 5. Johnson (Suzuki); 6. Shand (Yamaha); 7. Palmer (Suzuki); 8. Jackson (Yamaha); 9. Zanotti (I, Suzuki); 10. Mainwaring (Yamaha).
Race II: 1. Beaumont (Yamaha); 2. Da Costa (F, Kawasaki); 3. J. Laverty (Yamaha); 4. Jackson (Yamaha); 5. Shand (Yamaha); 6. Zanotti (I, Suzuki); 7. Mainwaring (Yamaha); 8. Johnson (Suzuki); 9. Wylie (Yamaha); 10. Neill (Suzuki).

FINAL CLASSIFICATION
1. Danny Beaumont	(Yamaha)	214
2. Andrew Tinsley	(Suzuki)	187
3. Ben Wilson	(Suzuki)	172

4. Palmer (Suzuki), 170; 5. Shand (Yamaha); 6. Da Costa (F, Kawasaki), 90; 7. Allan (Kawasaki), 82; 8. J. Laverty (Yamaha), 70; 9. Neill (Suzuki), 69; 10. Mainwaring (Yamaha), 69.

(*): Darren Mitchell suffered a fatal accident on 20th June at Brands Hatch.

Superbike

28th March – Silverstone
Race I: 1. Rutter (Honda); 2. Kiyonari (J, Honda); 3. Reynolds (Suzuki); 4. Kagayama (J, Suzuki); 5. Emmett (Ducati); 6. Nutt (Yamaha); 7. S. Smart (Kawasaki); 8. Thomas (AUS, Ducati); 9. Richards (AUS, Kawasaki); 10. Coxhell (AUS, Honda).
Race II: 1. Reynolds (Suzuki); 2. Kiyonari (J, Honda); 3. Rutter (Honda); 4. Emmett (Ducati); 5. S. Smart (Kawasaki); 6. Thomas (AUS, Ducati); 7. Easton (Ducati); 8. Mason (Yamaha); 9. Plater (Yamaha); 10. Hill (Yamaha).

12th April – Brands Hatch
Race I: 1. Reynolds (Suzuki); 2. Rutter (Honda); 3. Kagayama (J, Suzuki); 4. S. Smart (Kawasaki); 5. Mason (Yamaha); 6. Kiyonari (J, Honda); 7. Corke (Suzuki); 8. Kitkham (Suzuki); 9. Hill (Yamaha); 10. Clarke (Yamaha).
Race II: 1. Emmett (Ducati); 2. Rutter (Honda); 3. Reynolds (Suzuki); 4. S. Smart (Kawasaki); 5. Kagayama (J, Suzuki); 6. Kiyonari (J, Honda); 7. Richards (AUS, Kawasaki); 8. Thomas (AUS, Ducati); 9. Mason (Yamaha); 10. Hill (Yamaha).

25th April – Snetterton
Race I: 1. Kagayama (J, Suzuki); 2. Reynolds (Suzuki); 3. Rutter (Honda); 4. Emmett (Ducati); 5. S. Smart (Kawasaki); 6. Thomas (AUS, Ducati); 7. Kiyonari (J, Honda); 8. Hill (Yamaha); 9. Richards (AUS, Kawasaki); 10. Haydon (Ducati).
Race II: 1. Reynolds (Suzuki); 2. Rutter (Honda); 3. Emmett (Ducati); 4. Kagayama (J, Suzuki); 5. Thomas (AUS, Ducati); 6. S. Smart (Kawasaki); 7. Richards (AUS, Kawasaki); 8. Plater (Yamaha); 9. Kiyonari (J, Honda); 10. Hill (Yamaha).

3rd May – Oulton Park
Race I: 1. Kagayama (J, Suzuki); 2. Reynolds (Suzuki); 3. Rutter (Honda); 4. Thomas (AUS, Ducati); 5. S. Smart (Kawasaki); 6. Richards (AUS, Kawasaki); 7. Mason (Yamaha); 8. Emmett (Ducati); 9. Hill (Yamaha); 10. J. Ellison (Yamaha).
Race II: 1. Kagayama (J, Suzuki); 2. Reynolds (Suzuki); 3. Rutter (Honda); 4. Thomas (AUS, Ducati); 5. S. Smart (Kawasaki); 6. L. Haslam (Ducati); 7. Mason (Yamaha); 8. J. Ellison (Yamaha); 9. Richards (AUS, Kawasaki); 10. Haga (J, Ducati).

23rd May – Mondello – Irlande
Race I: 1. S. Smart (Kawasaki); 2. Reynolds (Suzuki); 3. Richards (AUS, Kawasaki); 4. Kagayama (J, Suzuki); 5. Thomas (AUS, Ducati); 6. Emmett (Ducati); 7. Buckingham (Suzuki); 8. Coxhell (AUS, Honda); 9. Haydon (Yamaha); 10. Clarke (Yamaha).
Race II: 1. Rutter (Honda); 2. Reynolds (Suzuki); 3. S. Smart (Kawasaki); 4. Richards (AUS, Kawasaki); 5. Kagayama (J, Suzuki); 6. Hill (Yamaha); 7. Emmett (Ducati); 8. Clarke (Yamaha); 9. Coxhell (AUS, Honda); 10. Buckingham (Suzuki).

6th June – Thruxton
Race I: 1. Rutter (Honda); 2. Reynolds (Suzuki); 3. Emmett (Ducati); 4. Lavilla (E, Suzuki); 5. Thomas (AUS, Ducati); 6. S. Smart (Kawasaki); 7. Mason (Yamaha); 8. J. Ellison (Yamaha); 9. Hill (Yamaha); 10. Clarke (Yamaha).
Race II: 1. Emmett (Ducati); 2. Rutter (Honda); 3. Lavilla (E, Suzuki); 4. S. Smart (Kawasaki); 5. J. Ellison (Yamaha); 6. Hill (Yamaha); 7. Clarke (Yamaha); 8. Kiyonari (J, Honda); 9. Coxhell (AUS, Honda); 10. Buckingham (Suzuki).

20th June – Brands Hatch
Race I: 1. Reynolds (Suzuki); 2. Emmett (Ducati); 3. McGuiness (Kawasaki); 4. Kagayama (J, Suzuki); 5. Rutter (Honda); 6. Haydon (Yamaha); 7. Hill (Yamaha); 8. L. Haslam (Ducati); 9. Corke (Suzuki); 10. Thomas (AUS, Ducati).
Race II: 1. L. Haslam (Ducati); 2. Emmett (Ducati); 3. Kagayama (J, Suzuki); 4. Haydon (Yamaha); 5. S. Smart (Kawasaki); 6. McGuiness (Kawasaki); 7. Reynolds (Suzuki); 8. Hill (Yamaha); 9. Coxhell (AUS, Honda); 10. Mason (Yamaha).

4th July – Knockhill
Race I: 1. S. Smart (Kawasaki); 2. Haydon (Yamaha); 3. Kagayama (J, Suzuki); 4. Reynolds (Suzuki); 5. Kirkham (Suzuki); 6. Mason (Yamaha); 7. J. Ellison (Yamaha); 8. MacPherson (Ducati); 9. Rutter (Honda); 10. Kiyonari (J, Honda).
Race II: 1. Haydon (Yamaha); 2. Emmett (Ducati); 3. Reynolds (Suzuki); 4. Rutter (Honda); 5. Kagayama (J, Suzuki); 6. S. Smart (Kawasaki); 7. McGuiness (Kawasaki); 8. Coxhell (AUS, Honda); 9. Thomas (AUS, Ducati); 10. J. Ellison (Yamaha).

18th July – Mallory Park
Race I: 1. Reynolds (Suzuki); 2. Kagayama (J, Suzuki); 3. S. Smart (Kawasaki); 4. Kiyonari (J, Honda); 5. Haydon (Yamaha); 6. Rutter (Honda); 7. Emmett (Ducati); 8. Thomas (AUS, Ducati); 9. McGuiness (Kawasaki); 10. Hobbs (Suzuki).
Race II: 1. S. Smart (Kawasaki); 2. Reynolds (Suzuki); 3. Kiyonari (J, Honda); 4. Haydon (Yamaha); 5. Emmett (Ducati); 6. Hill (Yamaha); 7. Mason (Yamaha); 8. Thomas (AUS, Ducati); 9. McGuiness (Kawasaki); 10. Plater (Yamaha).

15th August – Croft
Race I: 1. Rutter (Honda); 2. Kagayama (J, Suzuki); 3. S. Smart (Kawasaki); 4. Kiyonari (J, Honda); 5. Reynolds (Suzuki); 6. Haydon (Yamaha); 7. Emmett (Ducati); 8. Thomas (AUS, Ducati); 9. Hill (Yamaha); 10. McGuiness (Kawasaki).
Race II: 1. Rutter (Honda); 2. Smart (Kawasaki); 3. Reynolds (Suzuki); 4. Kiyonari (J, Honda); 5. Haydon (Yamaha); 6. Mason (Yamaha); 7. McGuiness (Kawasaki); 8. Coxhell (AUS, Honda); 9. J. Ellison (Yamaha); 10. Plater (Yamaha).

30th August – Cadwell Park
Race I: 1. Rutter (Honda); 2. Kiyonari (J, Honda); 3. Kagayama (J, Suzuki); 4. Haydon (Yamaha); 5. Hill (Yamaha); 6. Thomas (AUS, Ducati); 7. Richards (AUS, Kawasaki); 8. Clarke (Yamaha); 9. McGuiness (Kawasaki); 10. Emmett (Ducati).
Race II: 1. Kagayama (J, Suzuki); 2. S. Smart (Kawasaki); 3. Emmett (Ducati); 4. Thomas (AUS, Ducati); 5. Richards (AUS, Kawasaki); 6. Haydon (Yamaha); 7. Clarke (Yamaha); 8. Reynolds (Suzuki); 9. McGuiness (Kawasaki); 10. Ellison (Yamaha).

12th September – Oulton Park
Race I: 1. Reynolds (Suzuki); 2. Rutter (Honda); 3. Kagayama (J, Suzuki); 4. Emmett (Ducati); 5. Plater (Yamaha); 6. Richards (AUS, Kawasaki); 7. Thomas (AUS, Ducati); 8. S. Smart (Kawasaki); 9. Hill (Yamaha); 10. Brown (Ducati).
Race II: 1. Reynolds (Suzuki); 2. Rutter (Honda); 3. Kagayama (J, Suzuki); 4. Emmett (Ducati); 5. Thomas (AUS, Ducati); 6. Kiyonari (J, Honda); 7. Plater (Yamaha); 8. Haydon (Yamaha); 9. Richards (AUS, Kawasaki); 10. Hill (Yamaha).

19th September – Donington
Race I: 1. Kiyonari (J, Honda); 2. Rutter (Honda); 3. Reynolds (Suzuki); 4. S. Smart (Kawasaki); 5. Emmett (Ducati); 6. Richards (AUS, Kawasaki); 7. Thomas (AUS, Ducati); 8. Haydon (Yamaha); 9. Mason (Yamaha); 10. Hill (Yamaha).
Race II: 1. Kiyonari (J, Honda); 2. Rutter (Honda); 3. Emmett (Ducati); 4. S. Smart (Kawasaki); 5. Kagayama (J, Suzuki); 6. Reynolds (Suzuki); 7. Thomas (AUS, Ducati); 8. Haydon (Yamaha); 9. J. Ellison (Yamaha); 10. Plater (Yamaha).

FINAL CLASSIFICATION
1. John Reynolds	(Suzuki)	446
2. Michael Rutter	(Honda)	417
3. Yukio Kagayama	(Suzuki)	335

4. S. Smart (Kawasaki), 330; 5. Emmett (Ducati), 315; 6. Kiyonari (J, Honda), 234; 7. Thomas (AUS, Ducati), 193; 8. Haydon (Yamaha), 181; 9. Hill (Yamaha), 137; 10. Richards (AUS, Kawasaki), 125.

Spain

125 cc

2003

16th November – Valencia
1. Bautista (Aprilia); 2. Talmacsi (H, Malaguti); 3. Gadea (Aprilia); 4. Hernandez (Aprilia); 5. Fröhlich (D, Honda); 6. Pasini (I, Aprilia); 7. Pirro (I, Aprilia); 8. Ortega (Aprilia); 9. Catalán (Aprilia); 10. De Rosa (I, Malaguti).

23rd November – Jerez de la Frontera
1. Bautista (Aprilia); 2. Talmacsi (H, Malaguti); 3. Ortega (Aprilia); 4. Carchano (Honda); 5. Pasini (I, Aprilia); 6. Pirro (I, Aprilia); 7. A. Aldrovandi (I, Malaguti); 8. Gadea (Aprilia); 9. Fröhlich (D, Honda); 10. Jerez (Honda).

FINAL CLASSIFICATION
1. Alvaro Bautista	(Aprilia)	161
2. Sergio Gadea	(Aprilia)	82
3. Manuel A. Hernandez Junior	(Aprilia)	64

4. Ortega (Aprilia), 64; 5. Carchano (Honda), 49; 6. Bonache (Honda), 45; 7. Talmacsi (H, Malaguti), 40; 8. J. Miralles Junior (Aprilia), 36 ; 9. Catalán (Aprilia), 34; 10. Ballesteros (Aprilia), 33.

2004

23rd May – Catalunya
1. Carchano (Aprilia); 2. Perren (ARG, Honda); 3. Catalán (Aprilia); 4. Terol (Aprilia); 5. Danese (I, Aprilia); 6. Sandi (Aprilia); 7. Espargaro (Honda); 8. Petrini (I, Aprilia); 9. Tamburini (I, Aprilia); 10. Kyyhkynen (SF, Honda).

20th June – Jarama
1. Espargaro (Honda); 2. Terol (Aprilia); 3. J. Miralles Junior (Aprilia); 4. Catalán (Aprilia); 5. Tamburini (I, Aprilia); 6. Morelli (I, Aprilia); 7. Bonache (Honda); 8. Tutusaus (Honda); 9. Naverrete (Aprilia); 10. Belloso (Honda).

11th July – Albacete
1. M. Hernandez Junior (Aprilia); 2. Jerez (Honda); 3. Espargaro (Honda); 4. Bonache (Honda); 5. Terol (Aprilia); 6. Carchano (Aprilia); 7. Perren (ARG, Honda); 8. Danese (I, Aprilia); 9. Antonelli (I, Aprilia); 10. Iannone (I, Aprilia).

26th September – Jerez de la Frontera
1. M. Hernandez Junior (Aprilia); 2. J. Miralles Junior (Aprilia); 3. Jerez (Honda); 4. Espargaro (Honda); 5. Iannone (I, Aprilia); 6. Petrini (I, Aprilia); 7. Terol (Aprilia); 8. Saez (Aprilia);

9. Tamburini (I, Aprilia); 10. Bonache (Honda).

24th October – Albacete

1. J. Miralles Junior (Aprilia); 2. Iannone (I, Aprilia); 3. M. Hernandez Junior (Aprilia); 4. Carchano (Aprilia); 5. Sandi (I, Aprilia); 6. Saez (Aprilia); 7. Danese (I, Aprilia); 8. Petrini (I, Aprilia); 9. Maestro (Honda); 10. Jerez (Honda).

The final two races of the season (Valencia 14th November and Jerez 21st November) took place after publication of this book.

Supersport

2003

16th November – Valencia

1. Carrasco (Honda); 2. Jara (Yamaha); 3. Forés (Honda); 4. Mazuecos (Yamaha); 5. Cárdenas (COL, Yamaha); 6. Silva (Yamaha); 7. Tiberio (F, Honda); 8. Jimenez (Yamaha); 9. Tizon (Yamaha); 10. Piñera (Yamaha).

23rd November – Jerez de la Frontera

1. Cárdenas (COL, Yamaha); 2. Forés (Honda); 3. Mazuecos (Yamaha); 4. Silva (Yamaha); 5. Piñera (Yamaha); 6. Jara (Yamaha); 7. Del Moral (Yamaha); 8. Cestino (Yamaha); 9. Pandilla (Kawasaki); 10. F.-J. Oliver (Yamaha).

FINAL CLASSIFICATION

1. Iván Silva	(Yamaha)	143
2. Raúl Jara	(Yamaha)	115
3. Javier Forés	(Honda)	103

4. Carrasco (Honda), 95; 5. Piñera (Yamaha), 61; 6. Delgado (Yamaha), 57; 7. Cárdenas (COL, Yamaha), 54; 8. Tiberio (F, Honda), 48; 9. Sánchez (Kawasaki), 36; 10. Mazuecos (Yamaha), 34.

2004

23rd May – Catalunya

1. Carrasco (Honda); 2. Lozano (Yamaha); 3. Cárdenas (COL, Yamaha); 4. Forés (Suzuki); 5. Perez (Honda); 6. Delgado (Yamaha); 7. Tizon (Suzuki); 8. Arquer (Yamaha); 9. Salom (Yamaha); 10. Pandilla (Kawasaki).

20th June – Jarama

1. Carrasco (Honda); 2. Mazuecos (Yamaha); 3. Forés (Suzuki); 4. Salom (Yamaha); 5. Jara (Yamaha); 6. Lozano (Yamaha); 7. Pandilla (Kawasaki); 8. Arquer (Yamaha); 9. Juárez (Yamaha); 10. Delgado (Yamaha).

11th July – Albacete

1. Cárdenas (COL, Yamaha); 2. Tizon (Yamaha); 3. Pandilla (Kawasaki); 4. Delgado (Yamaha); 5. Moral (Yamaha); 6. Torres (Honda); 7. Arquer (Yamaha); 8. Steenhoudt (NL, Yamaha); 9. Cestino (Suzuki); 10. Salom (Yamaha).

26th September – Jerez de la Frontera

1. Carrasco (Honda); 2. Cárdenas (COL, Yamaha); 3. Tizon (Suzuki); 4. Jara (Yamaha); 5. Mazuecos (Yamaha); 6. Forés (Suzuki); 7. Perez (Honda); 8. Cestino (Suzuki); 9. Salom (Yamaha); 10. Torres (Honda).

24th October – Albacete

1. Cárdenas (COL, Yamaha); 2. Mazuecos (Yamaha); 3. Tizon (Yamaha); 4. Moral (Yamaha); 5. Jara (Yamaha); 6. Forés (Suzuki); 7. Delgado (Yamaha); 8. Lozano (Yamaha); 9. Piñera (Honda); 10. Carrasco (Honda).

The final two races of the season (Valencia 14th November and Jerez 21st November) took place after publication of this book.

Formula Extreme

2003

16th November – Valencia

1. Cardoso (Yamaha); 2. De Gea (Suzuki); 3. Morales (Suzuki); 4. Ribalta (Suzuki); 5. Tomás (Suzuki); 6. Fernández (Suzuki); 7. Ramirez (Suzuki); 8. Sardá (Suzuki); 9. Del Amor (Yamaha); 10. Cabana (Suzuki).

23rd November – Jerez de la Frontera

1. Cardoso (Yamaha); 2. Sardá (Suzuki); 3. Del Amor (Yamaha); 4. L. Oliver (Suzuki); 5. Fernández (Suzuki); 6. Tomás (Suzuki); 7. Noyes (Honda); 8. Cabana (Suzuki); 9. De Gea (Suzuki); 10. Casas (Suzuki).

FINAL CLASSIFICATION

1. José David De Gea	(Suzuki)	121
2. José Luis Cardoso	(Yamaha)	120
3. José Oriol Fernández	(Suzuki)	94

4. Tomás (Suzuki), 90; 5. Sardá (Suzuki), 68; 6. Morales (Suzuki), 67; 7. Ribalta (Suzuki), 58; 8. L. Oliver (Suzuki), 55; 9. Del Amor (Yamaha), 53; 10. Escobar (Suzuki), 34.

2004

23rd May – Catalunya

1. Silvá (Yamaha); 2. De Gea (Honda); 3. Cardoso (Yamaha); 4. Del Amor (Yamaha); 5. Ribalta (Yamaha); 6. Fernández (Yamaha); 7. Tomás (Yamaha); 8. Sardá (Honda); 9. Noyes (Honda); 10. L. Oliver (Suzuki).

20th June – Jarama

1. Cardoso (Yamaha); 2. Silvá (Yamaha); 3. Del Amor (Yamaha); 4. Fernández (Yamaha); 5. Tomás (Yamaha); 6. Ribalta (Yamaha); 7. Monge (Suzuki); 8. Sánchez (Suzuki); 9. Gómez (Suzuki); 10. Cabana (Kawasaki).

11th July – Albacete

1. Cardoso (Yamaha); 2. Silvá (Yamaha); 3. L. Oliver (Suzuki); 4. De Gea (Honda); 5. Tomás (Yamaha); 6. Monge (Suzuki); 7. Morales (Suzuki); 8. Sardá (Honda); 9. Ribalta (Yamaha); 10. Noyes (Honda).

26th September – Jerez de la Frontera

1. Cardoso (Yamaha); 2. Silvá (Yamaha); 3. Morales (Suzuki); 4. De Gea (Honda); 5. Del Amor (Yamaha); 6. Tomas (Yamaha); 7. Ribalta (Yamaha); 8. Monge (Suzuki); 9. Castillejo (Honda); 10. Gomez (Suzuki).

24th October – Albacete

1. Cardoso (Yamaha); 2. Del Amor (Yamaha); 3. Silvá (Yamaha); 4. Tomas (Yamaha); 5. Ribalta (Yamaha); 6. L. Oliver (Suzuki); 7. De Gea (Honda); 8. Monge (Suzuki); 9. Fernández (Yamaha); 10. Sardá (Kawasaki).

The final two races of the season (Valencia 14th November and Jerez 21st November) took place after publication of this book.

Germany

125 cc

9th May – Sachsenring

1. Lüthi (CH, Honda); 2. Giuseppetti (Honda); 3. Fröhlich (Honda); 4. Unger (Aprilia); 5. Hommel (Honda); 6. Ranseder (A, KTM); 7. Cortese (I, Honda); 8. S. Bradl (KTM); 9. Kalab (CZ, Honda); 10. Mickan (Honda).

23rd May – Hockenheim

1. Ranseder (A, KTM); 2. Hommel (Honda); 3. Minnerop (Honda); 4. Mickan (Honda); 5. S. Bradl (KTM); 6. Unger (Aprilia); 7. Bittman (CZ, Honda); 8. Walther (Honda); 9. Wirsing (Honda); 10. März (Honda).

20th June – Nürburgring

1. Ranseder (A, KTM); 2. Minnerop (Honda); 3. Mickan (Honda); 4. Hommel (Honda); 5. Unger (Aprilia); 6. Walther (Honda); 7. Litjens (NL, Honda); 8. Kalab (CZ, Honda); 9. D. Sutter (CH, Honda); 10. Mayer (Aprilia).

4th July – Salzburgring – Autriche

1. Ranseder (A, KTM); 2. S. Bradl (KTM); 3. Hommel (Honda); 4. Eitzinger (A, Honda); 5. Unger (Aprilia); 6. Fröhlich (Honda); 7. Cortese (I, Honda); 8. Mickan (Honda); 9. Litjens (NL, Honda); 10. Krummenacher (CH, Honda).

1st August – Lausitz

1. Ranseder (A, KTM); 2. Unger (Aprilia); 3. S. Bradl (KTM); 4. Hommel (Honda); 5. Cortese (I, Honda); 6. Wirsing (Honda); 7. Eitzinger (A, Honda); 8. Litjens (Honda); 9. Krummenacher (CH, Honda); 10. Aegerter (CH, Honda).

29th August – Schleiz

1. Ranseder (A, KTM); 2. Minnerop (Honda); 3. S. Bradl (KTM); 4. Walther (Honda); 5. März (Honda); 6. Kalab (CZ, Honda); 7. J. Miralles Jnr (E, Aprilia); 8. Lougher (IRL, Honda); 9. Mickan (Honda); 10. Unger (Aprilia).

12th September – Oschersleben

1. Ranseder (A, KTM); 2. Fröhlich (Honda); 3. Hommel (Honda); 4. Unger (Aprilia); 5. Minnerop (Honda); 6. Mickan (Honda); 7. Aegerter (CH, Honda); 8. Wirsing (Honda); 9. Litjens (NL, Honda); 10. Krummenacher (CH, Honda).

26th September – Hockenheim

1. März (Honda); 2. Ranseder (A, KTM); 3. Wirsing (Honda); 4. Aegerter (CH, Honda); 5. Kresse (FGR); 6. Unger (Aprilia); 7. Eismann (Aprilia); 8. Krummenacher (CH, Honda); 9. Mayer (Aprilia); 10. Lussiana (F, Honda).

FINAL CLASSIFICATION

1. Michael Ranseder	(A, KTM)	186
2. Patrick Unger	(Aprilia)	108
3. Sascha Hommel	(Honda)	102

4. Minnerop (Honda), 75; 5. S. Bradl (KTM), 74; 6. Mickan (Honda), 65; 7. Wirsing (Honda), 58; 8. März (Honda), 49; 9. Litjens (NL, Honda), 45; 10. Cortese (I, Honda), 39.

Supersport

9th May – Sachsenring

1. Wendel (Honda); 2. Tode (Yamaha); 3. Bauer (Suzuki); 4. H. Kaufmann (Yamaha); 5. Penzkofer (Yamaha); 6. M. Müller (Yamaha); 7. Gaisbauer (A, Yamaha); 8. C. Fernandez (F, Suzuki); 9. Defiori (GB, Yamaha); 10. Attnendoup (NL, Kawasaki).

23rd May – Hockenheim

1. Stamm (CH, Suzuki); 2. Andersen (N, Kawasaki); 3. Tode (Yamaha); 4. Penzkofer (Yamaha); 5. Kaufmann (Yamaha); 6. Gaisbauer (A, Yamaha); 7. Muff (CH, Kawasaki); 8. Wendel (Honda); 9. Bauer (A, Suzuki); 10. Prinz (Yamaha).

20th June – Nürburgring

1. Curtain (AUS, Yamaha); 2. Kaufmann (Yamaha); 3. Daemen (B, Honda); 4. Andersen (N, Kawasaki); 5. Penzkofer (Yamaha); 6. Vos (NL, Kawasaki); 7. Tode (Yamaha); 8. Kirmeier (Honda); 9. C. Fernandez (F, Suzuki); 10. Gaisbauer (A, Yamaha).

4th July – Salzburgring – Austria

1. Neukirchner (Honda); 2. Kirmeier (Honda); 3. Daemen (B, Honda); 4. Andersen (N, Kawasaki); 5. Kaufmann (Yamaha); 6. Stamm (CH, Suzuki); 7. Gaisbauer (A, Yamaha); 8. C. Fernandez (F, Suzuki); 9. Seidel (Honda); 10. Grammer (A, Kawasaki).

1st August – Lausitz

1. Daemen (B, Honda); 2. Kirmeier (Honda); 3. Andersen (N, Kawasaki); 4. Kaufmann (Yamaha); 5. Gaisbauer (A, Yamaha); 6. Bauer (A, Suzuki); 7. Stamm (CH, Suzuki); 8. Muff (CH, Kawasaki); 9. Günther (Honda); 10. Prinz (Yamaha).

29th August – Schleiz
1. Andersen (N, Kawasaki); 2. Daemen (B, Honda); 3. Kirmeier (Honda); 4. Kaufmann (Yamaha); 5. Bauer (A, Suzuki); 6. Penzkofer (Yamaha); 7. Stamm (CH, Suzuki); 8. Gaisbauer (A, Yamaha); 9. Seidel (Honda); 10. Günther (Honda).

12th September – Oschersleben
1. Daemen (B, Honda); 2. Tode (Yamaha); 3. Kaufmann (Yamaha); 4. Stamm (CH, Suzuki); 5. Kirmeier (Honda); 6. Penzkofer (Yamaha); 7. Bauer (A, Suzuki); 8. Müller (Yamaha); 9. Günther (Honda); 10. Schading (Kawasaki).

26th September – Hockenheim
1. Andersen (N, Kawasaki); 2. Kaufmann (Yamaha); 3. Bauer (A, Suzuki); 4. Daemen (B, Honda); 5. Penzkofer (Yamaha); 6. Stamm (CH, Suzuki); 7. Günther (Honda); 8. Papuuen (S, Kawasaki); 9. Müller (Yamaha); 10. Gaisbauer (A, Yamaha).

FINAL CLASSIFICATION
1. Werner Daemen	(B, Honda)	124
2. Herbert Kaufmann	(Yamaha)	124
3. Kai-Borre Andersen	(N, Kawasaki)	123

4. Kirmeier (Honda), 82; 5. Bauer (A, Suzuki), 80; 6. Stamm (CH, Suzuki), 77; 7. Penzkofer (Yamaha), 68; 8. Gaisbauer (A, Yamaha), 68; 9. Tode (Yamaha), 67; 10. Wendel (Honda), 54.

Superbike

9th May – Sachsenring
Race I: 1. Oelschläger (Honda)(*); 2. Schulten (Honda); 3. Wegscheider (I, Suzuki); 4. Meklau (A, Suzuki); 5. Zaiser (A, Suzuki); 6. Nebel (Yamaha); 7. Knobloch (A, Yamaha); 8. Hafenegger (Yamaha); 9. Teuchert (MV Agusta); 10. Sebileau (F, Kawasaki).
Race II: 1. Schulten (Honda); 2. Oelschläger (Honda)(*); 3. Zaiser (A, Suzuki); 4. Knobloch (A, Yamaha); 5. Sebileau (F, Kawasaki); 6. Nebel (Yamaha); 7. Hafenegger (Yamaha); 8. Hahn (Kawasaki); 9. Ulm (A, Suzuki); 10. Witzeneder (A, Honda).

23rd May – Hockenheim
Race I: 1. Schulten (Honda); 2. Oelschläger (Honda)(*); 3. Ulm (A, Suzuki); 4. Meklau (A, Suzuki); 5. Barth (Kawasaki); 6. Nebel (Yamaha); 7. Hafenegger (Yamaha); 8. Knobloch (A, Yamaha); 9. Hahn (Kawasaki); 10. Fritz (Suzuki).
Race II: 1. Schulten (Honda); 2. Oelschläger (Honda)(*); 3. Nebel (Yamaha); 4. Ulm (A, Suzuki); 5. Meklau (A, Suzuki); 6. Hafenegger (Yamaha); 7. Zaiser (A, Suzuki); 8. Knobloch (A, Yamaha); 9. Fritz (Suzuki); 10. Scheschowitsch (Yamaha).

20th June – Nürburgring
Race I: 1. Curtain (AUS, Yamaha); 2. Meklau (A, Suzuki); 3. Schulten (Honda); 4. Ulm (A, Suzuki); 5. Hafenegger (Yamaha); 6. Nebel (Yamaha); 7. Barth (Kawasaki); 8. Oelschläger (Honda)(*); 9. Ehrenberger (Suzuki); 10. Van Keymeulen (B, Yamaha).
Race II: 1. Curtain (AUS, Yamaha); 2. Schulten (Honda); 3. Hafenegger (Yamaha); 4. Van Keymeulen (B, Yamaha); 5. Ulm (A, Suzuki); 6. Zaiser (A, Suzuki); 7. Nebel (Yamaha); 8. Oelschläger (Honda)(*); 9. Knobloch (A, Yamaha); 10. Fritz (Suzuki).

4th July – Salzburgring – Austria
Race I: 1. Oelschläger (Honda) (*); 2. Schulten (Honda); 3. Meklau (A, Suzuki); 4. Ulm (A, Suzuki); 5. Scheschowitsch (Yamaha); 6. Zaiser (A, Suzuki); 7. Hafenegger (Yamaha); 8. Nebel (Yamaha); 9. Wegscheider (I, Suzuki); 10. Fritz (Suzuki).
Race II: 1. Schulten (Honda); 2. Ulm (A, Suzuki); 3. Meklau (A, Suzuki); 4. Zaiser (A, Suzuki); 5. Scheschowitsch (Yamaha); 6. Hafenegger (Yamaha); 7. Nebel (Yamaha); 8. Knobloch (A, Yamaha); 9. Wegscheider (I, Suzuki); 10. Fritz (Suzuki).

1st August – Lausitz
Race I: 1. Oelschläger (Honda)(*); 2. Meklau (A, Suzuki); 3. Ulm (A, Suzuki); 4. Hafenegger (Yamaha); 5. Wegscheider (I, Suzuki); 6. Zaiser (A, Suzuki); 7. Fritz (Suzuki); 8. Scheschowitsch (Yamaha); 9. Knobloch (A, Yamaha); 10. Witzeneder (A, Honda).
Race II: 1. Oelschläger (Honda)(*); 2. Hafenegger (Yamaha); 3. Ulm (A, Suzuki); 4. Meklau (A, Suzuki); 5. Nebel (Yamaha); 6. Knobloch (A, Yamaha); 7. Wegscheider (I, Suzuki); 8. Fritz (Suzuki); 9. Hahn (Kawasaki); 10. Manz (Suzuki).

29th August – Schleiz
Race I: 1. Schulten (Honda); 2. Teuchert (MV Agusta); 3. Ulm (A, Suzuki); 4. Oelschläger (Honda)(*); 5. Nebel (Yamaha); 6. Zaiser (A, Suzuki); 7. Sebrich (Kawasaki); 8. Meklau (A, Suzuki); 9. Hahn (Kawasaki); 10. Hafenegger (Yamaha).
Race II: 1. Teuchert (MV Agusta); 2. Schulten (Honda); 3. Nebel (Yamaha); 4. Hafenegger (Yamaha); 5. Ulm (A, Suzuki); 6. Zaiser (A, Suzuki); 7. Scheschowitsch (Yamaha); 8. Meklau (A, Suzuki); 9. Hahn (Kawasaki); 10. Barth (Kawasaki).

12th September – Oschersleben
Race I: 1. Teuchert (MV Agusta); 2. Meklau (A, Suzuki); 3. Knobloch (A, Yamaha); 4. Schulten (Honda); 5. Nebel (Yamaha); 6. Ulm (A, Suzuki); 7. Hafenegger (Yamaha); 8. Sofuoglu (TUR, Yamaha); 9. Wegscheider (I, Suzuki); 10. Wilding (Honda).
Race II: 1. Curtain (AUS, Yamaha); 2. Teuchert (MV Agusta); 3. Schulten (Honda); 4. Hafenegger (Yamaha); 5. Meklau (A, Suzuki); 6. Van Keymeulen (B, Yamaha); 7. Nebel (Yamaha); 8. Ulm (A, Suzuki); 9. Sofuoglu (TUR, Yamaha); 10. Wegscheider (I, Suzuki).

26th September – Hockenheim
Race I: 1. Meklau (A, Suzuki); 2. Ulm (A, Suzuki); 3. Nebel (Yamaha); 4. Schulten (Honda); 5. Hafenegger (Yamaha); 6. Teuchert (MV Agusta); 7. Fritz (Suzuki); 8. Wegscheider (I, Suzuki); 9. Knobloch (A, Yamaha); 10. Witzeneder (A, Honda).
Race II: 1. Hafenegger (Yamaha); 2. Nebel (Yamaha); 3. Ulm (A, Suzuki); 4. Wegscheider (I, Suzuki); 5. Leuthard (CH, Yamaha); 6. Kitsch (Suzuki); 7. Witzeneder (A, Honda); 8. Pölzleitner (A, Yamaha); 9. Peh (Suzuki); 10. Jansen (Suzuki).

FINAL CLASSIFICATION
1. Michael Schulten	(Honda)	276
2. Robert Ulm	(A, Suzuki)	212
3. Andreas Meklau	(A, Suzuki)	205

4. Hafenegger (Yamaha), 201; 5. Oelschläger (Honda)(*), 191; 6. Nebel (Yamaha), 179; 7. Teuchert (MV Agusta), 112; 8. Zaiser (A, Suzuki); 9. Knobloch (A, Yamaha), 105; 10. Wegscheider (I, Suzuki), 89.

(*): Jurgen Oelschlager (Honda) died ten days after an accident at Oschersleben.

Side-Cars

9th May – Sachsenring
1. J. Steinhausen/Hopkinson (D/GB, LCR-Suzuki); 2. Roscher/Hänni (D/CH, LCR-Suzuki); 3. Schlosser/Rückli (CH, LCR-Suzuki); 4. Doppler/Wagner (A, LCR-Yamaha); 5. Thalmann/Roth (CH, LCR-Suzuki); 6. Göttlich/Kölsch (LCR-Suzuki); 7. Centner/Helbig (LCR-Yamaha); 8. Kohlmann/Höss (LCR-Suzuki); 9. Eilers/Freund (LCR-Suzuki); 10. Bork/Ziegler (Honda).

23rd May – Hockenheim
1. J. Steinhausen/Hopkinson (D/GB, LCR-Suzuki); 2. Schlosser/Rückli (CH, LCR-Suzuki); 3. Göttlich/Kölsch (LCR-Suzuki); 4. Roscher/Hänni (D/CH, LCR-Suzuki); 5. Moser/Wäfler (A/CH, LCR-Suzuki); 6. Centner/Helbig (LCR-Yamaha); 7. Kiser/Schmied (CH, LCR-Kawasaki); 8. Eilers/Becker (LCR-Suzuki); 9. Arabin/Backmann(*) (LCR-Honda); 10. Zimmermann/Kolloch (LCR-Suzuki).

20th June – Nürburgring
1. S. Webster/Woodhead (GB, LCR-Suzuki); 2. J. Steinhausen/Hopkinson (D/GB, LCR-Suzuki); 3. Reeves/Reeves (GB, LCR-Suzuki); 4. Van Gils/Van Gils (NL, LCR-Suzuki); 5. Doppler/Wagner (A, LCR-Yamaha); 6. Roscher/Hänni (D/CH, LCR-Suzuki); 7. Schlosser/Rückli (CH, LCR-Suzuki); 8. Göttlich/Kölsch (LCR-Suzuki); 9. Moser/Wäfler (A/CH, LCR-Suzuki); 10. Arabin/Backmann(*) (LCR-Honda).

4th July – Salzburgring – Austria
1. J. Steinhausen/Hopkinson (D/GB, LCR-Suzuki); 2. Klaffenböck/Parzer (A, Yamaha); 3. Roscher/Hänni (D/CH, LCR-Suzuki); 4. Doppler/Wagner (A, LCR-Yamaha); 5. Centner/Helbig (LCR-Yamaha); 6. Moser/Wäfler (A/CH, LCR-Suzuki); 7. Schlosser/Rückli (CH, LCR-Suzuki); 8. Göttlich/Kölsch (LCR-Suzuki); 9. Hauzenberger/Wechselberger (A, RSR-Yamaha); 10. Arabin/Backmann(*) (LCR-Honda).

1st August – Lausitz
1. Schlosser/Rückli (CH, LCR-Suzuki); 2. Moser/Wäfler (A/CH, LCR-Suzuki); 3. Doppler/Wagner (D, LCR-Yamaha); 4. Arabin/Backmann(*) (LCR-Honda); 5. Centner/Helbig (LCR-Yamaha); 6. Eilers/Freund (LCR-Suzuki); 7. Hainbucher/Adelsberger (A, RSR-Yamaha); 8. Thalmann/Roth (CH, LCR-Suzuki); 9. Göttlich/Koloska (LCR-Suzuki); 10. Zimmermann/Kolloch (LCR-Suzuki).

29th August – Schleiz
1. J. Steinhausen/Hopkinson (D/GB, LCR-Suzuki); 2. Roscher/Hänni (D/CH, LCR-Suzuki); 3. Moser/Wäfler (A/CH, LCR-Suzuki); 4. Schlosser/Rückli (CH, LCR-Suzuki); 5. Hock/Becker (Kawasaki); 6. Doppler/Wagner (A, LCR-Yamaha); 7. Hainbucher/Adelsberger (A, RSR-Yamaha); 8. Centner/Helbig (LCR-Yamaha); 9. Thalmann/Roth (CH, LCR-Suzuki); 10. Foukal/Pertlicek (CZ, LCR-Yamaha).

12th September – Oschersleben
1. J. Steinhausen/Hopkinson (D/GB, LCR-Suzuki); 2. Roscher/Hänni (D/CH, LCR-Suzuki); 3. Moser/Wöfler (A/CH, LCR-Suzuki); 4. Doppler/Wagner (A, LCR-Yamaha); 5. Göttlich/Kölsch (LCR-Suzuki); 6. Schlosser/Ruckli (CH, LCR-Suzuki); 7. Hock/Becker (Hock-Kawasaki); 8. Eilers/Freund (LCR-Suzuki); 9. Thalmann/Roth (CH, LCR-Suzuki); 10. Hainbucher/Adelsberger (A, RSR-Yamaha).

26th September – Hockenheim
1. J. Steinhausen/Hopkinson (D/GB, LCR-Suzuki); 2. Moser/Wäfler (A/CH, LCR-Suzuki); 3. Göttlich/Kölsch (LCR-Suzuki); 4. Centner/Helbig (LCR-Yamaha); 5. Schlosser/Ruckli (CH, LCR-Suzuki); 6. Doppler/Wagner (A, LCR-Yamaha); 7. Hock/Becker (Hock-Kawasaki); 8. Eilers/Freund (LCR-Suzuki); 9. Schröder/Burkhard (CH, LCR-Suzuki); 10. Hainbucher/Adelsberger (A, RSR-Yamaha).

FINAL CLASSIFICATION
1. J. Steinhausen/Hopkinson	(D/GB, LCR-Suzuki)	175
2. Schlosser/Ruckli	(CH, LCR-Suzuki)	118
3. Roscher/Hänni	(D/CH, LCR-Suzuki)	109

4. Moser/Wäfler (A/CH, LCR-Suzuki), 104 ; 5. Doppler/Wagner (A, LCR-Yamaha), 102 ; 6. Göttlich/Kölsch (LCR-Suzuki), 80 ; 7. Centner/Helbig (LCR-Yamaha), 72; 8. Eilers/Freund (LCR-Suzuki), 60; 9. Thalmann/Roth (CH, LCR-Suzuki) ; 10. Arabin/Backmann (*) (LCR-Honda), 39.

(*): Gernot Backman, passenger to Siegfried Arabin, died in an accident during qualifying on 11th September at Oschersleben.

USA

Supersport

6th March – Daytona
1. Di Salvo (Yamaha); 2. R.-L. Hayden (Kawasaki); 3. T. Hayden (Kawasaki); 4. Aar. Gobert (AUS, Yamaha); 5. Hacking (Yamaha); 6. Barnes (Yamaha); 7. Yates (Suzuki); 8. Buckmaster (AUS, Yamaha); 9. Rapp (Suzuki); 10. Meiring (Kawasaki).

4th April – Fontana
1. T. Hayden (Kawasaki); 2. Spies (Suzuki); 3. R.-L. Hayden (Kawasaki); 4. Hacking (Yamaha); 5. Aar. Gobert (AUS, Yamaha); 6. Di Salvo (Yamaha); 7. Rapp (Suzuki); 8. Attard (Suzuki); 9. Barnes (Yamaha); 10. Meiring (Kawasaki).

2nd May – Sonoma
1. Spies (Suzuki); 2. Hacking (Yamaha); 3. T. Hayden (Kawasaki); 4. Di Salvo (Yamaha); 5. Aar. Gobert (AUS, Yamaha); 6. R.-L. Hayden (Kawasaki); 7. Yates (Suzuki); 8. Attard (Suzuki); 9. Buckmaster (AUS, Yamaha); 10. Meiring (Kawasaki).

16th May – Birmingham
1. R.-L. Hayden (Kawasaki); 2. T. Hayden (Kawasaki); 3. Aar. Gobert (AUS, Yamaha); 4. Hacking (Yamaha); 5. Rapp (Suzuki); 6. Yates (Suzuki); 7. Spies (Suzuki); 8. Barnes (Yamaha); 9. Meiring (Kawasaki); 10. Attard (Suzuki).

23rd May – Fountain
1. T. Hayden (Kawasaki); 2. Aar. Gobert (AUS, Yamaha); 3. Di Salvo (Yamaha); 4. R.-L. Hayden (Kawasaki); 5. Hacking (Yamaha); 6. Rapp (Suzuki); 7. Spies (Suzuki); 8. Yates (Suzuki); 9. Attard (Suzuki); 10. Meiring (Kawasaki).

6th June – Elkhart Lake
1. T. Hayden (Kawasaki); 2. Hacking (Yamaha); 3. Aar. Gobert (AUS, Yamaha); 4. Di Salvo (Yamaha); 5. R.-L. Hayden (Kawasaki); 6. Spies (Suzuki); 7. Attard (Suzuki); 8. Barnes (Yamaha); 9. Yates (Suzuki); 10. Farrell (Kawasaki).

27th June – Brainerd
1. T. Hayden (Kawasaki); 2. R.-L. Hayden (Kawasaki); 3. Di Salvo (Yamaha); 4. Hacking (Yamaha); 5. Aar. Gobert (AUS, Yamaha); 6. Spies (Suzuki); 7. Rapp (Suzuki); 8. Yates (Suzuki); 9. Barnes (Yamaha); 10. Perez (Yamaha).

11th July – Laguna Seca
1. R.-L. Hayden (Kawasaki); 2. Di Salvo (Yamaha); 3. T. Hayden (Kawasaki); 4. Spies (Suzuki); 5. Attard (Suzuki); 6. Rapp (Suzuki); 7. Meiring (Kawasaki); 8. Barnes (Yamaha); 9. Peris (Suzuki); 10. Perez (Yamaha).

25th July – Lexington
1. R.-L. Hayden (Kawasaki); 2. Spies (Suzuki); 3. Aar. Gobert (AUS, Yamaha); 4. T. Hayden (Kawasaki); 5. Barnes (Yamaha); 6. Rapp (Suzuki); 7. Howard (Yamaha); 8. Peris (Suzuki); 9. Acree (Suzuki); 10. Ulrich (Suzuki).

5th September – Braselton
1. R.-L. Hayden (Kawasaki); 2. T. Hayden (Kawasaki); 3. Di Salvo (Yamaha); 4. Aar. Gobert (AUS, Yamaha); 5. Spies (Suzuki); 6. Buckmaster (AUS, Yamaha); 7. Attard (Suzuki); 8. Rapp (Suzuki); 9. Barnes (Yamaha); 10. Eslick (Suzuki).

10th October – Alton
1. Di Salvo (Yamaha); 2. Hacking (Yamaha); 3. Aar. Gobert (AUS, Yamaha); 4. R.-L. Hayden (Kawasaki); 5. Rapp (Suzuki); 6. T. Hayden (Kawasaki); 7. Spies (Suzuki); 8. Attard (Suzuki); 9. Barnes (Yamaha); 10. Acree (Suzuki).

FINAL CLASSIFICATION

1. Tommy Hayden	(Kawasaki)	352
2. Roger Lee Hayden	(Kawasaki)	343
3. Aaron Gobert	(AUS, Yamaha)	284

4. Spies (Suzuki), 279; 5. Di Salvo (Yamaha), 274; 6. Rapp (Suzuki), 255; 7. Barnes (Yamaha), 248; 8. Hacking (Yamaha), 233; 9. Attard (Suzuki), 190; 10. Peris (Suzuki), 170.

Superstock

6th March – Daytona
1. Aar. Gobert (AUS, Yamaha); 2. Hacking (Yamaha); 3. T. Hayden (Kawasaki); 4. Buckmaster (AUS, Yamaha); 5. R.-L. Hayden (Kawasaki); 6. Di Salvo (Yamaha); 7. Hayes (Kawasaki); 8. Spies (Suzuki); 9. Rapp (Suzuki); 10. Haner (Suzuki).

4th April – Fontana
1. Spies (Suzuki); 2. Buckmaster (AUS, Yamaha); 3. Hacking (Yamaha); 4. Di Salvo (Yamaha); 5. Aar. Gobert (AUS, Yamaha); 6. R.-L. Hayden (Kawasaki); 7. T. Hayden (Kawasaki); 8. Rapp (Suzuki); 9. Pridmore (Suzuki); 10. May (Suzuki).

2nd May – Sonoma
1. Hacking (Yamaha); 2. Buckmaster (AUS, Yamaha); 3. Aar. Gobert (AUS, Yamaha); 4. T. Hayden (Kawasaki); 5. Di Salvo (Yamaha); 6. Spies (Suzuki); 7. Rapp (Suzuki); 8. Hayes (Kawasaki); 9. Haskovec (Suzuki); 10. Holden (Suzuki).

16th May – Birmingham
1. Hacking (Yamaha); 2. T. Hayden (Kawasaki); 3. R.-L. Hayden (Kawasaki); 4. Aar. Gobert (AUS, Yamaha); 5. Hayes (Kawasaki); 6. Rapp (Suzuki); 7. Di Salvo (Yamaha); 8. Al. Gobert (AUS, Honda); 9. Buckmaster (AUS, Yamaha); 10. Wood (Suzuki).

23rd May – Fountain
1. Hacking (Yamaha); 2. Aar. Gobert (AUS, Yamaha); 3. R.-L. Hayden (Kawasaki); 4. Di Salvo (Yamaha); 5. Pridmore (Suzuki); 6. T. Hayden (Kawasaki); 7. Spies (Suzuki); 8. Rapp (Suzuki); 9. Al. Gobert (AUS, Honda); 10. Holden (Suzuki).

6th June – Elkhart Lake
1. T. Hayden (Kawasaki); 2. Hayes (Kawasaki); 3. Aar. Gobert (AUS, Yamaha); 4. Di Salvo (Yamaha); 5. Spies (Suzuki); 6. R.-L. Hayden (Kawasaki); 7. Holden (Suzuki); 8. Pridmore (Suzuki); 9. Rapp (Suzuki); 10. Greenwood (Suzuki).

27th June – Brainerd
1. Hacking (Yamaha); 2. Hayes (Kawasaki); 3. Di Salvo (Yamaha); 4. T. Hayden (Kawasaki); 5. R.-L. Hayden (Kawasaki); 6. Spies (Suzuki); 7. Aar. Gobert (AUS, Yamaha); 8. Holden (Suzuki); 9. Al. Gobert (AUS, Honda); 10. Rapp (Suzuki).

11th July – Laguna Seca
1. T. Hayden (Kawasaki); 2. R.-L. Hayden (Kawasaki); 3. Aar. Gobert (AUS, Yamaha); 4. Hayes (Kawasaki); 5. Di Salvo (Yamaha); 6. Hacking (Yamaha); 7. Spies (Suzuki); 8. Pridmore (Suzuki); 9. Holden (Suzuki); 10. Al. Gobert (AUS, Honda).

25th July – Lexington
1. Di Salvo (Yamaha); 2. Spies (Suzuki); 3. R.-L. Hayden (Kawasaki); 4. Aar. Gobert (AUS, Yamaha); 5. Hayes (Kawasaki); 6. Pridmore (Suzuki); 7. Haskovec (Suzuki); 8. Holden (Suzuki); 9. Rapp (Suzuki); 10. T. Hayden (Kawasaki).

5th September – Braselton
1. Spies (Suzuki); 2. Aar. Gobert (AUS, Yamaha); 3. T. Hayden (Kawasaki); 4. R.-L. Hayden (Kawasaki); 5. Di Salvo (Yamaha); 6. Hacking (Yamaha); 7. Haner (Suzuki); 8. Holden (Suzuki); 9. Haskovec (Suzuki); 10. Rapp (Suzuki).

10th October – Alton
1. Di Salvo (Yamaha); 2. Spies (Suzuki); 3. Hacking (Yamaha); 4. Aar. Gobert (AUS, Yamaha); 5. Holden (Suzuki); 6. T. Hayden (Kawasaki); 7. Buckmaster (AUS, Yamaha); 8. Hayes (Kawasaki); 9. Rapp (Suzuki); 10. Pridmore (Suzuki).

FINAL CLASSIFICATION

1. Aaron Gobert	(AUS, Yamaha)	320
2. Jamie Hacking	(Yamaha)	317
3. Tommy Hayden	(Kawasaki)	313

4. Di Salvo (Yamaha), 312; 5. Spies (Suzuki), 297; 6. R.-L. Hayden (Kawasaki), 268; 7. Rapp (Suzuki), 244; 8. Hayes (Kawasaki), 235; 9. Holden (Suzuki), 232; 10. Al. Gobert (AUS, Honda), 204.

Formula Xtreme

6th March – Daytona
1. Mi. Duhamel (CAN, Honda); 2. B. Bostrom (Honda); 3. Zemke (Honda); 4. Al. Gobert (AUS, Honda); 5. Picotte (CAN, Yamaha); 6. Haskovec (Suzuki); 7. Holden (Suzuki); 8. Wood (Yamaha); 9. Eaton (Suzuki); 10. Trombino (Yamaha).

4th April – Fontana
1. Mi. Duhamel (CAN, Honda); 2. Zemke (Honda); 3. Pridmore (Suzuki); 4. Al. Gobert (AUS, Honda); 5. Haskovec (Suzuki); 6. Pegram (Yamaha); 7. Holden (Suzuki); 8. Palazzo (Yamaha); 9. Eaton (Suzuki); 10. Eslick (Suzuki).

2nd May – Sonoma
1. Mi. Duhamel (CAN, Honda); 2. Zemke (Honda); 3. Al. Gobert (AUS, Honda); 4. Crevier (Suzuki); 5. Holden (Suzuki); 6. Pridmore (Suzuki); 7. Pegram (Yamaha); 8. Barnes (Buell); 9. Eslick (Suzuki); 10. Eaton (Suzuki).

23rd May – Fountain
1. Zemke (Honda); 2. Mi. Duhamel (CAN, Honda); 3. Chandler (Ducati); 4. Haskovec (Suzuki); 5. Pridmore (Suzuki); 6. Al. Gobert (AUS, Honda); 7. Holden (Suzuki); 8. Eslick (Suzuki); 9. Barnes (Buell); 10. Moore (Suzuki).

6th June – Elkhart Lake
1. Mi. Duhamel (CAN, Honda); 2. Zemke (Honda); 3. Al. Gobert (AUS, Honda); 4. Chandler (Ducati); 5. Crevier (Suzuki); 6. Haskovec (Suzuki); 7. Cicotto (Buell); 8. Pegram (Yamaha); 9. Picotte (Yamaha); 10. Young (Suzuki).

27th June – Brainerd
1. Mi. Duhamel (CAN, Honda); 2. Zemke (Honda); 3. Haskovec (Suzuki); 4. Al. Gobert (AUS, Honda); 5. Picotte (Yamaha); 6. Barnes (Buell); 7. Young (Suzuki); 8. Pegram (Yamaha); 9. Small (Yamaha); 10. Moore (Suzuki).

11th July – Laguna Seca
1. B. Bostrom (Honda); 2. Mi. Duhamel (CAN, Honda); 3. Zemke (Honda); 4. Al. Gobert (AUS, Honda); 5. Haskovec (Suzuki); 6. Chandler (Ducati); 7. Pridmore (Suzuki); 8. Pegram (Yamaha); 9. Moore (Suzuki); 10. Cicotto (Buell).

25th July – Lexington
1. Mi. Duhamel (CAN, Honda); 2. Pridmore (Suzuki); 3. Haskovec (Suzuki); 4. Pegram (Yamaha); 5. Small (Yamaha); 6. Howard (Suzuki); 7. Al. Gobert (AUS, Honda); 8. Rojas (Yamaha); 9. Caylor (Suzuki); 10. Farrell (Kawasaki).

5th September – Braselton
1. Mi. Duhamel (CAN, Honda); 2. Zemke (Honda); 3. Chandler (Ducati); 4. Pridmore (Suzuki); 5. Pegram (Yamaha); 6. Smith (Yamaha); 7. Caylor (Suzuki); 8. Young (Suzuki); 9. Small (Yamaha); 10. Young (Suzuki).

10th October – Alton
1. Mi. Duhamel (CAN, Honda); 2. Haskovec (Suzuki); 3. Chandler (Ducati); 4. Cicotto (Buell); 5. Caylor (Suzuki); 6. Moore (Honda); 7. Small (Yamaha); 8. Edwards (Suzuki); 9. Keyes (Suzuki); 10. Gagliardo (Yamaha).

FINAL CLASSIFICATION

1. Miguel Duhamel	(CAN, Honda)	395
2. Jake Zemke	(Honda)	308
3. Vincent Haskovec	(Suzuki)	263

4. Al. Gobert (AUS, Honda), 254; 5. Pegram (Yamaha), 215; 6. Pridmore (Suzuki), 199; 7. Small (Yamaha), 197; 8. Hester (Yamaha), 178; 9. Chandler (Ducati), 166; 10. Melneciuc (Suzuki), 152.

Superbike

6th March – Daytona
1. Mladin (AUS, Suzuki); 2. Zemke (Honda); 3. Mi. Duhamel (CAN, Honda); 4. Pfeifer (Suzuki); 5. Acree (Suzuki); 6. Orlando (Suzuki); 7. Picotte (CAN, Yamaha); 8. Caylor (Suzuki); 9. Jensen (Suzuki); 10. Wood (Suzuki).

4th April – Fontana
Race I: 1. Mladin (AUS, Suzuki); 2. E. Bostrom (Ducati); 3. Mi. Duhamel (CAN, Honda); 4. Zemke (Honda); 5. May (Suzuki); 6. Crevier (Suzuki); 7. Pegram (Yamaha); 8. Cragill (AUS, Suzuki); 9. Haner (Suzuki); 10. Caylor (Suzuki).
Race II: 1. Mladin (AUS, Suzuki); 2. E. Bostrom (Ducati); 3. Zemke (Honda); 4. Mi. Duhamel (CAN, Honda); 5. B. Bostrom (Honda); 6. Crevier (Suzuki); 7. May (Suzuki); 8. Pegram (Yamaha); 9. Acree (Suzuki); 10. Wood (Suzuki).

2nd May – Sonoma
Race I: 1. Mladin (AUS, Suzuki); 2. Mi. Duhamel (CAN, Honda); 3. Zemke (Honda); 4. B. Bostrom (Honda); 5. E. Bostrom (Ducati); 6. Hayes (Kawasaki); 7. Stanton (Suzuki); 8. Pegram (Yamaha); 9. May (Suzuki); 10. Yates (Suzuki).
Race II: 1. Mi. Duhamel (CAN, Honda); 2. Zemke (Honda); 3. Yates (Suzuki); 4. Mladin (AUS, Suzuki); 5. B. Bostrom (Honda); 6. Crevier (Suzuki); 7. Hayes (Kawasaki); 8. Pegram (Yamaha); 9. May (Suzuki); 10. Higbee (Suzuki).

16th May – Birmingham
Race I: 1. Mladin (AUS, Suzuki); 2. Zemke (Honda); 3. Mi. Duhamel (CAN, Honda); 4. E. Bostrom (Ducati); 5. Hayes (Kawasaki); 6. Haner (Suzuki); 7. May (Suzuki); 8. Toye (Yamaha); 9. Wood (Suzuki); 10. Higbee (Suzuki).
Race II: 1. Mi. Duhamel (CAN, Honda); 2. Zemke (Honda); 3. Mladin (AUS, Suzuki); 4. Yates (Suzuki); 5. B. Bostrom (Honda); 6. Hayes (Kawasaki); 7. E. Bostrom (Ducati); 8. Haner (Suzuki); 9. May (Suzuki); 10. Toye (Yamaha).

23rd May – Fountain
1. E. Bostrom (Ducati); 2. Zemke (Honda); 3. Yates (Suzuki); 4. Mi. Duhamel (CAN, Honda); 5. B. Bostrom (Honda); 6. Mladin (AUS, Suzuki); 7. Hayes (Kawasaki); 8. Higbee (Suzuki); 9. Orlando (Kawasaki); 10. May (Suzuki).

6th June – Elkhart Lake
Race I: 1. Mi. Duhamel (CAN, Honda); 2. Mladin (AUS, Suzuki); 3. Zemke (Honda); 4. B. Bostrom (Honda); 5. E. Bostrom (Ducati); 6. Crevier (Suzuki); 7. Yates (Suzuki); 8. May (Suzuki); 9. Higbee (Suzuki); 10. Wood (Suzuki).
Race II: 1. Mi. Duhamel (CAN, Honda); 2. Zemke (Honda); 3. Mladin (AUS, Suzuki); 4. Yates (Suzuki); 5. B. Bostrom (Honda); 6. E. Bostrom (Ducati); 7. Crevier (Suzuki); 8. Pegram (Yamaha); 9. May (Suzuki); 10. Wood (Suzuki).

27th June – Brainerd
1. Zemke (Honda); 2. Mi. Duhamel (Honda); 3. Mladin (AUS, Suzuki); 4. E. Bostrom (Ducati); 5. B. Bostrom (Honda); 6. Hayes (Kawasaki); 7. Yates (Suzuki); 8. Picotte (Yamaha); 9. Holden (Suzuki); 10. May (Suzuki).

11th July – Laguna Seca
1. B. Bostrom (Honda); 2. Mladin (AUS, Suzuki); 3. Mi. Duhamel (CAN, Honda); 4. Yates (Suzuki); 5. E. Bostrom (Ducati); 6. Hayes (Kawasaki); 7. Zemke (Honda); 8. Holden (Suzuki); 9. Pegram (Yamaha); 10. May (Suzuki).

25th July – Lexington
Race I: 1. Mladin (AUS, Suzuki); 2. Mi. Duhamel (CAN, Honda); 3. Yates (Suzuki); 4. B. Bostrom (Honda); 5. Zemke (Honda); 6. Hayes (Kawasaki); 7. E. Bostrom (Ducati); 8. Holden (Suzuki); 9. Haner (Suzuki); 10. Pegram (Yamaha).
Race II: 1. Zemke (Honda); 2. B. Bostrom (Honda); 3. Mladin (AUS, Suzuki); 4. Yates (Suzuki); 5. Hayes (Kawasaki); 6. Holden (Suzuki); 7. E. Bostrom (Ducati); 8. Pegram (Yamaha); 9. Wood (Suzuki); 10. Haner (Suzuki).

5th September – Braselton
Race I: 1. Mladin (AUS, Suzuki); 2. Mi. Duhamel (CAN, Honda); 3. B. Bostrom (Honda); 4. Zemke (Honda); 5. Yates (Suzuki); 6. Haner (Suzuki); 7. May (Suzuki); 8. Wood (Suzuki); 9. Higbee (Suzuki); 10. Caylor (Suzuki).
Race II: 1. Mladin (AUS, Suzuki); 2. Mi. Duhamel (CAN, Honda); 3. B. Bostrom (Honda); 4. Zemke (Honda); 5. Hayes (Kawasaki); 6. Haner (Suzuki); 7. Pegram (Yamaha); 8. Craggill (AUS, Suzuki); 9. Wood (Suzuki); 10. May (Suzuki).

10th October – Alton
Race I: 1. Mi. Duhamel (CAN, Honda); 2. Yates (Suzuki); 3. B. Bostrom (Honda); 4. Lanzi (I, Ducati); 5. Laconi (F, Ducati); 6. Mladin (AUS, Suzuki); 7. Hayes (Kawasaki); 8. Holden (Suzuki); 9. May (Suzuki); 10. Smith (Suzuki).
Race II: 1. Mi. Duhamel (CAN, Honda); 2. Yates (Suzuki); 3. B. Bostrom (Honda); 4. Mladin (AUS, Suzuki); 5. Laconi (F, Ducati); 6. Hayes (Kawasaki); 7. Craggill (AUS, Suzuki); 8. Smith (Suzuki); 9. May (Suzuki); 10. Toye (Yamaha).

FINAL CLASSIFICATION
1. Mathew Mladin	(AUS, Suzuki)	584
2. Miguel Duhamel	(CAN, Honda)	551
3. Jake Zemke	(Honda)	490

4. B. Bostrom (Honda), 422; 5. May (Suzuki), 388; 6. Yates (Suzuki), 363; 7. E. Bostrom (Ducati), 336; 8. Hayes (Kawasaki), 316; 9. Wood (Suzuki), 314; 10. Haner (Suzuki), 312.

Switzerland

Promosport 600
11th April – Lédenon – France
Race I: 1. Grosjean (Suzuki); 2. Rüegg (Yamaha); 3. F. Millet (F, Honda); 4. Aufdenblatten (Yamaha); 5. Balestra (Yamaha); 6. O. Andenmatten (Yamaha); 7. Schmid (Yamaha); 8. Savary (Suzuki); 9. Chèvre (Suzuki); 10. Pahud (Suzuki).
Race II: 1. Aufdenblatten (Yamaha); 2. F. Millet (F, Honda); 3. Rüegg (Yamaha); 4. O. Andenmatten (Yamaha); 5. Grosjean (Suzuki); 6. Schmid (Yamaha); 7. Balestra (Yamaha); 8. Savary (Suzuki); 9. Chèvre (Suzuki); 10. Kroug (Suzuki).

16th May – Oschersleben – Germany
Race I: 1. Grosjean (Suzuki); 2. Graf (Kawasaki); 3. Junod (Suzuki); 4. Brodard (Honda); 5. Castellan (Suzuki); 6. Schröder (Yamaha); 7. Schmid (Yamaha); 8. Rohner (Suzuki); 9. Chèvre (Suzuki); 10. O. Andenmatten (Yamaha).
Race II: 1. Aufdenblatten (Yamaha); 2. Balestra (Yamaha); 3. F. Millet (F, Honda); 4. Junod (Suzuki); 5. O. Andenmatten (Yamaha); 6. Savary (Suzuki); 7. Grosjean (Suzuki); 8. Schmid (Yamaha); 9. Chèvre (Suzuki); 10. Lehmann (Yamaha).

13th June – Magny-Cours – France
Race I: 1. Aufdenblatten (Yamaha); 2. O. Andenmatten (Yamaha); 3. Grosjean (Suzuki); 4. F. Millet (F, Honda); 5. Chèvre (Suzuki); 6. Schmid (Yamaha); 7. Rüegg (Yamaha); 8. Castellan (Suzuki); 9. Junod (Suzuki); 10. Balestra (Yamaha).
Race II: 1. Aufdenblatten (Yamaha); 2. O. Andenmatten (Yamaha); 3. Chèvre (Suzuki); 4. F. Millet (F, Honda); 5. Schmid (Yamaha); 6. Rüegg (Yamaha); 7. Junod (Suzuki); 8. Balestra (Yamaha); 9. Grosjean (Suzuki); 10. Lehmann (Yamaha).

18th July – Dijon – France
Race I: 1. Grosjean (Suzuki); 2. Junod (Suzuki); 3. Chèvre (Suzuki); 4. O. Andenmatten (Yamaha); 5. Schmid (Yamaha); 6. Balestra (Yamaha); 7. Graf (Kawasaki); 8. F. Millet (F, Honda); 9. Brodard (Honda); 10. Amgwerd (Yamaha).
Race II: 1. Chèvre (Suzuki); 2. Grosjean (Suzuki); 3. O. Andenmatten (Yamaha); 4. Balestra (Yamaha); 5. F. Millet (F, Honda); 6. Schmid (Yamaha); 7. Rüegg (Yamaha); 8. Brodard (Honda); 9. Lehmann (Yamaha); 10. Graf (Kawasaki).

31st October – Lédenon – France
Race I: 1. Aufdenblatten (Yamaha); 2. F. Millet (F, Honda); 3. Chèvre (Suzuki); 4. Schmid (Yamaha); 5. Grosjean (Suzuki); 6. Savary (Suzuki); 7. Brodard (Honda); 8. Graf (Kawasaki); 9. Lehmann (Yamaha); 10. Rohner (Suzuki).
Race II: 1. Chèvre (Suzuki); 2. Brodard (Honda); 3. O. Andenmatten (Yamaha); 4. Schröder (Yamaha); 5. Schmid (Yamaha); 6. Amgwerd (Yamaha); 7. Savary (Suzuki); 8. Grosjean (Suzuki); 9. F. Millet (F, Honda); 10. Grange (Ducati).

FINAL CLASSIFICATION
1. Pascal Grosjean	(Suzuki)	157
2. Alain Aufdenblatten	(Yamaha)	143
3. Olivier Andenmatten	(Yamaha)	130
3. Raphaël Chèvre	(Suzuki)	130

5. F. Millet (F, Honda), 125; 6. Schmid (Yamaha), 102; 7. Balestra (Yamaha), 77; 8. Junod (Suzuki), 69; 9. Rüegg (Yamaha), 67; 10. Brodard (Honda), 65.

Supersport FIM
11th April – Lédenon – France
Race I: 1. Stamm (Suzuki); 2. Gantner (Honda); 3. Muff (Kawasaki); 4. Leemann (Honda); 5. Mähr (A, Honda); 6. Raschle (Kawasaki); 7. Bachmann (Honda); 8. Codiroli (Honda); 9. Villiger (Yamaha). 9 finishers.
Race II: 1. Gantner (Honda); 2. Portmann (Yamaha); 3. Raschle (Kawasaki); 4. Mähr (A, Honda); 5. Leemann (Honda); 6. Bachmann (Honda); 7. Codiroli (Honda); 8. Villiger (Yamaha). 9 finishers.

16th May – Oschersleben – Germany
Race I: 1. Stamm (Suzuki); 2. Portmann (Yamaha); 3. Muff (Kawasaki); 4. Borgelt (D, Honda); 5. Raschle (Kawasaki); 6. Brandt (D, Honda); 7. Gantner (Honda); 8. Bödewadt (D, Yamaha); 9. Zech (D, Yamaha); 10. Leemann (Honda).
Race II: 1. Stamm (Suzuki); 2. Gantner (Honda); 3. Muff (Kawasaki); 4. Portmann (Yamaha); 5. Raschle (Kawasaki); 6. Borgelt (D, Honda); 7. Mähr (A, Honda); 8. Kohnke (D, Yamaha); 9. Brandt (D, Honda); 10. Villiger (Yamaha).

13th June – Magny-Cours – France
Race I: 1. Muff (Kawasaki); 2. Portmann (Yamaha); 3. Raschle (Kawasaki); 4. Bachmann (Honda); 5. Villiger (Yamaha); 6. Codiroli (Honda); 7. Leemann (Honda); 8. Gantner (Honda). 8 finishers.
Race II: 1. Gantner (Honda); 2. Portmann (Yamaha); 3. Villiger (Yamaha); 4. Leemann (Honda); 5. Raschle (Kawasaki); 6. Bachmann (Honda); 7. Muff (Kawasaki); 8. Codiroli (Honda). 8 finishers.

18th July – Dijon – France
Race I: 1. Muff (Kawasaki); 2. Portmann (Yamaha); 3. Hofer (Honda); 4. Gantner (Honda); 5. Raschle (Kawasaki); 6. Koch (Yamaha); 7. Villiger (Yamaha). 7 finishers.
Race II: 1. Gantner (Honda); 2. Portmann (Yamaha); 3. Raschle (Kawasaki); 4. Hofer (Honda); 5. Koch (Yamaha); 6. Villiger (Yamaha). 6 finishers.

31st October – Lédenon – France
Race I: 1. Muff (Kawasaki); 2. Gantner (Honda); 3. Portmann (Yamaha); 4. Villiger (Yamaha). 4 finishers.
Race II: 1. Gantner (Honda); 2. Villiger (Yamaha); 3. Raschle (Kawasaki). 3 finishers.

FINAL CLASSIFICATION
1. Hervé Gantner	Honda	193
2. Ruedi Portmann	Yamaha	149
3. Patric Muff	Kawasaki	130

4. Raschle (Kawasaki), 120; 5. Villiger (Yamaha), 102; 6. Stamm (Suzuki), 75; 7. Leemann (Honda), 57; 8. Bachmann (Honda), 42; 9. Mähr (Honda), 31; 10. Codiroli (Honda), 28.

Superstock
11th April – Lédenon – France
Race I: 1. Stamm (Suzuki); 2. Devoyon (Suzuki); 3. Wildisen (Suzuki); 4. Hofmann (Honda); 5. Künzi (Yamaha); 6. A. Andenmatten (Suzuki); 7. Bucher (Suzuki); 8. Leibundgut (Honda); 9. Parolari (Suzuki); 10. Geisser (Suzuki).
Race II: 1. Stamm (Suzuki); 2. Devoyon (Suzuki); 3. Künzi (Yamaha); 4. Hofmann (Honda); 5. Wildisen (Suzuki); 6. Bucher (Suzuki); 7. A. Andenmatten (Suzuki); 8. Leibundgut (Honda); 9. Parolari (Suzuki); 10. Brunner (Suzuki).

16th May – Oschersleben – Germany
Race I: 1. Künzi (Yamaha); 2. Flückiger (Kawasaki); 3. Dähler (Yamaha); 4. Bucher (Suzuki); 5. Wildisen (Suzuki); 6. Monney (Suzuki); 7. A. Andenmatten (Suzuki); 8. Forster (Yamaha); 9. Brunner (Suzuki); 10. Devoyon (Suzuki).
Race II: 1. Stamm (Suzuki); 2. Künzi (Yamaha); 3. Flückiger (Kawasaki); 4. Devoyon (Suzuki); 5. Bucher (Suzuki); 6. Dähler (Yamaha); 7. Monney (Suzuki); 8. A. Andenmatten (Suzuki); 9. Leibundgut (Honda); 10. Brunner (Suzuki).

13th June – Magny-Cours – France
Race I: 1. Devoyon (Suzuki); 2. Stamm (Suzuki); 3. Künzi (Yamaha); 4. Bucher (Suzuki); 5. Dähler (Yamaha); 6. Flückiger (Kawasaki); 7. A. Andenmatten (Suzuki); 8. Forster (Yamaha); 9. Wildisen (Suzuki); 10. Brunner (Suzuki).
Race II: 1. Stamm (Suzuki); 2. Künzi (Yamaha); 3. Bucher (Suzuki); 4. Dähler (Yamaha); 5. Devoyon (Suzuki); 6. A. Andenmatten (Suzuki); 7. Wildisen (Suzuki); 8. Forster (Yamaha); 9. Brunner (Suzuki); 10. Huldi (Yamaha).

18th July – Dijon – France
Race I: 1. Künzi (Yamaha); 2. Flückiger (Kawasaki); 3. Stamm (Suzuki); 4. Devoyon (Suzuki); 5. A. Andenmatten (Suzuki); 6. Monney (Suzuki); 7. Dähler (Yamaha); 8. Brunner (Suzuki); 9. Wildisen (Suzuki); 10. Peter (Honda).
Race II: 1. Hofmann (Honda); 2. Bucher (Suzuki); 3. Devoyon (Suzuki); 4. Brunner (Suzuki); 5. Künzi (Yamaha); 6. Stamm (Suzuki); 7. Huldi (Yamaha); 8. Lavaggi (Kawasaki); 9. Dähler (Yamaha); 10. Monney (Suzuki).

31 October – Lédenon – France
Race I: 1. Hofmann (Honda); 2. Stamm (Suzuki); 3. M. Lagrive (F, Suzuki); 4. Bucher (Suzuki); 5. Künzi (Yamaha); 6. Flückiger (Kawasaki); 7. Sonderer (Kawasaki); 8. A. Andenmatten (Suzuki); 9. Leibundgut (Honda); 10. Huldi (Yamaha).
Race II: 1. Stamm (Suzuki); 2. Huldi (Yamaha); 3. Monney (Suzuki); 4. Flückiger (Kawasaki); 5. Künzi (Yamaha); 6. M. Lagrive (F, Suzuki); 7. Bucher (Suzuki); 8. Dähler (Yamaha); 9. Hofmann (Honda); 10. Brunner (Suzuki).

FINAL CLASSIFICATION
1. Roman Stamm	Suzuki	191
2. Christian Künzi	Yamaha	166
3. Jean-Louis Devoyon	Suzuki	124

4. Bucher (Suzuki), 114; 5. Flückiger (Kawasaki), 89; 6. Hofmann (Honda), 83;

7. Dähler (Yamaha), 74; 8.A. Andenmatten (Suzuki), 74; 9. Monney (Suzuki), 71; 10. Brunner (Suzuki), 66.

SUPERMOTARD

Prestige

2nd May – Eschenbach

Race I: 1. Götz (KTM); 2. D. Müller (Yamaha); 3. Zachmann (Suzuki); 4. Wehrli (KTM); 5. Ferrari (Husqvarna); 6. Singele (Yamaha); 7. Alpstäg (KTM); 8. Jappert (KMS-Husaberg); 9. Gysi (KTM); 10. Waeber (Yamaha).
Race II: 1. Götz (KTM); 2. Gautschi (Husqvarna); 3. Wunderlin (Honda); 4. Müller (Yamaha); 5. Ferrari (Husqvarna); 6. A. Marti (Yamaha); 7. Wehrli (KTM); 8. Möri (Yamaha); 9. Gsell (Husqvarna); 10. Singele (Yamaha).

27th June – Malters

Race I: 1. Götz (KTM); 2. D. Müller (Yamaha); 3. Wunderlin (Honda); 4. Zachmann (Suzuki); 5. Wehrli (KTM); 6. Alpstäg (KTM); 7. Ferrari (Husqvarna); 8. Rohner (KTM); 9. Singele (Yamaha); 10. Gysi (KTM).
Race II: 1. Götz (KTM); 2. Müller (Yamaha); 3. Wunderlin (Honda); 4. Zachmann (Suzuki); 5. Ferrari (Husqvarna); 6. Rohner (KTM); 7. Herger (KTM); 8. Gysi (KTM); 9. A. Marti (KTM); 10. Alpstäg (KTM).

11th July – Buchs

Race I: 1. Götz (KTM); 2. Wehrli (KTM); 3. Ferrari (Husqvarna); 4. Alpstäg (KTM); 5. Möri (Yamaha); 6. Gautschi (Husqvarna); 7. Meusburger (A, Yamaha); 8. Wunderlin (Honda); 9. Waeber (Yamaha); 10. Kromer (KTM).
Race II: 1. Götz (KTM); 2. D. Müller (Yamaha); 3. Zachmann (Suzuki); 4. Wunderlin (Honda); 5. Wehrli (KTM); 6. Singele (Yamaha); 7. A. Marti (KTM); 8. Waeber (Yamaha); 9. Herger (KTM); 10. Möri (Yamaha).

15th August – Büron

Race I: 1. Götz (KTM); 2. D. Müller (Yamaha); 3. Wunderlin (Honda); 4. Gautschi (Husqvarna); 5. Ferrari (Husqvarna); 6. Zachmann (Suzuki); 7. Welink (D, KTM); 8. Wehrli (KTM); 9. Alpstäg (KTM); 10. Möri (Yamaha).
Race II: 1. Götz (KTM); 2. Wunderlin (Honda); 3. Gautschi (Husqvarna); 4. Welink (D, KTM); 5. Zachmann (Suzuki); 6. D. Müller (Yamaha); 7. Alpstäg (KTM); 8. Wehrli (KTM); 9. Laimbacher (KTM); 10. Rohner (KTM).

29th August – Frauenfeld(*)

Race I: 1. Götz (KTM); 2. Wunderlin (Honda); 3. Ferrari (Husqvarna); 4. Wehrli (KTM); 5. D. Müller (Yamaha); 6. Rohner (KTM); 7. Grauf (D, Honda); 8. Welink (D, KTM); 9. Alpstäg (KTM); 10. Herger (KTM).
(*): The second race was cancelled, after an accident which cost the life of Stefan Scharer in the "rookie" event.

5th September – Tourtemagne

Race I: 1. Götz (KTM); 2. Wunderlin (Honda); 3. Ferrari (Husqvarna); 4. Gautschi (Husqvarna); 5. Zachmann (Suzuki); 6. D. Müller (Yamaha); 7. Welink (D, KTM); 8. Wehrli (KTM); 9. Herger (KTM); 10. Gysi (KTM).
Race II: 1. Götz (KTM); 2. D. Müller (Yamaha); 3. Wunderlin (Honda); 4. Ferrari (Husqvarna); 5. Zachmann (Suzuki); 6. Welink (D, KTM); 7. Rohner (KTM); 8. Wehrli (KTM); 9. Singele (Yamaha); 10. Herger (KTM).

26th September – Aarberg

Race I: 1. Götz (KTM); 2. D. Müller (Yamaha); 3. Wunderlin (Honda); 4. Welink (D, KTM); 5. Alpstäg (KTM); 6. Laimbacher (KTM); 7. Zachmann (Suzuki); 8. Rohner (KTM); 9. Herger (KTM); 10. Meusburger (Yamaha).
Race II: 1. Götz (KTM); 2. Ferrari (Husqvarna); 3. Alpstäg (KTM); 4. Zachmann (Suzuki); 5. Wunderlin (Honda); 6. Züger (KTM); 7. Meusburger (A, Yamaha); 8. Herger (KTM); 9. Jappert (Husaberg); 10. D. Müller (Yamaha).

FINAL CLASSIFICATION

1. Marcel Götz	(KTM)	325
2. Beat Wunderlin	(Honda)	242
3. Daniel Müller	(Yamaha)	229

4. Ferrari (Husqvarna), 205; 5. Zachmann (Suzuki), 171; 6. Wehrli (KTM), 164; 7. Alpstäg (KTM), 147; 8. Singele (Yamaha), 124; 9. Rohner (KTM), 118; 10. Herger (KTM), 110.

Challenger

2nd May – Eschenbach

Race I: 1. Notari (Husqvarna); 2. Monsch (Honda); 3. Griette (Husqvarna); 4. Barmettler (Husqvarna); 5. Terraneo (Honda); 6. Studer (GTS); 7. Schüpbach (Kawasaki); 8. Fässler (KTM); 9. Kieliger (KTM); 10. Faust (Husaberg).
Race II: 1. Notari (Husqvarna); 2. Schüpbach (Kawasaki); 3. Terraneo (Honda); 4. Kammermann (Honda); 5. Studer (GTS); 6. Fässler (KTM); 7. Kieliger (KTM); 8. Lugemwa (Yamaha); 9. Moroso (Husqvarna); 10. Faust (Husaberg).

27th June – Malters

Race I: 1. Schüpbach (Kawasaki); 2. Kammermann (Honda); 3. Notari (Husqvarna); 4. Studer (GTS); 5. Wiler (Husqvarna); 6. Stoff (KTM); 7. Tarraneo (Honda); 8. Dähler (Honda); 9. Spörri (KTM); 10. Barmettler (Husqvarna).
Race II: 1. Schüpbach (Kawasaki); 2. Terraneo (Honda); 3. Kammermann (Honda); 4. Notari (Husqvarna); 5. Schlatter (KTM); 6. Studer (GTS); 7. Zimmermann (Husqvarna); 8. Spörri (KTM); 9. Stoff (KTM); 10. Barmettler (Husqvarna).

11th July – Buchs

Race I: 1. Schüpbach (Kawasaki); 2. Notari (Husqvarna); 3. Terraneo (Honda); 4. Wirth (KTM); 5. Kammermann (Honda); 6. Dähler (Honda); 7. Kieliger (KTM); 8. Schlatter (KTM); 9. Lugemwa (Yamaha); 10. Studer (GTS).
Race II: 1. Notari (Husqvarna); 2. Terraneo (Honda); 3. Dähler (Honda); 4. Schlatter (KTM); 5. Spörri (KTM); 6. Faust (Husaberg); 7. Schüpbach (Kawasaki); 8. Studer (GTS); 9. Moroso (Husqvarna); 10. Lugemwa (Yamaha).

15th August – Büron

Race I: 1. Notari (Husqvarna); 2. Terraneo (Honda); 3. Kammermann (Honda); 4. Spörri (KTM); 5. Wiler (Husqvarna); 6. Dähler (Honda); 7. Griette (Husqvarna); 8. C. Müller (Suzuki); 9. Schlatter (KTM); 10. Lechthalter (A, KTM).
Race II: 1. Notari (Husqvarna); 2. Terraneo (Honda); 3. Wiler (Husqvarna); 4. Dähler (Honda); 5. Spörri (KTM); 6. Kammermann (Honda); 7. Schlatter (KTM); 8. Nyffeler (Husaberg); 9. Zimmermann (Honda); 10. Lechthalter (A, KTM).

29th August – Frauenfeld(*)

Race I: 1. Notari (Husqvarna); 2. Terraneo (Honda); 3. Wirth (KTM); 4. Monsch (Honda); 5. Spörri (KTM); 6. Dähler (Honda); 7. Schlatter (KTM); 8. Kammermann (Honda); 9. Barmettler (Husqvarna); 10. De Simone (KTM).
(*): The second race was cancelled, after an accident which cost the life of Stefan Scharer in the "rookie" event.

5th September – Tourtemagne

Race I: 1. Notari (Husqvarna); 2. Monsch (Honda); 3. C. Müller (Suzuki); 4. Spörri (KTM); 5. Studer (GTS); 6. Barmettler (Husqvarna); 7. Kieliger (KTM); 8. Dähler (Honda); 9. Frommelt (KTM); 10. Kammermann (Honda).
Race II : 1. Notari (Husqvarna); 2. Monsch (Honda); 3. Studer (GTS); 4. Terraneo (Honda); 5. Barmettler (Husqvarna); 6. Schlatter (KTM); 7. C. Müller (Suzuki); 8. Kammermann (Honda); 9. Frommelt (KTM); 10. Griette (Husqvarna).

26th September – Aarberg

Race I: 1. Notari (Husqvarna); 2. Studer (GTS); 3. Barmettler (Husqvarna); 4. Kieliger (KTM); 5. Terraneo (Honda); 6. Kammermann (Honda); 7. Aegerter (Husqvarna); 8. Monsch (Honda); 9. Dähler (Honda); 10. Murer (KTM).
Race II: 1. Notari (Husqvarna); 2. Terraneo (Honda); 3. Zimmermann (Husqvarna); 4. Spörri (KTM); 5. Moroso (Husqvarna); 6. Barmettler (Husqvarna); 7. Kaufmann (Husqvarna); 8. Griette (Husqvarna); 9. Monsch (Honda); 10. Dähler (Honda).

FINAL CLASSIFICATION

1. Andrea Notari	(Husqvarna)	310
2. Paolo Terraneo	(Honda)	236
3. Kurt Kammermann	(Honda)	183

4. Studer (GTS), 165; 5. Spörri (KTM), 157; 6. Dähler (Honda), 151; 7. Barmettler (Husqvarna), 127; 8. Schüpbach (Kawasaki), 125; 9. Schlatter (KTM), 119; 10. Kieliger (KTM), 118.

Rookie

2nd May – Eschenbach

Race I: 1. Züger (KTM); 2. S. Scheiwiller (Yamaha); 3. Saxer (KMS-Husaberg); 4. Schnegg (Yamaha); 5. Ricklin (KTM); 6. Burch (Yamaha); 7. Calabresi (Yamaha); 8. Pouchon (Suzuki); 9. Schöb (Husaberg); 10. M. Aeschbacher (KTM).
Race II: 1. Züger (KTM); 2. Schnegg (Yamaha); 3. Saxer (KMS-Husaberg); 4. Aggeler (Yamaha); 5. Calabresi (Yamaha); 6. S. Scheiwiller (Yamaha); 7. Von Gunten (Honda); 8. Pouchon (Suzuki); 9. Burch (Yamaha); 10. M. Aeschbacher (KTM).

27th June – Malters

Race I: 1. Züger (KTM); 2. Calabresi (Yamaha); 3. Kummer (Honda); 4. Schöb (Husaberg); 5. Schnegg (Yamaha); 6. Ricklin (KTM); 7. Tschupp (Husqvarna); 8. Imboden (Yamaha); 9. Vallotton (Honda); 10. Zurfluh (Yamaha).
Race II: 1. Züger (KTM); 2. Aggeler (Yamaha); 3. Von Gunten (Honda); 4. S. Scheiwiller (Yamaha); 5. Schnegg (Yamaha); 6. Burch (Yamaha); 7. Meyer (Yamaha); 8. Tschupp (Husqvarna); 9. Imboden (Yamaha); 10. Calabresi (Yamaha).

11th July – Buchs

Race I: 1. Von Gunten (Honda); 2. Züger (KTM); 3. S. Scheiwiller (Yamaha); 4. Schnegg (Yamaha); 5. Aggeler (Yamaha); 6. Tschupp (Husqvarna); 7. Burch (Yamaha); 8. Saxer (KMS-Husaberg); 9. Teutschmann (Honda); 10. Minoggio (Suzuki).
Race II: 1. Züger (KTM); 2. S. Scheiwiller (Yamaha); 3. Schnegg (Yamaha); 4. Aggeler (Yamaha); 5. Tschupp (Husqvarna); 6. Imboden (Yamaha); 7. Saxer (KMS-Husaberg); 8. Von Gunten (Honda); 9. Hofstetter (F, Vertemati); 10. Calabresi (Yamaha).

15th August – Büron

Race I: 1. Züger (KTM); 2. S. Scheiwiller (Yamaha); 3. Schnegg (Yamaha); 4. Aggeler (Yamaha); 5. Calabresi (Yamaha); 6. Ricklin (KTM); 7. Saxer (KTM); 8. Zurfluh (Yamaha); 9. Valloton (Honda); 10. Kummer (Honda).
Race II: 1. Züger (KTM); 2. S. Scheiwiller (Yamaha); 3. Hofstetter (F, Vertemati); 4. Ricklin (KTM); 5. Burch (Yamaha); 6. Tschupp (Husqvarna); 7. Schöb (Husaberg); 8. Aggeler (Yamaha); 9. Calabresi (Yamaha); 10. Von Gunten (Honda).

29th August – Frauenfeld(*)

Race I: 1. Züger (KTM); 2. S. Scheiwiller (Yamaha); 3. Aggeler (Yamaha); 4. Von Gunten (Honda); 5. Saxer (KMS-Husaberg); 6. Baruth (D, KTM); 7. Zurfluh (Honda); 8. Schnegg (Yamaha); 9. Burch (Yamaha); 10. Hofstetter (F, Vertemati).
(*): The second race was cancelled, after an accident which cost the life of Stefan Scharer in the "rookie" event.

5th September – Tourtemagne

Race I: 1. Aggeler (Yamaha); 2. Baruth (D, KTM); 3. Züger (KTM); 4. Tschupp (Husqvarna); 5. Zurfluh (Honda); 6. Von Gunten (Honda); 7. Kummer (Honda); 8. Hofstetter (F, Vertemati); 9. Schnegg (Yamaha); 10. Meyer (Yamaha).
Race II : 1. Aggeler (Yamaha); 2. S. Scheiwiller (Yamaha); 3. Züger (KTM); 4. Von Gunten (Honda); 5. Schnegg (Yamaha); 6. Baruth (D, KTM); 7. Saxer (KMS-Husaberg); 8. Burch (Yamaha); 9. Hofstetter (F, Vertemati); 10. Werfeli (KTM).

26 September – Aarberg

Race I: 1. S. Scheiwiller (Yamaha); 2. Aggeler (Yamaha); 3. Baruth (D, KTM); 4. Calabresi (Yamaha); 5. Schnegg (Yamaha); 6. Tschupp (Husqvarna); 7. Imboden (Yamaha); 8. Aeschbacher (KTM); 9. Minoggio (Suzuki); 10. Lechthaler (A, Honda).
Race II: 1. Aggeler (Yamaha); 2. Baruth (D, KTM); 3. Imboden (Yamaha); 4. Tschupp (Husqvarna); 5. Lechthaler (A, Honda); 6. Calabresi (Yamaha); 7. Von Gunten (Honda); 8. Burch (Yamaha); 9. Aeschbacher (KTM); 10. Debrunner (Husaberg).

FINAL CLASSIFICATION

1. Stephan Züger	(KTM)	262
2. Michael Aggeler	(Yamaha)	241
3. Serge Scheiwiller	(Yamaha)	226

4. Schnegg (Yamaha), 197; 5. Von Gunten (Honda), 160; 6. Burch (Yamaha), 152; 7. Calabresi (Yamaha), 151; 8. Tschupp (Husqvarna), 140; 9. Saxer (Husaberg), 123; 10. Ricklin (KTM), 109.

Youngster

2nd May – Eschenbach

Race I: 1. Zimmermann (Yamaha); 2. Birrer (Husqvarna); 3. Reinhard (Honda); 4. Darani (Husqvarna); 5. Joos (Yamaha); 6. Kalberer (Yamaha); 7. Würsch (KTM); 8. Jonas (KTM); 9. Rychlik (Yamaha); 10. Graf (KTM).

Race II: 1. Kalberer (Yamaha); 2. Zimmermann (Yamaha); 3. Reinhard (Honda); 4. Birrer (Husqvarna); 5. Würsch (KTM); 6. Joos (Yamaha); 7. Darani (Husqvarna); 8. Rychlik (Yamaha); 9. Rüdisüli (KTM); 10. Jonas (KTM).

27th June – Malters

Race I: 1. Kalberer (Yamaha); 2. Würsch (KTM); 3. Rüdisüli (KTM); 4. Reinhard (Honda); 5. Darani (Husqvarna); 6. Birrer (Husqvarna); 7. Jonas (KTM); 8. Graf (KTM); 9. Walker (Yamaha); 10. Meier (Yamaha).

Race II: 1. Birrer (Husqvarna); 2. Kalberer (Yamaha); 3. Würsch (KTM); 4. Zimmermann (Yamaha); 5. Joos (Yamaha); 6. Reinhard (Honda); 7. Rychlik (Yamaha); 8. Rüdisüli (KTM); 9. Walker (Yamaha); 10. Limacher (Yamaha).

11th July – Buchs

Race I: 1. Zimmermann (Yamaha); 2. Birrer (Husqvarna); 3. Würsch (KTM); 4. Kalberer (Yamaha); 5. Graf (KTM); 6. Darani (Husqvarna); 7. Joos (Yamaha); 8. Walker (Yamaha); 9. Rychlik (Yamaha); 10. Hunkeler (Yamaha).

Race II: 1. Kalberer (Yamaha); 2. Zimmermann (Yamaha); 3. Würsch (KTM); 4. Waldburger (Yamaha); 5. Rüdisüli (KTM); 6. Darani (Husqvarna); 7. Graf (KTM); 8. Birrer (Husqvarna); 9. Hunkeler (Yamaha); 10. Walker (Yamaha).

15th August – Büron

Race I: 1. Birrer (Husqvarna); 2. Zimmermann (Yamaha); 3. Würsch (KTM); 4. Kalberer (Yamaha); 5. Walker (Yamaha); 6. Darani (Husqvarna); 7. Joos (Yamaha); 8. Reinhard (Honda); 9. Rüdisüli (KTM); 10. Waldburger (Yamaha).

Race II: 1. Birrer (Husqvarna); 2. Würsch (KTM); 3. Kalberer (Yamaha); 4. Reinhard (Honda); 5. Graf (KTM); 6. Hunkeler (Yamaha); 7. Rüdisüli (KTM); 8. Jonas (KTM); 9. Blöchlinger (Yamaha); 10. Rychlik (Yamaha).

29th August – Frauenfeld(*)

Race I: 1. Birrer (Husqvarna); 2. Würsch (KTM); 3. Darani (Husqvarna); 4. Joos (Yamaha); 5. Zimmermann (Yamaha); 6. Kalberer (Yamaha); 7. Rüdisüli (KTM); 8. Graf (KTM); 9. Meier (Yamaha); 10. Frei (Yamaha).

(*): The second race was cancelled, after an accident which cost the life of Stefan Scharer in the "rookie" event.

5th September – Tourtemagne

Race I: 1. Zimmermann (Yamaha); 2. Darani (Husqvarna); 3. Kalberer (Yamaha); 4. Birrer (Husqvarna); 5. Würsch (KTM); 6. Meier (Yamaha); 7. Rychlik (Yamaha); 8. Reinhard (Honda); 9. Limacher (Yamaha); 10. Graf (KTM).

Race II: 1. Zimmermann (Yamaha); 2. Darani (Husqvarna); 3. Birrer (Husqvarna); 4. Joos (Yamaha); 5. Meier (Yamaha); 6. Reinhard (Honda); 7. Rüdisüli (KTM); 8. Mabillard (Husqvarna); 9. Reinisch (Yamaha); 10. Würsch (KTM).

26th September – Aarberg

Race I: 1. Zimmermann (Yamaha); 2. Kalberer (Yamaha); 3. Würsch (KTM); 4. Birrer (Husqvarna); 5. Joos (Yamaha); 6. Walker (Yamaha); 7. Darani (Husqvarna); 8. Graf (KTM); 9. Reinhard (Honda); 10. Rüdisüli (KTM).

Race II: 1. Zimmermann (Yamaha); 2. Kalberer (Yamaha); 3. Würsch (KTM); 4. Birrer (Husqvarna); 5. Darani (Husqvarna); 6. Joos (Yamaha); 7. Walker (Yamaha); 8. Graf (KTM); 9. Reinhard (Honda); 10. Rychlik (Yamaha).

FINAL CLASSIFICATION

1. Simon Birrer	(Husqvarna)	264
2. Mario Zimmermann	(Yamaha)	260
3. Andreas Kalberer	(Yamaha)	256

4. Würsch (KTM), 243; 5. Darani (Husqvarna), 187; 6. Reinhard (Honda), 167; 7. Joos (Yamaha), 156; 8. Rüdisüli (KTM), 148; 9. Graf (KTM), 138; 10. Rychlik (Yamaha), 122.

Ladies

FINAL CLASSIFICATION

1. Angela Haag	(Yamaha)	175
2. Myriam Sandoz	(KTM)	146
3. Vera Andexlinger	(KTM)	138

4. Nadia Bucher (Yamaha), 116; 5. Irène Berglas (Husaberg), 110; 6. Andrea Rey (KTM), 98; 7. Barbara Düsel (Gas-Gas), 81; 8. Virginia Vieser (Husaberg), 13. 8 finishers.

SHARE THE
GLORY
MOTUL
46
GO!!!!!!!